PELICAN BOOKS

The Pelican Guides to European Literature

THE AGE OF REALISM

F. W. J. Hemmings was born in Southampton in 1920 and was educated at Taunton's School, Southampton and Exeter College, Oxford. During the war he served in Intelligence, but returned to Oxford in 1946 as a post-graduate. He began his teaching career at the University of Leicester in 1948, and became a Reader in French in 1954. In 1966–7 he was a Visiting Professor at Yale University. He has been Professor of French Literature at the University of Leicester since 1963.

His other publications include *The Russian Novel in France 1884–1914* (1950); *Émile Zola* (1953); *Stendhal, a study of his Novels* (1964); *Balzac: an interpretation of 'La Comédie humaine'* (1967); *Culture and Society in France 1848–1898* (1971).

THE
AGE OF REALISM

G. M. CARSANIGA

R. H. FREEBORN

F. W. J. HEMMINGS
(EDITOR)

J. M. RITCHIE

J. D. RUTHERFORD

PENGUIN BOOKS

Penguin Books Ltd, Harmondsworth, Middlesex, England
Penguin Books Inc., 7110 Ambassador Road, Baltimore, Maryland 21207, U.S.A.
Penguin Books Australia Ltd, Ringwood, Victoria, Australia
Penguin Books Canada Ltd, 41 Steelcase Road West, Markham, Ontario, Canada
Penguin Books (N.Z.) Ltd, 182-190 Wairau Road, Auckland 10, New Zealand

—

First published 1974

—

Copyright © Penguin Books, 1974

—

Made and printed in Great Britain by
Richard Clay (The Chaucer Press) Ltd,
Bungay, Suffolk
Set in Monotype Bembo

Contents

Contents

Contents

ONE

Realism and the Novel: the Eighteenth-Century Beginnings

THE Age of Realism was the age of railways and of wireless telegraphy and of countless other mechanical inventions that collectively revolutionized the nature of society and the quality of human life within a short span of time. It was the age during which what used to be called 'natural philosophy' was rechristened 'science', having finally ridded itself of the few shreds of speculative idealism that still adhered to it. It was the age of the expansion of Europe into Asia and Africa, after which the legend 'terra incognita' disappeared from the atlases. It was the age of nationalism and rampant commercialism, but also the age when international revolutionary movements began to threaten the security of the wealthy governing classes. The Age of Realism was, in short, the age of George Stephenson, Marconi, Darwin, Cecil Rhodes and Karl Marx; it was the nineteenth century.

Not all the aspects of the age, as we have listed them, can be subsumed under the general category, realism, though most of them can be related to it. These broader implications can be left on one side, however, since in this volume we shall be concerned solely with the specific shape and content that the realist approach gave to the literary forms that seemed most naturally to embody it. The term itself, realism, was in this context of fairly late minting. If anyone had called Jane Austen a realist, it is hard to say whether she would have been flattered or indignant; it is certain that she would have been puzzled. The earliest recorded use of the word with a literary, as distinct from a philosophical application, was in a Parisian periodical, *Le Mercure français*, in the year 1826.[1] The journalist, having defined realism as a 'literary doctrine . . . which would lead to the imitation not of artistic masterpieces but of the originals that nature offers us', went on to predict that 'this might well emerge, to judge by certain signs, as the literature of the nineteenth century, the literature

9

of truth'. However, it was not until the 1850s that the word achieved any wide currency, even in France; and there – as in due course we shall see – it was applied by the critics to a certain style in painting even before it gained general acceptance as a term of literary criticism.

A question that arises naturally at this point is why it should have been at this particular period that the realist novel underwent its most vigorous development. The clue may lie in the connection that certain historians have traced between the emergence of realism and the abandonment, by many advanced thinkers in the nineteenth century, of the belief in transcendental values that had formerly characterized the European world-view. Those traditionalists who denounced realism, when it first appeared on the scene, as godless were not altogether mistaken, even though by no means all, and perhaps only a minority, of the great realists whose work will be discussed in the following pages professed a materialistic or atheistic philosophy. But it is a fact that the novel, which Lukács in a famous formula once called 'the epic of a world forsaken by God', depends on a willingness on the part of the writer and his public to suspend any belief they may have in 'a divinity which shapes our ends'; for if the characters in a novel are not shown to be shaping their own ends, then the reader will find them less interesting and their histories less meaningful. When Hardy informs us that 'the President of the Immortals . . . had ended his sport with Tess', we judge that he has forgotten, in the excitement of writing his final paragraph, that he is 'only' a novelist and is posing too grandly as a modern Aeschylus. To the marriage of realism and determinism no impediment may be admitted, but realism and fatalism make uneasy bedfellows.

Thomas Hardy, in fact, like most of the great Victorian novelists, was fundamentally concerned with other things than realism. We do not think of him – or, for that matter, of the Brontë sisters, Dickens, or even George Eliot – as being in the first place and above all else realists, though of course there is an abundance of what we call 'realistic observation' in their books. The novel, as it developed in the English-speaking world during the nineteenth century, differed in a number of ways from the novel as it took shape on the continent of Europe and in Russia. The reasons for the rift need not concern us here; but the fact of its existence will be regarded as justifying the second of the two limitations set on our present inquiry. Our concern will be with realist prose fiction, above all with the novel; and we shall confine ourselves to a consideration of how the novel developed, once it had adopted the mode of realism, in the principal literatures of the European mainland.

REALISM AND THE MIDDLE CLASSES

In this introductory chapter, which will be devoted to what we may call the larval stage of realism, it will nevertheless be necessary to give some account of developments in England, since it was in England and in France that preliminary experiments were made, during the first half of the eighteenth century, in the various techniques appropriate to realism in fiction; furthermore it was in England that the first two really influential novelists of the modern age – Richardson and Fielding – emerged. We shall regard them, for our purpose, principally as pathfinders for the realist literature still to be written; but of course, literary history not being at any point wholly discontinuous, they themselves had predecessors, whom Fielding, at least, was generous enough to name: his list starts with Cervantes and includes three early or contemporary French novelists, Scarron, Lesage, and Marivaux. Even so, Fielding himself, who prefaced *Joseph Andrews* (1742) with a few remarks about 'this new kind of writing which I do not remember to have seen hitherto attempted in our language', was fully aware that what he and a few like-minded authors were venturing on was something in many respects without precedent.

Others, practitioners and observers both in France and in England, were commenting about the same time on this novelty that had intruded itself on the literary scene, and incidentally offering the first tentative definitions of the doctrine which was not to be given its universally accepted name for another hundred years. A minor French novelist, Gaillard de la Bataille, wrote in 1744: 'People want speaking likenesses, natural relations of the truth or at least of what may be true. They want the reflection of the world as it is, the history of society, of the vices and virtues of the age, the portrayal of existing characters.'[2] And Dr Johnson, in 1750, described the new literature in closely similar terms: 'The works of fiction, with which the present generation seems more particularly delighted, are such as exhibit life in its true state, diversified only by the accidents that daily happen in the world, and influenced by those passions and qualities which are really to be found in conversing with mankind.'[3] These descriptions and definitions of the realist novel can still stand, as far as they go; a twentieth-century scholar, René Wellek, expresses no differently his own understanding of what the realist novel became in the nineteenth century when he formulates its aim as 'the objective representation of contemporary social reality'.[4] By 'objective', he means no more than what his eighteenth-century predecessors were referring to as 'the reflection of the world as it is', 'works . . . such as exhibit life in its true state'; a representation, in other words, undistorted by any subjective or partial vision. The realist must strive to see things clear and see them whole.

It sounds like a prescription for dullness: who would want to hear tiresome recitals of what everyone knows already and can see for himself? However, once it has attained a certain stage of development, a society is bound to include plenty of literate members with leisure to read who welcome the kind of 'guided tour' that the novelist offers him. Particularly if he stands on the threshold of life, the reader may be grateful for the advance warnings of lurking dangers and the intimation of opportunities he might otherwise miss. The point was made by Dr Johnson, elsewhere in the essay we have just quoted: novels, he observed, 'are written chiefly for the young, the ignorant, and the idle, to whom they serve as lectures of conduct and introductions into life'. Harry Levin drew attention to the same aspect of the realist novel in the eighteenth century when he called it 'a courtesy-book for successful merchants and their families'.[5] The very first of the important eighteenth-century novels, Lesage's *Gil Blas* (1715–35), conducts its ambitious and intelligent hero through almost every rank and level of society; he starts as a green boy fallen among thieves, and ends, a respectable man of property, experienced, middle-aged, and married. The formula was almost too obvious, and no writer after Lesage applied it as blatantly as he did, though something like the same structure underlies a great number of subsequent 'success-stories' and *Bildungsromane* that turn up at different periods in all European literatures.

A society, then, needs to have achieved a certain degree of complexity, diversification and internal mobility for the realist novel to come into being, and, further, it needs to be able to draw for its patrons on an energetic, ascendant group within that society – what Levin denotes perhaps too narrowly as 'successful merchants and their families'. An isolated work of art is rarely aimed at a particular social group: but for a whole literary tradition to arise and flourish it is almost essential that there should be a predetermined market, in other words a recognized class of people among whom exists or can be created a demand for its products. In times past there had been specific literatures for warriors, for courtiers, for clerics; and it is almost a commonplace of criticism to attribute the rise of realism to the emergence in the eighteenth century, in the two countries we are concerned with, of a pushful, self-confident, literate middle class.

The theory has had its opponents and it is true that some of its implications are troublesome. There were successful burghers – merchants and professional men – in Italy and in the Netherlands before the eighteenth century, but nothing that we should recognize as a tradition of realistic novel-writing arose among them. Possibly their city-state societies were too restricted, too ingrowing to support this kind of literature. Even in France the development of the novel does not fit as precisely as one might wish the hypothesis that it was basically a response to middle-class aspirations. Although the court at Versailles never recovered after 1715 the cultural prestige it enjoyed under Louis XIV, polite society, which at any rate in the first half of the century continued to dictate the canons of taste, remained aristocratic in outlook if not predominantly so in composition. This circumstance may have affected the novel less than it did other forms of literature, but it remains true that the French novelist felt rather more uneasy than his English colleague about introducing heroes who bore no titles and writing about ordinary, humdrum, middle-class life. Prévost gives us the story not of a mere commoner but of the Chevalier des Grieux (in the work best known by its abbreviated title, *Manon Lescaut*). Louvet de Couvray tells us of *Les Amours du Chevalier de Faublas*. Crébillon's best book, with its deceptively moralistic title *Les Égarements du cœur et de l'esprit* (*The Froward Heart and Wayward Mind*), is concerned with the adventures of a young sprig of the nobility newly introduced into the fashionable Paris world of drawing-room intrigue. Marivaux's Marianne moves in some rather low company at the outset; no one knows who her parents are, but there is a certain innate refinement in her speech and deportment which makes it clear enough that she is not of plebeian origin, however plebeian her upbringing. In any case the full title of the novel, which was *La Vie de Marianne ou les Aventures de madame la comtesse de* ✱ ✱ ✱, made it perfectly apparent that the butterfly was merely recounting her past history as a grub.

Whether for political, historical, or cultural reasons, it appears that in eighteenth-century France the educated classes ignored the lower classes to the point almost of pretending they were not there. If one overlooks the occasional brothel-novel, like Fougeret de Montbron's *Margot la Ravaudeuse*[6] – pornography in the true, etymological sense of the word – the only novelist who showed a sustained interest in the way of life of the less fortunate members of Parisian society before the Revolution was Restif de La Bretonne, whose works appeared in the latter part of the century. In form and technique, the French realists made immense strides at this period, as we shall see; nevertheless, it remains true that all the most gifted writers were singularly reluctant to penetrate beneath the polished surface represented by 'good society'. Fear of the hostility of critical opinion may have been partly the reason, or else one must explain this exclusiveness with reference to the great gulf that existed between the literate upper reaches of society and the Great Unwashed, the rabble in the lower depths. Certainly the realists – again with the exception of Restif and, perhaps, Sébastien Mercier – are a great disappointment to the inquiring social historian, as Hippolyte Taine discovered when he was investigating conditions in pre-Revolutionary France. 'It seems', he wrote, 'that for literature, nothing existed but drawing-rooms and men of letters. The rest does not count; outside the conversations of polite society, France appears a vacuum.' And Taine went on to compare the very different case of English literature of the same period.[7]

When they were translated into French, the novels of Richardson and Fielding, not to speak of Smollett, were regarded by many as inexpressibly crude and tasteless. The dialogue was so often quite vulgar; there were brawls, described in disgusting detail, in which the hero, on occasion even the heroine, might join. It was all too full-blooded for a fine gentleman like Horace Walpole, French by culture if not by parentage. In one of his letters to Mme Du Deffand (the original is couched in the most elegant French) he confessed:

Tom Jones has afforded me scant pleasure; parts are burlesque, and what I like even less is the depiction of the manners of the vulgar. I will grant that it is very natural, but nature, when it admits not taste, does not move me . . . Our novels are coarse. In *Gil Blas*, man-servants are introduced, and people of that sort, but never, never once do they disgust one. In Fielding's novels there are country clergymen who are real hogs.[8]

Such *ancien-régime* fastidiousness as Horace Walpole exhibits here no more affected the English novel in the eighteenth century than Victorian genteelness was to affect the French novel in the nineteenth. Leaving Fielding and his tavern scenes aside, there is something admirably robust about the way in which the heroes of the novels of DEFOE (1660?–1731) – each in his own way a glorified replica of the author – set about so unashamedly to 'better themselves', that is, to accumulate enough money to allow them to live in comfort and respectability once their adventures are over. Neither Crusoe nor Moll Flanders are particularly scrupulous about how they make their fortunes, but then neither was Defoe himself, if certain stories about his activities as a government spy are to be believed. We should not be misled by the fact that *Robinson Crusoe* (1719) fails to comply with one basic requirement of a realist novel, in that the action is mostly set not in the contemporary English society that Defoe knew so well and described in his other fictional works, but in distant regions of the earth either totally uninhabited or populated by savages. The book bears only a superficial resemblance to the traditional travel-yarn, since it is not out of desire for adventure but in the hope of a fat profit that Crusoe takes ship. In this story Defoe expressed his own intimate longings, his own sense of what constituted the proper business of a man: feelings and assumptions which were shared by most members of the lower middle class from which he sprang and which provided him with his public. What they all wanted to do was to 'make good'; and, short of reaching this pinnacle of success them-selves, they liked to read about some imaginary superman who brought it off in a convincing fashion; so, Robinson Crusoe was their hero, 'Robinson who, thrown back on his own resources, triumphs over the stubbornness of nature and creates prosperity, security, order, law and custom out of nothing, is the classical representative of the middle class'.[9] It is, indeed, possible to interpret this strange and powerful book, which stands at the fountain-head of the English realist novel, as an extended metaphor translating the situation of the lower middle classes at the start of their slow rise to prominence. Crusoe demonstrated how their practical skills and crafts, their narrow range of utilitarian values, their disregard of idle, time-wasting romanticism in such matters as sex and their firm belief that God was on their side and ready to lend them a hand – how all this could allow them to cope with the hostile environment in which they found themselves, though of course this environment was not, in reality, an island far away from the centres of civilization. Crusoe survived (realistically speaking, he would have gone melancholy-mad, dashed out his brains or reverted to brutishness): this was the lesson, with its further implication that in his position the 'gentleman' would have floundered and gone under. The myth persisted for generations: *The Admirable Crichton* is simply *Robinson Crusoe* brought up to date, made into a cautionary tale for Edwardian theatre audiences.

The ready-made public that existed for *Robinson Crusoe* and for Defoe's technically more realistic but morally less exemplary sub-sequent novels, *Moll Flanders* (1722), *Colonel Jacque* (1722), *The Fortunate Mistress (Roxana)* (1724), was no doubt chiefly composed of small *entrepreneurs* like the author himself, of tradesmen like his father, plain Master Foe, a tallow-chandler turned butcher, and especially of the very numerous group of apprentices, footmen, and servant-girls, as the contemporary jingle testified:

> Down in the kitchen, honest Dick and Doll
> Are studying Colonel Jack and Flanders Moll.

Strict limits were set on the size of this reading public by widespread illiteracy – even by the end of the century there may have been no more than 100,000 persons in the country who could read print with any facility – and by the high price of books which was due in those days not so much to labour costs as to the relative dearness of paper and movable type: it has been reckoned, for example, that *Tom Jones*, originally issued in six volumes at three shillings each, cost more than a labourer would earn in a week. At this time, one must remember, up to half the population even of so rich a country as England, which had a sizeable grain surplus for export, was living at bare subsistence level. However, then as now, more people read books than actually purchased copies. Newspapers could serialize them – without, incidentally, remitting a penny or a sou to the original author or publisher – and, midway through the century, the circulating library came into being. No doubt the young lady who paid her half-guinea subscription would now and then lend the novel she had borrowed to her favourite maid. In Paris, largely as a consequence of the vast popular demand for Rousseau's *Nouvelle Héloïse*, the *cabinet de lecture*, a different sort of institution though one which served approximately the same purpose, made its appearance for the first time: it was to supply the needs of non-book-buying readers in French towns for generations. Finally, in rural areas particularly, simple folk used to forgather of an evening to hear one of their number read aloud to them. There is a story that at Slough one such group, touched to learn that Pamela's wedding had taken place in their own village, repaired to the parish church and began pealing a joyful carillon.

Pamela (1740–41), the first novel published by Samuel RICHARDSON (1689–1761), gave as great a fillip, in its own way, to the morale of the common people as had Defoe's first novel. Prigs might scoff at the vulgarity of the heroine's manner of expressing herself – but this was, after all, a tribute to the accuracy of the author's ear and thus to his realism. A few fashionable ladies turned up their noses at *Pamela*, 'the joy of chambermaids of all nations', as Lady Mary Wortley Montagu called it; but this very sneer provides involuntary evidence of the immensely enlarged reading public that Richardson had tapped: women in humbler stations of life, chambermaids to be sure, but also the wives and daughters of men in a middling way of business who, a generation or two back, would have been absorbed in the multifarious domestic activities that used to afford employment to the female members of a household. As the developing industrial revolution relieved them of many of these duties (particularly spinning and weaving), they found themselves with time to spare both for instruction and for entertainment. Pamela, as Ian Watt has put it, became 'the culture-heroine of a very powerful sisterhood of literate and leisured waiting-maids',[10] and this sisterhood continued, probably all through the nineteenth century, to constitute an important pool of potential readers for a certain kind of novelist. Stendhal, in 1832, divided the current French output of fiction into two categories: 'chambermaids' novels' ('romans pour femmes de chambre') and 'drawing-room novels' ('le roman des salons').

Richardson's design, in *Pamela*, was essentially very simple: to take the stock *soubrette* of French comedy, as she appears in Molière and Marivaux and as she would later appear in Beaumarchais – the pert, pretty, intriguing, hard-headed little minx – and to transform her, thanks to a stiff dose of middle-class self-respect, into a virtuous heroine, obstinately repelling the licentious landowner's assaults on her chastity. This had little to do with realism. Pamela's convenient fainting-fits, which so effectually check her persecutor when he has her cornered, suggest a more delicate constitution than one would expect to find in a girl of her nurture. The realistic, i.e. typical, outcome of Pamela's predicament is better represented by the fate of Hardy's dairymaid, of Tolstoy's Maslova (in *Resurrection*), and of the chambermaids in Zola's *Pot-Bouille*, none of them resisting for long the sexual advances of their masters. But Richardson did succeed in embodying, in *Pamela*, the democratic dream of his heroine's class. 'For the first time in English literature a person of low social status was portrayed seriously as a complex and admirable human being.'[11] The question whether Pamela was as admirable as Richardson no doubt thought her to be was warmly contested at the time and can still be argued today. Her steady refusal to admit the squire to her bed before he makes her mistress of his estate laid her open to the charge of following a cynically prudential morality. Pamela, in one of the current lampoons, was an alias for Shamela. 'I thought once of making a little fortune by my person. I now intend to make a great one by my virtue.' But if Pamela was a gold-digger, she was an unconscious one: she regards herself rather as the representative, perhaps the standard-bearer, of her class, and as championing the egalitarian theory, recently reinforced by the spread of methodism, that there is no distinction of rank in the sight of the Almighty:

> When Adam delved and Eve span,
> Who was then the gentleman?

The question had first been asked four centuries earlier, at the time of the Peasants' Revolt; it was none the less topical as rephrased by this subversive, somewhat sanctimonious domestic in one of her letters home:

One may see how poor people are despised by the proud and the rich! yet we were all on a footing originally: and many of those gentry, who brag of their ancient blood, would be glad to have it as wholesome and as *really* untainted as ours . . . O keep me, heaven, from *their* high condition, if my mind shall ever be tempted with *their* vice, or polluted with so cruel and inconsiderate a contempt of that humble estate they behold with so much scorn.[12]

In the six-year interval separating the publication of *Pamela* from that of *Clarissa* (1747–8), the middle-aged printer turned novelist had ample occasion to broaden his experience of society. The astounding success of his first novel caused him to be lionized in certain polite drawing-rooms, so that when he came to write his second he was less handicapped by ignorance of the manners and speech of refined society. Even so, and although Clarissa is no undowered lady's maid but a young lady herself, with property of her own, it is not too hard to discern the same element of class conflict underlying her dealings with her would-be seducer. The aristocratic Lovelace affects to despise the Harlowes, as 'sprung up from a dunghill, within every elderly person's remembrance'; in abusing Clarissa's innocence, he is partly concerned to humiliate her family, which had had the temerity to slight him.

FICTION AND HISTORY: THE MEMOIR-NOVEL

The strongly moralistic, dissenting middle-class bias of Richardson's novels must be regarded as in part an instinctive or unconscious response to the unexpressed demands of the new reading public; but it is also true that the didactic element of his work can be construed as an attempt to allay the suspicions of those whose moral objections to novels arose not from any assessment of their contents but from a general aversion to the very concept and nature of fiction. Such critics had formed a powerful opposition, admittedly more active, or more effectively active, in France than in England, and one which the new realists had either to disarm or to overcome if they were to make any progress: for the gravamen of the charge here laid against fiction was, quite simply, that fiction by definition was not truth; novelists were liars, and lying was sinful. Where this fundamentalist objection to fiction is encountered in the history of English literature, it is usually attributed, perhaps a little glibly, to the workings of the Puritan conscience. But the Puritans had not colonized France, where the same argument was heard and, indeed, so successfully pressed that about 1738 the authorities introduced an almost total ban on the publication of new novels in the kingdom, effective enough to cause novelists thereafter to have their works published abroad. The prejudice against this new type of fiction arose more probably from a misunderstanding of what the novelists were trying to do. To accept fiction as fiction, to 'believe in' people whose acts and words are recorded in a book while realizing all the time that they have never had any historical existence, this requires a certain cultural sophistication even today; in the late seventeenth and early eighteenth centuries, among the reading public the novelists were hoping to sweep into their net, so advanced an attitude of mind must have been rather unusual.

Often enough the readers' misgivings were allayed – or so it was hoped – by firm assurances, usually provided in the foreword, that the narrative they were about to peruse was 'gospel truth'. Thus Mrs Behn protested, in a prefatory note to *Oroonoko* (1688): 'I do not pretend to entertain my reader with the adventures of a feigned hero, nor, in relating the truth, to adorn it with any accidents but such as arrived in earnest to him.' Defoe, in the unsigned preface to *Robinson Crusoe*, was a little more circumspect: 'The editor', he wrote, 'believes the thing to be a just history of fact; neither is there any appearance of fiction in it.' For sheer brazen impudence, there was nothing to beat the author of *The English Hermit* (1727), who evidently worked on the principle that the best way to gain credit for a tall story was to call all one's rivals liars. 'Now it may without the least arrogance be affirmed', he wrote, 'that though this surprising narrative be not so replete with vulgar stories as [*Robinson Crusoe*] or so interspersed with a satirical vein as [*Gulliver's Travels*] ... yet it is certainly of more use to the public than either of them because every incident herein related is matter of fact.'[13]

In England, the educated reader had probably little difficulty in distinguishing between fiction and genuine statements of fact. In France, the problem was complicated by the accident that the realist novel, in its beginnings, had sometimes deliberately masqueraded as authentic historical writing. A kind of historical novel had become popular in the latter part of the seventeenth century. Its earliest exponents were careful to distinguish their work from that of *bona fide* historians. Mme de La Fayette, in the prefatory note to *La Princesse de Montpensier* (1662), warned her readers not to look on her story as a true account of the life and loves of the rather obscure historical figure she had chosen to write about. It was a narrative deriving, she said, 'from no manuscript that has come down to us from the time of the persons to whom it relates. The author, having wished, for her own amusement, to write a story with incidents invented according to her fancy, decided it was more fitting to take names known in our history than to use such as are found in novels.' Later authors were far less scrupulous than Mme de La Fayette. Saint-Réal, for example, published in 1672 a *Conjuration de Venise* (*Conspiracy in Venice*) which was for a long while regarded as a serious contribution to history; actually, like Defoe's *Journal of the Plague Year* much later, it was history enlivened and embellished by the author's imagination. In the same year (1672) a certain Mme de Villedieu brought out, under the title *Mémoires de la vie de Henriette-Sylvie de Molière*, a work of fiction which the public of the time were encouraged to treat as authentic autobiography. The prolific and popular romancer Courtilz de Sandras caused still greater confusion by producing a whole series of spurious autobiographies under the names of various personages, like the celebrated duellist D'Artagnan, who were known to have lived and to have been involved in many of the adventures they were supposed to be writing about. Serious students of history began to take alarm at these misleading incursions of colourful invention into the hallowed realm of established fact. In one of the entries of his famous *Dictionary*, published right at the end of the seventeenth century, Pierre Bayle denounces the practice of authors who attempt to

deceive people into thinking that their 'secret histories' have been drawn from manuscript sources: they know well that love intrigues and suchlike adventures give more pleasure when they are believed to be real than when it is realized they are mere inventions. Thus it has come about that the new novels avoid as far as possible the appearance of being novels; but by the same token a thick shadow is cast over true history, and I believe that eventually the authorities will be constrained to enact that these new novelists should make a choice: let them write either pure history or pure novels.

But Bayle's protest went unheeded. Pseudo-memoirs continued to pour from the presses, and a number of them crossed the Channel. This time it was Steele's turn to complain, as he did in *The Tatler* (22 October 1709), about

some merry gentlemen of the French nation, who have written very advantageous histories of their exploits in war, love, and politics, under the title of memoirs ... The most immediate remedy I can apply to prevent this growing evil is, that I do hereby give notice to all book-sellers and translators whatsoever, that the word *Memoir* is French for a novel; and to require of them that they sell and translate it accordingly.

In fact, the word novel (*roman*) was scarcely ever used by French novelists in the first half of the eighteenth century to describe their works: they were nearly all denoted on the title-page either as memoirs or as histories.

The vogue of fictitious memoirs must have owed something to the appearance, about this time, of a number of authentic memoirs written by various illustrious or well-placed personages living under the previous two reigns. The memoirs of Bussy-Rabutin were published in 1696, those of Cardinal de Retz in 1717, of the Abbé de Choisy in 1727, of Mme de La Fayette in 1731. (The work of the most gifted memorialist of them all, the Duc de Saint-Simon, was not brought to light till the nineteenth century.) Certain features of this kind of writing were naturally copied by those who were trying to produce passable imitations: the setting, whether in France or in some foreign land, needed to be given an air of authenticity; and the authors of fake memoirs had to make credible the behaviour of the various men and women with whom the supposed writer had had dealings. Here, already, were two basic ingredients of the realist novel: local and psychological verisimilitude. Unfortunately, there were other features common to both genuine and fictitious memoirs that were responsible for discouraging the new novelists from attempting a serious presentation of social reality and orientating them instead towards a more popular art of ephemeral interest. Authentic memoirs were very often the record of a life full of stirring adventure or dark intrigue, in the field, at court, or under foreign skies: the novelists – among them Antoine-François, Abbé PRÉVOST (1697–1763) – took their cue from this and wrote rambling, episodic compositions full of coincidences and strange twists of fortune. If the author feared that his readers' powers of belief might be strained by the multiplicity of surprising incidents in his hero's life, he could always fall back on the perennial device of the subsidiary story, recounted to the main character by some garrulous stranger he chances to fall in with. The one novel for which Prévost is universally remembered today, *Manon Lescaut*, was originally an intercalated 'episode' in the multi-volume *Mémoires d'un homme de qualité*, published between 1728 and 1731: the story was supposedly related to the principal narrator by a young man whom he chances to meet on the road to Le Havre. If *Manon Lescaut*, exceptionally, has power to move us still, it is for qualities quite other than those on which Prévost normally relied for literary success: in a couple of hundred pages he plumbs the depths of a powerful but irrational passion – that of a young man of fine sensibility for a corrupt but fascinating wanton – thus creating the kind of type-situation to which reference will always be made so long as literature lasts and people remain baffled by the inconceivable follies of their fellow creatures.

Having completed the *Mémoires d'un homme de qualité*, Prévost went on to produce a couple more lengthy fake memoirs, on which he conferred a semblance of authenticity by introducing important political events and personages of the previous century. Thus, the hero of *Le Philosophe anglais, ou Histoire de Monsieur Cleveland* (1731–9) is an imaginary bastard son of Oliver Cromwell who visits the exiled Stuart court at Bayonne, travels to America, and returns to England at the Restoration to become a privy councillor. The plot (in so far as there is one) of *Le Doyen de Killerine* (1735–40) turns on the efforts of the Irish Catholics to restore James II to the throne after 1688. It should be noted that, for all the care he took to get the historical and topographical details right, Prévost was honest enough in his other writings not to attempt to deny the fictional nature of these works: the stories of Cleveland and the Dean of Colerayne were, he wrote, 'books of no historical value, their only merit being to provide decent and diverting reading matter'.[14]

The gap between Prévost's pseudo-memoirs and realism as we

understand it yawns wide; it was closed, to some extent, by his successors, who abandoned the pretence of historicity and set their stories squarely in contemporary France. The Parisian street scenes of Marivaux's *Vie de Marianne* (1731–41), the interiors of Crébillon's *Les Égarements du cœur et de l'esprit* (1736), were recognizable copies of ordinary life among the quality, and to a minor degree among the low-born, of the reign of Louis XV. Jacob, the ploughboy on the make in Marivaux's second novel, *Le Paysan parvenu* (1735–6), was a lively portrait of a cheerful rustic of the period, and as for Duclos's *Confessions du comte de * * * (1742), it created something of a scandal at the time, so faithfully did it reflect the dissolute manners of high society.

Probably the most important respect in which the vogue of the pseudo-memoir interfered with the normal development of the realist novel was that it necessarily implied a first-person narrative technique. Now, in what we are calling the 'age of realism', fictitious autobiographies account for a very small minority of the novels written, since by the beginning of the nineteenth century the convention of the 'omniscient narrator' had been firmly established. But in the first part of the eighteenth century, virtually up to the appearance of *Tom Jones* (1749), it was felt to be essential that all the events related in a novel should be presented as witnessed by the supposed author. This had not always been so: neither Cervantes nor Mme de La Fayette had thought it incumbent on them to adopt the first-person narrative technique in writing *Don Quixote* (1605–15) and *La Princesse de Clèves* (1678). The reason for the universality of the practice in the Age of Reason, as it was so complacently denominated, was that no story that was not vouched for by a principal participant – active or passive – was thought to warrant belief. There could be no narrative without a narrator. The reading public was in the position of the members of a jury who must hear what happened from the witness's own lips and who will accept neither hearsay evidence nor inspired guesses. Hence the extraordinary and – for a modern reader – childish lengths to which authors went to make plausible not only the writing of a 'true confession' but its subsequent discovery and publication: the yellowing manuscript found in a locked cupboard in an empty house, or in a trunk left behind in an inn by a traveller who never returns to reclaim it. Hence too the solemn assertions provided in prefaces by 'editors', the glib and patently mendacious pretence that, of course, *this is not a novel*, the writer having no inventive talent; and also the cunning adaptation of the alleged narrator's style to his or her supposed position in society, age and education: something at which Marivaux especially excelled.

There is nothing inherently primitive in the convention of the first-person narrative *per se*: Conrad, in *Lord Jim*, handled the device with great subtlety, and Proust, when he came to write *À la Recherche du temps perdu*, decided finally in its favour after experimenting earlier (in *Jean Santeuil*) with the alternative, 'omniscient narrator' technique. All the same, it has its limitations – or, perhaps one should say, its employment presents certain difficulties – which are sufficient to explain why it fell largely into abeyance during the great age of the realist novel. It may be true that an outsider sees most of the game, but it is unlikely that he ever sees it all; and for the most part the narrators in memoir-novels were not outsiders at all, but active participants in the plot. This meant that authors had to rely far too heavily on confidences received and chance eavesdropping. Further, since the events related were often supposed to have taken place long ago, it was necessary to credit the 'narrator' with a phenomenal memory for the detail of conversations and the like: Philip Stewart instances the case of a letter reproduced 'word for word' by the heroine of Mouhy's *Paysanne parvenue*, even though she admits that she only scanned it 'hurriedly' at the time she read it.[15]

THE EPISTOLARY NOVEL

In due course the novelists came to realize that their business was not to hoax the reader with these elaborate and, finally, transparent confidence-tricks, but rather to persuade him that what he experiences when reading is as real as what he might experience in the ordinary transactions of life. Between childhood and the grave, we all of us come into contact with hundreds of our fellow beings; but our knowledge of most of them, and hence their reality for us, is for the most part sketchy, superficial, and monochrome. If we were honest with ourselves, we would have to admit that they are a good deal less real to us than many of the characters in the novels we read. How many unmarried girls can anyone of us say we have known as we know Emma Woodhouse or Natasha Rostov? For what young man's romantic aspirations and foolish daydreams can we be as indulgent as we are for Lucien Leuwen's or Frédéric Moreau's? All this is tanta-mount to saying that – reality being what the mind perceives as reality – these creations of Jane Austen or Tolstoy, Stendhal or Flaubert, which never had any 'real' existence, are possessed none the less of a superlative reality thanks to some mystery or other of the novelist's craft.

We may say that these authors compel us to respond to their creations, to sympathize, in extreme cases to identify with them in a way we should find it almost impossible to identify with a living man or woman of our private acquaintance. Possibly the first occasion in literary history when a novel achieved a widespread effect of this kind was when Richardson's *Clarissa* started to come off the press. Just as, a century later, his readers wrote to Dickens with passionate pleas to spare this or that doomed child-hero or stricken heroine, so after the appearance of the first volumes of Richardson's masterpiece the author was beset by anxious followers of Clarissa's fortunes begging him to have Lovelace relent and marry her as Mr B— had married Pamela. Even Fielding hoped this might happen; and Richardson's friend Laetitia Pilkington reported to him the wild lamentations that Colley Cibber had broken into when he learned what fearful fate lay in store for this latter-day virgin and martyr.

Clarissa was quickly and badly translated into French by Prévost, and was soon as well known to Parisians as to Londoners. Diderot waited till he could read it in the original and then penned his *Éloge de Richardson* (published 1762), an extravagant and highly emotional encomium which, translated into German in 1766 and praised by Herder, served to propagate the cult of Richardson still further afield. The essential passage in this essay, where Diderot analyses in glowing terms the English novelist's gift of enlisting the reader's sympathy for his characters, runs as follows:

O Richardson! one cannot but act a part in thy works, intervene in the dialogues, approve, disapprove, admire, wax wrathful or indignant. How many times have I not caught myself, like children taken to see a play for the first time, exclaiming: *Do not believe him, he deceives you! If you go thither, you are lost.* My soul was held in a constant state of agitation . . . I had encountered in the space of a few hours a great number of situations such as the longest life scarcely offers in its fullest span. I had heard the true accents of the passions; I had seen the motive forces of self-interest and self-love working in a hundred different ways; I had been the spectator of countless incidents, I felt I had acquired experience.

It would seem that Richardson's realism was valued by Diderot because it was a substitute for, or an augmentation of, 'real' experience. And, as he goes on to say, this realism was fortified by the very ordinariness of everyone and everything in the book:

The world in which we live is his setting; the backcloth of his drama true; his characters have the greatest possible reality; his types are drawn from the middling part of society; his incidents are compatible with the way of life of any civilized nation; the passions he depicts are such as I experience myself; the same factors provoke them, they have the strength that I know them to have; the misfortunes and afflictions of his characters are of the sort that threatens me ceaselessly; he shows me the general course of the stream that bears me along.

That such banality should excite such enthusiasm is something that cries out for explanation. Partly it is that Richardson's novels were bound to strike Diderot as breaking quite new ground in literature. As he wrote at the very beginning of his essay: 'By a novel, we have meant hitherto a string of fanciful and frivolous incidents, to read which was dangerous for one's taste and one's morals. I wish some other word could be found for the works of Richardson . . .' But the novelty did not lie simply in the absence of 'fanciful and frivolous incidents'. The impact of *Clarissa* on the contemporary reading public was due above all to the form in which Richardson had couched his story. *Pamela* had been a novel-in-letters; but since nearly all the letters in it had been written by the heroine, the book might as well have been presented entirely as her diary. Equally, it would have been conceivable as an autobiographical novel, presenting the memoirs of the servant-girl graduating to squire's lady – another *Paysanne parvenue*. But in *Clarissa* Richardson made far more extensive use of the resources of the epistolary novel, and in consequence the book is scarcely imaginable written in any other way. There are two principal sets of correspondence: the exchange of letters between Clarissa and her friend Miss Howe, and that between Lovelace and his fellow rake Belford. The same intrigue is thus seen under a double perspective and, with no sacrifice of plausibility, we are allowed greater insight into the heroine's predicament than she obtains herself – something the memoir-novel by its very nature can never give us. Moreover, Clarissa Harlowe could never have written her own confessions, since her story ends, and has to end, with her death. Here we touch on yet another of the drawbacks of the autobiographical novel: the reader is necessarily conscious that, whatever distressful circumstances may at any moment beset the writer, he must have survived them or he would not be relating them to us. If death is the ultimate calamity, then the first-person novel can never achieve the ultimate in tragedy.

None of this altogether explains why Diderot, and others like him but less articulate about their reactions, should have experienced so overwhelming a sense of oneness with the rather silly girl that Clarissa was, if one considers her conduct in cold blood; nor why they should have followed her fortunes with bated breath and, at the end, with horror and compassion. It may be noted in passing that when, in 1761, Jean-Jacques ROUSSEAU (1712–78) brought out *La Nouvelle Héloïse*, which must count as the first entirely successful epistolary novel in France, it was greeted with similar excitement: the eagerness to read it was so great that booksellers found they could make more money renting the volumes at twelve sous an hour than by selling them to would-be purchasers. La Harpe commented with sardonic ambiguity that 'the ladies whiled away the nights reading it which they could not employ any better'. Rousseau himself was astonished to receive letters from all manner of good people who were evidently completely persuaded that Julie, Saint-Preux, Lord Bomston and Baron Wolmar were real people: there could have been no better proof of his success as a literary illusionist.

Both these novels, Richardson's and Rousseau's, were extremely long. Each provided the most detailed account of every scene in which the characters were involved, the most meticulous analysis too of their emotional reactions to each scene. Sometimes this verged on the ridiculous: Saint-Preux goes so far as to indite a letter to Julie, describing his state of rapturous anticipation, when he is actually in her bedroom waiting for her to come upstairs and fulfil her promise to give herself to him. Such exhaustiveness may jar with modern tastes, but the eighteenth-century reader had the delicious feeling that, for the first time, nothing was being kept from him. This was life itself in all its fullness, in all its dullness too, enlivened by apprehensive shudders; for in these novels the events, tiny and insignificant though they may appear to be, are relayed to us by those whom they touch most closely and who have no means of knowing, at the moment of writing, whither these events are tending and what the outcome will be. The emotional impact was bound to be more powerful than in the memoir-novel, where everything was presented through the lens of retrospective knowledge. Richardson himself took care to point out the difference, and the immense advantage of the epistolary form, in his preface to *Clarissa*:

Much more lively and affecting . . . must be the style of those who write in the height of a *present* distress, the mind tortured by the pangs of uncertainty (the events then hidden in the womb of fate); than the dry, narrative, unanimated style of a person relating difficulties and dangers surmounted, can be; the relater perfectly at ease; and if himself unmoved by his own story, not likely greatly to affect his reader.

After *Clarissa* and *La Nouvelle Héloïse* the epistolary novel had a brief vogue, culminating in *Les Liaisons dangereuses* (1782), the only work of fiction ever composed by the artillery officer Pierre Choderlos de LACLOS (1741–1803). The subject apart, which caused this work to be twice banned by the civil courts in France, *Les Liaisons dangereuses* represented the high-water mark of technical achievement in the genre. It is relatively short, and very few of the component letters are of any great length. Laclos avoided the trap of including letters which obviously serve only the purpose of giving the reader of the novel – as distinct from the intended recipient – information about the development of events: every one of the letters is prompted by a clear need on the part of the writer to communicate something or other of importance to the addressee. He made splendidly ironic use of the 'multiple viewpoint', by which the same event is reported by two or three different witnesses, each knowing a little more than the other about the true circumstances underlying the event. Letters are used not merely to disclose what has happened, but to instigate new happenings; there is, indeed, one letter that drives the woman who receives it mad. Finally, Laclos showed himself a past master in the art of revealing character through the quirks of style of each of his letter-writers: we gain a remarkable insight into their standard of education, maturity of outlook, and degree of sophistication not just by noting what they say, but by observing how they say it.

It was a virtuoso performance which perhaps discouraged any further exploitation of the genre. The example Laclos gave, of so triumphantly overcoming the difficulties inherent in the epistolary novel, incidentally demonstrated how formidable were those difficulties for a would-be realist. For to present a narrative entirely through the medium of private letters is, as one of Richardson's early biographers admitted, 'the most natural and the least probable way of telling a story'.[16] The most natural because, after all, people do write letters – or did, at all events, in the eighteenth century. The least probable because it is hard to believe that a multitude of connected events are likely to be found all duly chronicled in an assortment of letters from various writers, or that all these letters should by some happy chance have been preserved. To carry conviction, the novelist had so to arrange matters that letters were not exchanged between two people who could more conveniently meet and converse by word of mouth. He had, if he could, to dispense with the give-away device of the inactive confidant who has to be kept faithfully posted regarding every development. He had to arrange sufficient privacy and leisure to make letter-writing not just a possible but a plausible occupation even for persons in the thick of some highly charged emotional drama. And when he had done all this, he was still faced with the fundamentally unrealistic assumption lying at the very heart of this form of novel, that a man or a woman is ever likely confidently and candidly to set out on paper, for perusal by a friend, a relative or a lover, all that he thinks, all that he feels, all his anxieties and expectations.

FIELDING: 'TOM JONES'

Little wonder that the epistolary novel fell so rapidly into disuse, even more completely than the fictional autobiography. Balzac's vast output includes only one novel-by-letters (*Mémoires de deux jeunes mariées*) and only one novel written in the first person (*Le Lys dans la vallée*). Nineteenth-century realism rejected both the forms that eighteenth-century fiction writers had spent most of their time and energy in developing, and preferred instead to concentrate on a third type of novel, of which there had been only one really outstanding example, Fielding's *Tom Jones* (1749).

Henry FIELDING (1707–54), unlike Richardson, had received the education of a gentleman (at Eton College), which meant that he was well-versed in the Greek and Latin classics and could read French. His first novel, *Joseph Andrews* (1742), which started as a satire on Richardson's *Pamela* but in its later stages developed a momentum of its own, owed something to *Gil Blas* and rather more than something to Marivaux's *Paysan parvenu*. But by the time he came to write *Tom Jones* he seems to have freed himself from the influence of the French authors of fictional memoirs, and of their anxious concern to maintain the pretence that their novels were not novels at all but authentic accounts of the actual experiences of real people. Fielding cast his eyes further back, and took as his models the sturdy story-tellers of antiquity, the authors of the old epics. One need not take too seriously the intention he proclaimed, in the preface to the second part of *Joseph Andrews*, to write 'a comic epic poem in prose': the two qualifications effectively cancel out the central concept. What does need to be seen is how Fielding grasped the artistic possibilities of a long narrative capable of being held together by its own internal logic, without needing to be buttressed by any claims to external authentication. As a classicist, he believed that the chief function of art was 'to copy nature'; in the prefatory chapters to the various component books of *Tom Jones*, the theme recurs constantly: 'our business is only to record truth'; 'it is our province to relate facts, and we shall leave causes to persons of much higher genius.' The common run of fertile story-tellers were denounced for the arbitrary subjectivity of their creations: 'truth distinguishes our writings from those idle romances which are filled with monsters, the productions not of nature, but of distempered brains.' The truth in question was, of course, the truth about human nature: psychology, as we should call it today, but psychology in breadth, not in depth. Here, life itself, multifarious contacts with all manner of men, could alone give the novelist his schooling. 'A true knowledge of the world is gained only by conversation, and the manners of every rank must be seen in order to be known.' The word *conversation*, in eighteenth-century English, meant more than just talk; it included 'the action of consorting with others', and clearly Mr Henry Fielding, the London magistrate, ex-playboy who was on familiar terms with the great as well as being in daily contact, professionally, with the riff-raff of the streets and the hardened criminal, was well-placed to write the first realist novel to mirror the whole range of English society, from the forelock-pulling rustic to the city fop and from the village hoyden to the luxurious lady of fashion. The mirror was, of course, angled: we are not given an entirely neutral account of the scene. Only a London-based Whig could have sketched the grotesque lineaments of the choleric, high-tory, sottish father of Sophia Western. Fielding, as Walter Allen has said, 'populated a whole world, but it exists as a considered criticism of the real world'.[17] But then, realism can never be altogether free of bias, and it is doubtful indeed whether a flatly photographic repro-duction of human diversity should constitute the prime objective of art. Even at this time, the point had been taken by the greatest English critic of the age: 'If the world be promiscuously described, I cannot see of what use it can be to read the account; or why it may not be as safe to turn the eye immediately upon mankind, as upon a mirror which shows all that presents itself without discrimination.'[18]

Fielding exercised his discrimination not merely in his portraiture but in the formal organization of his work. To find a novel as carefully wrought as *Tom Jones* one needs to go back to *La Princesse de Clèves*: significantly, a product of classicism in its finest flowering. It has been suggested that in respect of the impeccable construction of his master-piece Fielding may have been indebted to his earlier study of the French classical dramatists: he had started his literary career as a play-wright. Only Sophocles' *Oedipus* and Ben Jonson's *Alchemist* seemed to Coleridge worthy to be compared to *Tom Jones* in point of struc-tural perfection, while a professional novelist of a later generation (Thackeray) showed himself full of admiration for the 'literary providence' that Fielding displayed: 'Not an incident ever so trifling but advances the story, grows out of former incidents, and is connected with the whole.'[19] But, of course, such artifice, however well hidden, could be judged a distraction from the 'truth' that Fielding was aim-ing at. Life is not so tidy, and, as we have seen, the realist has to manage without providence, literary or divine.

This might seem an appropriate cautionary point with which to close this introductory chapter. All through the 'age of realism' novelists will be faced with the same dilemma: social institutions, human relationships, the separate courses of individual lives, all these cannot be presented in a work of art without a certain measure of trimming and tailoring. An accurate reproduction of any 'slice of life' would be hopelessly unsatisfactory as literature: too formless, full of false trails and pointless anticlimaxes. However firm his allegiance to realism, a novelist has to impose his own peculiar vision on what he sees, partly because this vision is inseparable from his artistic consciousness, and partly because without it his work would lack shape and point and would finally prove unreadable. This underlying dilemma amounts to an internal contradiction at the very core of realism, one which was destined in the long run to discredit it, or at least to discredit its pretensions; but not before the struggle to achieve the impossible – a faithful representation of contemporary social reality which should yet be integrated into a smoothly consistent work of art – had resulted in the production of a series of striking literary masterpieces.

Notes

1 See E. B. O. Borgerhoff, '*Réalisme* and kindred words: their use as terms of literary criticism in the first half of the nineteenth century', *Publications of the Modern Language Association*, Vol. LIII (1938), p. 839.

2 Preface to *Jeannette seconde, ou la Nouvelle Paysanne parvenue*. Quoted in Jacques Rustin, '*L'histoire véritable* dans la littérature romanesque du XVIIIᵉ siècle français', *Cahiers de l'Association Internationale des Études françaises*, Vol. XXVIII (1966), p. 89.

3 *The Rambler*, Vol. I, No. 4 (31 March 1750), p. 27.

4 *Concepts of Criticism* (New Haven and London, 1963), pp. 240–41.

5 *The Gates of Horn* (New York, 1963), p. 36.

6 A useful analysis of this work may be read in 'Literature and Society: Eighteenth Century', *Yale French Studies*, No. 40 (1968), pp. 142–55.

7 *Les Origines de la France contemporaine: l'Ancien Régime* (Paris, Hachette, 1904), Vol. II, p. 314.

8 Walpole, *Correspondence with Madame du Deffand*, ed. W. S. Lewis and W. H. Smith (London, 1939), Vol. III, p. 390.

9 Arnold Hauser, *The Social History of Art* (London, 1962), Vol. III, p. 44.

10 *The Rise of the Novel* (London, 1957), p. 49.

11 Lionel Stevenson, *The English Novel* (London, 1960), p. 82.

12 *Pamela* (Everyman's Library edition, 1969 reprint), Vol. I, p. 229.

13 Quoted in A. J. Tieje, 'A peculiar phase in the theory of realism in pre-Richardsonian fiction', *Publications of the Modern Language Association*, Vol. XXVIII (1913), p. 234.

14 *Le Pour et le Contre*, Vol. VI (1735), No. 90, p. 354. *Le Pour et le Contre* was a literary periodical edited by Prévost from 1733 onwards.

15 *Imitation and Illusion in the French Memoir-Novel* (New Haven and London, 1969), p. 104.

16 Anna Laetitia Barbauld, 'A Biographical Account of Samuel Richardson', introduction to the first volume of Richardson, *Correspondence* (1804). Quoted in Miriam Allott, *Novelists on the Novel* (London, 1959), p. 259.

17 *The English Novel* (1954), Pelican Books edition, p. 63.
18 S. Johnson, quoted in R. Wellek, *A History of Modern Criticism: the Later Eighteenth Century* (London, 1955), p. 85.
19 Thackeray, *Critical Papers in Literature* (London, Macmillan, 1911), p. 207.

TWO

Realism in the Age of Romanticism

ROMANTICISM AND REALISM

IT has been urged often enough that the terms romanticism and realism are not susceptible to precise and comprehensive definition; however, a simple inventory of their commonest connotations is sufficient to show how completely opposed the two concepts are. The realist is supposed to deal with contemporary life and commonplace scenes; the romantic succumbs to the lure of the past and delights in dreaming of far-off places. The realist fixes his gaze on the world of men, the streets where they jostle and the rooms where they meet and converse; the romantic seeks solitude and finds it in nature, in the woods, the fields, the lonely seashore and the lonelier mountain crag. The realist is drawn into the social vortex, charts the cross-currents of ambition and self-interest, is familiar with all the processes of getting and spending; the romantic disdains such prosaic preoccupations; instead, he idealizes the purer passions and cultivates the darker ones, having leanings towards the satanic as well as the spiritual; whereas the typical realist, more especially in France, levels passion down to the play of the senses and has no patience with intimations of immortality. The romantic exalts the creative spirit and puts his faith in intuition; the realist's approach to his material is detached and analytic. On a strictly literary plane, the value the realist sets on stylistic sobriety contrasts with the romantic's cultivation of exuberance and emotive imagery; the former, in short, sticks to prose, while poetry remains the authentic, if not the exclusive, medium for the expression of the romantic mood and the romantic world-view.

Literary romanticism reached its apogee in France in 1830: later than in neighbouring countries, but the reasons need not detain us here. Victor HUGO (1802–85), the acknowledged leader of the movement, produced his provocatively romantic verse drama, *Hernani*, in March of that year; its stormy performances were universally taken to signalize the triumph of the new school. His verse collection *Les Feuilles d'automne* (1831), taken in conjunction with the *Orientales* which had been published two years before, exemplified the two sides of romantic poetry, the colourfully dramatic and the more muted and meditative strain. As if anxious to show equal virtuosity in every domain of literature, Hugo also published at this time his historical novel *Notre-Dame de Paris*. This romance was set in the late Middle Ages; his *Orientales*, largely inspired by the Greek War of Independence, had evoked the contemporary barbarity of the Ottoman Empire; while for the spectators at the Comédie Française Hugo contrived a double displacement in time and space: the action of *Hernani* takes place in Spain and Germany at the time of Charles V. Romanticism was manifesting itself, intentionally or not, as a literature of escapism.

Now 1830 was also the year of the July Revolution, the moment in time when the French nation decided it had lived long enough in the pallid afterglow of the *ancien régime* represented by the rule of the restored Bourbon sovereigns. The failed autocrat Charles X fled the country and Louis-Philippe, the 'bourgeois king', was enthroned in his place. For the next eighteen years, ostensibly France was to be governed by a bicameral parliament; in reality, it was the hard-headed bankers and businessmen who exercised control. This period of middle-class rule was marked by steady industrial expansion and occasional industrial unrest, remorselessly suppressed as soon as it became really troublesome. Railways spread, factories smoked, labourers left the land and flocked to the towns, where they found inadequate lodgings and were paid starvation wages. The contrast between swashbuckling or inward-turning romanticism and the harshly positivistic spirit of the age could hardly have been more striking. But the discrepancy between literature and life was more apparent than real, especially if one turns from poetry to prose: for it was in these years that the earliest works which we would today be inclined to denominate 'realist' were composed and published. Stendhal was actually writing *Le Rouge et le noir* while *Hernani* was attracting tumultuous audiences; and at the same moment (in April 1830) Balzac brought out the first edition of his *Scènes de la vie privée*, a collection of six novellas which represent the first spurt of the torrent later to broaden out into the magnificent flood of *La Comédie humaine*.

Stendhal and Balzac, respectively forty-seven and thirty-one years of age in 1830, can be called romantic novelists only in the very limited sense that they were novelists writing in the period when romanticism was the dominant literary mode. Their art owed nothing to the writers of fiction who immediately preceded them in France: neither to Ducray-Duminil, author of immensely popular mystery yarns, nor to Paul de Kock, the master of the *roman gai*, nor yet to the band of insipid lady novelists, Mme de Genlis, Mme Cottin, Mme de Souza and the rest of them, whose genteel and edifying romances were one of the most oddly inappropriate literary products of the stressful reign of Napoleon I. If one disregards Constant's unique masterpiece *Adolphe*, only semi-fictional and in any case too condensed, perhaps, to rate as a full-scale novel, the history of prose narrative in France over the fifty years that separated *Les Liaisons dangereuses* from *Le Rouge et le noir* affords nothing to engage the attention of posterity.

WALTER SCOTT AND THE FRENCH

The writer who gave Stendhal and Balzac the stimulus they needed was Walter SCOTT (1771–1832), the last of the trio of novelists writing in English (the others being of course Richardson and Fielding) whose art can be said to have made a significant contribution to the development of European realism. On the evidence of one of his marginal notes, it would appear that Stendhal read at any rate some extracts from *Waverley* as early as 1815, the year after it was published.[1] Domiciled, at that time, in Milan, he instructed his bookseller in Paris to send him all the novels of the series, *The Abbot*, *The Antiquary*, *Rob Roy* etc., as soon as they could be procured. His letters in 1819 and 1820 show him to be devouring Scott's 'divine novels' with an enthusiasm that caused him to rate the author's genius even higher than Byron's.[2] As for Balzac, the first mention of Scott in his writings occurs in a letter to his younger sister Laure in 1821. She had told him she was reading Richardson's *Clarissa*; he advises her, when she has finished, to go on to *La Nouvelle Héloïse*, and strongly recommends in addition '*Kenilworth*, Scott's last novel; it is the finest thing in the world'.[3] The following year, Balzac paid Scott the compliment of imitating him, publishing under a coy pseudonym a historical novel of his own composition.[4] It was, however, hastily written, ill researched and of negligible literary value.

In the fervour with which they flung themselves on the Waverley Novels, Stendhal and Balzac were entirely typical of their generation. The translators had gone to work in 1817; in the half-dozen years that followed, enthusiasm built up rapidly among the lettered public in France. Victor Hugo, in one of his earliest critical essays, eulogized Scott for having achieved an amalgam of the two kinds of novel which, before, had been practised quite separately: that is, the novel of plain narrative, and the novel-by-letters. Scott had succeeded in renovating fiction by borrowing from drama; he presented events as no one had presented them before, in a succession of lively scenes and conversational exchanges.[5] Such technical considerations may have accounted for the esteem in which Scott was held among literary professionals; his unprecedented sales testify to his popularity among the broader reaches of the public. This popularity was reflected in borrowings by practitioners of the sister arts: the plots of the Waverley Novels were used in operas, while the more memorable scenes were made the subject of paintings. For those who had the time and the money, literary pilgrimages to Edinburgh and points north became almost as fashionable as, at the end of the century, musical pilgrimages to Bayreuth when Wagner was all the rage.

Reporting in the *London Magazine* on the Paris scene, Stendhal observed that Scott had brought about

a revolution in French literature. Without being conscious of it, probably, or aspiring to the honour, he is the chief of what is called in France *le parti romantique* . . . Moreover, the strong attachment felt or feigned by Sir Walter Scott, for all that smacks of ancient institutions, and his consequent want of enthusiasm for those innovations and improvements, which tend to ameliorate the present social state of mankind, have rendered him a distinguished favourite with the Ultra party.[6]

The *ultras* were the right-wing extremists of the Restoration period who, more royalist than the king, regarded the constitutional settlement of 1815 as a shameful sell-out; they had been greatly heartened when the reactionary Charles X succeeded his brother Louis XVIII in 1824. At the time Stendhal was writing, the romantics – those of them, at any rate, who took their cue from Hugo – shared the political out-look of the *ultras*: if not exactly court poets, they were certainly dedicated defenders of throne and altar. Stendhal, a lifelong liberal, had little patience either with the *ultras* or with the romantics, or for that matter with the toryism of the Scottish baronet whose talent as a novelist he nevertheless so genuinely admired. It is here that we come up against the double paradox involved in tracing the ancestry of the French realist movement back to Scott and his literary example. In the first place, Scott's political conservatism would almost seem to disallow from the start any claim that he might have inspired a school of writers who, on the whole and with significant exceptions, tended to align themselves with the more socially progressive forces in what-ever country they happened to belong to. And secondly, perhaps more importantly, there would appear to be an inherent contradiction in the proposition that a man who had made his name as the author of historical novels, whose source-material was all drawn from the recent or distant past, could be said to have fathered a movement which prided itself on its lucid analysis of the contemporary condition of society.

The first chapter of Georg Lukács's *Historical Novel* provides a plausible explanation of how it came about that Scott, 'like so many great realists, such as Balzac and Tolstoy, became a great realist despite his own political and social views'. The core of Lukács's argument, which is that insight and honesty must always be more highly valued in a writer than correct (i.e. politically progressive) views, is surely unassailable; the most one can do is to breathe a passing regret that the conclusions of Marxist theorists, in this area as in others, seem not always to be very carefully applied by Marxist ministers of culture. For our immediate purpose, it will be sufficient to mention two aspects of Scott's treatment of his cast of characters which show him both as an innovator in his own right and as the founder of a durable tradition.

In the first place, his art has a markedly democratic stamp which it owes to the fact that Scott was, as George Sand observed, 'the poet of the peasant, soldier, outlaw and artisan'. His most memorable characters are by no means always the kings and queens, the lords and ladies, the generals and the ministers. The great and the powerful play their part in his novels, though it is often a sorry one, but the characters who engage our interest and affections come mostly from much lowlier social strata. They are the old bedesman, Edie Ochiltree, in *The Antiquary*; the simple-minded, steadfast Jeanie Deans in *The Heart of Midlothian*; honest Simon Glover, the father of the fair maid of Perth, and Henry Smith, the armourer, her lover; besides many another representative of the stalwart Scottish artisan and peasant classes. Similarly, in the novels set farther back in time, it is not unusual to find the forefront occupied by commoners or serfs, members of a nameless throng ignored by the chroniclers of the period. The opening scene of *Ivanhoe*, with its lively interchanges between the swineherd Gurth and Wamba, the Saxon jester, struck all readers as startlingly original. 'Low' characters had, of course, been employed in minor roles by earlier novelists, by Marivaux, Fielding, Smollett, and others, but mainly to provide comic relief; Scott was the first to take them seriously. Balzac imitated him here directly in *Les Chouans* (1829), a straightforward historical novel centring on the 1799 royalist rising in Brittany; later, he used the same convention in stories with contemporary settings, such as *Le Curé de Tours* (1832) and *Histoire de la grandeur et de la décadence de César Birotteau* (1837). In these three novels we find that the most fully developed and sympathetic characters are, respectively, an honest sergeant in the Republican army, a bumbling minor canon, and a Parisian tradesman of exceptional honesty, but not otherwise noteworthy. In *La Chartreuse de Parme* similarly, the novel above all others in which Stendhal echoes Scott, an unusual prominence is given to ill-educated men of low rank, like Ludovic, Fabrice's manservant, Giletti, the strolling player, and Ferrante Palla, the self-styled 'tribune of the people'; while Blanès, the oddly impressive village priest who dabbles in astrology, is bound to put any reader of *Quentin Durward* in mind of Galeotti Martivalle. George Sand's fondness for working-class heroes, in novels published in the late 1840s, admittedly owes more to her admiration of Fourier than to the by now much attenuated influence of Scott, but it remains true that without the example he set it is improbable that the realists would have so readily incorporated the humble dramas of lower-class life into their fiction.

An even more portentous technical innovation of the Waverley Novels was the downgrading of the central character. The typical protagonist in a novel by Scott is a young man of breeding, with sound moral principles and a modicum of practical intelligence. Essentially a colourless figure, he is the decent, average Englishman (or Scotsman), stirred by no very deep passions and not intended to arouse more than a mild sympathy in the reader. In a word, Scott may be said to have invented the 'unheroic hero' and in this he was most sharply at odds with the whole spirit of romanticism: there is nothing Byronic about Waverley. Neither Stendhal (except perhaps in *Lucien Leuwen*) nor Balzac can be said to have adopted this particular feature of Scott's narrative method. It was a device, however, which was to prove admirably suited to the realist novel as it developed later in the century, especially in Russia, the breeding ground of the 'superfluous man'. By placing at the centre of his novel an unremarkable, basically uninteresting character, the realist would find it easier to concentrate attention on the social scene which he conceived it as being his main business to depict.

The point has already been made that, as the author of historical novels (*St Ronan's Well* was his only attempt at a story set in his own times, and it was a conspicuous failure), Scott cannot in any obvious sense be regarded as a forerunner of the realists, whose principal concern would be with contemporary life. At the same time, the critical acclaim he won in France in the 1820s was in no small measure due to the impression of reality that his novels conveyed. Amédée Pichot, in a literary travel-book written in 1825, praised Scott for remaining on 'the prosaic ground of commonplace realities', while the anonymous author of an essay, 'De la réalité en littérature', which appeared the same year in *Le Mercure du XIXe siècle*, attributed Scott's mastery to his uncanny success in associating himself imaginatively with the period he was describing: hence 'the *reality* of the landscapes, sites, characters, customs and people that he depicts'.[7] His more educated readers felt – not altogether wrongly – that they were absorbing history under the guise of entertainment; by conferring on it a certain instructional value, Scott succeeded in raising immeasurably the prestige of the novel, which, as a form of literature, had lost much of the critical esteem that Richardson, Fielding and Rousseau had secured for it in the previous century. 'Ten years ago,' observed a contributor to *Le Globe* in 1826, 'serious men went into hiding to read a novel; today, short of being a Jansenist, nobody makes a mystery of his taste for such reading matter. Ten years hence, it will be said that the fiction of *Ivanhoe* is just as noble as that of [Tasso's] *Jerusalem Delivered*.'[8]

As we saw in the previous chapter, it was from historical and pseudo-historical writing that the early realist novel largely stemmed; Fielding himself had called the novelist the 'historian of private life'. A feeling for history, in its broadest sense, is a feeling for the changes that time brings about; and for those who, like Stendhal, had been born on the eve of the French Revolution and were in middle age when the romantic revolution was subverting all the old literary canons, nothing was more evident than that everything was subject to change. A sense of the entirely provisional nature of laws, customs, and social institutions, of the impermanence of men's most cherished beliefs and most settled convictions, marked the romantic generation as it had no previous one. The neurosis bred by this new instability informs works as various as Constant's *Adolphe* and certain celebrated odes of the romantic period, Lamartine's 'Le Lac' and Hugo's 'Tristesse d'Olympio'. It accounts for the cult of ruins found in Chateaubriand's *Génie du christianisme* and for the dread of approaching industrialization that Vigny expressed in 'La Maison du Berger'. The vogue of the historical novel is but one aspect of this generalized nostalgia for the past; the fact that the vogue was short-lived must be attributed less to any sudden resolution of the neurosis than to a change in the way it expressed itself. Regret at the mutability of human affairs can lead – and did, in the case of Balzac particularly – to an anxiety that everything in the evanescent texture of present reality should be preserved; much as a man might prefer to photograph changing cloud effects rather than the unaltering contours of the hills. Thus the realist began by thinking of himself as a conservationist, with a particularly tender regard for anything in the life of the community that he judged might be threatened with extinction. He was the historian of the present, whose mission was to capture the spirit of his own period, with all its minute and fugitive particularities, before it was swept away by the rising tide of future change.

BALZAC, STENDHAL, AND THE HISTORICAL PERSPECTIVE

In the foreword (*Avant-propos*) to his collected works, which dates from 1842 and was therefore posterior to most of the novels and short stories subsumed under the collective title *La Comédie humaine*, Honoré de BALZAC (1799–1850) described his aim as being 'to write the history that so many historians have forgotten about, the history of manners [or morals: *mœurs*]'. 'Manners' is a word with narrower implications than '*mœurs*', which in turn has narrower implications than 'morals'. Balzac meant that he wanted to describe how people lived and how they behaved towards others, to enumerate and analyse the social and economic factors that controlled to a large extent the way they lived and behaved; he wanted to achieve for his own age what academic social historians are compelled to attempt, usually with inadequate data, for past periods. This might extend even to such apparently trivial matters as the clothes and items of personal adornment worn by his characters. The details he gives of Mme de Barge-ton's provincial finery, Charles Grandet's waistcoats and dressing-gown, Pons's old-fashioned 'spencer' and the yellow kid gloves of a lady-killer like Maxime de Trailles, have a value comparable with that of Scott's descriptions of the garb of a medieval serf or the panoply of a crusading knight: they constitute so much historical evidence, carefully recorded by Balzac for the benefit of posterity, for whom such evidence will possess a genuine antiquarian interest.

Living as he did in a period of rapid social change, Balzac was particularly careful to describe, in loving detail, any social institution, any manifestation of community life which he guessed might be doomed to disappear.

The railways, in the very near future, are destined to destroy certain industries and modify others, particularly as concerns the various modes of transport employed in the neighbourhood of Paris. For this reason, before long the characters and institutions that form the elements of this story will give it the value of an archaeological study. Will not our children be delighted to learn of the social arrangements of a period they will call the good old times?

These are the opening sentences, roughly translated, of a short novel entitled *Un Début dans la vie* (*A Start in Life*) which was first published in 1842: the principal characters are all passengers in a horse-drawn public conveyance of the type that commonly plied, some twenty years earlier, between the capital and the small outlying towns. The first sentence of another story, *La Maison du Chat-qui-Pelote* (*At the Sign of the Cat and Racket*, 1830), has the same ring: 'Half way down the Rue St Denis, almost at the corner of the Rue du Petit Lion, there existed until recently one of those precious houses which give' historians the opportunity of reconstructing by analogy the Paris of olden times.' The house in question is in fact a mercer's shop, recognizable by its quaint signboard (a cat wielding a racket), and still operating, at the period of which Balzac was writing, in accordance with eighteenth-century commercial principles, the shopkeeper with his wife and daughters living under the same roof as his apprentices. (The establishment is in fact astonishingly similar to the Varden household described by Dickens only a few years later in his own historical novel, *Barnaby Rudge*.) When his story has a provincial setting, Balzac seems to take even greater delight in pointing out the relics of the past: the more untouched the town is by modern ways, the more scrupulously he records its appearance and the way of life of its inhabitants.[9]

His belief in the importance of preserving word-pictures of reality, because reality was nothing but a flux of evanescent forms – buildings, costumes, trades and professions alike – accounts in large measure for the frequency of descriptive passages in Balzac's works. In Stendhal's novels descriptions are, by contrast, something of a rarity, and up to a point one can explain the discrepancy in terms of a difference in the assumptions made by each novelist concerning human psychology. Balzac was a firm believer in the influence of environment on personality and, conversely, in the extent to which human beings leave on their surroundings the imprint of their character and way of life. The oft-quoted phrase in the first chapter of *Le Père Goriot*, about the fat, slovenly landlady whose 'whole person explains the boarding-house, as the boarding-house implies her person', is only one instance of this reciprocity of influence, equally observable in the action-and-reaction process between Grandet and his cold, dark house in Saumur (*Eugénie Grandet*), the Claës family and their ancestral home at Douai (*La Recherche de l'absolu*), and the Baroness de Rouville, her daughter, and their shabby-genteel apartment in the early story *La Bourse* (*The*

Purse); it is in this last text that Balzac puts the significant question: 'Are not our sentiments, so to speak, written on the things that surround us?' The deep impression made on Balzac by the theories of Lavater, the Swiss clergyman who founded the pseudo-science of physiognomy, is clearly traceable here. In his treatise on the art of telling character by facial study, Lavater had written:

It is true that everything that surrounds man acts on him; but conversely he acts on external objects and if he is modified by them, in turn he modifies his environment. Hence it becomes possible to assess a man by observing his dress, his house, his furniture.[10]

Though STENDHAL (pseudonym of Henri Beyle, 1783–1842) was in some ways a more impenitent materialist than Balzac, his reading of Montesquieu had taught him that men were governed far less by the pressures of their physical environment than by their passions, their ambitions, their fears and their greed, these motivations being implanted and nurtured by the social circumstances in which they happened to find themselves. Thus, for Stendhal, a shopkeeper's personality, or a doctor's, would be determined not by the conditions in which he worked but by whatever feelings he entertained about his position, privileged or otherwise, in the total social structure.

Hence Stendhal rarely bothered to do more than sketch in his backgrounds, preferring to leave it to the reader to picture for himself the material setting of any particular scene; whereas Balzac dictates to his readers precisely what they should see, down to the minutest particular. In his autobiographical *Souvenirs d'égotisme* (*Memoirs of an Egotist*), after giving a series of lively pen-portraits of the various members of Destutt de Tracy's circle, Stendhal interjects: 'I have forgotten to describe the drawing-room. Sir Walter Scott and his imitators would have sagely started by doing so, but for myself, I abhor material description. The tedium of composing descriptive passages is what prevents me writing novels.' After he had overcome this inhibition and had written two or three, he still felt they suffered from the lack of picturesque details, and made plans to write these in when the novels were due for new editions.

Another difference, seldom remarked, between Stendhal's form of realism and Balzac's arises from the fact that Stendhal did not subscribe to the theory of the novelist as the 'historian of the present'.

Although nearly all Balzac's works were set in post-Napoleonic France, that is, in the span of time that coincided with his own adult life, it is noteworthy that the majority of them are situated at some small remove from the moment of writing, as though Balzac felt a time-lag to be essential. Thus, out of the ninety novels and short stories that make up *La Comédie humaine*, only seventeen are set in the period of the July Monarchy, yet all except the very first were composed by the author during this period. *Le Père Goriot*, published in 1834, deals with events in the year 1819; *La Rabouilleuse* (*The Black Sheep*, 1840) stretches from the closing years of the First Empire to the early stages of the conquest of Algeria; but the principal episodes must be considered to have occurred around 1820. By contrast, Stendhal's novels – those at any rate that are set in France – deal as a matter of course with current events. *Armance*, the first, bore the subtitle: 'Quelques scènes d'un salon de Paris en 1827'; it was actually published in August 1827. *Le Rouge et le noir* (*Scarlet and Black*), which followed *Armance*, seems to have been largely written in the early months of 1830: there are allusions in the text to the first performances of *Hernani* and other events of the spring of that year, though none to the July revolution, since Stendhal had written the concluding page before it broke out. This time, the book was sub-titled 'Chronique de 1830'. As for *Lucien Leuwen*, which Stendhal composed at Civitavecchia between June 1834 and November 1835, though he never dared publish it during his lifetime, it is stuffed with allusions to workers' insurrections, electoral gerrymandering, and other unsavoury features of the early years of the reign of Louis-Philippe. It is evident that Stendhal's brand of realism was in this respect rather different from Balzac's: he preferred to dispense with the retrospective view enjoyed by the historian and, like a leader-writer in a newspaper, to deal with social reality as it was in the process of revealing itself at the very moment he was writing. The word *chronique*, incidentally, which he used to describe *Le Rouge et le noir*, is applied in French to newspaper reports of current happenings: *chronique financière*, for example, is that part of the paper devoted to financial news, stock-exchange intelligence and the like.

Stendhal's concept of the novel is perfectly conveyed in the celebrated analogy of the mirror, which he seems to have invented even before he started on his career as a novelist.[11] In the foreword to

Armance he asked of his reader the same indulgence as was accorded to the authors of a comedy recently produced on the Paris stage: 'they held a mirror up to the public; is it their fault if people with ugly faces walked past the mirror? What are the political allegiances of a mirror?' The same argument is used in the much better known passage that occurs in Chapter 19 of the second part of *Le Rouge et le noir*. Stendhal imagines how he would answer a reader who might object to the somewhat scabrous sequence of incidents he has been narrating:

Why, sir, a novel is a mirror carried along a highroad. One moment it will reflect into your eyes the azure of heaven, the next the mire in the pot-holes along the road. And you would accuse the man who carries the mirror on his back of immorality! His mirror shows the mire, and you blame the mirror! Oughtn't you rather to blame the road with the pot-holes, or even better, the inspector of highways who lets the water gather and the pot-hole form?

The simile is treacherously attractive. Variants on it were used by realist novelists through the rest of the century whenever critics accused them of partiality, distortion or prurience. The fallacy in the argument emerges as soon as it is pressed too far, and the apologist finds himself brought up short by the same objection as we have noted already: if realism is an art-form at all, then it must involve selection and invention, it must go beyond mere reflection.

POLITICS AND THE NOVEL

Stendhal will refer once more to the mirror analogy in the course of *Le Rouge et le noir*, this time linking it with another famous simile, that in which he likens the intrusion of politics in the novel to the firing of a pistol at a concert. This second passage occurs as a typically nonchalant parenthesis, which takes the form of an imaginary dialogue between the author and his publisher inserted into the narrative with little regard for the maintenance of dramatic illusion. At this juncture the hero, Julien Sorel, is about to be involved in a mysterious conspiracy to bring about some kind of a right-wing putsch. Stendhal pretends he would like to draw a veil here, or in other words replace the whole episode by a row of dots; but the publisher dislikes dots.

'Politics,' retorts the author, 'is a stone tied to literature's neck, which drowns it inside six months. Politics in the middle of a work of imagination is like a pistol-shot in the middle of a concert: an ear-splitting noise which lacks point. It's in tune with none of the instruments. This political passage is going to offend mortally half my readers, and bore the other half who read it all in this morning's paper and found it a lot more apposite there . . .'

'If your characters don't talk politics,' answers the publisher, 'they aren't Frenchmen of the year 1830 and your book is no longer a mirror as you claimed . . .'

The danger here so clearly foreseen by Stendhal was of a political partisanship almost unavoidable in his type of up-to-the-minute realism. Topicality carries its penalties. In addition, his fiction risked sinking into premature obsolescence, since he was not at a sufficient distance from events to distinguish the accidental and the ephemeral from the truly significant. This was a pitfall he usually avoided, thanks to his keen sense of the direction events were taking; even so, it has to be admitted that certain portions of his novel (as, here, the so-called episode of the 'secret note') have become dead wood by now.

This is not to say, of course, that his grasp of contemporary reality, its general contours and its underlying currents, was in any way less firm than Balzac's. The similarity, broadly speaking, of the account each novelist gave of the state of the country during the third and fourth decades of the century is all the more remarkable when one considers that, as far as private political convictions went, the two were poles apart. This means no more, of course, than that they proposed contrary remedies for the political evils of which each provided an identical diagnosis. Stendhal had greeted the news of the execution of Louis XVI with secret exultation; admittedly, he was only a boy at the time, but precocious in more ways than one. He was slow in reconciling himself to Napoleon's seizure of power in 1799; he was so depressed at the restoration of the Bourbon dynasty in 1814 that he went into voluntary exile. The revolution of 1830 delighted him until he realized that it had merely strengthened the power of the bankers and captains of industry; even so, he seems to have come round to the persuasion that the new régime was the best that France could hope to have at the time. Stendhal was never a republican, except in his hot-headed youth. He hated the very notion of democracy based on universal suffrage, as in the United States, and saw great merit in the system of bicameral government with a monarch who reigned but did not rule, after the British fashion. He believed that the lower classes should be kept in their place, though he was not in favour of actually shooting them down. He was, in short, the typical left-of-centre moderate of the period. Balzac, on the other hand, a republican sympathizer in his early manhood, perversely moved over to the right in the early 1830s, swayed initially by certain liaisons, flattering to his self-esteem, that he formed with women of rank, and later influenced intellectually by the doctrines of two reactionary political thinkers, Joseph de Maistre and Louis de Bonald, notable upholders of the theory of the divine right of kings and the infallibility of the Roman Catholic Church. In the foreword to *La Comédie humaine* Balzac went so far as to proclaim, provocatively, that he wrote his novels 'by the light of two eternal verities, Religion and the Monarchy, two necessities proclaimed by the current trend of events and back towards which every sensible writer must try to guide our country'. At the time (1842) nearly every novelist in France, from George Sand to Eugène Sue, was straining in the opposite direction, but although he can hardly have been unaware of this Balzac continued obdurately, for the rest of his life, to support a forever lost cause.

His conservatism, however, interfered no more with the acuteness of his analysis of society and with the penetration of the gaze he turned on the human condition than, a generation or so later, did Dostoyevsky's. Hardly any of his books – perhaps only one, *Le Médecin de campagne* (*The Country Doctor*), which is a special case – can be called works of overt propaganda. In the novels, his political creed emerges in the occasional parenthetical remark, but his principles never distorted the clarity of his observation nor did he ever construct a plot to prove a point. This is why, despite his retrograde opinions, left-wing thinkers as diverse as Engels and Zola have judged him to have contributed more to the discrediting of the nineteenth-century establishment than all the self-proclaimed middle-class 'friends of the people' from Hugo down. It is arguable, even, that his denunciation of the governing and property-owning classes was more devastating than Stendhal's, simply because it was more thorough; but the two novelists concurred in their conclusions, particularly as regards the evolution of the class system over the thirty years that followed the collapse of the Empire at Waterloo.

PORTRAIT OF A CONDEMNED CLASS: THE ARISTOCRACY

'Every Stendhal novel', remarks one of the wittiest of his modern commentators, 'is a concerto for passionate soloist and social orchestra.'[12] The passionate soloist in his first novel, *Armance*, bears the name Octave de Malivert, and bears it with an ill grace: he is the last representative of one of the 'old' aristocratic families whose line was founded by some semi-mythical crusader. The Maliverts enjoyed great wealth and privileges before the Revolution, which reduced them to penury and impotence. Now that the old royal dynasty has been restored in the person of Louis XVIII, they hope that a proportion at least of their former affluence will be restored too. Alone, the young man Octave has noted the bitter paradox: it is with the wealth amassed by the middle-class industrialists who have displaced them that the 'indemnity' to which the Maliverts believe they are entitled will be financed. They themselves have not contributed to this wealth, nor do they intend to put it to productive use; Octave's father and uncle want the profits of the counting-house without having to put in office hours. Under the *ancien régime*, perhaps, the Maliverts had an identifiable function in the body politic: the nobility did at least officer the king's armies and navy. Since the political revolution of 1789 the state has had no real use for them, and with the newer industrial revolution they exist simply as an embarrassing anachronism. 'Now that the steam-engine's become the monarch of the world, a title's an absurdity, but it's one I'm saddled with,' sighs Octave. It seems that only two courses are open to the young viscount: to idle away his time as a social butterfly; or to change his name and enter some useful profession. He is too serious-minded to be content with the first choice and too lacking in drive to try the second alternative. In the end he marries, and shortly after sets sail for the East to join the forces engaged in helping the Greeks win their independence, in much the same way as an earlier aristocrat, the

Marquis de La Fayette, had fought in America on the side of the rebellious colonists. This seems a dignified dénouement until one looks more closely at the implications. His marriage is meaningless, for Octave knows himself to be sexually impotent: the line of the Maliverts finishes with him; and he never reaches Greece, nor intends to: he takes a dose of laudanum and dies on board ship. Both his marriage and his suicide are the acts of a desperate man and have obvious symbolic significance.

As for the 'social orchestra', this is composed of various fashionable folk who buzz distractingly round the unfortunate Octave, chattering, flirting, dabbling in crank religions, pontificating about the menace of democracy. It is, as Victor Brombert has said, Stendhal's 'constant awareness of a socio-political background' that 'makes this minor novel a milestone in the history of literary realism'.[13] Stendhal broadened his picture of the restoration aristocracy in the second part of *Le Rouge et le noir*, adding such unforgettable figures as that elegant fop, the Chevalier de Beauvoisis; the tender-hearted prude Mme de Fervaques (an aristocrat by marriage only), who has more say in the appointment of bishops than anyone else in the kingdom; and above all, of course, the Marquis de La Mole, a true grandee, rich, powerful, busily intriguing to maintain and consolidate his position: an intelligent man too, no snob, steeped in the old-world courtesies, though deadly if anyone crosses his path. The *salon* of the Marquise de La Mole is magnificent but horribly dull, conversation being limited to 'safe' topics; the *habitués* consist of the effete young noblemen who are courting the daughter of the house, and a mixed bunch of spies, academicians on the make, and newly ennobled millionaires. The revolution of 1830 was shortly to disperse this unillustrious company. The old families retired to their country houses, where Stendhal shows them (in his third novel, *Lucien Leuwen*) fretting and fuming and ineffectually plotting the return of the pretender, the grandson of Charles X whom they call 'Henry V'.

The authenticity of this class-portrait can be checked against a score of novels and short stories in *La Comédie humaine*, though, as a man who would have liked to see the nobility assuming their 'proper place' in the social hierarchy, Balzac was more disappointed than Stendhal at their failure to live up to the old principle 'noblesse oblige'; his general account is therefore even more scathing. As a rule, the older aristocrats in Balzac's novels are either mercenary or hopelessly behind the times, lost, like Baron du Guénic in *Béatrix*, in dreams of a feudal past. The womenfolk – the married ladies living in the capital at any rate – are interested only in amorous intrigue. Their children are badly brought up: the daughters, once they are safely married off, behave much as their mothers did, the sons, trained to no profession, grow up fit only for cards, betting on the horses, or seducing village maidens. Some run foul of the law and find themselves in prison (Savinien de Portenduère in *Ursule Mirouet*); others, like Victurnien d'Esgrignon in *Le Cabinet des antiques* (*The Collection of Antiques*), are saved from this fate only by the strenuous efforts of their high-placed friends. A few become 'bohemians', living in near-destitution, but conserving all the old arrogance of their caste. Once turned forty they 'settle down', that is, marry into the wealthy middle class. This is how the best-known of them all, Eugène de Rastignac, finishes up, taking for wife the daughter of his first mistress, whose husband was Nucingen, a multimillionaire banker.

Though as a class they are indolent, dishonourable, and pleasure-loving, there are individuals among them who do display a certain crude energy. The Comte de La Bastie does what Octave de Malivert recoiled from doing: he changes his name to the more bourgeois one of Charles Mignon and, having lost his original fortune, builds up another through trade in distant parts of the world. M. de La Baudraye (in *La Muse du Département* (*The Provincial Muse*)), whose estates had been badly dilapidated during the revolutionary years, sets himself single-mindedly to make good the losses by dint of stringent economy. Like Stendhal's Octave, he is impotent; needing heirs, he imperturbably claims as his own the children his wife bears to the Parisian hack-writer whom she takes as a lover. Not all Balzac's studies of aristocratic *mores* are as unedifying. Félix de Vandenasse, after a wild youth described in *Le Lys dans la vallée* (*The Lily in the Valley*), turns into a model husband in *Une Fille d'Ève* (*A Daughter of Eve*), exerting himself discreetly to save his young wife from committing a folly she might regret. True nobility of character allied to nobility of race is shown in one story only, called *L'Interdiction* (*The Petition in Lunacy*): the Marquis d'Espard, having discovered that his family's fortunes were founded on an act of despoliation committed two centuries previously by one of his ancestors, traces the descendants of the

Huguenot family who suffered the wrong and does all in his power to make restitution. But as if to show how untypical such a delicate sense of family honour was, Balzac placed alongside D'Espard his wife, a woman of fashion so out of sympathy with her husband's idealism that she tries to set the law in motion to stop him spending his money to still the reproaches of his incomprehensibly tender conscience.

THE LOWER CLASSES IN STENDHAL AND BALZAC

At the other end of the social scale from the aristocracy were the plebs, the 'fourth estate': peasants, artisans, domestics, and the small but growing body of factory-workers and miners, who, as the century wore on, came to be known as the proletariat. Except in *La Chartreuse de Parme* Stendhal paid very little heed to the 'lower orders' either in his novels or, it must be confessed, elsewhere in his writings. It is true that Julien Sorel, the discontented hero of *Le Rouge et le noir*, pretends to regard himself as a 'poor peasant', a 'carpenter's son'; but in fact his father, uneducated workman though he may be, strictly speaking counts as a member of the propertied class, since he owns a sawmill and does quite well out of it. Julien encounters the children of the downtrodden poor, numerically no doubt the largest section of the population at the time, when he enters the seminary at Besançon as a theological student. The dull intellects, servile spirit and mere boorish gluttony of the other seminarists fill him at first with a fine contempt, but later he comes to understand them better: 'it had happened to the fathers of most of his class-mates to return home to their cottages of a winter's evening and find nothing to eat – neither bread nor chestnuts nor potatoes. "It's hardly surprising," thought Julien, "that happiness, in their eyes, consists firstly in having dined well, and secondly in possessing a good suit of clothes." ' Most of the *curés* in country parishes had no stronger vocation than the desire to escape the rags and periodic starvation which had been their fathers' lot: or so at least Stendhal, no friend of the Church, would have us believe.

This is a far cry from the idealized picture of the honest yeoman that George Sand – no realist – was to provide a little later in her series of rural stories.[14] The millennial pastoral tradition, in art as well

54

as literature, complicated the task of rendering contemporary country life as it really was; the writers, who were, besides, in general town-dwellers, were rarely in close and prolonged contact with the labouring classes in the fields and villages. Balzac made more than one attempt to get at the truth, and did not finally arrive at it until almost the end of his life. He signed a contract for the publication of *Les Paysans* (*The Peasants*) in 1841; at his death, nine years later, the novel was still unfinished, but even in its fragmentary state it represents a fearful indictment of rural pauperism which must have been valid for large parts of the French countryside. The plot of *Les Paysans* turns on the fierce but finally unavailing attempt on the part of a big land-owner to keep his estate intact and draw a reasonable income from it. Montcornet is not a member of the old aristocracy: he bought his manor in 1815 with the booty he had won during the wars as one of Napoleon's generals. Previously, the estate had belonged to an opera singer, who out of timidity and indolence had winked at the encroachments of her tenants. Montcornet tries to stop the rot, and of course arouses the bitter hostility of the peasants. 'Qui terre a, guerre a' ('He who owns land has war on his hands') is an old proverb that Balzac adopted as the title of the first volume of his novel. He declared his impartiality, as between Montcornet and his opponents, in the very opening chapter:

The historian must never forget that his business is to give each his due: the unfortunate and the fortunate are equal before his pen; for him, the peasant has the greatness of his sufferings, as the rich man has the pettiness of his foibles; in a word, the rich have passions, the peasants have only needs, the peasant is therefore twice poor; and if, politically speaking, his acts of aggression need to be pitilessly repressed, from the human and religious point of view he is sacred.

Even though, in accordance with this programme, Balzac does his best to be scrupulously fair, it is clear that he viewed the inescapable outcome – the defeat of Montcornet and the partitioning of the estate among the peasant smallholders – as in every sense catastrophic: for without a ruling class of territorial magnates, Balzac could not see how France was to be governed and remain a civilized country, boasting a culture that had put her in the forefront of the nations of the world. However, the most remarkable aspect of the social analysis he provides in *Les Paysans*, one which has made it almost a sacred text for Marxist critics, is that the conflict involves not just the two classes, the land-owning aristocracy and the landless peasantry; the true villains are the moneyed class in the middle, a small group of intelligent, unscrupulous men led by the unfrocked monk Rigou, the very type of the village usurer as he still exists in many an agrarian community outside Europe today. Rigou will help a small farmer to purchase a plot of land, but will charge him an extortionate rate of interest on the loan. The peasant in these circumstances is as badly off as when he was working for the large landowner under the 'share-cropping' system; though he does not realize it, he has simply changed masters. Rigou is as much his class enemy as Montcornet; if anything, Rigou is the more efficient parasite of the two. But as the peasant sees it, Rigou's money loans have enabled him to increase his personal holdings, and his age-old land hunger has to that extent been satisfied. In the last chapter of *Les Paysans* we are shown the whole of the territory that used to form the Montcornet demesne, now split up into dozens of smallholdings, all intensively cultivated by the peasants, who are toiling as hard as ever, but still not keeping for themselves the product of their labour. Rigou and the other small capitalists like him are drawing a bigger income from the land than Montcornet, representing the seignorial class, ever succeeded in extracting.

MONEY MATTERS

The central place occupied by the money-lender, not only in *Les Paysans* but in several other of the major novels (*Illusions perdues, César Birotteau, La Cousine Bette*), is one of the features of *La Comédie humaine* which makes it seem, to a reader today, most quaintly primitive. But Balzac was simply reporting a reality of his time. In a slowly expanding economy, when enterprise was still largely individualistic (the joint-stock bank, the limited liability company, were things of the future), there was a chronic shortage of capital, and no means of remedying it by the creation of paper credit. Money was ordinarily specie – gold, silver, and copper – hoarded in strongrooms or, at best, lent to property-owners in good standing in the form of mortgages. The eerie spectacle of old Grandet gloating over the heaps of gold coin in his sick-room would not have seemed nearly so fantastic to Balzac's contemporaries as it does to us. Though the letter of credit was by no means a recent invention, it was still customary to effect cash transfers by transporting money physically from place to place: when Eugène de Rastignac begs his parents, living on their small estate in the south-west, to send him a subsidy, it arrives in the shape of two bags of coin brought on the mail coach. Otherwise, large payments were regularly made by means of promissory notes, redeemable in six or twelve months' time, for which the needy could get ready cash on application to the money-lenders, who also acted as professional discounters. The size of the discount would depend both on the good standing of the issuer and the estimated need of the holder for cash. In the cut-throat economic conditions of the time, to be short of liquid assets was to invite a ruinous take-over. The business failure of César Birotteau, when his prospects are so good and his credit-worthiness so high, or David Séchard's inability to raise the capital that would permit him to complete his researches into process-ing a cheap paper from vegetable fibre, are 'commercial dramas' of a kind scarcely imaginable today; but Balzac, who in spite of his relatively high earnings as an author was perpetually trembling on the edge of bankruptcy himself, knew well enough what he was talking about.

There was, besides, another reason why the profession of money-lender should have held a horrid fascination for a realist like Balzac – as, for that matter, it later did for Dostoyevsky. In the ordinary course of business, the money-lender necessarily found himself the recipient of so many strange and lamentable confessions that the novelist could not help envying him and hence, in the long run, empathizing with him. The would-be borrower, like the doctor's patient or the solicitor's client, cannot afford to be reticent, even about those secrets he is most ashamed to divulge. There are usurers, Balzac would have us believe, who ply their trade simply for the feeling of power it gives them to be afforded these privileged glimpses into private or domestic dramas. As one of them, Gobseck, says in the short story that bears his name: 'My eye is like the Eye of God, which can look into the hearts of men. Nothing is hidden from me. No one has anything to refuse to the man who can tie or untie the strings of the money-bag.' Gobseck speaks of a secret fraternity of financiers like himself, 'all silent, unknown monarchs who control your destinies', and whose custom is regularly to meet in a certain coffee-house and there discuss and decide the affairs of all and sundry.

The enormous emphasis laid on money transactions is peculiar to Balzac; it is a feature of his art that repels many of his readers, who find these feverish calculations incomprehensible and in any case devoid of human interest. There is nothing of the sort in Stendhal's novels, though for part of his life at least (between 1814 and 1830) he was as much plagued by money worries as Balzac ever was. But Stendhal found the whole subject distasteful and boring. In his fictional world there is only one banker, Lucien Leuwen's father. We see him in his wife's drawing-room, in the Chamber, at the Palace, in his box at the opera; but hardly ever at his desk in the bank. Business he leaves to his partner; and it is hardly surprising that he dies almost poor. What might astonish us is that he ever became rich. François Leuwen is an autobiographical projection, a modified self-portrait or an essay in wish-fulfilment, anything rather than a typical member of the banking community under the July Monarchy. Almost any one of Balzac's financial wizards, Nucingen, Keller, Du Tillet, Pierre Graslin (in *Le Curé de village*), is more credible as a specimen of the reality.

The importance Balzac attributes to financial motivations (and it is hard to think of a novel of any substance in *La Comédie humaine* where such motivations do not loom large) is part of his peculiar realism. Alone in his generation of writers, he saw clearly the implications of the final triumph of the bourgeoisie in 1830. Wealth, the private ownership of property, conferred every kind of power, permitted every imaginable licence. As yet another banker, Taillefer, remarks in *La Peau de chagrin* (*The Wild Ass's Skin*), the opening words of the Constitution, 'all Frenchmen are equal before the law', do not apply to a millionaire, for 'he shall not be subject to the laws, the laws are subject to him; there is no scaffold, no public hangman for million-aires.' And Crevel, a millionaire himself, observes in *La Cousine Bette* that even the king on his throne has not the power that his effigy possesses when stamped on the standard silver coin of the realm, the five-franc piece. The desire for riches is stronger than any other; no indulgence of the senses or gratification of the affections can compen-sate for poverty, which is the only truly deplorable state of being. A middle-class girl with an inadequate dowry has hardly any chance of marrying, for no young man of sense will take as wife one whose father cannot amply provide for her: this is the hard truth that experience teaches Cécile Camusot de Marville and her parents in *Le Cousin Pons*. In *La Vieille Fille* (*The Old Maid*) a poet, a youth of refinement and sensibility, drowns himself when the middle-aged lady he is courting, who has a double chin but a handsome property, rejects his suit and marries his rival, a thick-set, middle-aged business-man.

All this gives a certain grossness to Balzac's realism which is quite absent from Stendhal's, and yet, since the same society was being depicted, the same underlying conditions apply. The difference is that in Balzac's fictional world everyone, even the most virtuous and other-worldly, accepts the rule of the five-franc piece, whereas Stendhal's main characters hold values totally alien, in this respect, to those of society. Armance is perfectly aware that Octave's sudden acquisition of a fortune, at the beginning of the novel, makes him a 'good catch'; however, this only increases her anxiety not to seem to be angling for him. Lucien Leuwen cannot possibly doubt that it is his father's reputed millions, and not his own personal qualities, that have made him an object of the keenest interest to the mothers of every un-married young lady in the town of Nancy where, as a lieutenant of dragoons, he is temporarily stationed. In *Le Rouge et le noir* several of the minor characters, especially in the scenes set in Verrières, are obsessed by calculations of profit and loss: old Sorel, Julien's father; M. de Rênal, his first employer; and Valenod, Rênal's political rival in the small town. But it is equally clear that all this haggling and competition, from which Balzac would have distilled such excitement and drama, was for Stendhal something quite sordid and hateful. The characters intended to engage our interest and sympathy, such as Julien himself, Mme de Rênal, Mathilde de La Mole, the Abbé Pirard, even Fouqué the timber-merchant, Julien's boyhood friend, are utterly disinterested in money matters. Their motivations are nobler or more passionate, and it is in this respect that Stendhal shows him-self more idealistic, more of a romantic, it might be said, than the lusty materialist who begot *La Comédie humaine*.

RESIDUAL ROMANTICISM IN STENDHAL

The degree to which romanticism, so pervasive an element in the cultural atmosphere of the period, can be said to have 'rubbed off' on to these two writers whose inspiration was nevertheless primarily realistic – this is the last remaining major question to be dealt with in this chapter. In Stendhal's novels it is above all the youthful protagonists – Octave, Julien, Lucien, and Lamiel in the last, unfinished novel – who strike us as embodying the spirit of romanticism. While Balzac offers us a series of social studies involving, each of them, up to a dozen principal characters, Stendhal invariably organizes his narrative round the lifetime experiences of a solitary young hero who dies before the book ends. Now Balzac too made use of the convention of the young man newly launched on the world – *Un Début dans la vie* (*A Start in Life*) is indeed the title of one of his minor works – but death rarely, if ever, cuts short his heroes' careers. Eugène de Rastignac, Lucien de Rubempré, Félix de Vandenasse, are all alive and in good health on the last page of the novels in which they first figure, *Le Père Goriot, Illusions perdues, Le Lys dans la vallée*: necessarily so, indeed, for the author knew he would need them again in later works. The device of the 'recurrent character', which Balzac adopted fairly early in the writing of *La Comédie humaine*, is in itself, incidentally, a powerful adjunct to his realism, since the reappearance of the same name in different works somehow confers an air of authenticity on the person named: this is, we feel, no artificial creature who lives only between the two covers of a book. A further difference is that Balzac's young men accommodate themselves on the whole fairly readily to the social order: no rebels, they agree to the rules of the game and win or lose accordingly. Stendhal, on the other hand, conceived his heroes always as being romantically at odds with society, either at war with it[15] or superciliously condemning it and opting out. And society takes its revenge, driving them to exile, to suicide, or, if all else fails, sending them to the scaffold.

Whether intentionally or not, his choice of the eternal *outsider* as hero served Stendhal admirably in one respect: it meant that the critique of society that he aimed to give in his novels could be conveyed – as it would be later (1942) by Albert Camus in the novel called *The Outsider* (*L'Étranger*) – directly through the private observations and reflections of his hero.[16] There was no need for extraneous comment; the occasional authorial intervention merely serves the purpose of ironically underlining this or that reaction on the part of the central character. Thus, when tears start to Julien's eyes at discovering how heartlessly Valenod treats the workhouse inmates he has in his charge, Stendhal needs only to observe 'I must confess that the weakness Julien betrays in this monologue gives me a poor opinion of him' for the shocked reader immediately to embrace the opposite view. These ironical intrusions by Stendhal, which are sometimes none too easy to interpret, are utterly different in nature from the relatively heavy passages of didactic commentary that Balzac inserts in order to air his opinions. Balzac's seriousness is all on the surface; Stendhal hides his in the depths of his work, under a superficial play of lightly humorous *persiflage*.

Each of Stendhal's heroes is representative of a particular social trend or phenomenon. Octave embodies the predicament of the old families in a world which offers no employment tailored to the blue-blooded aristocrat. Julien typifies the educated and pushful lower-class man in a society still quite rigidly stratified. Lucien exhibits in a concentrated form all the moral uncertainties of the triumphant middle class under Louis-Philippe. Yet each stands apart from the crowd, unwilling or unable to make contact, *singular*, to use the special word that Stendhal applies to each of them in turn and even to Fabrice in *La Chartreuse de Parme*, though his case is slightly different.

Their best chance of establishing lines of communication and arousing human sympathies is through the emotion of love. There is a love-story, and sometimes two or three, in each of Stendhal's novels. Here again, a sharp distinction can be drawn between him and Balzac, whose occasional attempts at basing a novel on the relations between two lovers were never particularly successful: either the novel is insipid (*Modeste Mignon*, *Ursule Mirouet*) or the love-interest is overshadowed by some darker theme (*Eugénie Grandet*, *Pierrette*). In *La Cousine Bette* Balzac achieved a remarkable study of male lust, and in the short novel *Honorine* an equally memorable account of a husband's frantic obsession with a young wife who cannot endure living with him; while *La Duchesse de Langeais* and *La Fille aux yeux d'or* (*The Girl with the Golden Eyes*) are two powerful, if melodramatic, transcriptions of frustrated or unnatural passion. But in tracing the delicate process whereby sympathy is gradually converted into intimacy, Stendhal remains unrivalled; it is the best thing there is in *Armance*, and in his succeeding novels he was able to repeat the achievement without repeating the effects. Outside of Tolstoy's novels, there are no girls or young women in fiction quite so tenderly observed as those that Stendhal displayed to us.

It is true that they owe their vitality, and perhaps their charm, to something that must be called 'psychological realism', which is of course a variety of realism, but a variety not specific to the 'age of realism' as we characterized it at the outset of this study. Psychological realism is encountered in all the great creative writers of the Renaissance and the classical age, and Stendhal's heroines are no more bewitchingly alive than Shakespeare's, no more moving than Racine's. In this respect as in many others, Stendhal is too universal an artist to be understood wholly in terms of the fashions and movements of his own age. What many regard as his masterpiece, *La Chartreuse de Parme* (*The Charterhouse of Parma*), is not strictly classifiable as a work of realism. It has a complex love-plot of tragical potential, involving a clever middle-aged statesman, a brilliantly vivacious court-lady who is his mistress, a reckless young gallant, and a demure, devout, and melancholy girl. The interweaving threads of love, jealousy, and friendship between these four produce as romantic a pattern as one could find in any novel. Then again, the setting is not (except for one important interlude in Flanders) the grey skies and muddy fields of northern Europe: the action takes place in Italy, which in the romantic age was regarded as the most romantic of countries, and all the characters are Italians. Finally, in place of the tedious banality of the power centres of a modern democracy – ministerial offices, business offices, newspaper offices – Stendhal gives us in *La Chartreuse de Parme* the picture of an anachronistic court society and the captivating if disgraceful spectacle of government by intrigue and favouritism.

There is, admittedly, one area of writing in which *La Chartreuse de Parme* set a new standard for realism: in the presentation of modern warfare. The confusion and discomfort, the absence of heroism or grandeur, that characterize most large-scale military actions is conveyed by Stendhal, in the chapters devoted to the battle of Waterloo, in an entirely convincing way thanks to the simple but effective device, which he was the first to employ, of showing everything from the point of view of a puzzled raw recruit, a young man whose head is full of ideas of death or glory, and whose only real worry is that he cannot be sure whether or not he is really in the middle of a battle; ironically, the battle in question is possibly the only one that can be said to have radically changed the course of world history in the nineteenth century. The limited, fragmentary viewpoint that Stendhal chose functions far better in the optics of realism than the grandiose bird's-eye view adopted later by Hugo, in *Les Misérables*, to describe the same historical event; and Tolstoy freely admitted that as a war-novelist he had learned more from Stendhal than from any other writer. This episode apart, however, the general impression left by *La Chartreuse de Parme* is of a work having closer links with romanticism than with realism. However contemptuous he may have shown himself of the French romantic movement and its leaders, Stendhal could not help catching the infection of the time. Nor was Balzac immune; but it affected him differently.

RESIDUAL ROMANTICISM IN BALZAC

'I have many a time been astonished', confessed Baudelaire, 'that Balzac's great glory should be his reputation as an observer; it had always seemed to me that his primary merit was that he was a vision-ary, and a passionate visionary at that. All his characters are endowed with the vital ardour with which he himself was imbued. All his fictions are as deeply coloured as dreams. From the lofty heights of the aristocracy down to the social outcasts in the lower depths, all the actors of his *Comedy* are more ardently alive, more active and wily in the struggle, more patient under suffering, more greedy in enjoyment, more angelic in devotion, than the comedy of the real world shows people to be.'[17] Oscar Wilde, who quoted part of Baudelaire's observation in his essay on 'The Decay of Lying', added a gloss to the effect that Balzac's characters 'have a kind of fervent, fiery-coloured existence. They dominate us, and defy scepticism . . . But Balzac is no more a realist than Holbein was. He created life, he did not copy it.' Certainly, readers with a fixed hostility to realism such as Wilde had, who none the less have fallen under Balzac's spell, will always fasten on this aspect of his work to justify whatever seems contradictory in their critical reactions. The excessive luridness and the excessive sombreness of Balzac's reflection of the world, above all the excessive intensity of passion with which his characters pursue their objectives – these are features that make his work unlike any other; and it is not hard to see how they can always be invoked to challenge the claim, which so many literary historians have made for Balzac, that his art represents a primary source of modern realism. To this objection one reply is possible: without these 'visionary' qualities of which Baudelaire spoke, Balzac could never have conveyed the full force and flavour of reality as he himself apprehended it. To bring familiar matters to the attention of the common reader, a writer is compelled to show them 'in a new light', as the saying is; and in certain circumstances this may well entail what the common reader will call 'exaggeration'. Such an artist will not be content to photograph a grassy, sunlit meadow as it is – he will arrange to have it sprayed first with bright green paint.

In some of his writings – usually short stories and very often set in past ages – Balzac deliberately transgressed the limits of ordinary, day-to-day experience and what is called real life. Such works were classified, inside the general scheme of *La Comédie humaine*, as 'études philosophiques': they were habitually concerned with certain phenomena of para-psychology like thought-transference which had always excited Balzac's interest; sometimes – as in *La Peau de chagrin*, where a piece of leather is found to have the power of granting every wish uttered by the person who owns it – they involve accessories more in keeping with fairy-stories or 'science fantasy'. The works that purported to be scenes from the real life of the times were classified under a different heading, as 'études de mœurs'; they comprise the great bulk of *La Comédie humaine*, and in so far as they do diverge from the accustomed norms of everyday reality, such divergence is traceable always to the presence in them of a certain type of character: a man (or, in one or two rare instances, a woman) dominated by a single, devouring passion, who strains every nerve to achieve one particular, often chimerical goal, or to gratify some frantic, all-consuming desire. Such characters do not appear in every one of the 'études de mœurs', but they occur in sufficient numbers to constitute a recognizable category, normally referred to, by the name Balzac himself sometimes used, as 'monomaniacs'.

Obsessional passions range from the most inoffensive – De Watteville in *Albert Savarus* has devoted his whole life to enlarging his geological and entomological collections – to the most reprehensible; but even an apparently innocuous passion, like Balthazar Claës's for chemistry, or a normally worthy one, like the widower Goriot's devotion to his daughters, can take a sinister turn if the 'monomania' blinds the patient to ordinary social or moral obligations. The fascination of the phenomenon for Balzac lay probably in the witness it bears to the enormous strength of the human personality, which can withstand every assault, however violent, that the social order can mount against its independence. Like the creative artist himself, the monomaniac lives in a world of his own; whatever penetrates his consciousness from outside is immediately and infallibly reinterpreted in terms of his own fantasmic universe. The ravages of these obsessional passions are highlighted by small but significant sayings, turns of phrase symptomatic of the grave imbalance of the monomaniac's system of values. Grandet, for instance, the miser of Saumur, learns that his brother's business has failed and that he has taken his own life, sending on his son Charles to Saumur in the hope that the young man's uncle will help him. Grandet tells his wife of the suicide and all she can say, thinking of Charles, is: 'The poor boy!' 'Yes,' answers Grandet, 'poor indeed; he hasn't a penny to his name.' Or there is Claës, whose mania is scientific research: seeing his wife weeping broken-heartedly, he tells her exultantly that he has analysed tears – would she be interested to hear the chemical formula of the lachrymal fluid? Or there is the old Baron Hulot, who cannot live without mistresses, however vulgar or even ugly. His hobby is as ruinously expensive, in the long run, as Claës's, but instead of dying frustrated, as does the hero of *La Recherche de l'absolu*, Hulot escapes from disgrace into the Paris slums, where his long-suffering wife eventually finds him living in utter squalor, but as much a slave to his lusts as ever. When she suggests that he return to the modest comfort and respectability of their home, the only question he puts is: 'And can I bring my little girl with me?'

*

If it were possible to formulate concisely the difference between these two forerunners, Stendhal and Balzac, and the writers of the realist and naturalist schools that arose after their deaths, one would need to refer above all to the very personal vision they brought to bear on the social scene that each one, in his own way, tried to render. The problem that confronted all the realists, as we enunciated it at the end of our first chapter, was solved by these two along lines which accorded closely with the spirit of their age. Romanticism is nothing if not self-expression, and both Stendhal and Balzac were romantics at least in the limited sense that their work expressed their own individualities in a strongly marked and clearly recognizable fashion. Stendhal's self-betrayal in his novels is more apparent to posterity than it was to his contemporaries, since we have the advantage of access to his private journals and letters, to his essays in autobiography, and to the factual results of all the patient research that has been directed towards elucidating the obscure meanderings of his erratic journey through life. This mass of detailed knowledge demonstrates at least this, that if none of his novels is a direct transcription of the experiences of the man Beyle who sheltered behind the writer Stendhal, all of them are deeply coloured by Beyle's personal beliefs, prejudices, attitudes, hopes and dreams. As for Balzac, something of his burly physique and magnetic gaze is everywhere apparent in his books, in which no page is quite bad, no passage is altogether without its interest, and which, taken together, surely amount to one of the most extraordinary creative achievements in the history of literature. *La Comédie humaine* may not be realism in the sense in which the word came finally to be understood, but its reality is unmistakable: strident, coarsely flavoured, vividly coloured, with a tumultuous and multitudinous presence which later novelists (Émile Zola, Pérez Galdós, Teixeira de Queirós) were to emulate though none could match him.

1 See K. G. McWatters, 'Stendhal, Walter Scott et la *Bibliothèque britannique*', *Stendhal Club*, No. 16 (1962), pp. 344–5.

2 Stendhal, *Correspondance*, ed. H. Martineau and V. Del Litto (Paris, 1962), Vol. I, pp. 917, 1030, 1053.

3 Balzac, *Correspondance*, ed. R. Pierrot (Paris, 1960), Vol. I, p. 108.

4 *Clotilde de Lusignan ou le Beau Juif, manuscrit trouvé dans les archives de Provence et publié par Lord R'hoone*. 'R'hoone' was, of course, an anagram of Balzac's first name, Honoré.

5 *La Muse française*, July 1823 (review of *Quentin Durward*); reprinted in *Littérature et philosophie mêlées* (1834).

6 'Letters from Paris (II)', *London Magazine*, new series, Vol. I, p. 205 (February 1825).

7 Quoted in Marguerite Iknayan, *The Idea of the Novel in France* (Geneva and Paris, 1961), p. 111.

8 Quoted in L. Maigron, *Le Roman historique à l'époque romantique* (Paris, 1912), pp. 227–8.

9 Examples are Angoulême in *Illusions perdues*, Issoudun in *La Rabouilleuse*, Bayeux in *La Femme abandonnée*, Provins in *Pierrette*, etc.

10 Lavater, *L'Art de connaître les hommes par la physionomie*, quoted in A. J. Mount, *The Physical Setting in Balzac's 'Comédie humaine'* (Hull, 1966), p. 18.

11 It occurs first in a review he wrote of L.-B. Picard's novel, *L'Honnête Homme ou le niais* (*New Monthly Magazine*, 1 August 1825). In a notice Stendhal composed on Rossini's opera *La Donna del lago* (*Journal de Paris*, 21 December 1826), there occurs the sentence: 'It has been said that a poet is a mirror which reflects every image and retains the impression of none.'

12 R. M. Adams, *Stendhal: notes on a novelist* (London, 1959), p. 144.

13 V. Brombert, *Stendhal: fiction and the themes of freedom* (New York, 1968), p. 56.

14 *La Mare au diable* (1846), *La Petite Fadette* (1848), *François le champi* (1850), *Les Maîtres Sonneurs* (1852).

15 'C'était l'homme malheureux en guerre avec toute la société' is

how Stendhal describes Julien at a critical point in *Le Rouge et le noir* (Part II, Chapter 13).

16 The connections between these aspects of the two writers' works have been emphasized in a number of critical studies, notably G. Sandstrom, 'The Outsiders of Stendhal and Camus', *Modern Fiction Studies*, Vol. X (1964), pp. 245–57, and A. Abbou, 'Camus et Stendhal à travers l'*Étranger* et le *Rouge et le noir*', *Revue des Lettres humaines*, Nos. 170–74 (1968), pp. 93–146.

17 Baudelaire's remark occurs in section IV of his essay on Théophile Gautier, published in 1859. It forms the basis of Albert Béguin's 'Balzac visionnaire', originally published in 1946 and reprinted in Béguin, *Balzac lu et relu* (Paris, 1965).

THREE

Realism in Russia, to the Death of Dostoyevsky

THE HISTORICAL BACKGROUND

ALTHOUGH historical circumstances naturally contributed much to the emergence of realism as the dominant literary manner in nineteenth-century Russia, there are certain less tangible facets of the Russian character and national attitude towards culture which made realism, or a concern with the *realia* of experience, more accessible to Russian sensibilities than classicism, sentimentalism or romanticism. The historical fact that Russia, although situated to the east of Europe, was cut off from Renaissance influences by the Mongol invasion meant that it never experienced at first hand the impact of Latin culture. Until the eighteenth century, when French neo-classicism began to exert a certain influence, little was known of classical culture, and this circumstance accounts for the relatively slight indebtedness of nineteenth-century Russian literature to classical example. Classicism remained, even in its most brilliant exponents, an acquisition rather than a native habit of mind. Its most marked effect was probably to be seen in that sense of formal balance – the architectural sense of literature, in fact, which derived no doubt from the neo-classical architecture of St Petersburg, of Tsarskoye Selo (where Pushkin was educated), of innumerable country mansions of the nobility – which distinguishes the work of Pushkin, or of Turgenev and Tolstoy, who were like him in receiving at least the rudiments of a classical education. But sentimentalism, for all that it greatly enlarged the emotional range of literature, as can be seen in the work of Karamzin and his immensely popular and influential sentimental novelette, *Poor Liza* (1792), was an insufficiently robust literary manner to have appeal beyond the *salon* or drawing-room; and romanticism was a wild yeast to Russian sensibilities which produced all manner of liberating effects but reached far beyond the confines of literature and became virtually synonymous with revolutionary aspiration, radicalism and, in due course, nihilism. For it has to be stressed that the Russian concern with 'the real' rather than 'the ideal' must in part be due to an un-Germanic rejection of philosophy in favour of facts, an un-French liking for the austerities of progress rather than the luxuries of culture, and, more fundamental than these, to a rather blunt, fairly unsubtle, if devious, conservative, often xenophobic, endearing, unpretentious lack of imagination. Russian literature has a rich folkloristic tradition, at least one great fabulist in Krylov, and an extremely rich memoir literature, but it is noticeably deficient in such branches of imaginative writing as the adventure story, historical fiction, children's tales on the pattern of *Treasure Island*, and stories requiring imaginative plotting, such as tales of crime and detection. Russian literature, when not obviously imitative, has tended to rejoice in factuality and the finiteness of experience in a way which always suggests that Russian sensibilities are happiest when located, fixed or rooted, when horizons are known and seasons have a predictable rotation. There is volatility, splendid eccentricity, an abundance of curiosity and sympathy towards the rest of the world, to be found within the confines of the realistic Russian attitude, but it is the realism of a land-conscious people which relates to places and does not have the easy, rather fluid, predominantly narrative characteristics of English fiction.

The beginnings of Russian realism are traceable to the Russian defeat of Napoleon in 1812. It was an event which put the final seal of authenticity on the Russian claim to be a European power of imperial proportions. Continuing Russian expansion along the Baltic littoral and in the Crimea throughout the eighteenth century had demonstrated this to European eyes but had hardly seemed conclusive evidence. It gave Russia almost overnight a kind of missionary role towards Europe as the ostensible liberator of Europe from Napoleonic oppression. It proved, needless to say, the greatness of Russia and her military power, and it brought Russia directly into a position of dominant authority in the councils of Europe for at least a decade, if not for the forty years remaining until her defeat in the Crimean War (1854–5). But it also released contrary tendencies which alerted the Russians themselves to increasingly profound scrutiny of their vast country's relationship with Europe, its meaning as a nation, its terrible internal contradictions and the course it should adopt in order to prove its right to a place in the civilized world. Two salient facts emerged from the Russian defeat of Napoleon. The first was that, for all the military prowess of the Russian commander-in-chief, Kutuzov, the victory had been gained partly through the rigours of the Russian climate and partly through the stoicism of the ordinary Russian masses, who had risen as one man to defend their fatherland. The second fact was that, as the educated and liberal-minded soon realized, the Russian liberators of Europe were in much greater need of liberation from the tyranny of ignorance, feudalism and autocracy than were those whom they aspired to liberate. Briefly, what the Russian defeat of Napoleon brought sharply into focus was not only Russian imperial power but also a vision of Russia cast in some special, almost holy, role, as saviour and mendicant in its relationship to Europe.

The capacity for understanding Russia's *real* power, the *real* situation both internally and in relation to Europe, the *real* meaning of Russian nationhood, was integral to what may now be understood as Russian realism. There are many quotable examples of realism in Russian literature dating from the eighteenth century and the first decade of the nineteenth, but when such works as Fonvizin's comedies (*Brigadier*, 1769; *The Minor*, 1782) or Radishchev's famous *Journey from St Petersburg to Moscow* (1790) are itemized as instances of early Russian realism, as happens in Soviet literary histories, it is their concern with the realities of the Russian situation – poorly assimilated foreign influences, the evils of serfdom, the divisions in Russian society – which receives greatest emphasis. They are treated, in other words, as items in a process of growing national self-awareness. Literature had to be above all a mirror to life; the need to entertain, excite, even interest, had a lesser priority in the Russian understanding of the real purpose of literature. The mirror with which Russian literature needed to confront life after 1812 had to reflect vaster meanings than any before that date, and in reflecting truthfully it could hardly fail to reflect critically the real implications of an ostensibly European power racked by so many internal contradictions.

Alexander I, whose destiny it was to wear the laurels of the victory over Napoleon, promised sweeping reforms at the beginning of his reign, in 1801, but at his reign's end, in 1825, all thought of reform had long since been replaced by an excessively repressive internal policy which included the suppression of freemasonry, hostility towards all forms of learning not sanctioned by the Bible, and the establishment of the notorious 'military settlements' where peasants were dragooned into working in the fields to the sound of martial drumbeats. Alexander devoted a great deal of his time to foreign policy relationships, chiefly the promotion of his Holy Alliance, and left the execution of his internal policies to the brutal Arakcheyev. The fact that constitutions had been granted to such non-Russian areas of the empire as Poland and Finland was a further cause of dissatisfaction among the better educated and more liberal sections of the Russian nobility. Gradually, in the decade between the final defeat of Napoleon (1815) and Alexander's death (1825), the dissatisfaction took the form of active sedition. By 1821 the first, rather loose, revolutionary organizations, such as the Union of Salvation and the Union of Welfare, had evolved into Northern and Southern Societies of army officers and other members of the nobility who were generally agreed that serfdom would have to be abolished and the autocracy replaced by some kind of constitutional monarchy or republic.

These aristocratic plotters were no more than enthusiastic amateurs in the art of revolution. Though the Southern Society, established among army officers in the Kiev area, argued the need for a kind of socialization of the Russian economy, the more aristocratic Northern Society in St Petersburg contemplated nothing more drastic than the establishment of a constitutional monarchy on the English pattern. How such changes were to be effected and how far precisely they were to be taken were questions never satisfactorily decided. The revolutionaries were forced to acknowledge their unpreparedness through a combination of unhappy circumstances. Alexander I died suddenly in Taganrog in November 1825. The news took some while to reach St Petersburg and when it did confusion arose over the succession to the throne. The presumed successor, Grand Duke Constantine, then in Warsaw, had already renounced his right to the throne, though this fact was not publicly known, and the new successor, Grand Duke Nicholas, would not accept the succession until Constantine had made public renunciation. A state of interregnum ensued. For the revolutionaries of the Northern Society the time for open avowal of their dissent now seemed ripe. Their plans for an uprising were, however, already known to Nicholas. Rather than await inevitable exposure, the Northern Society decided, largely unprepared though it was, to show its hand, and on 14 December, when the regiments quartered in St Petersburg were called upon to swear allegiance to Nicholas as the new tsar, leading members of the Northern Society marched their troops on to the Senate Square before the Winter Palace and declared themselves in favour – among other things – of Constantine and Constitution (assumed by the rank and file, so legend has it, to be Constantine's wife). After this somewhat indecisive show of strength and some attempts to parley, a stalemate developed which was finally resolved by Nicholas's belated decision to bring up cannon and disperse the insurgents. The revolution of December 1825, which gave birth to the legend of Decembrism and endowed the amateur noblemen-revolutionaries with the honoured title of Decembrists, ended abruptly with some grapeshot, the spilling of quantities of blood on the Senate Square and in the river Neva, and the collapse within a week of the attempt by the Southern Society to organize a revolt among troops quartered in the Kiev area. In 1826 five of the ringleaders were hanged and more than a hundred Decembrists were dispatched into Siberian exile.

For all its romantic associations and the glamour of martyrdom in the cause of liberty which came to surround it, Decembrism marked the beginning of very real opposition to tsarism and all its reactionary paraphernalia of government. Seemingly ready as they were to abolish their own privileged roles as serf-owners by abolishing serfdom, the Decembrists appeared to set an example of self-sacrifice and altruistic dedication to the ideal of a liberated, rejuvenated Russia which was to influence successive generations of the intelligentsia throughout the remaining years of the century. But the Decembrist revolt naturally also put the autocracy on its guard against any kind of change that might endanger its position. Nicholas I, always a suspicious disciplinarian, could hardly fail to regard even the supposedly loyal 'official class' of the nobility with suspicion and mistrust after the opening of his reign had been so clouded by this revolt of amateur noblemen-revolutionaries.

His thirty-year reign (1825–55) was marked by growing reaction in his internal policies, designed at all costs to maintain the *status quo*, and a policing attitude towards Europe (when imperial Russia became known as the gendarme of Europe) combined with colonial expansion in the Caucasus and active hostility towards Turkey in the Eastern Mediterranean and Black Sea areas. Nicholas I ruled Russia as a military autocrat through an enormous, parasitic and stifling bureaucracy. His suspiciousness manifested itself chiefly in the establishment of the notorious Third Department, which acted as a kind of secret police. Its purpose was to seek out all forms of sedition and to eradicate any activity which might be considered dangerous to the well-being of the state. All forms of cultural innovation were considered suspect. Literature was subjected to severe censorship, and journals were placed under rigorous surveillance. If these policies were unjustly repressive when considered in isolation, they were in reality no more than symptoms of a body politic undermined by the fundamental social injustice of serfdom. Russia under Nicholas I was an overwhelmingly agricultural country in which tens of millions of peasants were held in servile subjection to scarcely more than 100,000 members of the land-owning nobility. Various half-hearted attempts were made by successive government-appointed committees to find means of alleviating the serf problems but the fundamental issue, that of its abolition, was never faced.

Despite the repression and para-military character of the tsarist government, Russian intellectual life first acquired an independent national vigour during the reign of Nicholas I. During the 1830s the first stirrings of a Russian intelligentsia become discernible in the student circles of Moscow University. By the beginning of the 'remarkable decade' of the 1840s the intelligentsia, as a body of educated opinion independent of officialdom and predominantly anti-tsarist and anti-authoritarian in its bias, was beginning to formulate divergent, polemical viewpoints on Russia's future course of development. The Westernists (*Zapadniki*) believed that Russia should in the main follow a course of Westernization, which meant in most cases the advocacy of socialism, whereas the Slavophils (*Slavyanofily*) upheld the romantic notion that Russia should repudiate the West and its revolutionary ideas in favour of her own national ideal based on an indigenous culture and the teachings of the Orthodox Church. There were many shades of opinion occupying the ideological bands within the limits of this spectrum and all were determined by their respective attitudes toward the people, the *narod*, in whose name the intelligentsia sought always to speak and act. Out of this concern for the people grew the humanism and sense of moral purpose which permeated all the best literature of the forties and gave such a special moral character to the Russian realistic tradition.

The vigorous intellectual and literary life which had sprung up during the forties was halted by the 1848 revolutions in Europe. The tsarist government, fearful that the constitutionalist movement might spread to Russia, imposed such severe restrictions that for seven years (1848–55), until the death of Nicholas I during the Crimean War, Russia underwent a period of suspended cultural animation. The most conspicuous victims of this final repressive phase of Nicholas's reign were those members, including Dostoyevsky, of the Petrashevsky group who were arrested in 1849, sentenced to death, had their sentences commuted to penal servitude at the last moment, and were then sent off into Siberian exile.

On learning that the Emperor (*Imperator*) Nicholas was dead, Herzen, in his self-imposed London exile, threw coins to the urchins outside his house, who ran about the streets giving hurrahs and shouting 'Impernickel is dead! Impernickel is dead!' There was cause for rejoicing. His death, like the defeat in the Crimean War, offered a chance for Russia to escape from the hidebound conservative policies of the preceding three decades. The initiative was taken by the new tsar, Alexander II, who proposed in 1856 that the nobility should contemplate the idea of liberating the serfs 'from above'. The nobility reacted with a hostility born of generations of greed and privilege. They used every kind of filibustering tactic to delay and erode the reformative activities of the commissions which had been set up to draft the Emancipation Act. But slowly the work went forward and was accompanied, after 1858, by increasing polemic and public debate in the press.

This was the era when the journal *The Contemporary*, founded by Pushkin shortly before his death in 1837, and influential as the platform for Belinsky's publicism in 1847 and 1848, achieved its supreme ascendancy in Russian journalism. It became the mouthpiece of a new generation of the intelligentsia. Their leading spokesman was N. G. Chernyshevsky, who became actively associated with *The Contemporary* in 1855 and dominated its publicism until his arrest in

1862. He was abetted and in some ways even outshone by the precocious literary critic N. A. Dobrolyubov. These two men fostered in the younger generation, 'the men of the sixties', as they were called, or *raznochintsy*, a 'classless' intelligentsia belonging neither to the nobility nor to the peasantry, the desire to rebel against their past and against all authority that was not justified by the laws of the natural sciences. From this teaching grew a spirit of nihilism which made the younger generation scrutinize everything in terms of practical, social utility. They were soon urged by the most iconoclastic of the radical critics of the sixties, Dmitry Pisarev, to become 'Realists' – that is to say, to fight for the survival only of what could be regarded as having real socio-economic value for the future of Russia. Although unstated, the revolutionary implications of such ideas were obvious. This was merely one of several dangers courted by an autocracy intent on trying to modernize Russia without modernizing itself.

The first step in the process of modernization was completed with the promulgation of the Emancipation Act in 1861. Millions of peasants were delivered from slavery in name if not in fact. This piece of legislation, for all its cumbersome and ineffectual apparatus, at least freed the enserfed peasantry of Russia without the catastrophe of civil war which accompanied the same process in the United States of America. The release of capitalistic forces which such a change entailed and the proportionate reduction in the social authority and the economic power of the land-owning nobility caused tremors, which in turn began to open fissures, in the social structure of Russia. Partly to offset these consequences of the Emancipation and partly to update some of the country's archaic institutions, reforms were introduced in local government and the judiciary, in finances and in certain areas of education. The most significant of those changes was the introduction of trial by jury in criminal cases, and the establishment of local councils or *zemstva* at provincial level and in municipalities. This latter reform introduced the elective principle into Russian government, and the *zemstva* brought manifest improvements to the country as a whole; but this only accentuated the anomaly of an elective principle at local level while the central government remained unswervingly autocratic.

This anomaly and disillusionment with the Emancipation Act,

which seemed to do no more than substitute the burden of redemption payments for the former burden of servitude to a feudal master, alienated the younger intelligentsia and caused revolutionary feeling to grow. The era of reforms came to an end in 1866 when the first attempt was made to assassinate the tsar-liberator, as the Emperor Alexander II had come to be known. The attempt failed, but an immediate consequence was the suppression of *The Contemporary*, since the assassin, a young man of noble extraction named Karakozov, was supposed to have admitted that the journal had influenced him. If the government adopted a reactionary course from now on, the revolutionary intelligentsia resorted to extreme and increasingly bizarre measures. The most notorious of such activities have come to be associated with the name of Nechayev. The ruthlessness of his dedication to the cause of revolution made him instigate the murder of one of his fellow conspirators in an attempt to ensure loyalty to the revolutionary cell. When the conspirators were brought to trial, even though Nechayev had escaped abroad, the affair became a *cause célèbre* which excited wide interest and attracted the attention of several writers, including Dostoyevsky, who based the murder of Shatov in *The Possessed* on the Nechayev affair.

Though Nechayev was himself finally captured and brought to trial in 1872, the decade known as 'the seventies' or the 'epoch of great endeavours' (*epokha velikikh del*) was already being dominated by much weightier issues. In the first place, the Franco-Prussian War of 1870–71 seemed to prove to the nationally conscious Russian intelligentsia that Europe was being torn apart by the jingoistic feelings induced by imperialistic greed and rampant capitalism. Russia had to be preserved from the effects of such capitalism, and the most articulate sections of the intelligentsia devoted themselves to an educative, propagandist drive among the peasantry to encourage various forms of agrarian socialism. Their motivations were very mixed: they wanted to avert the stage of capitalism in Russia; they wanted to make the peasants themselves realize that the Emancipation had been a farce, and to foster in them a spirit of dissatisfaction which would eventually lead to the overthrow of the autocracy; they wanted also to simplify themselves, to refresh themselves morally, by drinking at the fount of popular wisdom, and thereby, perhaps, to discharge the moral debt owed by the so-called 'repentant nobleman' to the peasants who had for so many centuries of serfdom supported him by their labour. These and many other ideas came together under the general heading of Populism (*Narodnichestvo*). The Populists, chiefly ardent young students, had begun to make their appearance at the end of the 1860s, but the first major campaign for their ideas occurred in 1874 when more than 3,000 of them participated in the famous 'going into the people' (*khozhdeniye v narod*) of that year. The movement was spontaneous and had no single clearly defined aim. Although certain of the young agitators were successful in establishing co-operatives, the majority had little effect, it seems, and many of them were denounced by the peasantry to the authorities. The whole episode ended in mass arrests. Although there were later such 'goings into the people', the mood of most Populists began to change.

In the second place, the messianism of the Populists, if the peasantry tended to turn a deaf ear to it, at least had the effect of causing all intelligent members of Russian society to reappraise the moral bases of the society in which they lived. Such tendencies are to be seen in all the major literary works of the decade, especially in the novels of Dostoyevsky and Tolstoy. But if the messianism of the intelligentsia sought, among other things, to prove that Russia was morally superior to Europe, a similar proselytizing messianism informed certain aspects of Russian official foreign policy, though its causes and effects were very different. Panslavism united a starry-eyed belief in the brotherhood of the Slav peoples with abhorrence for Roman Catholicism and devout hatred of the infidel Turks. Russian foreign policy became largely dictated by Panslav ideals in the second half of the 1870s, when a conflict arose in the Balkans over Turkish persecution of the Orthodox Slavs. Russia came to the aid of the Serbians who had rebelled against Turkish rule. The ensuing Russo-Turkish War (1877–8), described by the Russians as a 'war of liberation', ended after a protracted and ill-run campaign with the humiliation of the Turks, but the spoils of the victory were snatched from the Russians by the Treaty of Berlin, largely through the activities of Lord Beaconsfield. Russia's messianic hopes of becoming the leading spirit in a movement for liberating all the Slav peoples ended in diplomatic squabbles and financial crises.

The internal Russian situation had become dangerously insecure.

By 1876 Populism had begun to acquire the doctrines and forms of an avowedly revolutionary organization. When those Populists who had been imprisoned after the 'going into the people' of 1874 and on other occasions were brought to trial in 1877 and 1878, virtually at the height of the Russo-Turkish War, public opinion had swung so strongly against the authorities that the accused received relatively light sentences. Then, in January 1878, Vera Zasulich attempted to assassinate the governor-general of St Petersburg. She was subsequently tried and, to the consternation of the authorities, acquitted, but her example quickly sparked off a new phase of the Populist movement – the terrorist activities associated with the organization known as The People's Will (*Narodnaya volya*). Populism now became synonymous with a succession of fanatical attempts to bring down the autocracy by acts of terrorism directed against government ministers and principally against the life of the Emperor. The People's Will was so successful that during 1880 it seemed that the government might be forced into conceding a constitution. The campaign of terrorism reached its climax on 1 March 1881, when bomb-throwers finally succeeded in assassinating the Emperor Alexander II. So profound, though, was public reaction to this murderous deed and so swift was the retaliation of the authorities that the assassins were soon brought to trial, organized terrorism was stamped out and the 'epoch of great endeavours' ended in so much apparently useless bloodshed. What ensued was the reactionary obscurantism of Alexander III's policies and the period known as the 'epoch of small endeavours' (*epokha malykh del*), celebrated so profoundly and touchingly in the muted, tragi-comic world of Chekhov's writings. With the ending of the 'epoch of great endeavours' there also ended the era known as the golden age of Russian literature and its most important genre, the realistic novel.

PUSHKIN: 'EUGENE ONEGIN'

It is worth bearing in mind, when considering realism as a literary manner, the irreverent attitude of Oscar Wilde towards the notion that art necessarily imitates life. 'Literature', he claimed, 'always anticipates life. It does not copy it, but moulds it to its purpose. The nineteenth century, as we know it, is largely an invention of Balzac.' Nineteenth-century Russia, as we know it, is largely the invention of Russian novelists from Pushkin to Dostoyevsky. Novelists, if they are to be at all realistic, cannot fail to be image-makers. What we remember of their work is usually reducible to the images of their heroes and heroines imagined in their several settings. What seems most memorable about the greatest Russian realists is their power of evoking a visualization of heroes and heroines related to places; but since the 'placing' of character was important to them, they tended to be almost as scrupulous about giving specific dates and times to their fiction, limning it in with the pretence of a watch tick. We should not be tempted to forget Oscar Wilde's irreverence, for it imposes a surreal sanity on the whole vexed question of which is more real, fiction or history; but in the case of the Russian realistic novel in the nineteenth century one cannot overlook its topical character, its fusion of *belles lettres* and journalism and therefore its often quite conscious role as a chronicle and criticism of its time. From the beginning Russian critical comment was directed chiefly towards appraising the relative success or failure of a novel in offering a topical picture of the social scene. But the realism of this picture depended very much upon a demonstration of the way in which the social scene gave rise to certain particular psychological traits in the hero or heroine and by that means conditioned their behaviour, made them typical and served to illumine the paradoxes and contradictions observable in Russian society.

'Realism' in Russian nineteenth-century critical usage – and it has to be stressed that the term did not become common currency until after the Crimean War – tended to mean principally a *critical* attitude towards the blemishes in Russian reality and the adoption of a style of social-psychological portraiture which always related psychological characteristics to social background. The more extensive the work of literature, the greater the scope for the criticism and the more detailed and profound could be the portraiture. The novel as the most expansive of literary genres became the principal vehicle of Russian realism, and the history of Russian realism can be equated with the history of the Russian novel. The novel had such size, such a propensity for encompassing all manner of estates and occasions. In its ability to create closed worlds of experience which revealed the private

truth behind the public façade and elicited sympathy for the meanest
of human conditions, it had a power to be, in the beautiful Lawrentian
phrase, 'the one bright book of life'.

No book is brighter in the whole canon of the Russian realistic
novel than *Eugene Onegin*, the 'novel in verse' composed by Aleksandr
Sergeyevich PUSHKIN (1799–1837) over seven or so years (1823–31)
during the fullest flowering of his talent. Though it reflects his own
evolution as much as it does his hero's or his heroine's, it is in no sense
autobiographical. The term masterpiece may be used only with
glibness of this delicately wrought miniature offered to us as if seen
through the magic crystal of Pushkin's art. It is charming, playful,
parodistic, and as much a motley of diverse manners and moods as
the dedicatory lines at its opening suggest:

> Take this gathering of motley chapters,
> Half-jocular, half-sad,
> Unsophisticated, idealistic,
> The careless fruit of leisure hours,
> Sleeplessness, slight inspirations,
> Of callow and long-faded years,
> The mind's chill observation
> And heartache's bitter tears.

The 'story' of this 'novel in verse' is so simple as to seem faintly
implausible in the telling. The hero, Eugene Onegin, a St Petersburg
dandy, abandons the society of the Russian capital because he professes
to be bored by it and travels to the country, where, as Fate has conveniently ordained, he has inherited an estate from his uncle. He enjoys
the bucolic pleasures of his inheritance for a while, wards off incipient
boredom through friendship with his eighteen-year-old neighbour,
the aspiring Romantic poet, Vladimir Lensky, and is eventually
persuaded by this young man to accompany him on a visit to a local
family, the Larins. Lensky is in love with Olga, the younger of the
Larin daughters, but Onegin on his first visit is more impressed by
the elder daughter, Tatyana. She, dreamy and remote though she is,
falls instantly in love with Onegin, mistaking him perhaps for a hero
of a romantic novel, and writes him a love-letter. He repulses her
love with a reproving lecture on the need for her to control her
feelings. It becomes winter. Onegin is invited to attend Tatyana's
nameday ball. He does so reluctantly, finds himself surrounded by

country bumpkins, discovers Tatyana tearful and taciturn (she has had an ominous dream full of sinister portents), and revenges himself both on the boorish provincial society and on the wretched Lensky by dancing with Olga. Lensky challenges him to a duel, in which Onegin kills him. At this point in the work the emphasis shifts from Onegin, who has departed on his travels, to the heroine, Tatyana, who gradually, through visiting his country house, comes to realize that her hero was not the man she imagined him to be, though exactly what he is – a melancholy and dangerous eccentric, a creation of heaven or hell, an angel or a scheming devil, an imitation, a Muscovite in Childe Harold's cloak, a parody – she is unable to discover. Shortly afterwards she is whisked away from the countryside she loves to Moscow, where she is quickly betrothed to a stout General. In the final chapter Onegin returns from his travels (it is not at all clear, incidentally, why he should have spent so long on these travels) and discovers that Tatyana, now the General's wife, has been transformed into an imperious and haughty adornment of St Petersburg society. The hardly unexpected reversal of roles occurs: Onegin now falls in love with Tatyana, and she, at their final meeting at the novel's end, declares that she loves him but cannot abandon her marriage for his sake. She leaves the room and we leave Onegin at that inauspicious moment when, thunderstruck by her rejection of him, he hears her husband's footsteps resound beyond the door.

Why should so simple a story be regarded as the starting-point of Russian nineteenth-century realism? At a first glance it would seem to owe more to romanticism or the novel of sentiment than to the plain-spoken ways of a realistic tradition.[1] Doubtless the Sternian playfulness which Pushkin exhibits in his digressive commentaries, the unhesitating claim he makes to authorial rights in the fiction, his playing with the subject of his story as though he were turning the relationship between hero and heroine into a game of hide-and-seek, his framing of the whole work in classical allusions are whimsical features which reveal the parodistic, transitional and indefinite form of this unique 'novel in verse'. Exaggerated claims for it as the first realistic work in nineteenth-century literature can be discounted.[2] It is realistic only because it consciously attempts to 'document' the backgrounds of Onegin and Tatyana in order to make them recognizably Russian characters.

Onegin is documented as a character both through the biographical information which Pushkin sardonically offers in introducing him to the reader and through an amusing account – Pushkin's manner in Chapter 1 is always light, even flippant – of his day-to-day life in the Russian capital. Onegin's inadequate education, his father's penury, his mastery of the art of seduction, his epicureanism and pursuit of fashion, his dandyism and his visits to the theatre – all is told to us by a fond narrator who knows intimately the world and its types but is not to be identified with his hero. Narrator and hero both planned to leave St Petersburg, both sought freedom. For all his apparent spleen and boredom, it may well be that Onegin took leave of St Petersburg because he could not afford to live there.[3] What matters is that, when transported to the countryside, Onegin cannot but feel superior to his surroundings. In such *hauteur* and incomprehension he is revealed as dangerously eccentric, not to say superfluous.

Tatyana is deeply immersed in her rural world, representative of its innocence and absorbed in its perennial cycles. We know little about her childhood and upbringing, for there is essentially very little to be told, but we know that the peacefulness of her life disposes her to day-dreaming and reading romances. She sees Onegin cast in the role of her fated lover and exhibits a spontaneity of feeling in writing to him which seems entirely in keeping with the candour of her rural innocence.

Her approach is no doubt precipitate; his rejection of her love is callous. Each, though, acts in accordance with the precepts of his or her character, she in accordance with her 'innocence', he with his 'sophistication'; and as the cycle of the year moves on towards winter they become frozen in their respective roles, the one misapprehending the other and both demonstrating the tragic divide which separates town from country, imitative from indigenous, new from old, as well as sex from sex, in Russian society.

Although, so far as we know, hero and heroine confront each other only twice and both confrontations have the form of monologues, the second and final such meeting reveals not only a reversal of roles but also an acknowledgement of the new-found equality of status which exists between them. They are equals in their love and their regret at lost opportunities in the past, but this is an equality of a most private, individual character. Their relationship, although perhaps doomed from the start if interpreted exclusively in terms of the differentiating factors which derive from their social backgrounds, can only be seen to have really tragic meaning when regarded as one between individuals who discover far too late that mutual happiness would have been possible. They learn the realities of their own feelings and simultaneously how incompatible are such things with the realities of his cynical dandyism and her lifelong commitment to marriage. Russian realism receives, in this final moment of *Eugene Onegin*, a kind of formula for its future evolution. The social and psychological realities which divide Onegin and Tatyana acquire moral reinforcement with Tatyana's dutiful rejection of his love in the name of a higher moral code than the *beau monde* of St Petersburg may recognize, and with his consequent isolation when he is seen to be morally unworthy of her, superfluous alike to his society and to himself.

Pushkin never carried the exploration of this dilemma further, though the relationship of the individual to society or of man to his destiny is examined in deeply ironic and understanding ways in such masterpieces as *The Queen of Spades* (1834) and *The Bronze Horseman* (composed in 1833; first published in 1837). Pushkin's conviction that prose should be used only for narrative purposes naturally limited its scope as a medium for expressing the *realia* of life. His only prose work of any length, *The Captain's Daughter* (1836), a short historical novel related in the first person, contains much clear simple character drawing but is so dominated by the narrative element that there is no room for elaboration of either realistic detail or character relationships.

LERMONTOV: 'A HERO OF OUR TIME

Mikhail Yur'evich LERMONTOV (1814–41) is commonly regarded as a 'Byronic' poet, though his lyric poetry has a fiercer and far more deeply embittered tone to it than is generally found in Byron. *A Hero of our Time* (1840), his only long work in prose, can clearly be seen to have Byronic antecedents,[4] but the character of the hero, Pechorin, is so autobiographical and simultaneously so profound a psychological case-book study that Byronism seems irrelevant to its understanding.

The five sections, or stories, of which the work is composed – *Bela, Maksim Maksimych, Taman, Princess Mary, Fatalist* – are related to each other in such a way that the portrait of Pechorin is gradually elaborated and deepened, despite the fact that the chronological order is purposely violated and at best uncertain. There are three narrators – an anonymous itinerant author who is making travel notes, a *shtabs-kapitan* (or junior captain) called Maksim Maksimych, who tells him the story of Pechorin's relationship with Bela, the daughter of a Circassian prince, and, finally, Pechorin himself. The elaborate and experimental form of the work must be ascribed chiefly to Lermontov's attempts to disguise the autobiographical subject-matter and simultaneously to avoid the difficulty of having to motivate the whole work with a single first-person narrator, the problem of every autobiographer. The first two stories consequently offer what may be regarded as an 'objective' portrait of the hero, which is followed in the final three stories, described as Pechorin's journal, by the hero's subjective, confessional examination of his own *malaise*.

The first portrait, filtered to us through the garrulous reminiscences of Maksim Maksimych and the rather *blasé*, coolly appraising eye of the itinerant author, naturally miniaturizes and generalizes the image of Pechorin. The simple honesty of Maksim Maksimych brings credibility to his exciting tale of love and vengeance – and *Bela* is a splendidly exciting story – but so unsophisticated a narrator can hardly be expected to understand the boredom and coldness of heart which Pechorin finally exhibits when Bela dies. It is left to the itinerant author to comment that such characteristics are symptoms of a Byronic pose. It is also left to him to offer the only first-hand portrait of Pechorin in the whole work. But it is not hard to see that this portrait, for all its seemingly specific detail, is really composed of a series of generalizing observations which tend to leave the impression that Pechorin, seen as it were from the outside, is simply a Byronic young man with all the fashionable social habits and attributes of such a type.[5]

Pechorin's own picture of himself, which begins with the brilliant and famous *conte, Taman*, is distinguished by its irony, its display of prejudice and its vengefulness. *Taman* tells of the hero's involvement with a group of smugglers – an episode which at once throws doubt on his supposedly heroic role. Only at the end of the story does he realize that he has been their victim rather than the agent of fate who uncovers their nefarious activities. As in the other sections comprising Pechorin's journal, we are offered all the events on Pechorin's own terms, and this 'subjective' approach necessarily blurs, confines and on occasion deliberately mystifies.

The most important confessional section of the work, composed almost wholly in diary form, is *Princess Mary*. It reveals a Pechorin who is obsessively concerned with acting the part of a vengeful fate in his deliberate seduction of Princess Mary herself and his eventual destruction of his *alter ego*, the Byronic parody of himself, Grushnitsky. He excuses his conduct by emphasizing that duality in his nature which can also be discerned in Onegin and in many other 'superfluous' heroes, definable perhaps as a division between the mind and the heart. In Pechorin's case it led to his becoming a moral cripple:

I became a moral cripple: one half of my soul ceased to exist, it wilted, languished and died; I cut it off and threw it away – while the other half became alive and lived to be of service to everyone, and no one noticed this, because no one knew of the existence of its perished other half.

What Pechorin achieves in the killing of Grushnitsky and the calculated humiliation of Princess Mary resembles an allegorical enactment of the moral crippling of his own innocence which society's mistrust had enforced upon him. There is no doubt that Pechorin is maladjusted: he has delusions of grandeur, a cruel arrogance, an embittered cynicism, but his conflict with society is motivated chiefly, it seems, by his desire to experiment with his own force of will in order to prove himself independent of morality and the laws of fate. Happiness is defined by him as 'satiated arrogance' and he enjoys the satiety in his relations with women and in a persistent, overweening display of cleverness. He appears serious only in his experiments with fate, which culminate in the last section, *Fatalist*, with a testing of the idea of predestination that leads him to choose the freedom to doubt rather than the assurance of knowledge.

The realism of the work springs both from the psychological veracity of the portrait and from the authenticity of the characters and the settings which assist Pechorin in his process of self-revelation. *Princess Mary* especially has a forcefulness and candour, despite the artifice of the diary form, which make it the most mature piece of realistic prose literature to appear in Russia until that time.

GOGOL: 'DEAD SOULS'

Eugene Onegin and *A Hero of our Time* represent the beginnings of a realistic tradition which did not begin to establish its dominance in Russian literature until the 1840s. With the deaths of Pushkin in 1837 and Lermontov in 1841 poetry ceased to be the most popular vehicle of literary expression. An interest in prose and a particular interest in writing for the theatre attracted all the literary figures who first became prominent during the 1840s. Realism in Russian prose literature is very largely a consequence of close association between theatrical experience and the use of the set scene as the basis of prose fiction. The supreme example of this close association is Nikolay Vasilievich GOGOL (1809–52), whose famous stage comedy, *The Inspector General* (1836), laid the foundations of a realistic tradition in the Russian theatre and also served as a model for the way in which he presented his finest creation, the ingratiating rascal Chichikov, in his major prose work, *Dead Souls*.

Gogol's earlier works had been predominantly romantic in spirit, by which one means simply that they were more imaginative than empirical in their treatment of Ukrainian life, its folklore and legends. Though it is doubtful whether Gogol ever became a realist in the sense that the term may be used of a Turgenev or a Tolstoy, he could hardly help depending on reality for the material of his fiction, despite the exuberant verbal richness which may seem to compromise his every attempt to be an objectively representational author. The first work of his which, however exaggeratedly and grotesquely, attempted to offer a realistic picture of Russian society was *The Quarrel between the Two Ivans* from his famous collection *Mirgorod* (1835). This study of Ivan Ivanovich and Ivan Nikiforovich, who quarrelled over a gun and the fact that the one called the other a goose, is elaborated and enriched by a wealth of quirkily observed detail as well as by Gogol's sprightly and whimsical humour. There is also a recognition that property values and social status are the mainsprings of human conduct and a consequent saddening realization that, no matter how trivial and fatuous such things may seem, they can be the source of real tragedy and spiritual despair in this life, as the final words of the story make clear: 'Gentlemen, this world of ours is a bore!' ('Skuchno na etom svete, gospoda!').

The first part of *Dead Souls* appeared in 1842, and though he intended to expand this extraordinary work into a trilogy, on the lines of Dante's *Divine Comedy*, Gogol never succeeded in completing, after claiming to have burnt much of it, more than fragments of the work's second part before his death in 1852. What remains in Part I of *Dead Souls* is complete in itself and assessable as a single entity. It tells the story of the arrival in a Russian provincial town of an apparently respectable stranger with the comic, *'atishoo'*-sounding name of Chichikov. He quickly ingratiates himself with the town's officials and meets some of the local landowners. He then embarks on a series of visits to landowners in the surrounding district – to Manilov, Korobochka, Nozdryov, Sobakevich and Plyushkin – from whom he tries, with varying success, to buy 'dead souls', meaning those serfs who have died since the previous census but whose names still appear on the tax registers. His object, it turns out, is to use such 'dead souls' as a means of obtaining land on which to resettle his fictitious purchases and so establish himself as a landowner in his own right. He returns to the town, registers his lists of serfs, and is feted as a millionaire, until the news that he has only bought *dead* souls takes the town by storm and he is impelled into hurried departure in his carriage drawn by a birdlike troika, which becomes equated in the final lyrical lines of the work with Russia racing into the future.

Gogol subtitled it 'a poem' and there is little doubt that in the splendid rolling periods of the lyrical digressions he makes his prose into an intricate and sinuous combination of poetic expression and biblical oratory. This highly personal and idiosyncratic manner necessarily imposes a subjective bias on the fiction that must partly invalidate its claim to offer a realistic picture of Russian provincial life. Gogol, born in the Ukraine, had very little intimate knowledge of the Russian provinces and he wrote practically all of *Dead Souls* while he was abroad, chiefly in Rome, between 1836 and 1842. If we are to believe what he had to say about it, he began writing it simply for entertainment, on the basis of an idea given him by Pushkin, and thought of it as 'all my own invention'. Was this Gogol's imaginary Russia? The question is not easy to answer, and the whole issue is complicated by the fact that, after Pushkin's death, Gogol apparently regarded himself as cast in the role of Pushkin's successor and a writer summoned by fate to speak some special word of encouragement and salvation to a Russia threatened by evil ideas from the West. As the work progressed Gogol became increasingly concerned about the moral worthlessness of his grotesque characters and the moral effect of the whole enterprise. His lyrical digressions, in which he speaks of his task as a creator of character and refers guardedly to his own role as one who seeks to achieve Russia's spiritual renewal, are the only serious elements in an otherwise grotesquely comic fiction. After the book was published he sought to justify the 'poshlust' (Vladimir Nabokov's coinage from the Russian *poshlost'*, lit. 'mediocrity', 'spiritlessness', 'commonplaceness'[6]) of his characters by claiming that they could be regarded as emanations of his own spiritual problem, just as all his latest work was to be considered the biography of his own soul. Whether or not we accept Gogol's own view of his work, there seems to be little doubt that he never regarded it as a realistic exposure of serfdom, that most serious of the social evils in the Russia of his day, and he never considered himself a realistic writer.

The critic Vissarion Belinsky never entertained any such doubts. He welcomed *Dead Souls* as what he called 'a social work' and he commended Gogol's talent as one

which consists not simply in the exclusive gift of luminously depicting the commonplaceness [*poshlost'*] of life but also of penetrating into the fullness and reality of the phenomena of life. By his nature he is disinclined to idealization, he does not believe in it; it seems to him to be an abstraction and not reality; in reality as he understands it good and evil, nobility and commonplaceness are not separate but mixed together in unequal doses. He has succeeded in depicting not commonplace man but man in general, as he is, unembellished and unidealized.

For all Gogol's protestations to the contrary, Belinsky stuck to his view and finally went to the lengths of attacking Gogol in his famous *Letter to Gogol* (1847) as 'a preacher of the knout, an apostle of ignorance, a champion of obscurantism and darkness, a panegyrist of Tatar customs . . .'

This disagreement over *Dead Souls* was crucial and tends to become a perennial bone of contention between those who assert, like Gogol, that literature has its own autonomy and those, like Belinsky, who argue that it has a social responsibility. For fear of the censorship Belinsky could not speak his mind plainly, but he evidently applauded *Dead Souls* because, in his estimation, it 'mercilessly ripped the cover from reality', by which he meant that it illustrated the evil of serfdom. It did so by caricaturing the serf-owners and the whole system on which serfdom rested. But in so doing it naturally served to illustrate the further, and more universal, evil of man's acquisitiveness, his craving after possessions which help him hide his spiritual impoverishment. In retrospect this was what Gogol claimed to have depicted in his work. Belinsky's and Gogol's views are at different ends of the same spectrum and have a similar kind of moral intent. What chiefly emerges from the polemic which raged, and still rages, about *Dead Souls* is the necessarily paradoxical character of all realism in literature, how it presumes to reflect a reality that must needs be apprehended subjectively by a writer who has nothing more adequate than language with which to objectify his own version of the real.

Gogol's was a genius obsessed by the magic of language. The abundance and expressiveness of the Russian language inspired him to flights of grotesque fancy in which proportion and form tend to disappear under the sheer pressure of his talkativeness. In *Dead Souls* the theatrical form of the various confrontations between Chichikov and the landowners is blurred by the ubiquitous authorial comment and the often outrageously funny, long-winded and aimless exchanges between the participant characters. Gogol digresses from his central theme, his characters digress like inveterate chatterboxes, and whole worlds of peripheral experience are suggested by the extended similes, by the garrulous arabesques of Gogol's commentary and by such an interpolated short narrative as the story of Captain Kopeykin. The chief characters exist in elaborately depicted settings which both reflect and illustrate their respective types of 'poshlust': Manilov with his spurious charm of manner dwells in an ambience which combines genteel pretentiousness with an aimless squalor; Korobochka (lit. 'a little box') exists in a boxroom of a world full of domestic *realia*, an abundance of food, shrieking animals and noisy clocks. The names tend to suggest the character – Nozdryov, 'the nostril', suggests one who is always trying to sniff out a bargain but never knows when to stop; Sobakevich has a canine nature and a bear-like shape which make him the most solid, clumsy and hard-headed of those with whom Chichikov has to negotiate. Plyushkin, whose name suggests lichen, has a miserly character which the luxuriously elaborate squalor of his setting simultaneously embalms and enhances. All have human lineaments in which one aspect has been exaggerated, but none is so grotesque as to be unrecognizable as a human type.

The most splendid of the portraits is Chichikov, so plumply respectable and mediocre, so outwardly presentable like his box but hiding a rapacious acquisitiveness which makes money his god and human weakness his prey, as the final biographical excerpt shows. Chichikov's portrait gradually emerges from the anonymity of his arrival in the town of NN, revealing first one aspect then another during the successive meetings with the landowners, until he acquires so dominant a position in the book that it seems in retrospect as if *Dead Souls* were simply a portrait of *his* dead soul. But the work is elusive, its meaning open to many interpretations, just as the presumed realism of its representation of Russian provincial life has anachronisms and ambiguities in it. It may be regarded as Gogol's own Bosch-like vision of hell, as a grotesque satire on contemporary morals, as critical realism of a Hogarth-like candour, as a gallery of portraits whose exaggerations owe much to theatrical example; but no interpretation can overlook the sheer comic invention which enlivens so many aspects of this masterpiece.

Gogol's laughter-dominated art presupposes, as he put it, 'a laughter visible to the world and invisible tears unknown to it'. Although the conspicuous element is the laughter, the tears are there in the sadness which is an inevitable aftertaste to any encounter with the grotesques of Gogol's world. Nowhere is this more obvious than in his study of the wretched copying clerk, Akaky Akakiyevich, from the story *The Greatcoat* (1842), who achieves a sense of personal identity in the new greatcoat for which he sacrificed so much, only to have it stolen from him and to become, in Gogol's final vision of an after-life, a lost soul haunting St Petersburg in search of its identity in a greatcoat. For all the grotesque attributes of his penury and impoverishment of spirit, Akaky Akakiyevich appeals to our compassion as one of the injured and insulted of this life. His image, evoking the presence in Russian society of an oppressed, inarticulate mass of urban and rural poor, was more affecting and disturbing than Pushkin's principal study of the type of 'poor official', Samson Vyrin, the keeper of a post-station in his *Tales of Belkin* (1831).

THE FORTIES

By accident, it seems, although Belinsky always insisted otherwise, Gogol's work brought to Russian realism a compassionate spirit of solicitude for all the dispossessed in Russian life. There was no tradition of the heroic in Russian literature, nor was there anything comparable to the Miltonic Christian example in English literature. The Christian ideal found its expression in Russian literature in a semi-Dickensian campaigning on behalf of those who, like Akaky Akakiyevich, would have no other legitimate means of voicing their grievance to the full. For Belinsky – and for the majority of the Russian intelligentsia of the 1840s – this Christianity was secularized into socialism and endorsed the closer identity of literature and society. The superfluous, misunderstood, disenfranchised and oppressed became the 'heroes' of Russian realism.

The closest successor to Akaky Akakiyevich in Russian literature was Dostoyevsky's first literary creation, the poor copying clerk, Makar Devushkin, of *Poor Folk* (1846). Fyodor Mikhailovich DOSTOYEVSKY (1821–81) had been trained as a military engineer, but his principal passion in life had always been literature and when he had completed his training he embarked on his career as a writer by translating Balzac's *Eugénie Grandet*. As the son of a doctor at the Hospital for the Poor in Moscow, he early acquired a knowledge of the way the poor lived: later, personal experience of poverty when he was a writer in St Petersburg added to this knowledge. *Poor Folk*, composed in the form of a series of letters exchanged between the middle-aged Makar Devushkin and Varenka, the youthful object of his love, is a work which studies both the psychology of poverty and the compensatory, addictive effect of the emotional attachment which impels Devushkin into making his blurted, compulsive, epistolary confessions to his beloved. Despite critical opinion to the contrary, there is, in this first work of Dostoyevsky's, much evidence of careful literary craftsmanship and very sure command both of style and of characterization.[7] The heroine appears from her letters to be the conventional sentimental type, but Devushkin's characterization, thanks to its confessional form, is a profound psychological study which represents in part Dostoyevsky's answer to Gogol's Akaky Akakiyevich and, more significantly, an astonishingly mature examination of the volatility and caprice by which the injured and insulted triumph over their poverty and assert their individuality.

Dostoyevsky brought to Russian realism in the 1840s not only a unique awareness of the alienating effect of the city upon urban man but also a willingness to experiment with this theme and explore its literary potential. All his important literary creations in this period are solitaries who seek to emerge from their isolation but cannot sustain a normal relationship with another person. He experimented with studies of abnormal psychological and emotional conditions, all of which could be attributed to the enforced isolation of his urban characters. The most important of these studies is that of Golyadkin in *The Double* (1846), who is literally driven into insanity by an insolent replica of himself, Golyadkin junior. The work is less successful as literature than *Poor Folk* and yet in form and subject it anticipates several features of Dostoyevsky's maturity. For instance, it employs a concentrated time-scheme of only four days' duration, and it shows Dostoyevsky's interest in the tragi-comic potential of the revelatory 'scandal' scene. Its chief innovation is the study of the split or schizophrenic personality; from this beginning sprang such later, very complex, dual-personality figures as Raskolnikov in *Crime and Punishment* or Ivan Karamazov. What Golyadkin lacks as a character is ideological interest, and it has to be stressed that none of Dostoyevsky's creations during this first stage of his evolution as a writer possesses the ideological consciousness of his later characters. They are possessed rather by dreams, as is the dreamer-hero in *White Nights* (1848), or by pathological emotional conditions, as is Netochka Nezvanova in the eponymous fragment of a novel. Dostoyevsky's realism displays its uniqueness in his readiness to examine man's fundamental need to escape from reality. Dostoyevsky does this not by resorting to the fairy-tale or the stratagems of romanticism (though the work of the romantics, particularly Schiller, was a lasting literary inspiration to him) but by stressing the warped psychological and emotional conditions which a hostile urban environment appears to cause in sensitive individuals. His is an urban world peopled by hypersensitive solitaries who find solace only in such escape.

Dostoyevsky had an intimate knowledge of the world of which he wrote. So did the poet N. A. Nekrasov (1821–77), whose realism evolved from a dreamy romanticism into a harsh, deliberately prosaic, yet touchingly lyrical 'civic' poetry devoted – at least in the 1840s – to a depiction of urban poverty, to satire of officialdom, and to violent, embittered repudiation of the supposed idyll of squirearchal life. This attack on the idea of the countryside as somehow more tranquil and ideal than the city took several quite specific forms in the prose literature of the period. The work of D. V. Grigorovich (1822–99), especially his studies of peasant life in *The Village* (1846) and *Anton Goremyka* (1847), is an example of the naturalistic manner which deliberately set out to make Russian literature into a form of realistic, documentary criticism of the injustices in Russian life. Grigorovich's work met with considerable success, but he knew the world of which he wrotel ess nearly than did Ivan Aleksandrovich GONCHAROV (1812–91), whose first novel, *An Ordinary Story* (1847), examines the dichotomy between town and country more profoundly than any other work of the period. It is the story of the young Alexander Aduyev who brings with him a naïve provincial romanticism when he sets out to seek fame and fortune in St Petersburg, but finds there, epitomized by the figure of his uncle, a hardheaded, materialistic realism to which his romantic nature eventually succumbs. The novel is a carefully composed series of dialogue confrontations between nephew and uncle which plot the gradual collapse of the nephew's illusions and also succeed in demonstrating the purity of his youthful idealism.

The conflict between romanticism and realism was demonstrated most effectively during the 1840s in a number of characterizations of 'superfluous' intellectuals. Such studies owed something to the very influential portraits of Onegin and Pechorin, but they were concerned with a later generation, the so-called 'men of the forties', whose problems had little connection with the Byronic flamboyance of their two literary predecessors. The most fully developed portrait of this type is the figure of Beltov in A. I. Herzen's novel *Who is Guilty?* (1847). He is a wealthy and bored young man, of wit and intelligence, who returns to Russia in the hope of finding a suitable role for himself in provincial life, is rejected by the provincial gentry and succeeds only in wrecking the previously happy marriage of a young couple when the wife falls in love with him. The novel is written with Herzen's eloquent acerbity and is more successful as special pleading on Beltov's behalf than as a piece of well-constructed fiction. It is a realistic work in that it clearly delineates the provincial society which forms its setting, but it also points up the contrast between Beltov's ideal in life and the final tragi-comic reality of his situation as a would-be idealist turned squalid adulterer. Herzen obviously lays the guilt for such a situation at the door of Russian society by asking the question in his novel's title. More subtle portraits of this type are to be found in Turgenev's *The Diary of a Superfluous Man*[8] (1850) and his only full-length play, *A Month in the Country* (1850); but the most profound and touching of such studies is to be found in the anonymous *Hamlet of Shchigrovsky District* (1849), which he included among his famous *Sketches from a Hunter's Album* (*Zapiski okhotnika*).

Ivan Sergeyevich TURGENEV (1818–83) first achieved prominence with the publication of a little sketch of peasant life, *Khor and Kalinych*, which he deposited in the editorial office of the journal *The Contemporary* before he left Russia to go abroad early in 1847. Turgenev was of wealthy gentry background, but he had been educated in Germany and had returned at the beginning of the 1840s convinced that Russia must follow the example of the West. This commitment to what was known as Westernism (*Zapadnichestvo*) brought him close to Belinsky and Belinsky's view that literature should take account of the needs of society. It was also one of the reasons why he fell in love with the famous singer Pauline Viardot and followed her across Europe. Many of the most ostensibly 'Russian' of his famous *Sketches* devoted to pictures of Russian rural life were composed when he was in the West, particularly while he was staying at the Viardot home of Courtavenel north of Paris, between 1847 and 1850.

The success of his *Sketches* must be attributed partly to their realistic candour in depicting representatives of the peasantry and the rural gentry and partly to the lyrical power of the descriptive writing which made the finest of them into small-scale literary masterpieces. The most famous are those devoted to such peasant portraits as the Khor and Kalinych of the first *Sketch*, the peasant boys of *Bezhin Lea*, Kasyan of *Kasyan from the Beautiful Lands*, Yakov of the magnificent and expressive voice in *Singers*, and Lukeria, the victim of paralysis, in *Living Relic*, the most poignant of all the studies. Turgenev's is the realism of an observer of peasant life, but he brought to such realistic observation a spirit of compassionate understanding allied to a magically evocative, lucid and poetic style. There is no idealization of the peasantry; there is acknowledgement of their inadequacies and their very real talents. Chiefly, these are portraits based on glimpses, chance meetings between Turgenev, the hunter, and the peasants he met on his hunting trips, and the result of these encounters is practically always to place the peasant portraits in a setting of nature and to make their existences seem the more precious, the richer and more touching for being so ephemeral. Not the least of Turgenev's services was to rescue the peasants he portrays from the virtual anonymity of serfdom, to give human lineaments to the nicknames which for so many were their sole identity. But the power of his realism is seen to best advantage in those *Sketches* – the majority, in fact – which deal with rural conditions as seen from the point of view of the land-owning gentry. Here Turgenev exhibits an intimate knowledge of his subject which gives him the right to satirize, though by laconic inference rather than by anything so overt as the grotesque exaggeration of Gogol.

His study, for example, of the ostensibly civilized Penochkin in *Bailiff*, who orders one of his serfs to be flogged for failing to warm the wine, is acidly critical of the whole miserable condition of serfdom, especially in the revelation of the arbitrary authority wielded by the bailiff himself. The illustration of a landowner's capricious cruelty in *Two Landowners* reminds one that behind the seeming idyll of peasant life is the ubiquitous brutal fact of serfdom. The injustice of the system is suggested in many subtle ways, but Turgenev is careful always to maintain a correctly objective, almost non-committal, stance in relation to the cruelty and fundamental lack of human dignity upon which the system was based. He can laconically satirize the loquacious guests assembled at the house which forms the setting for *Hamlet of Shchigrovsky District*, or poke fun, in a mild, understanding way, at such neighbouring landowners of his as Radilov and Ovsyani-kov, but what his treatment of the land-owning gentry reveals by inference is their general inadequacy both as feudal liegemen and – in the most important cases – as human beings with wills and emotions of their own. Perhaps the gravest indictment of serfdom concerned not the oppressive burden which it meant for the peasantry but the oppressive, brutalizing effect which it could be seen to have on those who presumed to be leaders of Russian society, its masters and intellectual mentors. The realism of his *Sketches*, when they were first published in book form in 1852,⁹ for all its careful understatement, proved to be too much for the authorities and Turgenev was arrested, imprisoned and then exiled to his country estate of Spasskoye. His work concluded the period known as 'the forties' and yet served to elevate Russian realism from the confines of literature into a moral influence which was eventually to have a profound, if indirect, effect on state policy, leading to the liberation of the serfs in 1861.

THE FIFTIES

Turgenev was not the first, nor was he the last, to suffer a kind of martyrdom in the name of literature. Dostoyevsky was arrested in 1849 and sent into a ten-year exile. Herzen voluntarily left Russia in 1847, never to return. Along with the disappearance of such figures, new forces were beginning to emerge which would soon radically change the composition and attitudes of the Russian intelligentsia. But in the first half of the 1850s, before the Crimean War of 1854–5, the land-owning gentry remained the dominant influence, and the most significant newcomer in these years was Count Lev Nikolaye-vich TOLSTOY (1828–1910), who published his first work, *Childhood*, in 1852.

Tolstoy's emergence as a writer caused instantaneous interest. His *Childhood* differed from previous studies in being a brilliant recon-struction of childish experience which involved an apparently total recall of the feel, the psychological and emotional state, the direct apprehension of being a child. This was a much profounder realistic manner than the realism current in the previous decade in the sense that it presupposed that growth, change and flux were indispensable elements in any literary portrayal of character. Chernyshevsky described Tolstoyan portraiture as 'a dialectics of the soul', and though this description has been used indiscriminately in Soviet criticism it is of value if used to emphasize the way Tolstoy, in psychologizing his portraiture, establishes a particular reciprocal relationship between the viewed object and the viewing eye, between object and subject, and creates from this a dialectic of growth in his characters. Tolstoy's realism involved an enlargement not only of the means which can be used for representing reality but also of the frame of reference of realistic literature: it took the experimentation of the 1840s a stage further by indicating that the totality of human experience must involve the evolution from childhood to adulthood. His *Childhood, Boyhood and Youth* explored this process in semi-autobiographical form and led him, whether in the figure of Irtenev (of the autobiographical trilogy) or in Nekhlyudov, another literary *persona*, to examine chiefly the morality of human relationships in a social context and the moral growth which could ensue. He examined similar moral issues in a much keener way in his studies of war, both in his military tales from the Caucasus and in his fictionalized re-portage of the Crimean War, *Sevastopol Sketches* (1855).

Tolstoy's essay in autobiography was symptomatic of a nostalgic mood which had a marked influence on Russian literature in the 1850s. It is to be explained by – among other things – a sense, which literature is especially fitted to articulate, that change was either imminent or already occurring in Russian life. With the revolutionary situation in Europe in 1848 and the increased vigilance exercised by the government, the intelligentsia of the forties found itself forced to acknowledge, as the Crimean War approached, that its Westernist ideals had proved inadequate and its knowledge of Russia insufficient. Since the land-owning intelligentsia was largely educated in the West, it could hardly fail to feel isolated, even superfluous, in Russia once the links with the West came under strain.

Realism in literature always tends to be more dependent on memory than on imagination for its sources, and in the stagnant atmosphere of Russia in the first half of the 1850s the desire to recapture the past brought a sense of history to the realistic manner and, naturally enough, led to a reappraisal of the significance of the national heritage. Sergey Timofeyevich AKSAKOV (1791–1859) offered, very late in his own life, an act of homage to the Slavophil ideal, which he had done so much to foster, with his remarkable, lovingly executed reconstruction of patriarchal life, *A Family Chronicle* (1852). It is a masterpiece of carefully re-created items from the times of Aksakov's grandfather, celebrating both the patriarchalism of the old gentry and the past experience from which Aksakov's own story, as told in the *Childhood Years of the Bagrov Grandson* (1858), grew. Some degree of idealization is perhaps forgivable in such marvellously evocative pieces of writing. The most famous example of memoir literature begun in the 1850s had a merciless realism which repudiated all idealization. This was Herzen's *Past and Thoughts* (1852–68), begun in his London exile; it recounts his experiences and offers his evaluations of the world of 'the forties', bringing into focus an album of brilliant portraits which suggest more vividly than any other source the splendours and miseries of the early years of the Russian intelligentsia.

This concern with the past enriched the realistic fiction of the period by turning it into a type of chronicle. If Turgenev turned his novels into a chronicle of the growth of the Russian intelligentsia, Pisemsky and Goncharov also turned to the chronicle novel as a means of examining, in a spirit of realistic nostalgia, the slow erosion of old standards and ideals. Both created memorable portraits of figures typical of their epochs which yet transcended the limitations of their time and place.

Aleksey Feofilaktovich PISEMSKY (1821–81) brought the practice of 'critical realism' to the point of making his picture of Russian life so critical that little positive good could be found in it. His story is one of misfortune and misjudgement. He fell foul of the censorship in the 1840s, which meant that his first major work, *Boyarshchina*, had to wait ten years for publication; in 1862, after he had achieved widespread literary popularity, he became critical of the younger nihilist intelligentsia, which meant that he forfeited the good will of the radical press and virtually doomed himself to premature extinction as a writer. His reputation never recovered, in part deservedly, though a certain amount of scholarly attention has been given to him since the republication of his works in the 1950s. His only major achievement as a novelist was the four-part novel *A Thousand Souls* (1858), which traced the career of a bureaucrat, Kalinovich, from youthful obscurity to success, power and eventual disgrace. Pisemsky could create characters: his novel is packed with them; he found difficulty in sustaining a story, or argument, in his fiction. Kalinovich's portrayal has a sensible veracity, the dialogue of the novel has realistic pungency, but only at a very few points does Kalinovich's story have the power to move, memorable though the portrait may be in its delineation of the hero's growing realization that the ideals of happiness and achievement which belonged to his youth have been relinquished for ever in his later pursuit of wealth and power. But no amount of wealth and power can finally bridge the gap which exists between his lowly social status and the hereditary nobility to which his wife belonged.

The hero of Goncharov's masterpiece *Oblomov* (1859) is likewise a study in the gradual collapse of illusory ideals and the recognition of the real facts of Russian life. The figure of Ilya Ilyich Oblomov in his dressing-gown has become a classic image of slothfulness. Whether he be considered, as Dobrolyubov in his famous review, 'What is Oblomovism?', considered him, the ultimate corruption of the gentry hero familiar to us already from such types as Onegin and Pechorin, or whether he be regarded as possessing universal attributes which place him alongside such universally recognizable types as Hamlet or Don Quixote, there is no doubt that Oblomov is the first example of large-scale portraiture in Russian literature. For the first time characterization has been assumed to mean not only the relationship of character to setting or to another character, but the relating, as nearly as is feasible, of the totality of a character's experience, from boyhood to death. We know Oblomov principally in the squalid setting of his St Petersburg apartment, where at the opening of the novel he spends a whole day in a dressing-gown rejecting the overtures of visitors from the cold outside world or quarrelling with his serf Zakhar. We also know him principally as a man momentarily roused from his dressing-gown torpor by the attractions of the novel's heroine, Olga. He spends an enchanted summer in gentle courtship of her (Parts II and III of the novel), only to retreat again into his dressing-gown existence when winter approaches. But beyond this twofold portraiture, principally static and fluidly episodic, are the lovingly designed vistas of 'Oblomov's Dream' or the chorus-like commentaries of the novel's 'positive' hero, Stolz, and these give perspectives of time and meaning to Oblomov's characterization. We can glimpse from them the private cause of his lethargy, the evasion of adult responsibility which is arguably at the source of his *oblomovshchina* (Oblomovism) and the presumption of superiority to 'them', meaning those who have to dress themselves or occasionally move house (this crisis faces Oblomov at the novel's opening), no doubt the fondest of Oblomov's private illusions. In the end even his lethargy is idealized into a demonstration of what he considered to be an ideally tranquil aspect of human existence, his Oblomovism can be seen to be not an excuse for inactivity so much as a deliberate rejection of all normal human activity as fatuous and irrelevant, and his superiority to 'them' is indeed the superiority of his 'crystal, pellucid soul', as Stolz describes it, to the showy falsehoods and oceans of evil which surge round him in his life.

The realism of this masterpiece is founded on much more than the lovingly detailed *Kleinmalerei* of Goncharov's descriptive manner, though this aspect of the work is outstanding even in a literature so rich in examples of detailed realistic word-painting as is nineteenth-century Russian literature. The intricacy of the descriptions devoted to Oblomov's St Petersburg apartment, the complexity of the imagery describing his mental processes, the fond, clock-ridden, soporific abundance of the lyrical narrative which tells of Oblomov's last years are high points only in a work that has a marvellously substantial feel about its realistic manner in all its parts. Its realism embraces, in a more intimate and explorative sense than any hitherto, the real character of the mutual interdependence existing between master and serf in mid-nineteenth-century Russia. There is also a profounder awareness than in earlier literature of the real socio-economic forces that were threatening to engulf the nobility isolated and cocooned in their respective Oblomovkas, their respective country estates. The tensions between the new and the old in Russian society, although seemingly offered in excessively black-and-white terms if Oblomov be compared with the positive hero, Stolz, are suggested more subtly by the conflict between Oblomov's embodiment of a decayed idealism and the guileful realism of the money-grubbing world surrounding him. If in the end Goncharov seems over-indulgent towards his hero by allowing him a kind of metaphysical redemption, the realism of his work, by its very scale and profundity, invites us to sympathize just as much as to censure, to understand and therefore to forgive, though without proselytizing, simply by offering us a likeness. If we do not recognize the reality of Oblomov, we simultaneously do not recognize the Oblomov in each of us.

The stature and importance acquired by the figure of Oblomov was an acknowledgement of the extent to which literature in the post-Crimean-War period had begun to exert an authority, albeit unofficial, which tended to usurp the authority of church and state. Turgenev contributed to this process as much as any literary figure of the period, but the importance of literature as a moral and educative influence was appreciated more fully by the younger generation of the intelligentsia. The review of *Oblomov* by the young radical critic Dobrolyubov, which appeared in *The Contemporary* in May 1859, was not only a masterly critical examination of the novel, it was also a remarkable publicistic document which used the novel as a means of demonstrating the Oblomovism of the older generation of the gentry intelligentsia and the consequent need for their replacement, as an influential force in Russian society, by a younger generation with radical ideas. There is little doubt that what Dobrolyubov sought was revolution. The impulse for change in Russian society, present among sections of the nobility since the beginning of the century, held less appeal for them as soon as it began to acquire the revolutionary characteristics which led Dobrolyubov, as a spokesman of the *raznochintsy*, to proclaim, no matter how circumspectly for fear of the censorship, the cause of peasant revolution and the role of the *raznochintsy* as its leaders. His review of *Oblomov* became one of the first shots fired in an incipient internecine warfare between the 'fathers' and 'sons', between the older liberal-inclined intelligentsia, who came almost entirely from the nobility, and the younger radical intelligentsia drawn from among the less privileged elements of Russian society, the *raznochintsy*.

To a great extent Dobrolyubov was following in the footsteps of the acknowledged leader of the younger intelligentsia, N. G. Chernyshevsky. He had proclaimed a philosophical materialism and a commitment to Feuerbach from the very beginning of his publicistic career in 1855. His attack on Hegelian aesthetics in his extremely eloquent dissertation *The Aesthetic Relations of Art to Reality* (1855) demanded that literature should be not only a representation of life but also 'a textbook on life' ('uchebnik zhizni'). In his only major piece of literary criticism devoted to post-Crimean-War literature, he attacked Turgenev's story *Asya* (1858) for the spinelessness of its nobleman hero and suggested by implication that the future of Russia would lie not with the nobility but with the *raznochintsy* who would replace it. He enunciated in several important articles between 1858 and 1862 a programme of change designed to introduce socialist principles into Russian life. The fullest and most coherent statement of his views came only after his arrest in 1862 when, incarcerated in the Peter and Paul fortress in St Petersburg, he wrote a highly didactic novel that has since become his best-known work. Its title, *What Is To Be Done?* (*Chto delat'?*, 1863) reveals that it was intended as a blue-print for social change. Through the story of the heroine's relations with Lopukhov, her first husband, and Kirsanov, her second, it indicated how female dignity and emancipation could be achieved in marriage, while simultaneously demonstrating, through Vera Pavlovna's activities in organizing seamstresses, how labour could be dignified if it were based on co-operative, socialist principles. In addition to being a blue-print, the novel was a vision of the socialist future which inspired many revolutionaries in later generations, especially Lenin, and it is not surprising that it has become one of the fundamental texts of Russian socialism. Its place in the history of literature is less certain, but its contribution to the evolution of Russian realism is inestimable. It showed how the realistic manner could, in an extreme case, evolve from representation to inspiration, from being a book about life to becoming a textbook on life. The moral impulse behind such an evolution was present in the very earliest works of Russian realism, and became most obvious in Gogol's striving to speak 'a new word' of salvation to the Russia of his time through *Dead Souls*. But inherent in such an impulse is the danger, experienced so tragically by Gogol, that the morality may simply sound sententious and the impeccably moral purpose may reduce the work of literature to a moral tract. We may wonder why Chernyshevsky's novel exerted such an appeal. There is no denying that it did. Its effects were to be felt in a new emphasis on the educative role of literature in the 1860s and 1870s. It also enshrined a principle about the utilitarianism of art which has since come to be regarded as essential to the literature of socialist realism.

THE NOVELS OF TURGENEV

After his arrest in 1852, ostensibly for his obituary of Gogol but mainly for the publication in book form of his *Sketches from a Hunter's Album*, Turgenev was forced to reappraise his role as a writer. Dissatisfied with the *Sketch* as a genre, he attempted to write a long prose work, though he seems to have doubted whether Russian literature was mature enough to accommodate itself to large prose forms. This hesitancy is characteristic. Turgenev's approach to the novel as a form was tentative and he never attempted to enlarge its scope beyond certain precise limits which owe much to theatrical example.

All his first four novels are 'months in the country'. They are, like his only full-length play, *A Month in the Country* (1850), circumscribed in time, occupying barely more than a couple of summer months, and similarly circumscribed in spatial terms by the limiting of the action to a particular place. They also run to a formula like his play in that they are concerned by and large with the impact of a stranger from the outside world on the world in which the fiction is placed. More significantly, Turgenev's visual sense demanded that the world of his fiction should be offered to us as if it were staged. As author, he was keen to seem invisible, unlike Gogol, for example, who never lets us forget that he is the author of *Dead Souls*. Turgenev will introduce his characters with explanatory biographies sufficient to make their roles comprehensible, but he will then leave them to demonstrate their respective dilemmas and difficulties much as a playwright will leave the actors to play out the roles assigned to them. His success both in evoking a sense of place, a particular atmosphere, and in conveying the subtle weave of human relationships through admirably poised dialogue was technically his greatest achievement. His novels, though, were dependent for their distinctive character on a combination of elements which may seem at first glance un-suited to each other – the love-story and socio-political interest. Each of his novels contains an inevitably doomed love-story between hero and heroine in the course of which, by one means or another, the significance of the hero's socio-political role is gradually revealed and judgement is passed on his credibility.

Though on occasion Turgenev liked to protest that he was un-interested in politics, he was in fact as concerned with mirroring the political 'body and pressure' of his time as any conscientious and objective observer of the contemporary scene must be. In his role of observer he had to contend with other dangers than those offered by a fickle reading public; he faced a suspicious, and often repressive, censorship which was in turn merely the instrument of a callous bureaucracy. His success in appearing to offer an objective picture of his time was due not only to the way in which he dissociated him-self technically from his fiction by 'staging' it, but also to his very real ability to suggest the universality of the human experience, principally the love-story, which was at the centre of his fiction. As I have said elsewhere:

The two aims which Turgenev always had before him – that of depicting 'the body and pressure of time' and the rapidly changing face of cultured Russian society – unite in the primary artistic consideration of his novels: the fact that they are 'realistic'. Turgenev's realism is to be defined, firstly, in common human terms. His novels give us pictures of real life which are true to life and acceptable in terms of a reality that every man can experience. Secondly, his novels are realistic in the sense that they are 'social-psychological' representations of epochs in the development of Russian society. The two definitions are complement-ary: the reality of the artistically transformed experience must neces-sarily complement the reality of the particular social-psychological problem which Turgenev sets out to identify and depict.[10]

The universality of the human experience is suggested by Tur-genev's assumption that human relationships, meaning those chiefly between his heroes and heroines, must always be short-lived and foredoomed; and that man must realize his ultimate insignificance in the face of nature and eternity. The assumption is fundamentally pessimistic and can seem grotesquely maudlin, but Turgenev lightened his picture of life by illustrating its dependence on a subtle balance between the poles of human experience, between love and death, joy and sadness, youth and age, innocence and maturity. The ephemeral happiness which such a balance offers is at the centre of Turgenev's tragi-comic vision of the world

His first novel, *Rudin* (1856), written at the height of the Crimean War, tells of the unexpected arrival at a country estate of an intellectual, Dmitry Rudin, whose eloquence exerts a powerful charm over the guests assembled at a kind of provincial *salon* presided over by the lady of the estate, Darya Lasunskaya. His talk of duty and self-sacrifice in the name of the future of Russia appeals chiefly to the younger generation, and Darya Lasunskaya's daughter, Natalya, an eighteen-year-old girl, falls in love with him. Rudin is not young – he is thirty-five – and when challenged by her to live up to his words he rather ignominiously prefers to submit to fate. When Darya Lasunskaya discovers his relationship with her daughter, she orders him to leave and Rudin obeys. We learn in an extended epilogue how he tries to put his talents to some practical, educative use, and how all his efforts end in failure. The last glimpse we have of him – a final section added by Turgenev in 1860, four years after the novel first came out – shows how he dies clutching a red flag on the Paris barricades in 1848.

Rudin's failure was in part an admission by Turgenev that his own generation, the so-called 'men of the forties', had failed. This apart, Rudin's weaknesses are attributable in some measure to Turgenev's own failure to keep the portrait in focus; there are hesitancies and blurrings in the picture that emerges. The main features, though, are clear: Rudin suffered from a division between the head and the heart; he had no spontaneity of emotional response, just as, for all his eloquence, he could not enact his ideals of service and self-sacrifice for the good of Russia, save in the final, rather uncharacteristic, apotheosis of his heroism on the Paris barricades. Chiefly Rudin could not meet the challenge of the younger generation personified by Natalya. We may find this heroine a tiresomely serious-minded young lady, but there is no doubt that Turgenev was successful in evoking her youthful sense of dedication and readiness to sacrifice herself in the name of a better future. Rudin misjudged her and in so doing was forced to acknowledge his own 'superfluousness' both as an individual and as a representative of the 'men of the forties'.

The portrait of Rudin is saddening because it strikes chords of truth. We can easily recognize Rudin as a type of intellectual who would fail in life through lack of practical sense. His is not a phenomenon exclusive to Russia, but his failure is all the more poignant when seen as the squandering of talent and intelligence in a society which so badly needed an enlightened intelligentsia. Rudin could disseminate ideas, and this role, even if cosmopolitan and rootless, had enormous value. The veracity of the portrait may suffer through Turgenev's own ambivalence toward the sitter, but its relevance as a realistic study struck home very strongly in the immediate post-Crimean-War period, when the Russian intelligentsia was beginning to face the new, practical problems of peasant reform.

Turgenev's second novel, *Home of the Gentry (Dvoryanskoye gnezdo*, 1859), indicated obliquely and elegiacally what attitude the older intelligentsia would have to adopt towards their own country, the peasant problem, the next generation and such issues as Slavophilism and Westernism. Fyodor Lavretsky, the hero, has a divided heritage, being the son of a rich noble family with a mother who was originally a serf. His background is explained in a very extensive biographical section which not only establishes him in the fiction but is also a historical microcosm of the Russian intelligentsia from the Napoleonic period through Decembrism to the 1840s. Lavretsky's father had become infected, like many others of his class and generation, by indiscriminate admiration for the West, meaning in this case everything English, and the most serious effect of this was the curious, unbalanced, Spartan style of education which he inflicted on his son. So distorting was this education that, on his father's death, Lavretsky was quite unprepared for the world at large, knew nothing of women and consequently made a most unfortunate marriage which ended in separation. The novel opens with his return to his 'home', the nest (*gnezdo*) of his boyhood, where he hopes gradually to be able to recover from the collapse of his marriage.

Here he meets and falls deeply in love with Liza Kalitina, a character exceptional in the portrait gallery of Turgenevan heroines by reason of her devout religious nature. It is already assumed that she will marry a promising young civil servant, Panshin, but the superficial plausibility of this young man is contrasted, as are his vaguely Westernist ideas, with the genuine need to readjust to Russia which is central to Lavretsky's problem and personality. Liza seems to Lavretsky to epitomize his native land. When, in a brief episode, he demonstrates to Panshin the falseness of the idea that all change can be introduced from above, by government decree, and makes a plea for greater understanding of Russia's youth and independence, he is exhibiting a patriotic or Slavophil attitude which makes an instant appeal to Liza. They make confession of their love, but the news of his wife's death which Lavretsky had recently read in a French newspaper turns out to be incorrect. His wife suddenly returns; his chance of happiness with Liza is destroyed. Liza enters a convent and he resigns himself to ensuring as best he can that his peasants are guaranteed a living. This is his only practical contribution to the welfare of his country. At the end he is bound to accept that a younger generation has come to take his place in the 'home of the gentry'.

The novel has that special realistic atmosphere, uniting summer warmth and a luxuriantly evoked rural background with carefully observed characterization and dialogue, which one associates with Turgenev. As a novel it belongs to its age in the very obvious sense that the love-story between hero and heroine tends to be overladen with such Victorian bric-à-brac as nightingale song and moonlight. It is more successful precisely in those areas which are most commonly associated with the realistic manner: the characterization of minor figures, the psychological portrayal of the hero and the documentation of a particular way of life – in this case, the patriarchal way of life of the Russian gentry.

By the time he published *Home of the Gentry* in 1859 Turgenev was already aware of the revolutionary aspirations of the younger generation. Although he did not share these, he was fascinated by their spontaneous, untutored desire for change. Theoretically – and the revolutionary impulse was always more theoretical than real to him – he attempted, in his article 'Hamlet and Don Quixote' of 1860, to diagnose their altruism and self-sacrifice by contrasting these Quixotic characteristics with the predominantly Hamlet-like attributes of his own generation. The contrast and its meaning are explored more fully in his third novel, *On the Eve*, of the same year.

The contrast becomes apparent at the very opening of the novel when two young Russians, Shubin, a dilettante sculptor and aesthete, and Bersenyev, a recently graduated student who aspires to be a professor, argue their respective Hamlet-like and Quixotic viewpoints on the banks of the Moscow River. Both are attracted to the same girl, Yelena, the heroine, but she cannot discern in either of them the active revolutionary vocation which would satisfy her own craving for moral change. Instead she is drawn to a young Bulgarian patriot, Insarov, and eventually, after marrying him, accompanies him on his return journey to his own country, where he aims to take part in a national liberation struggle. He dies in Venice before he has a chance of reaching Bulgaria, and Yelena herself takes his coffin back to his native land, where she is last heard of among the gathering armies of liberation. The eve referred to in the title of the novel is not so much that of national liberation before the incidents leading to the Crimean War (the action takes place in 1853) as the eve of the liberation of the Russian serfs which was to occur in 1861.

The novel is more loosely constructed than its predecessors and suffers from Turgenev's inability to make Yelena an intellectually interesting character. Her moral strength, her purity, her evident attractiveness and her femininity are suggested sufficiently well to make this the most fully developed portrait of a woman to appear in Russian literature before Anna Karenina. The realism of Yelena's portrayal depends to some extent on the introduction of such private or 'subjective' material as letters, diaries (the basic story of the novel derived from a diary belonging to one of Turgenev's neighbours), and passages devoted to describing her emotional state. The introduction of such material seems contrived, and Turgenev was never at his best when describing emotional states. When he lets his painter's eye rest on a subject, as he does with the incomparable description of Venice towards the novel's end, he is brilliant. Moreover, Yelena's portrait is not balanced by a matching portrayal of the hero. Insarov is a pale figure whose antecedents Turgenev clearly did not understand; as a result his revolutionary impulse appears counterfeit. There is no denying, though, that Turgenev managed to suggest the spirit of change and hope for the future which was present among the younger intelligentsia after the Crimean War. He also captured the poignancy of this youthful optimism, forlorn and doomed though it may have been in his opinion. In this he was true to the reality of the times, but he demonstrated his realistic view of things not so much in his pessimistic attitude towards Yelena's sacrifice as in his many brilliantly depicted scenes of Moscow life, in many exquisite sketches of minor figures, and in a satirical tone, especially directed at the older generation, which for all its malicious exaggeration lent an asperity and sharpness to his picture of the Russian social scene.

His seemingly deliberate refusal to acknowledge the existence of specifically Russian revolutionary aspirations in *On the Eve* provoked

Dobrolyubov to launch his most outspoken attack. Turgenev, who sought to mirror the 'body and pressure' of his time in his novels, was hurt by this criticism and reacted to it by portraying the younger generation of the Russian intelligentsia in the hero of his fourth novel, Bazarov, who appeared to flatter the tough-minded pragmatism of the younger generation quite as much as he apparently offended their sense of literary decorum.

Turgenev conceived Bazarov during three rather wet and windy weeks spent at Ventnor on the Isle of Wight in August 1860. The place may have depressed him and the portrait may have been initially conceived as that of an apostle of revolutionary ideals who was doomed to premature death. In the course of the gestation of this figure over the next eighteen months Turgenev turned Bazarov into the most vital of his literary creations, a young erstwhile doctor whose directness of approach and repudiation of all authority save that exercised by the natural sciences endowed him with a stature and authority clearly greater than any enjoyed by the representatives of the nobility in the novel. As its title indicates – *Fathers and Children* – the novel was a study in the conflict between two generations of the Russian intelligentsia; it was also a study in the confrontation between the *raznochintsy* and the nobility on the eve of the emancipation of the serfs in 1861. Bazarov, the representative of the *raznochintsy* and nihilism, is not only a remarkably powerful portrait; he is also represented as the victor in the conflict and a model for a whole succeeding generation of nihilists who strove to renounce the past and work for a revolutionary future.

The action of *Fathers and Children* (1862) takes place in the summer of 1859. The novel shows us first the return home from the university of young Arkady Kirsanov, who is accompanied by a fellow student, Bazarov. Apart from Arkady's widowed father, Nikolay Petrovich Kirsanov, his uncle Pavel Petrovich also lives on the estate, a man who at one time aspired to be a spokesman of the nobility but has since retired to this country backwater as a result of an unhappy love-affair. Bazarov and Pavel Petrovich quarrel over Bazarov's respect for science and Pavel Petrovich's reverence for art. Bazarov's scientism may seem unduly naïve in its assertion that 'a good chemist is twenty times more useful than any poet'; similarly, Pavel Petrovich's defence of art in the name of civilization may seem little more than an aristocratic apologia for idleness; but for all that, each line of argument is closely relevant to the contemporary Russian situation and to the problems of the peasantry, of economic survival, of coming revolutionary change. Bazarov, in his hard-headed, pragmatical way, can see little merit in peasant ignorance or in such peasant institutions as the commune, whereas Pavel Petrovich, whose knowledge of such matters is at best second-hand, likes to represent himself as a liberal-minded devotee of the peasantry and their customs. Bazarov believes in the need to sweep away the clutter of the past and start again by learning the alphabet of the natural sciences, while Pavel Petrovich, though having little except the *status quo* to offer in place of Bazarov's programme, can see in the advocacy of change the threat of a mindless violence which could easily destroy the most precious things in civilization. Bazarov is a revolutionary only by implication. His chief concern is practical change, and, as the novel finally shows, he devotes himself to working for the peasantry whom he so despises by helping his father, a retired army doctor, in his medical practice. He dies of typhus, contracted while he is carrying out a post-mortem on a peasant who has died of the disease.

The novel contains its love-stories, as do all Turgenev's novels, but this aspect of the work, though significant in helping to reveal the social as well as the psychological contrasts, is generally made subservient to the principal business of portraying the hero. His relationship with the wealthy young widow Odintsova ends with his acknowledgement of his love, but they are also obliged to admit in their respective ways that they do not 'need' each other. The theme of 'needfulness' is central to Bazarov's problem: for all his evident strength of character and practical hard-headedness he is forced by the Hamlet-like qualities in his predominantly Quixotic personality to wonder how needful he is to life when his isolated, solitary existence is seen in the context of nature and eternity. Turgenev's pessimism here makes itself felt in the characterization of his greatest hero. The death of Bazarov may seem to demonstrate that, in Turgenev's view, Bazarov was not needed in Russian life, but this consideration is inevitably outweighed by the tragic grandeur which the portrait acquires through the hero's death. Turgenev's visualization of Bazarov has none of the uncertainties and blurrings that are to be found in Rudin's portrait. The reality of Bazarov as a character is poignantly highlighted by his death. Throughout the novel, realism is served by Turgenev's careful and sympathetic delineation of character in relation to background – the Kirsanovs against the background of their dilapidated estate, Odintsova's sumptuous world of Nikolskoye, Bazarov's parents and their modest home. Gradually, as Bazarov moves from one setting to another, his portrait is enlarged and deepened, until, revisiting each of the principal settings in turn towards the novel's close, he demonstrates his superiority to the older generation by wounding Pavel Petrovich in a fatuous duel, by his rejection of the nobility as the leading class of Russian society in his parting with Odintsova, and, finally, by his tragic destiny as the solitary man who has only one task in life, that of dying decently, as is illustrated by his premature death when he returns home to work among the peasantry.

Turgenev never achieved greater success as chronicler of the realities of his time than he did in *Fathers and Children*. His two later novels, *Smoke* (1867) and *Virgin Soil* (1877), lack the artistry, balance and objectivity of his masterpiece. They are realistic in that they offer us pictures of societies and we may in consequence judge the state of Russia from them, even though *Smoke* is set in Baden-Baden. But neither work adds anything to Turgenev's realistic manner.

The conventions of Russian realism were to be enormously enlarged by the contributions of Tolstoy and Dostoyevsky in the sense that they both multiplied the constituent parts of the novel until it acquired a formal resemblance to a latter-day epic or Greek tragedy. Both writers were concerned to represent the social realities as they saw them and the problem of the hero or principal figure in terms of a given society at a particular time. But realism tended to mean to them more than the copying of reality; it meant a search for the true verities, the true meaning of life and, in the end, a search for God. The novel tended to become in their hands a work of profound moral edification. Naturally, reality yielded symbolical meanings under this treatment. Dostoyevsky liked to think of his own realism as 'a penetration of reality' in which the real and the fantastic became interchangeable and almost identical. Realism as an artistic attitude of mind and a manner of writing did not so much degenerate as acquire profounder, ultimate meanings, but this in turn meant, as we can see from Dostoyevsky's *The Brothers Karamazov*, that it had perhaps reached the limits of its growth.

TOLSTOY'S EARLY FICTION

Tolstoy took almost two decades to make himself into a novelist of repute. Beginning with his essay in autobiography, *Childhood* (1852), he did not complete *War and Peace* until 1869, and the transformation from autobiographer who tended to invent his own childhood to historical novelist who tended to invent the supposed impulses of history was in its essentials no transformation at all but could never have been achieved without the intervening experience. The utterly candid eye of the young Nikolenka of *Childhood* is fundamentally the same eye as Pierre Bezukhov's in *War and Peace*: both perceive the world as fresh, novel, 'made strange' by the very candour of their perception. The principal difference between *Childhood* and *War and Peace* is one of range. *Childhood*, with its emphasis on the closed family world, achieves its remarkable verisimilitude by the very limitations of the child's viewpoint; *War and Peace* extends this principle by suggesting the existence of several interrelated viewpoints, of contiguous but separate worlds, and it enlarges the range of such relationships to encompass the epoch-making event of the Napoleonic invasion of Russia. In the process, quantitative change leads to a change in the quality of Tolstoyan art and the form of the novel.

Tolstoy's first experiment in suggesting range of experience by multiplying the viewpoints was conducted in the second of his famous *Sevastopol Sketches*, his *Sevastopol in May* (1855). Here war is presented through several different eyes and the realism which results, even if primarily pictorial, evokes the fragmented, intense, baffling impact of a military engagement with startling immediacy. In *Two Hussars* (1856), Tolstoy enlarged his range of subject by introducing contrasts such as those between the older and the younger generation, between town and country, past and present, hero and heroine, but he was far more preoccupied with minutely examining his own moral dilemma as a liberal-minded aristocrat in the period after the Crimean War when the whole land-owning and serf-owning ethos of the Russian nobility was being challenged by the need for reform and the emergence of the *raznochintsy*. In *A Landowner's Morning* (1856), *Lucerne* (1857) and *Albert* (1858) he examined the problem of his relationship to the peasantry, the problem of social inequality and the role of art in society, though in each case he wore the disguise of a fictitious *persona* and in each case what emerged most conspicuously from the exercise was the ambivalence of his attitude. All his life Tolstoy attempted to deny his fundamentally aristocratic heritage while demonstrating the nobility of his attitude in all things. The nobility of his attitude barely concealed its abhorrence of the lower orders while pretending to revere the noble savage in man. In each instance one can easily discern the Tolstoy who not only had to share his personal dilemma with his readers but also sought to turn the ostensible fiction into a moral lesson. The didactic intent, though often quite unobtrusive, is always present in Tolstoy's realism. He could not realistically represent life in his fiction without indicating in many subtle ways how far the norms of life fell short of being ideal.

This may be seen in the second and third parts of his autobiographical trilogy, *Boyhood* (1854) and *Youth* (1857), but it is most conspicuous in his first extended examination of a relationship between a hero and a heroine, *Family Happiness* (1859). The novella is something of a *tour de force* in the characterization of the heroine, who also narrates the events; it is much less striking in its treatment of the relationships between the heroine and the men in her life, and the final picture of her married life is dull if edifying. The work has atmosphere; what it lacks is the leaven of a sense of humour. Tolstoy could describe laughter and high spirits, but he took life too seriously to permit himself to smile at its comedy. He was always conscious of norms, proprieties, the checks and balances that contribute to social living, and in stressing these seeming permanencies in life he tended to impose moral limits on the conduct permitted to his characters just as he imposed a pictorial frame on the image of the world which his fiction offers us. He could never allow himself to compromise with the reality of life as he saw it: it had to be totally apprehended within the frame of his looking. In the last resort this involved him in an absolutist view of moral issues and a majestically Olympian view of his art which liked to give the impression that life happened *there*, on the page, remote from him as its author, vicariously known to us through the experience of his characters, exteriorized to the point where it almost seemed to be more real, more what life should be than was life itself. But Tolstoy achieved such extraordinary veracity chiefly by allowing the fiction to come to us through the sensibility of some character who acts as the reader's eyes and by relating that character to one or another society or social unit which explains the character, establishes his or her place in an intricate network of relationships and makes him or her known as an almost archetypally familiar spirit with whom the reader can intimately identify. That the Tolstoyan character was an amalgam of the prejudices and assumptions of his class or society had no seriously inhibiting effect upon the candour of his seeing eye, but it did tend to mean that for the Tolstoyan hero to learn, to acknowledge, that is, the existence of other truths beyond his own, he was obliged to suffer the trauma of revelation from without. Tolstoy did not begin to achieve success in elaborating this kind of characterization until, after a break of almost four years (1859–63), during which he was much concerned with his school for peasant children, he completed *Polikushka* and *The Cossacks*.

Polikushka is a study of peasant society dominated by the economic fact of money. The chief character, the horse-doctor Polikushka, is a masterly portrait of a feckless peasant who plays on the gullibility of other peasants and is in turn made the prey of the money-dominated society to which he belongs. When he discovers that the money entrusted to him by his mistress is apparently lost he hangs himself. The squalor of this suicide is symptomatic of the squalid, closed world of peasant penury and human deprivation which spawned Polikushka. It is the most powerful of Tolstoy's works before *War and Peace*, and its power is largely due to his evocation of a primitive, brutalized society. The same is true of *The Cossacks*. The society of Cossack frontiersmen springs vividly to life, and the whole work acquires realistic atmosphere through Tolstoy's success in showing us the Cossacks themselves – Uncle Yeroshka, Maryana, Lukashka – as carefully delineated characters given authenticity by their social setting. Less successful is the character of the central figure, Olenin. He travels to the Caucasus from Moscow and finds himself overwhelmed by the novelty and strangeness of the experience. The mountains of the Caucasus strike him initially as such a remarkable aesthetic experience that he can never satisfactorily adjust to their magnificence, and he tends to equate his own love for the Cossack girl Maryana and his admiration for the Cossack ethos with this incomprehensible magnificence of the mountains. His former assumptions about life are shaken. He believes that he has discovered in the idea of 'living for others' a formula for happiness, but he is eventually ready to acknowledge that, no matter how hard he tries, he cannot achieve the simple, uncomplicated purity of heart and mind that would permit him to become part of Cossack life. His failure to relate to this exotic world partly explains the failure of his portrait, but his moral and intellectual crisis represents Tolstoy's first successful essay in the kind of realistic portraiture which owed something to autobiographical experience but chiefly examined the dilemma of an intelligent member of the Russian nobility who sought to reconcile himself with society.

'WAR AND PEACE'

Tolstoy preached such reconciliation for the rest of his life. His masterpiece, *War and Peace* (1863–9), presupposes the possibility of reconciliation at many levels – between nations, between peoples, between classes, between apparently irreconcilable social and political currents – and seeks among other things to identify those elements in life which prevent and those which promote the reconciliation of all men. *War and Peace* cannot be said to be *about* any one thing: it is a multiform work concerned with multifarious themes; and the sheer impossibility of defining it in genre terms – Tolstoy himself simply called it a 'book', refusing to define it more precisely on the grounds that Russian novels were not definable in European terms – is a tribute to Tolstoy's skill in giving the whole work an appearance of being in motion. The verb forms are the clue, stylistically speaking. Tolstoy can suggest the way a person walks, speaks, smiles, gestures, laughs with incomparable art. Just as artfully, for there is artifice as well as artistry in this, he can suggest kaleidoscopic effects by moving us from scene to scene, from public occasions to private, from room to room, from city to battlefield to bedroom, from fictional colloquy to that 'intensification'[11] of historical fact which makes *War and*

Peace seem to be a truer replica of history than the most truthful of historical accounts could ever be. The animating of his fiction naturally depends on his success in creating credible characters; throughout *War and Peace* Tolstoy identifies characters by specifics of appearance and gesture, inviting the reader's instant recognition of Pierre Bezukhov's bulk and his bespectacled candour, Prince Andrey Bolkonsky's 'tired, bored look', Natasha Rostov's youthful brio, Napoleon's white hands, Speransky's mirror-bright eyes, to mention only a few. In certain subtle ways the use of mechanistic imagery, as in the description of Anna Scherer's *salon* at the novel's opening, or zoomorphic analogy, as in the description of the young Princess Bolkonsky's resemblance to a dog, serves not only to identify the characters but also to appraise them morally. As readers we are invited, though without conspicuous urging, to accept that certain styles of life and certain types of people exist but are not considered to have Tolstoyan approval. He offers them to us as the supremely truthful realist who can witness to their condition of being but cannot in the final estimate see how they act out their social roles except by using the analogy of clockwork.

War and Peace was written out of a sense of the inherent stability of life which Tolstoy acquired through his early years of marriage to Sonya Bers (whom he married in 1862). This autobiographical fact must account for the emphasis which Tolstoy gives to the role of the family. The Rostov and Bolkonsky families are the normative social groupings, as it were, by which all other types of social organization in *War and Peace* are to be known and judged. Whatever is genuinely true, morally right, healthy and right-minded in life can in the end be equated with the Rostov ideal – or this would seem to be the assumption we are to make. For the Rostovs represent the essentially Russian virtues, have their social centre in Moscow, not in the artificially Europeanized world of the imperial capital of St Petersburg, and it is their essentially private *understanding*, among each other and with those upon whom they shed their influence, that is the magic which makes the reader captive to their phantasy, their joy in living, and simultaneously places him on the side of the Russians against the French in the Napoleonic invasion of Russia. Although it can be regarded as a family chronicle, *War and Peace* celebrates only the family of the land-owning nobility. Notwithstanding its 500 or more characters, *War and Peace* is predominantly about a handful of members of the Russian nobility who exemplify what Tolstoy considered to be the best social elements in the period 1805–12 and who were destined, at least in the case of Pierre Bezukhov, to participate in the Decembrist movement. Written during the 1860s, when the prestige of the land-owning nobility had been undermined by the emancipation of the serfs, *War and Peace* may be considered partly a vindication of Tolstoy's own class, an attempt to show what the Russian nobility had done for Russia when her nationhood was most seriously threatened, partly – at least by implication – a work designed to oppose the revolutionary feeling of the decade by emphasizing the importance of an established *status quo*, partly a deliberately biased or idealized study (depending on one's feelings in these matters) of the nation's patriotic struggle against Napoleon and his defeat in 1812, in contrast to the humiliating defeat which imperial Russia had suffered in the Crimean War. The permanencies are more important in *War and Peace* than the variables; there are more known than unknown quantities; and the most obvious of these is that the work, being based on certain historical events, has an inevitability to it that must be tinged with fatalism.

War and Peace is no loose, baggy monster, as Henry James would have it, though it may seem in its truth to life to have the seeming formlessness of all immediate, unmeditated experience. It has a sensible architecture as a work of historical fiction which is naturally chronological and based on historical happenings. The first volume deals with events occurring in the six-month period from June to November 1805, the second with those occurring over as many years, from 1806 to 1811. The third and fourth volumes cover events between June 1812 and the beginning of the following year. The architecture is discernible rather in the total edifice of the work than in Tolstoy's plans for it, because he seems to have had no clear idea where it would end when he began writing it in 1863. Characters tended to be forgotten, chronology was not always carefully observed, items were overlooked in the cumulative onward sweep of the writing, but an architectural pattern can be seen to emerge. In the first volume each episode may be regarded as crucial in characterizing and explaining the problem of each character. Pierre Bezukhov, who first appears in Anna Scherer's *salon* as a footloose bachelor of limited means and dubious illegitimate background, is transformed in the course of the following six months into a possessor of great legitimate wealth and the husband of the great beauty, Hélène Kuragin. Andrey Bolkonsky, Pierre's close friend, is changed from the hero-worshipping devotee of Napoleon who aspires to further his military career by committing an act of unexampled heroism into the withdrawn, wounded Bolkonsky who discovers the emptiness of Napoleon's greatness as he lies on the battlefield of Austerlitz and stares up at the endless sky above, which makes all human ambition seem no more than deceit. Nikolay Rostov, the most 'loyal' of Tolstoy's heroes, receives his baptism of fire at the Enns bridge under the French grapeshot and is suddenly made to realize when wounded that he is no longer the little boy Nikolay protected by the love and loyalty of his family. Similarly, Natasha Rostov evinces her spontaneous love of life, Sonya her kittenishness, Vera her coldness, the old Prince Bolkonsky his tetchiness, Princess Marya Bolkonsky her shining goodness, and each predominant facet of character is illustrated – Natasha's by her childishly spontaneous declaration of love to Boris Drubetskoy in the conservatory, Princess Marya's by her good-natured sufferance of the attempt to betroth her to Anatole Kuragin – in beautifully composed scenes which have the startling clarity of animated pictures. So Tolstoy musters his characters, as it were, and moves readily from the artificial *salon* world of St Petersburg to the contrasting Moscow scenes of the nameday ball at the Rostovs and the deathbed of Count Bezukhov, from there to the Bolkonsky estate of Bald Hills and then to the military engagements of Enns and Schöngraben and finally to the battlefield of Austerlitz.

The dramatic tone of the first volume is followed by the evolving, slower pace of the second, which allows for gradual development of character. This involves principally a study of peaceful family life interspersed with descriptions of such public occasions as dinners and balls. Andrey Bolkonsky, whose wife dies in childbirth on the night of his return from the wars, gradually recovers something of his former poise and a renewed zest for life through his love for Natasha Rostov. Pierre Bezukhov, increasingly estranged from his wife, finds solace in freemasonry and attempted good works. Their respective philosophical viewpoints emerge during their conversation on the ferry, as they travel from Bogucharovo to Bald Hills. This is the point where *War and Peace* becomes more than a historical fiction in the commonly accepted sense: it transforms itself into a projection of Tolstoy's own search for moral self-improvement and reconciliation with his society. Pierre advocates recognition of an all-reconciling higher truth, while the more sceptical Andrey affirms the need for each man to concern himself primarily with his own interests. In the end each of them is to undergo a form of reversal of his attitude of mind which corresponds to the movement of peripeteia on which the whole work is constructed.

This process is chiefly apparent in the third and fourth volumes, which describe the single most remarkable reversal of fortune in nineteenth-century history, the total defeat of the Napoleonic armies invading Russia. The enormity of the event is splendidly matched in Tolstoy's panoramic, multifaceted picture of Borodino, the burning of Moscow and the French retreat. We witness it mostly through the candid, uncensorious eye of Pierre Bezukhov, and it is largely through him that history is made private, comprehensible and intimately felt by the reader. Such a multitude of happenings are touched on that they cannot even be mentioned here, but invariably they are offered to us in a pictorialized form, perhaps witnessed by one or another of Tolstoy's observer-narrators, perhaps explicated in elaborate metaphors such as the clockwork movements of armies or the beehive of Moscow invaded by decay and putrefaction. Tolstoyan realism becomes at this climactic point in his greatest work a representation of seen reality finely reinforced by striking imagery. The potential of the events to shock becomes all the greater through the seeming impartiality of Tolstoy's vivid manner. We are invited to assume that *en masse* human beings are governed by the mindlessness of a swarm life and that the individual human conscience is made doubly precious in such extreme circumstances. The individual consciences belong to Pierre Bezukhov and Andrey Bolkonsky: though victims of the historical process, they surmount the spiritual numbing which the swarm life can cause and discover out of chaos a knowledge of spiritual permanency.

Andrey Bolkonsky is mortally wounded at Borodino. Strictly speaking, his is the only 'death of a hero' in a work devoted to so many deaths, but Tolstoy repudiates the notion of martial heroism. Andrey Bolkonsky's death, when it eventually occurs at Yaroslavl, is not physically ennobling, though at the end, through his love for Natasha, who insists on nursing him, he discovers a kind of spiritual peace which involves the obliteration of selfhood and an acknowledgement that all love has a divine source. Pierre Bezukhov, after the appalling experience of capture by the French, and under the influence of the only 'popular' figure in the whole work, the peasant philosopher Platon Karatayev, realizes that truth is not to be equated only with higher things of the spirit but involves a recognition that God is to be discovered in life, in finite existence, and that through what Pierre later calls 'active virtue' life may be changed for the better.

If these, very briefly, are the principal private truths which Tolstoy enunciates through his two main characters in *War and Peace*, he also concludes the work with a publicistic discussion of the sources of power in history. After rejecting a number of rather dog-eared concepts, he propounds the ambivalent view that power in history rests less with those who ostensibly give the orders than with the mass of the people who enact the events. The argument at least serves to justify the guying of Napoleon as military genius and supreme master of his destiny; throughout *War and Peace* Tolstoy has contrived to represent Napoleon as self-important, behaving as a puppet deluded into thinking he was the grand puppeteer of all that happened, while Kutuzov, the Russian commander, is commended by contrast for his fatalistic acceptance of the inevitability of the historical process.

There is no doubt that Tolstoy's picture of history owes much to a fatalistic view of the human condition. Even where the motivation of history was lacking, he still offered a fatalistic interpretation of human destiny. His second novel, *Anna Karenina*, though it is related very closely to the period when it was written, presupposes a fatalism about human conduct that can only be due to Tolstoy himself as the omniscient creator of the fiction.

'ANNA KARENINA'

In *Anna Karenina* (1873–7) Tolstoy achieves a greater realism, especially in the portrayal of character, than he had in any previous work, largely because he is writing now directly out of his own experience. Simultaneously he invents more fully and daringly than in any previous work. There is no paradox here: it is simply that, if the figure of Konstantin Levin is more obviously a projection of his own experience and problems than is any character in *War and Peace*, the figure of Anna Karenina is a profounder invention, a creature of greater fictional art, than any piece of characterization achieved earlier. Anna is so vital, sentient, actual as a fictional creation that one is forced absurdly to think of her as a person, to wish to reach into the fiction and warn her, distract her from the awaiting fateful peril, persuade her that the passion which we can so readily understand is misdirected and tell her, almost scold her into promising, that she will go nowhere near trains.

Anna Karenina is of a piece; one can, given some effort of concentration, encompass it as a whole in one's recollection – and this cannot truthfully be said of *War and Peace*, except perhaps by those who may have devoted a lifetime to doing so. Of the two, *Anna Karenina* is the more finely constructed edifice, smaller in scale perhaps, certainly more domestic and easier to live in vicariously; what is more, it has the completeness of tragedy and the comprehensibility of a drama enacted within the constraints and proprieties of a realistic social setting. In *War and Peace*, Tolstoy tended to validate the historical fiction by emphasizing such 'subjective' experience as dreams, delirium, day-dreaming in representing his characters' reactions to events, especially wartime events. He uses such effects much more sparingly in *Anna Karenina*, and we are correspondingly more conscious of the fixed norms of reality, dependent upon times of day, the routines of living, almost impermeable divisions between classes and persons. Again, in *Anna Karenina* all is pictorialized; we are shown the world, as it were, but we are not required to attend to Tolstoy's own lengthy dilations on its problems, as we were in the later stages of *War and Peace*. The objectivity is evidently that much greater; so is the maturity, for the charm of a nursery world, which attaches to the Rostov ideal in *War and Peace*, is replaced in *Anna Karenina* by a concern for the complexities of adulthood, for the realities of adultery and marriage. The rather trite domestication of all the principal figures in *War and Peace*, especially the transformation of Natasha into Pierre's doting and matronly wife in the first Epilogue, is made to seem too easy a solution of human relationships by the harsher, less fairy-tale stand-ards that prevail in the world of *Anna Karenina*.

It is a strange but apparently incontrovertible fact of Tolstoy's evolution as a writer that because he began his career with his semi-fictional treatment of his own childhood he virtually expunged the childhoods of all his later principal heroes and heroines. No doubt we can guess at the Rostov childhoods, but there is no knowing exactly what the childhoods of Pierre and Andrey were, except for very occasional, fragmented recollections. Their self-sufficiency may seem to make the knowledge unnecessary. In Anna Karenina's case the omission is far more serious. If we had a clearer idea of her childhood and adolescence, we would have a better understanding of her reasons for marrying Karenin in the first place. The conse-quence is that Anna, despite all her remarkable vitality, must appear to illustrate a thesis rather than a psychological evolution. Her life in the fiction must seem to be fated in certain specific ways: by the moral absolutism of the Tolstoyan epigraph to the novel, 'Vengeance is mine, saith the Lord, and I will repay'; by the rigid symbolism of the parallel lines of the railway which carry her into the fiction and upon which she kills herself at the close of her story; by the way in which she is seen so often moving, as if pursued by the Eumenides.

The thesis is never obtrusive, but it is unmistakable, for the novel has a definite architecture formed largely from the parallel stories of Anna herself and Konstantin Levin, which complement and explain each other. Central to the thesis is the question of marriage as the basic social contract. The point is made at the novel's opening. Stiva Oblonsky's marital relations are precariously poised and are only righted by the – ironic, as it turns out – intervention of his sister, Anna Karenina. But strictly speaking Oblonsky's marital relations are always precarious; he epitomizes in his healthily sensual way the casual attitude towards marital fidelity characteristic of his class. The contrast to his view of these matters is offered by Konstantin Levin, who comes to Moscow to propose marriage to Kitty Shcher-batsky but is unhappily refused on this occasion. Levin cannot con-ceive of happiness and love save within the framework of a stable marriage. He is refused by Kitty because there is an ostensible rival for her affections: the elegant and attractive guards officer Vronsky. Anna becomes attracted to Vronsky – she is almost forced into the relationship through being placed next to Vronsky's mother on the train trip from St Petersburg – and as the infatuation grows she illustrates the thesis that those who violate the divinely sanctioned bond of marriage commit a crime and, as her husband portentously remarks to her when he first becomes aware of the indiscreet character of her relationship with Vronsky (Part II, Chapter 9), 'a crime of this sort incurs a heavy punishment'. Anna's story is the story of her punishment.

The novel falls into two halves not only in the parallel stories of Anna and Levin but also in the sense that a natural divide occurs between the fourth and fifth parts of this eight-part novel. Until the end of Part IV there is always the possibility that the relationship between Anna and Vronsky will not lead to the irreparable breakdown of her marriage to Karenin. At that point, after she has almost died in giving birth to her daughter by Vronsky, after Vronsky has almost succeeded in committing suicide and Karenin has almost forgiven, there is a promise of reconciliation; but at the last moment Anna and Vronsky leave for Italy and reconciliation is no longer possible. Simultaneously, at the beginning of Part V, Levin and Kitty get married. For Anna there is no longer any choice left, she appears doomed to a life of deceit and illicit passion which becomes increasingly pointless, whereas for Levin life begins gradually to acquire through marriage a much richer basis for understanding its true purpose.

It is not sufficient to contrast the parallel stories as pessimistic and optimistic; they are, but Anna's is tragic, and what the tragedy means is the loss for all who are affected by it of that which each most cherishes. Anna, for instance, loses Seryozha, her dearly loved son (her surreptitious visit to him on his birthday is profoundly touching); Seryozha loses her; Karenin loses all chance of further advancement in his bureaucratic career; Vronsky loses the possibility of securing a socially respectable name for himself and his children. In the end Anna loses even love; nor is she ever permitted to discover any but a rational answer to her dilemma and the reason merely obliges her to recognize the futility of her life. Perhaps she kills herself on the spur of the moment, out of spite at Vronsky's apparent disregard for her, or perhaps her final decision is precipitated by overhearing a woman enunciate an idea – 'Reason is given to man in order to escape from what troubles him' – whatever the cause she seems to be allowed no choice. She has violated a law and must be punished. Levin, by contrast, conforms to the law and finds that his marriage allows him to pass through the stage of rational futile discovery of the meaninglessness of life which naturally predisposes him to thoughts of suicide. As is always the case when a Tolstoyan hero discovers the truth, it comes from outside and always from a natural or unsophisticated source. Levin suddenly discovers from a peasant on his estate the axiom that 'one should live for the soul' and this immediately leads him to an awareness that good and evil are only comprehensible outside the rational chain of cause and effect. From this moment he reaches the conviction that he has discovered the true law of goodness, which has always been known to common people, and that henceforth his life 'is not only not meaningless, as it was before, but has an indubitable sense of goodness which I am able to impart to it.' Levin's discovery of this truth presupposes also that he has discovered a means of reconciling himself with the mass of the people, with his society and a concept of God that can reconcile all men.

The novel is full of echoes of the ideas and aspirations of the decade in which it was written. The role of women in society, the sanctity of marriage and the family, were matters under profound scrutiny in the Russia of the 1870s. They are reflected in other famous works of literature of the period, in Saltykov-Shchedrin's *The Golovlyov Family* (1880), a harshly realistic exposure of the forces that cause the breakdown of a land-owning family, and in Dostoyevsky's *A Raw Youth* (1875) and *The Brothers Karamazov* (1878–80). The last work also mirrors some of the ideas on self-perfection and new social bases which were fundamental to Populism and which must be assumed to find their reflection in Levin's 'conversion' in the final part of *Anna Karenina*. Both these masterpieces of the 1870s also contain echoes of the greatest real sources of tension and bloodshed in these years, the Russo-Turkish War which is the background to Levin's discovery of truth and the terrorism of the People's Will which was the real conflict of generations that Dostoyevsky in his last novel sought to diagnose and remedy. *Anna Karenina* may seem to suffer a little in the comparison. The lucid objectivity of its realistic depiction of Russian land-owning and metropolitan high society can serve to date it as surely as the most perfect photograph of those years. That society is dead and its issues with it, but such was Tolstoy's mastery that there is not a page in his novel which does not catch a vital resemblance, stir an echo of the real, set vibrating the tone of a voice more fully and roundly than could any photograph or phonograph. The uses of fashion have helped to enhance the majesty of this masterpiece and leave its purity undiminished.

DOSTOYEVSKY: THE PERIOD OF THE MASTERPIECES

At the end of 1849 Dostoyevsky was sent off into a ten-year Siberian exile for his part in the Petrashevsky affair. He was released from penal servitude after four years and gradually began writing again. The only work of his during this period which aspires to be a novel was *The Village of Stepanchikovo and its Inhabitants*; it suffered from being outmoded by the ideological standards of the time. Dostoyevsky was out of touch with the most recent ideas current in European Russia, but he still contrived to make his work a novel of ideas. For this very reason it differs from his pre-exile work and must be considered as a cornerstone of all his mature achievement. It analyses a society, whereas his pre-exile work was concerned almost entirely with the problem of the solitariness of urban man; it sets viewpoints in dramatic conflict, whereas before his exile he had not really been concerned with the opposition of ideas in pro and contra form. These are to become principal ingredients of his greatest novels as realistic works of literature.

His first object when he returned from exile in 1859 was to re-establish his literary reputation. As well as the remarkable *Notes from the House of the Dead* (1861), the reminiscences of his four years of penal servitude, he also published his first large-scale novel, *The Insulted and Injured* (1861). Hardly surprisingly, this combines some of the mannerisms conspicuous in his pre-exile writing with an attempt to offer an ideological justification of the metropolitan capitalism of the 1860s. The sentimental themes and love-stories belong to Dostoyevsky's past and are the less striking aspects of the novel. The figure of Prince Valkovsky, on the other hand, the arch-villain of the piece, is a study in egotistical sensualism which initiates a whole new *genus* of Dostoyevskian hero. Though grotesque in his sensuality, Valkovsky is powerfully drawn and easily outshines in interest the narrator-hero or the other stock types who are Valkovsky's victims; only the characterization of the young adolescent girl, Nelly, challenges by its accent on her own 'egoism of suffering' and precocious sexuality the blatant exercise of caprice which he exalts.

For Dostoyevsky, who knew more personally and painfully than any other writer of his day what the restriction of liberty can mean, the idea of 'free will' (*svoyevoliye, khoten'ye*) became a profound obsession which he plumbed to its limits. But to understand its full significance for Dostoyevsky one must recognize his own apparently contradictory but frequently repeated commitment to the idea that the Russian intelligentsia should humble itself and learn from the common people, the peasantry. This 'back to the soil' ideal (*pochvennost'*) presupposed reconciliation between classes; it also presupposed reconciliation between man and God, for the people were to be interpreted by Dostoyevsky as 'God-carrying', just as Russia's true role in regard to Europe was to be messianic. These were not rational commitments, and the least rational of the commitments that Dostoyevsky acknowledged, immediately after his release from penal servitude, was his personal commitment to the figure of Christ. But he was always paradoxical in his thinking. If the figure of Christ was the most perfect of ideals to which mankind could aspire, mankind for Dostoyevsky was always beset by the tempting ideals of some *advocatus diaboli* who offered a greater freedom than the moral law permitted. In seeking a means of expressing these and related ideas in a dialectical fashion, Dostoyevsky turned first to the type of paradoxical dreamer whom he had employed as a literary vehicle in some of his pre-exile works, particularly *White Nights*. The anonymous author of *Notes from the Underground* (1864) is engaged, at least in the first part of this two-part work, in tetchily dreaming aloud his paradoxical complaint about man's irrationality.

Notes from the Underground can be regarded as Dostoyevsky's answer to Chernyshevsky's apotheosis of man as a rational creature; it can also be considered the watershed of ideas for the four great novels of Dostoyevsky's maturity. Finding himself faced with the stone wall of the laws of the natural sciences, the Underground Man expresses his own paradoxical individuality by asserting his right to free will. By the exercise of free will man will never become a plaything either of the laws of nature or of the social utopians who would turn him into an ant-like member of the mathematically perfect society. The subsequent attempts of the Underground Man to assert his individuality are farcical and humiliating, but his *idea* is a key to all Dostoyevsky's later studies of the type of diabolical 'proud man' who endeavours to set himself above moral law. This idea was also at the centre of Dostoyevsky's treatment of nihilism – fairly obviously so, since the idea of free will must involve a denial of any authority, whether moral, religious or scientific, that limits man's total freedom.

Stricken by debts, overwhelmed by troubles, Dostoyevsky found himself in 1865 stranded in Wiesbaden and unable even to buy tea. From this perilous situation grew the perilous state of Raskolnikov in Dostoyevsky's first great novel, *Crime and Punishment* (1866). Raskolnikov, an impoverished drop-out from university, murders a pawnbroker both for her money (which he does not use) and for motives of free will: he seeks to prove, in other words, that he can do it, that he can overstep the moral barriers dividing the mass of obedient humanity from those who actually make the laws of right and wrong. He seeks to be a Napoleon, but, as he acknowledges at one point, he has succeeded in being no more than 'an aesthetic louse'. The motivation of Raskolnikov is in itself less important than the means employed by Dostoyevsky to illustrate his problem. Raskolnikov's feverish, almost delirious, apprehension of St Petersburg tenements and streets during a July heatwave, the deliberate concealment of his reason for acting as he does, the sense which the reader can easily get of living inside Raskolnikov's brain, endow this novel with a psychological realism that makes it one of the most powerful examples of the realistic manner in all fiction.

In specific ways, despite the detailed *realia* which lend such veracity to the St Petersburg scene, the novel transcends documentary realism: it has an intricate symbolism which highlights the moral and psychological condition of the principal characters by, for example, laying emphasis on the cramped, coffin-like room in which Raskolnikov conceives his idea or the deformed room where Sonya Marmeladova lives, which suggests the way prostitution may deform her life. The novel also invites interpretation as a kind of latter-day Attic tragedy or, as Vyacheslav Ivanov called it,[12] a 'novel-tragedy' in five acts, corresponding roughly to the five parts of the novel itself, with the sixth part in the form of an epilogue (though the novel contains an epilogue of its own). It may also be seen as a modern version of a mystery play in which Everyman in the person of Raskolnikov is faced by a choice between his good and his bad angels, meaning Sonya and Svidrigaylov.

Chiefly the novel invites an awareness of the morbid deeps of the human psyche. The catalyst, as it were, for Dostoyevsky's supreme achievements in the realistic novel was the notion of homicide. Equally, it seems, he was excited by the connection between homicide and the most extreme forms of Russian sectarianism, the flagellants and castrates.[13] A connection can be established between Raskolnikov and the religious schismatics, the Raskolniks. But for an understanding – even if only partial – of Raskolnikov's deed, his murder of the pawnbroker and her sister, the nihilism in Raskolnikov himself has to be plumbed. The wish to deny all authority and to usurp the place of God in the material universe is a very great part of Raskolnikov's motivation, despite his own attempts to excuse his crime on the grounds of utilitarianism or by referring to the example of Napoleon. The denial of all authority must involve a superman ideal in the moral sphere. The natural corollary is that humanity must be divisible into the ordinary and the extraordinary. But in the carefully judged ideological structure of the novel, in which idea is balanced against idea, Dostoyevsky opposes the seeming grandeur of Raskolnikov's nihilistic assertion of free will with the parody of this idea embodied in the figure of the enigmatic Svidrigaylov. In the tripartite plot pattern discernible in the novel, Svidrigaylov may be considered the central figure of the sub-plot dealing with the suitors of Raskolnikov's sister, Dunya.[14] He comes to Raskolnikov ostensibly in order to see his prospective brother-in-law, but it is not hard to feel that he is drawn to Raskolnikov because he knows and shares his criminality. He appears to Raskolnikov out of a delirium in which Raskolnikov has just re-enacted his crime and he taunts him, as the devil was later to taunt Ivan Karamazov, with a knowledge of the gross egoism of what he has done. Svidrigaylov represents a self-justifying nihilism which asserts the primacy of sensual satisfaction. Ultimately this may be assumed to reduce itself to the absurdity of supposing that if one claims supreme free will, meaning total power over life and death, then the supreme willed act should be the taking of one's own life. And Svidrigaylov takes his own life in the most superbly written passage of sustained surreal horror in the whole novel. Raskolnikov, then, can follow his example and act out his nihilism to the logical absurdity of suicide, or he can follow the advice of the prostitute Sonya, the central figure in the second sub-plot devoted to the Marmeladov family. She epitomizes the need of humanity to acknowledge and worship a God in whose name sin can be forgiven. She persuades Raskolnikov to confess to the authorities and to submit to the penal servitude which is the legal punishment exacted by society. Whether or not Raskolnikov, the 'proud man', will acknowledge a moral law higher than his own, remains in doubt right to the end of the novel. We are left to assume that his love for Sonya will redeem him.

Throughout the very brief period of time, barely two weeks, occupied by the main action of the novel Raskolnikov is portrayed as literally sick with his idea. His nihilism is a sickness from which he has to recuperate before he can become spiritually whole again. This concern with sickness as a manifestation of infection by ideas not only reflects Dostoyevsky's own 'divine' sickness, his epilepsy, but characterizes his anthropology. Humanity was prone to ideological infection in the Dostoyevskian view of things. Therefore, the purest being was the sick child, and the sick child is present in so many of Dostoyevsky's works as an image of the sickness attaching even to innocence in the society of his day. When he came to conceive the image of mankind redeemed, as an antidote to the nihilistic sickness of Raskolnikov, his realistic sense of the fitness of things obliged him to project the image in the form of the child-like epileptic Prince Myshkin of his novel *The Idiot* (1868–9).

Whenever Dostoyevsky writes about the Russian nobility an air of parody and Gogolian exaggeration surrounds his portraiture. The notes which he made both for *The Idiot* and for the other major novel written during his self-imposed European exile between 1867 and 1871, *The Possessed*, indicate the difficulties which he encountered in defining the character of the central figure in each novel. The result was an indecisiveness in the portrayal of both Myshkin and Stavrogin (the central character – one can hardly call him the hero – of *The Possessed*). These novels also do not have firm centres and balanced structures. They are great works of literature flawed by just that limpness or unsureness of form which *Crime and Punishment* so notably avoided.

The Idiot has a splendid opening and a powerful ending; its central sections tend to ramify into sub-plots and subsidiary themes which Dostoyevsky deliberately introduces for publicistic reasons of his own. As a work of realistic literature which criticizes the inadequacies of Russian life, the novel is packed with characters and scenes that satirize the hypocrisies and self-seeking of the nihilists, denounce the absurdity of Russian liberalism, and attack the evils of money and the danger of Roman Catholicism. The novel is correspondingly packed with enormously talkative characters who can recount anecdotes with a typical Dostoyevskian humour and trenchancy. But realism as an artistic manner which evokes a social background and embodies social attitudes in representative types is given a twist in the direction of parody or caricature; and, except in certain instances, the apprehension of the real world through one or another character does not have anything like the powerful effectiveness that was achieved in *Crime and Punishment* by the same method.

Myshkin's epilepsy and his child-like wonder at the upper-class world of St Petersburg are the principal ways in which Dostoyevsky penetrates the seeming reality of the visible and tangible. The onset of epilepsy, in which Myshkin's whole being is shaken to its core, is one instance of the way that Dostoyevsky, by the power of his descriptive writing, succeeds in suggesting how mental and physical states can coalesce. The mysterious eyes that pursue Myshkin among the hot city crowds contribute to the air of peril and menace. The dark interior of Rogozhin's house is as sinister in its uninhabited tomb-like silence, as if awaiting the occupancy of the murdered Nastasya Filippovna, as the crowded apartment of the Ivolgins is labyrinthine and ready to receive the fits of hysterics, discord and high-key emotion which its volatile inhabitants can so readily express.

In other words, the 'places' of the fiction have a symbolic relationship to the people and ideas that inhabit them. Myshkin, who comes from Switzerland to seek out the true nobility in Russian life, the 'positively beautiful man' (as Dostoyevsky described him) who tries to redeem Russian reality by offering a new image of the beautiful, finds himself pursuing a ridiculously Quixotic purpose in a world governed by money and rampant capitalism. Having no 'place' in the world of the fiction, Myshkin, the redeemer, is superfluous, just as Nastasya Filippovna who seeks redemption from him through love eventually falls victim to his murderous counterpart, Rogozhin, whose sinister 'place' is the heart of darkness at the centre of Dostoyevsky's vision of contemporary Russia. Looking back at Russia from his European exile, Dostoyevsky felt ready to condemn, not because he found Europe superior but because Russia had insufficiently realized her true role in relation to Europe. The aping of the West appalled him. He condemned it in many ways in this novel, nowhere more profoundly than in the semi-delirious 'Necessary Explanation' of the consumptive nihilist Ippolit. The only positively counterbalancing argument he could formulate – and it became part of the endearing but cloudy bombast with which so much of his publicism of the 1870s was filled – was messianic: the idea of a Russian Christ who would redeem a corrupt Europe. Russia herself had also of course to realize the extreme preciousness of her own national religion in order to play such a messianic role.

The Possessed (*Besy*, 1871–2) carries Dostoyevsky's condemnatory argument several steps further. It is the darkest, most portentous – and, for some, the greatest – of Dostoyevsky's novels. The Russian realistic novel here approximates more closely to a political work of art than any other example in the genre. *The Possessed* is about politics in its relationship to the contemporary Russian scene, insofar as Dostoyevsky understood it; and it is also concerned with that profounder action of political ideas upon the human psyche which can seem to lead to demoniac possession by them. The title has been more accurately translated by David Magarshack as *The Devils*, but '*The Possessed*', with its reference to the story from St Luke's gospel about the man possessed of devils which Christ suffered to enter into the herd of swine, explains the main idea of the novel. Dostoyevsky saw the history of the Russian intelligentsia as one of gradual possession by alien ideas from the West. He offers in this novel his own anatomy of the contemporary state of the Russian intelligentsia seen in a historical perspective.

The older generation is represented by the engaging elderly intellectual Stepan Trofimovich Verkhovensky, who lards his eloquence with French phrases and suffers from the harmless but amusing delusion that he is notorious enough to be under secret-police surveillance. A 'man of the forties' both ideologically and in temperament, he must be taken to be the initial source of demoniac influence, however unlikely that may seem, for he is Stavrogin's first teacher, and Stavrogin undoubtedly represents the dark source that has afflicted contemporary Russia with profoundly conflicting ideas and ideals. Stavrogin returns to Russia from Europe and makes contact with his two 'disciples', Shatov and Kirilov. Shatov has received from Stavrogin the idea of Russia as a God-carrying nation, yet paradoxically he does not believe in God. He will believe, he claims, and in this potential for belief in his divine purpose he symbolizes the possibility of a new Christian Russia. Kirilov has been infected by Stavrogin with the idea of suicide. By committing suicide in the name of combating the fear of death, he hopes to procure for mankind the freedom of ideal man-godhood, and yet paradoxically this alleged bridge-building into the future – Kirilov is supposed to be an engineer – is really no more than an atheism which symbolizes a future for Russia conceived in defiance of God and filled with a demoniac freedom.

These ideas are manipulated in the course of the novel by the most unscrupulous of the nihilistic figures, Pyotr Stepanovich Verkhovensky, son of Stepan Trofimovich, who, like Nechayev in real life, endeavours to achieve total conformity to his will among the members of a conspiratorial cell by involving them in the murder of one of their number. The victim is the one 'believer' among them, Shatov. He is murdered and his body cast into a pond.[15] Kirilov commits suicide after signing a statement that he was Shatov's murderer. The episode of Kirilov's suicide, attended in anxious solicitude by the watchful Pyotr Stepanovich, is one of unmatched nightmarish power. In the end Stavrogin, the erstwhile Prince Harry cast in the role of Russia's saviour, at least in the eyes of Pyotr Stepanovich, is seen as impotent both sexually and symbolically and commits the final nihilistic act of hanging himself. Stepan Trofimovich ends his life in a self-styled crusade among the peasantry, seized by a new-found belief in the 'Great Idea, the eternal, limitless Idea' of God. The only survivor is the petty nihilist, Pyotr Stepanovich, who departs on an errand of callous destruction elsewhere.

Though Dostoyevsky was concerned above all things with the problem of the existence of God, he does not suggest that the hand of

God is to be seen in the Russia of *The Possessed*. Only the faintest rays of light are discernible in this remarkable political pamphlet of a novel. By vicious, sombre caricature Dostoyevsky excoriates both Russian nihilism and the self-importance of the Russian bureaucracy. He attacks Turgenev in the devastatingly cruel portrait of the eminent writer Karmazinov. Through the earnest Shigalyov he shows how the planned utopia of total freedom becomes the planned utopia of total oppression. He shows how a national intelligentsia which has a godless intellectual vacuum at its heart, a vacuum personified in the novel by Stavrogin, can be possessed of legions of devils that spread mayhem and destruction in all quarters. The lunatic fete organized by the governor's wife, for example, gives rise to rioting among the local workers, arson and murder. But the darkness of Dostoyevsky's realism, surging from one scandal scene to another on a turbulent rip-tide of narrative, is never without its humour. Partly this is due to his gossipy, ubiquitous narrator; it is also due to Dostoyevsky's expert handling of the comic aspects of the boldly operatic ensemble scene in which a cast of loquacious characters is assembled and supposed to achieve a measure of accord.

By the time the publication of *The Possessed* was completed, Dostoyevsky had returned to Russia. With the exception of *A Raw Youth* (1875), a novel about an 'accidental' family which is not strictly comparable to his greatest works, he devoted most of his time during the 1870s to various forms of publicistic activity, especially his *Diary of a Writer*, but he continued to nurse the idea for his last and greatest novel. The idea had been conceived when he was preoccupied with plans for *The Possessed*. He allowed it to gestate for some ten years before expressing it in *The Brothers Karamazov*. As we know from his notebooks, this work came to him almost ready-made, requiring for the most part only the necessary lineaments of narrative and scene-setting to turn the draft idea into the replete fiction.

In formal terms no novel by Dostoyevsky shows greater dramatic compactness and intensity. It is in four parts with an epilogue. The first three parts occupy three days, during which we are told in great detail about the events and ideas which culminate in the murder of Fyodor Pavlovich Karamazov and the arrest of his eldest son, Dmitry, on the charge of parricide. The fourth part is devoted principally to the events of Dmitry's trial, at which a miscarriage of justice leads to Dmitry's conviction as the murderer. The epilogue points the way to the assumption by Alyosha, the youngest Karamazov brother, of his future role as a saviour of the children.

The novel is set in a small Russian provincial town which boasts a famous monastery nearby. The fame of the monastery is due chiefly to an 'elder' (*starets*), Zosima, who has become the spiritual father of Alyosha Karamazov. Alyosha's real father, a reprobate of a sensuality unequalled for grossness in any previous portrayal, is Fyodor Pavlovich, who lives in a large house in the town with his intellectual son Ivan for temporary company. He is looked after by an elderly retainer, Grigory, and a bastard son called Smerdyakov who is semi-literate and epileptic but has been trained as a cook. The novel opens with an attempt by Zosima to resolve a feud which has developed between Fyodor Pavlovich and his eldest son, Dmitry; the quarrel has arisen partly over the latter's claims to his inheritance and partly from a sexual rivalry between them over a girl of evident physical attractions, Grushenka. The feud is not resolved, and when Fyodor Pavlovich is found battered to death it is immediately assumed that Dmitry is guilty.

The novel is about the meaning of guilt and the nature of justice. The conflict is posed as one between generations, between a greedy, sensual father and his son's rightful claim to the patrimony; but it is also posed as a pro and contra, an opposition of ideas, which broaches the whole question of man's claim to total freedom in the moral sphere and the claims made upon him by the existence of God. There are two layers of meaning in the novel: it may be understood either as the breakdown of a family in consequence of disputes over money (significantly, and confusingly, the sum of 3,000 roubles has an ambiguous role to play in the feud between Fyodor Pavlovich and Dmitry) or as a conflict between the ideological viewpoints of Ivan Karamazov and Zosima. Both layers of the novel meet in the determining of the guilt for the parricide and the problem of human rather than divine justice.

Alyosha, the youngest brother, the neophyte monk, acts as the go-between in the feud between the members of the Karamazov family. To him Dmitry confesses his sensuality, his shame at being thought dishonest and his passion for Grushenka – all items in a view of things which exalts man's paradoxical state as a battleground of desires between the ideals of Sodom and the Madonna, between Satan and God. To Alyosha, in what have become the most famous chapters of the novel, 'Revolt' and 'The Grand Inquisitor', Ivan Karamazov confesses his intellectual arrogance. The first principles of Ivan's nihilistic rejection of God are simple to the point of being elementary: if there is no immortality, then there can be no such thing as virtue, consequently everything is permissible. In the chapter entitled 'Revolt' he sets out to demonstrate that there is no evidence for assuming that the world is inherently based on principles of right and wrong, so far as he can judge from the known facts. Ivan insists that he can only judge according to facts on the basis of Euclidean logic – rationally, that is. He instances many examples of appalling cruelty to children – examples which cry out, even to the loving, merciful spirit of Alyosha, for immediate retribution *on this earth*. What point is there – so Ivan's argument runs – in having a hell for sinners in an after-life if the tormentors of innocent children are not punished in this life? What point is there in assuming the existence of an all-merciful God in the face of such facts? Ivan will therefore 'most politely' hand back his entrance ticket into this world. It is not a just world. But, protests Alyosha, he has forgotten that there is someone who can redeem the world – the figure of Christ.

Ivan answers this charge with an idea for a poem which he plans to write. It is to be called *The Grand Inquisitor* and it describes how Christ returns to Seville at the height of the Inquisition, is recognized and imprisoned. He is visited in prison by the Grand Inquisitor, who reproaches Him for imposing upon weak mankind too great a burden with His new gospel of freedom of choice in the knowledge of good and evil. Roman Catholicism, in the person of the Grand Inquisitor, understanding weak humanity better than did Jesus, has taken this burden from man. In the name of the three temptations offered to Christ in the wilderness – miracle, mystery and authority – the Church has suborned human conscience by offering in place of Christ's freedom of choice the notion of immortality as a reward for virtue. Millions of simple believers can now live out their lives happy in the conviction that their sins will be forgiven and eternal life will await them after death. Had Christ chosen, argues the Inquisitor, to perform the miracle and let manna come from heaven, to reveal the source of the mystery of this life and acknowledge His authority in reality before all men, mankind would for ever have followed Christ unswervingly out of fear that the miraculous blessing of bread from heaven might be withdrawn. Christ chose to base His gospel not on mankind's subservience but on the freedom to choose. As a result, the 'elect' of the church, knowing, as does the Grand Inquisitor himself, that there are no real grounds for such a promise, have promised mankind out of pity that there *is* an after-life, that virtue *is* rewarded, though the solace they offer is in reality justified only in the name of the devil.

Christ's response to this 'modification' of His gospel is to kiss the Grand Inquisitor on his bloodless, nonagenarian lips. Alyosha greets Ivan's story with a similar response. For 'The Grand Inquisitor' does not demolish Christ's gospel of love and immortality so much as reveal the fundamental inadequacy of men's attempts to 'humanize' it, to render it atheist or socialist in the name of humanity's greater happiness. It presupposes, as did Raskolnikov's and Shigalyov's theories, a division of humanity into those who would play the role of God, the 'elect', who are beyond the law, and the mass of people, who must accept and obey. To it is opposed the teaching of Zosima, as revealed in Alyosha's recollections of what his spiritual father told him (in the Book called 'The Russian Monk'). It may seem that this teaching speaks too openly of an ideal condition of things in which the lion shall lie down with the lamb. All things are bright and beautiful in it, no doubt, but it makes two fundamental assumptions. Firstly, it denies any division in humanity by assuming that, as Zosima tells his brother monks on the day of his death, all men are responsible for all other men's sins. Secondly, it denies the notion of an after-life by assuming that, as Zosima learned from his brother, *this* life is potentially paradise if only men would realize it. The real and the heavenly, the now and the hereafter become indistinguishable in this teaching. What it also suggests, though by implication only, is that each generation should work for the resurrection of the fathers in order to establish the Kingdom of Heaven on earth. This idea provides a context for understanding the degree of seriousness attaching to the crime of parricide as it is posed in this novel.

The Brothers Karamazov is about the way in which a miscarriage of justice can occur when the real motives governing human conduct are obscured. The trial of Dmitry Karamazov was the public occasion, we are led to assume, when the real motivation was not disclosed. The novel tells us what the real motives were – in other words, it shows how Ivan's doctrine that 'all is permissible' infects the mind of the 'lackey' of his idea, Smerdyakov, and gives him a pretext for murdering Fyodor Pavlovich. Smerdyakov hangs himself, and Ivan at the trial, seemingly deranged, can do no more than claim in his evidence that 'we all desire the death of the father' and try to implicate Smerdyakov by producing the money (3,000 roubles) that the latter had stolen from his father when he murdered him. But the money is no proof at all: it could be any money. Ivan remains true to his nihilistic assertion of free will with his murderous claim that all men desire the death of their father, for fatherhood, both biologically and spiritually, must deny man's total independence. Again, though, this is no proof of Smerdyakov's guilt. Ivan has reached the point where phenomenal and noumenal coincide, the real and the surreal blend and the physical and metaphysical are no longer clearly separable, as they presumably should be if the world is ever to seem 'real'.

This point is the most daring exploration of the limits to which the realistic manner in literature can be taken without violating realistic appearances: it occurs when Ivan Karamazov is confronted by his eminently respectable devil. His devil amusingly turns Ivan's argument back upon him, acting as a distorting mirror to his ideas, while also pointing up the distinguishing characteristic of Dostoyevsky's realism, its concern with semi-conscious states of being and a reality founded as much on ideas as on things. Tauntingly his devil says to Ivan:

Listen: in dreams, and particularly in nightmares, whether from an upset stomach or some other cause, a person sometimes sees such artistic dreams, such complex and real actuality, such events or even a whole world of events, held together by a story with so many unexpected details, from the loftiest manifestations down to the last button on a shirt-front that, I swear to you, Lev Tolstoy couldn't spin such a yarn, and it isn't only story-tellers who see such dreams, but quite ordinary people, officials, feuilletonists, priests . . . It can even be a job: one government minister even confessed to me that he gets his best ideas in his sleep. As now. Although I'm your hallucination, still, as in a nightmare, I'm saying original things which have never before entered your head, so that it's no longer a case of my repeating your thoughts, but I'm still only your nightmare and no more.

Ideas have in Dostoyevsky's world this special quality of reality. Related though the ideas may be to particular Russian circumstances, they have the magnified intensity of the real brought into nightmarishly sharp focus. Dostoyevsky is, as he liked to think of himself, a realist 'in a higher sense', and nowhere does he endow his realism with higher meaning than in his exploration of the paradoxes of reality in *The Brothers Karamazov*. He carries not only the realistic manner further than did his great contemporary, Lev Tolstoy, but also the presumptions of realism, its preoccupation with mimesis and psychological verisimilitude. We are admitted deeper into the consciousness of a Dostoyevskian character than a Tolstoyan, and in the process the archetypal forms that guide the human spirit, no matter whether we call them religious, symbolical or psychological, are made vicariously real – always in conflict, striving, seeking redemption from sin, seeking to know in the sick conscience of mankind the way to a discovery of God's truth. But Dostoyevsky's realism does not affirm, though it may presuppose reconciliation between all men. Like all truth it has to be validated by doubt, and Dostoyevsky's realism excites by the very unsureness of its realistic premises. The secret of Dostoyevsky's greatness and his appeal to contemporary tastes lies both in his own intense involvement in the reality of the nightmarish moment and simultaneously in his penetrating sense of the illusory nature of the real. No Russian realist committed himself more surely to the reality of Christ than did Dostoyevsky, but he could never escape a proneness to doubt. As he said of himself in the first letter that he wrote after his release from penal servitude, he was a child of the nineteenth century, 'a child of disbelief and doubt up to this time and even (I know this) to the end of my life'. His doubt was the query about the meaning of life which gnawed at the heart of nineteenth-century Russian realism.

Notes

1 Dmitry Cizevsky (*Evgenij Onegin, a Novel in Verse*, Harvard U.P., 1953) claimed unequivocally that it 'belongs to the age of romanticism and bears clear marks of that period' (p. ix); Vladimir Nabokov in his brilliant commentary makes no claims for the work's realism (*Eugene Onegin*, Bollingen Foundation, 1964); John Bayley (*Pushkin, a Comparative Commentary*, Cambridge, 1971) assigns it to the category of novel of sentiment and argues the case most persuasively.

2 See, for example, G. A. Gukovsky, *Pushkin i problemy realisticheskogo stilya* (Moscow, 1957).

3 The suggestion made by D. D. Blagoy in his erudite and perceptive *Sotsiologiya tvorchestva Pushkina* (Moscow, 1931).

4 These are carefully examined in John Mersereau, *Mikhail Lermontov* (Southern Illinois U.P., 1962).

5 The name Pechorin derives from the river Pechora, Onegin from the river Onega, just as Pechorin superficially imitates Onegin in his Byronic derivation.

6 Vladimir Nabokov offered his own whimsical explanation of the term's relevance to Gogol's work in his entertaining study, *Nikolai Gogol* (Yale U.P., 1944).

7 These matters are expertly and comprehensively examined in the study by Victor Terrass, *The Young Dostoyevsky (1846–1849)* (The Hague, 1969).

8 The notion of 'superfluous man' comes from this source.

9 They were originally published in *The Contemporary* between 1847 and 1851. The 1852 edition contains 22 sketches; Turgenev later added three more.

10 Richard Freeborn, *Turgenev, the Novelist's Novelist: a study* (Oxford, 1960), p. 48.

11 Professor R. F. Christian has described Tolstoy as 'an intensifying rather than an inventive genius', an assertion amply demonstrated in his *Tolstoy's 'War and Peace': a study* (Oxford, 1962), and in his excellent 'critical introduction', *Tolstoy* (Cambridge, 1969).

12 V. Ivanov, *Freedom and the Tragic Life*, tr. N. Cameron (London, 1952).

13 See R. Peace, *Dostoyevsky: an Examination of the Major Novels* (Cambridge, 1971).

14 See K. Mochulsky, *Dostoevsky, his Life and Work* (Princeton U.P., 1967), pp. 298–9.

15 The description in Part III, Chapter 6, of 'the very sinister place at the far end of the large Stavrogin Park' is based, according to A. G. Dostoyevskaya (Dostoyevsky's wife), on her brother's description of the park and grotto of the Petrovsky Agricultural Academy in Moscow, where he was a student and where the student Ivanov was murdered on Nechayev's orders.

FOUR

The Realist and Naturalist
Movements in France

THE NOVEL OF SOCIAL PROPAGANDA, 1830–48

As a contributor to the *Revue de Paris* observed light-heartedly in 1832, only a few years earlier every educated young Frenchman with literary aspirations would have sat down as soon as he left school to write a tragedy; but now he would hopefully begin his career with a novel. Even before Louis-Philippe came to the throne, the more far-sighted critics had come round to the view that this form of literature, too disdainfully abandoned in the past to purveyors of light entertainment, had serious, not so say revolutionary, potentialities.

At the stage we have reached, the novel, as an expression of the civilization of our times, to which it has regularly adapted itself through every shift and turn, appears destined to assume a new character in response to the interest that contemporary minds take in important social questions and their readiness to challenge those interests and prerogatives that former generations took for granted. The novel of this century will thus necessarily be informed by an austerer and more profound spirit of observation than that which concentrates on the minutiae of social behaviour and the passing quirks of fashion. It will absorb the lessons taught by that experimental philosophy of purely human origin which is gaining increasing doctrinal credit among the nations as the dogmatic philosophy of revealed religion begins to lose its hold.

For an anti-establishment thinker like Charles Nodier, who made this remarkable prediction as early as 1823,[1] it is clear that the novel was valued more particularly for the help it would lend in the fight against obscurantism. In condemning, at least by implication, its use as a mere record of 'the minutiae of social behaviour and the passing quirks of fashion', Nodier states the case for the novel of ideas (provided the ideas were progressive ones) as against the conception of the novel as 'mirror' or as 'contemporary history' which, as we have seen, chiefly inspired the two most accomplished fiction writers of the age, Stendhal and Balzac.

All the way through the period known to historians as the July Monarchy (1830–48), a great number of minor authors were engaged in putting into practice the programme outlined by Nodier. Far from being the only writer concerned with depicting his period, Balzac was one of a host and – to contemporary readers – not so easily distinguished from the rest. Like him, these lesser and now forgotten novelists describe a society divided sharply between rich and poor, in which nothing was done to alleviate the harsh impact of economic laws. But whereas in Balzac's view this deplorable state of affairs could be remedied only by reinforcing the traditional framework of authority, spiritual and secular, these other writers, authors of the so-called 'social novels' of the period, pinned their hopes on political innovations to bring about the abolition of social injustice. Their main objective was to evoke, through their works, sympathy for the suffering masses, and the solutions they proposed to the problems facing the nation and its legislators were socialistic (as the word was understood before 1848) and mildly revolutionary, instead of being, as Balzac's were, retrogressive and paternalistic.

The reasons why the popular novel took on this particular radical colouring are to be looked for in the political rather than the literary history of the period. The revolution of 1830 had ended the autocratic rule of the last Bourbon king, but the sole beneficiaries had been the entrepreneurial class; the conditions of life of the poorer sections of the population remained as miserable as ever. Progressive political thinkers soon understood that a fresh revolution would be necessary if a more just society was to be constituted; but they had to wait eighteen years before conditions were ripe. In the meantime the novelists did what they could, by attacking the rich bourgeois (especially if his riches had been newly come by) as greedy, immoral, and oppressive, in contrast to the invariably virtuous and honest representatives of the less prosperous classes. Obviously such sharp distinctions had little to do with realistic observation, but realism in this sense was no part of their aim. The novelist's mission, as one of them (Émile Souvestre) expressed it, was 'to popularize progressive ideas, to give them shape and force by clothing them, as it were, with the authority of example. Like the old epics, the novel will furnish the common people with models, sum up human knowledge for them, name the gods they should worship.'

These words occur in the preface to a novel published in 1836, with the significant title *Riche et Pauvre (Rich and Poor)*. The plot devised by Souvestre is not untypical of the moralistic social novel of the time. It turns on the fortunes of two lawyers, one of whom has the advantage of aristocratic connections. They spent their childhood together, but Antoine never overcomes the handicap of low birth and is worsted at every turn by the more fortunate Arthur, who even seduces his fiancée, Louise, and then abandons her to her shame. There is a sentimental and highly implausible ending. Louise commits suicide and Antoine, intending to do the same, confronts Arthur with a bitter sermon on his thoughtless licentiousness. Arthur repents, and Antoine decides to live and devote his energies to the establishment of a more equitable social order.

Riche et Pauvre was, even so, one of the more sophisticated products of this school of novelists, who can be linked to the realist tradition only by virtue of their deep concern with the state of society in their time and their fumbling attempts to offer a critique of its shortcomings. Their methods, admittedly, were primitive, but the public they wrote for had not yet acquired even the rudiments of literary discrimination. These readers, for the most part clients of the *cabinets de lecture*, preferred a clear-cut dividing line between the good and the bad characters, and were flattered if this line coincided with class divisions, putting the greedy, selfish, depraved men of money on the one side and the high-principled, intelligent proletarians on the other. The fiction they revelled in is therefore full of virtuous young workers coming to the rescue of distressed girls, protecting them from designing aristocrats or else offering them shelter, finding them work and restoring their sense of dignity. Sometimes the heroine – a poor sempstress content with her lot – disdaining more flattering offers of marriage, remains faithful to the honest young artisan to whom she is betrothed; or else the working-class girl, having married some effete count, succeeds in shaming her husband into leading a less dissolute, more useful life. Marriage was, indeed, for many of these novelists a heaven-sent contrivance for effecting reconciliation between the opposed classes. George Sand was particularly fond of it in fiction, however little the institution had suited her in real life. In *André* (1835) we have a young nobleman marrying a florist's assistant in spite of the understandable opposition of his family, while in *Le Meunier d'Angibault* (*The Miller of Angibault*, 1845) she shows us a baroness in love with a commoner, a man of working-class origins who persuades her to sell up her possessions and distribute the proceeds to the poor.

Such sentimental wish-fulfilment stories can scarcely be said, of course, to reflect the realities of the age, except in the indirect sense that they can be held to testify to a widespread concern with the problems of a divided society. Too often the need to present the poor as heroic led these writers to gloss over the fact that poverty commonly results in human degradation. We are seldom made aware that this was a period when the labouring classes and factory workers were actually enduring a calamitous decline in their standard of living, with constant falls in the purchasing power of a wage which even so tended to be lowered as the influx from the countryside increased the available labour force in the towns. It is rare for a realistic glimpse to be given of the actual conditions under which the poor had to live before 1848. Just occasionally an author will risk describing some filthy, airless workshop, or a room in a slum stripped of all furniture during a period of unemployment. Yet often the writers themselves were the sons of working-class families and had personal experience of the way of life of the proletariat. They knew the real reason why the taverns were so powerful a magnet for the worker on his one free day of the week; they knew the difficulties that beset any attempt to organize a trades union so as to secure wage increases or improved working conditions. A collection of stories by Souvestre published in 1835 includes an account of such an attempt, speedily suppressed by the police. The working-class hero is caught stealing and sent to prison; his wife and daughter are left with the choice between starvation and prostitution.

EUGÈNE SUE AND THE 'ROMAN-FEUILLETON'

It was particularly in the 1840s that social protest became a recognizable element in the popular novel, not infrequently accompanied by predictions of violent revolution if nothing was done to relieve the desperate misery of the poor. This exacerbation of tone coincided with the invention of the *roman-feuilleton* or serial story, which at a stroke greatly enlarged the audience the novelist could reach. The first long work of fiction to be published in instalments in a daily newspaper was Balzac's *La Vieille Fille* in 1836. The fashion rapidly caught on, and rival newspaper editors started bidding against each other for publication rights in the works of star authors. The sums paid were sometimes prodigious: Véron, editorial manager of *Le Constitutionnel*, offered Sue 100,000 francs for *Le Juif errant* (*The Wandering Jew*), a speculation which paid handsomely, for the increased sales of his paper gave him a clear profit of 600,000 francs.

Opposition to the *roman-feuilleton* developed in different quarters for a variety of reasons. Booksellers feared their trade would be damaged. Sainte-Beuve denounced it as 'industrial literature', posing a threat to the purity of French prose style, since the writer of serial stories derived an obvious pecuniary advantage from prolixity. But the most serious objections came from those responsible for law and order. One of the principal objects of the press censorship during the Second Empire was to call a halt to the dangerous vogue of the *romans-feuilletons*, particularly, of course, those of the prince of the genre, Eugène SUE (1804-57).

It was Sue, rather than Balzac, George Sand, or even the indefatigable Alexandre Dumas the Elder, who emerged as the most truly popular French novelist of the century, at least until Zola started breaking sales records in the late 1870s. Sue's plots were extravagant and his characters quite incredible, but these defects were gladly overlooked by his devotees panting for the next instalment, hooked on *la suite à demain*. Everyone read Sue, including, said Théophile Gautier, 'those who can't read themselves and have it read aloud to them by some willing and erudite janitor'. But it is a fact that the proportion of Frenchmen in the category of 'those who can't read' was constantly diminishing. Though in 1819 the illiteracy rate was something like 15 out of 20 million adults, Guizot's educational reforms of 1833 changed this situation quite dramatically: at the end of Louis-Philippe's reign literacy among army conscripts was discovered to have risen to 64 per cent. For the first time in history the children of the poor were taught at least the 'three R's', and it was this generation that reached adulthood at the time Sue's ramshackle but exciting fictions were penetrating, thanks to collections of clippings from the *Journal des Débats* and *Le Constitutionnel*, into even the humblest households.

Les Mystères de Paris (1842–3), his first sensationally successful serial novel, appears to have been started (as the title indeed suggests) as a straightforward thriller. We follow the nocturnal perambulations through Paris of the mysterious Rodolphe, Grand Duke of Gerolstein, a sort of modern Haroun-al-Raschid bent on righting injustices, punishing villains, and succouring honest folk in distress. In response to a number of letters that Sue started receiving from his readers, he orientated the novel increasingly towards social criticism, by inserting detailed and harrowing accounts of the circumstances in which the poorer sections of the Parisian population had to live. In search of material, he conscientiously visited the slum areas of the city, and what he saw there fired his indignation; for Sue, who like Flaubert was the son of a successful doctor, had hitherto lived very much the life of a man-about-town with no real inkling of the hardships the great mass of the people had to contend with. As his working-class readership grew, so did the number of his informants; he came to be appreciated not just as a popular writer, but as a champion of the underdog. With a touching faith in the good intentions of their social superiors, his working-class readers felt convinced that the graphic picture he drew of the sordidness of their lives would infallibly persuade the 'authorities' to come to their help.

Eugène Sue's method of composition in *Les Mystères de Paris* was that of the true manufacturer of cliff-hangers. Nothing was planned in advance. He had not the slightest idea, when he sat down to write one instalment, how he could satisfactorily extricate his characters from the perilous predicament in which he had left them in the last; and at the end of the new instalment, he would as likely as not have placed them in as critical a situation as before. Not surprisingly, his characters often lacked all consistency and were apt to change, without warning and without prompting, from treacherous brutes to large-hearted philanthropists. Almost always, however, these inexplicable transformations were from bad to good, rather than the other way about: the *feuilletonniste* was an optimist where human nature was concerned. Furthermore, however defective his psychology might have been, he was a realist in the sense that some of his characters, at least, were copied from real life. To get properly acquainted with typical members of the working classes, Sue went much further than the Goncourts, Zola or Huysmans were to do: he disguised himself as a house-decorator and paid court to a working girl with whom he would spend his Sundays in popular places of amusement. The girl was put straight into the *Mystères de Paris* and one can be sure that the details Sue gave of her working life were absolutely truthful (an eighteen-hour day six days a week on a meagre diet of bread, milk, and vegetables – never any meat – with nearly half her earnings going on rent, light and heating). When Sue took his characters from higher social spheres he occasionally caused offence. There is the curious story of how Dr Véron, who as we have seen purchased the rights of *Le Juif errant* for his paper *Le Constitutionnel*, was surprised and indignant to recognize himself portrayed in Sue's next novel, *Les Sept Péchés capitaux* (*The Seven Deadly Sins*), as the incarnation of Greed. He insisted on changes, which the novelist proudly refused to make, and the contract had to be cancelled, *Les Sept Péchés capitaux* appearing instead in the columns of *Le Siècle*.

Sue showed himself a conscientious realist in another respect: he dealt in his novels only with those classes of society with which he had some personal acquaintance. These were, as it happened, the topmost and the bottommost; since Sue had never had much truck with the middle classes, they figure little in his novels. Lurid though it may seem today, contemporaries testified to the veracity of his portrayal of the fashionable world, which Sue, thanks to his large inherited fortune and the ease of manner which recommended him to society hostesses, knew inside out. In his writings, he represents the aristocracy much as Balzac does, as effete and corrupt: the older generation for ever exchanging reminiscences about the years they spent in exile at Coblenz and elsewhere, while the younger men pass their time in frivolous pursuits, it being quite unheard of for any of them to enter a worthwhile profession. The women are promiscuous, though confining their adulteries strictly to their own social sphere.

At the other end of the scale were the criminal classes. Here it was Balzac who followed in Sue's steps, rather than the other way round, since the novel in which he first introduced members of the underworld, *La Dernière Incarnation de Vautrin* (Part IV of *Splendeurs et misères des courtisanes*) was written after the appearance of *Les Mystères de Paris*, partly indeed in the hope of outdoing Sue if he could. But Sue followed Balzac in comparing his gangsters to Fenimore Cooper's redskins and also in insisting that the criminal type was recognizable at a glance by certain physical features (a thick neck, a receding forehead, etc.: both Balzac and Sue were disciples of the celebrated physiognomist Lavater). The question of the treatment of criminals preoccupied Sue, and he showed himself an enlightened reformer in bringing to public notice some of the more crying abuses of the penal system: the fatal corruption of young delinquents who were forced to associate in prison with hardened criminals, the lack of after-prison care, the way a prisoner's family was made to suffer when he was sentenced, and lastly the lamentable fact that conditions inside prison could hardly be made harsher than those obtaining outside. A convict, forced to work twelve hours a day, was at least lodged, fed and clothed. An unskilled workman putting in even longer hours might not earn enough to keep himself and his family alive.

The influence of Sue on the development of realism, and in particular on the shape realism took in France, has never been properly assessed. He was not, of course, the first French writer to introduce lower-class characters into his novels; Restif de La Bretonne had preceded him here, but no one before Sue had conceived the audacious idea of using the popular novel for purposes of social propaganda. The fact that his art and technique were so crude and that his greatest appeal was to the least enlightened sections of the population meant that his type of novel, in which realism was coupled with reforming zeal, stood little chance of further development in France. Perhaps the only important writer he inspired was Victor Hugo, and *Les Misérables* is even further removed from the general line of realist development than *Les Mystères de Paris*. The difference between realism as it eventually manifested itself in England and in France can be traced to the same cause: if France never produced a writer like Dickens, whose creative genius could be harnessed to humanitarian idealism, part of the reason may have been that Eugène Sue had discredited in advance this kind of literature with the immature and melodramatic specimens he had to offer.

THE FEMINIST NOVEL

Besides the half-starved worker with his anaemic, ragged family, there was another category of the underprivileged whose plight excited the indignation of the group of novelists we have been speaking of: this category embraced the whole of womankind, in every social class. The feminist novel of this period was totally different from the sentimental novel written chiefly by titled ladies under the Empire and the Restoration, the tone of which was loftily moral and the matter infinitely tedious.[2] It was still sentimental, but its moral assumptions were much less stuffy.

In the mythology of the left, women had long filled an important symbolical role. Some of the semi-legendary figures of the Great Revolution had been women: Charlotte Corday, Mme Roland. In the mystical socialist religions that developed in the early nineteenth century the figure of the priestess, the 'woman-messiah', occupied a place of some honour. Eugène Delacroix, when he incarnated the spirit of 'Liberty on the Barricades' (the reference was to the 1830 revolution) as a chaste but splendidly bare-bosomed girl, beautifully expressed the floating conviction that in the new, free society of the future woman would, somehow or other, be man's equal or even – why not? – his superior, his leader, the standard-bearer of universal emancipation. In stark contrast to this spirit of admiration and romantic devotion was the reality: women worse treated, more deeply degraded, in the France of Louis-Philippe than they had been under any previous régime. The new factories, the new industries exploited working women even more cruelly than they did men, while in the middle and upper classes women were still too often regarded as insensate chattels, useful instruments to swell the family holdings by attracting into marriage some propertied suitor.

The novelists recognized these abuses, exposed them, but then weakened their case by exaggeration. They were not content merely to pin responsibility for the scandal of prostitution on to the exploiting classes. The argument went further: 'fallen women' were not just innocent victims, they were, thanks to some freak inversion of the moral law, held to be actually superior to women of conventional virtue. Suffering purifies the soul; therefore, she who suffered by submitting to the embraces of strangers emerged purer than before, and it followed that acts of heroic self-abnegation were only to be expected from the 'saintly courtesan'. So in one novel a kept woman effects a reconciliation between the hero and his wife, and then dies. In another a ballet-dancer falls in love with a medical student, nurses him through a dangerous illness, and then cures him of his burgeoning passion for her. Yet another 'woman of easy virtue', named Emma, renounces her lover so that he may contract a suitable marriage, and from the height of her moral superiority reads the bride a lesson on her duties in the married state . . .[3] Occasionally, even so, realism crept into these fanciful representations of a rather horrible social evil. Thus, the heroine of Alphonse Karr's *Une Heure trop tard* (*One Hour Too Late*, 1833) was actually modelled on the actress Juliette Drouet, who was Karr's mistress before she acquired a permanent niche in the hall of fame as Victor Hugo's. Alphonse Esquiros's *Les Vierges folles* (*The Foolish Virgins*, 1840) was less a work of fiction than a serious, factual report on the ravages of prostitution, and as such earned the writer a prison sentence.

Esquiros wrote a sequel to this book, which he called *Les Vierges sages* (*The Wise Virgins*, 1842); it was another documentary inquiry, this time into the state of marriage in France. There were few subjects that evoked greater interest at this period, as well among major novelists like Balzac and George SAND (1804–76) as among the lesser luminaries. Balzac's traditionalist attitude to the question set him at loggerheads with the rest of his generation; he was almost alone in showing (in *La Femme de trente ans*, *Le Père Goriot*, and *Honorine*) what disastrous consequences ensued when wives strayed into adultery.[4] Most of his contemporaries felt, or at least argued, that husbands being what they are, married women were all more or less victims and therefore, even if they took lovers, fundamentally guiltless: deserving, at any rate, compassion rather than censure. George Sand's first novel on the subject, *Indiana* (1832), was also her best, since her heroine is not presented as an entirely admirable woman. Colonel Delmare, the husband, is admittedly a harsh and insensitive man, but he loves her after his fashion and depends on her; it is Indiana's masochism that brings out the worst in him. It seems strange, all the same, that at the time it was published *Indiana* should have been regarded as an outstanding work of realism. Sainte-Beuve, reviewing it in *Le National* (5 October 1832), praised the author for having created 'a true, living world, which is our world, a hundred leagues from the historical scenes, the rags and tatters of the Middle Ages which so many hack writers have glutted us with'. After this side-swipe at the Walter Scott industry, Sainte-Beuve went on to congratulate George Sand for having shown 'characters and manners just as we can observe them around us, natural conversations, scenes in familiar settings, violent, uncommon passions, but sincerely felt or observed and such as are still aroused in many hearts, under the apparent uniformity and monotonous frivolity of our lives.' Sainte-Beuve was too gallant. In fact, *Indiana* is a hybrid work, in which certain characters (like Sir Ralph Brown) are the purest products of an overheated imagination, while at the same time George Sand endeavoured with some success to anchor her novel firmly in contemporary time by including transparent references in a number of chapters to the political turmoil that heralded the 1830 revolution.

Other critics professed to see in her a disciple of Stendhal, whose *Rouge et noir* had appeared little more than a year before. George Sand herself seemed to be making obeisance to Stendhal's type of realism when, in the preface she wrote for the first edition of *Indiana*, she used the same analogy with the mirror as he had, and for the same purpose: to refute the charge that she was presenting too black an image of the world.[5] 'Let society bear the blame for its injustices, destiny for its caprices! The writer is but a mirror that reflects them, a machine that copies them, and is under no obligation to ask for indulgence if the print is exact, the reflection faithful.' George Sand was particularly anxious to defend the ending she had contrived, after some hesitation, for *Indiana*, an ending that had scandalized the more prudish of her readers. She declared that she would always give truthfulness precedence over morality; but it has to be said that a more truthful writer than George Sand would have shown Indiana sinking into destitution and worse, instead of being providentially rescued, cared for and consoled by her 'guardian angel', Sir Ralph.

It would need, however, another fifty years before realism had progressed to the point where an ending of that kind would be regarded not just as tolerable but as inevitable.

The solution George Sand adopted for her heroine's marital problems was to have her contract an 'irregular' union with the man who had always cherished her. However, the pair were to live together far from civilization and its conventions, on an idyllic tropical island in the Indian Ocean. Free love was not the usual answer, either in George Sand's novels or in those of her less talented feminist contemporaries. Very often, the heroine will contract a marriage, but under auspices that bode ill for the future. In *Valentine* (1832), her next novel after *Indiana*, a rich, nobly born heiress sacrifices her inclinations to marry the man her parents have chosen for her; in *Jacques* (1834), a self-sacrificing husband ends his life so as to enable his wife to marry the man she has fallen in love with. *Mauprat* (1837), which has an eighteenth-century setting, does show a happy marriage gladly entered into, though only after the young hero has shown himself fully worthy of the woman he loves. In none of these novels was the actual condition of the typical married couple, as it could be observed in mid-century France, the true subject. The first writer to attempt a realistic portrayal of this very common human situation was Gustave Flaubert, in his maiden novel, *Madame Bovary*.

'MADAME BOVARY'

The book was published in 1857, in a political and literary climate which, over the previous ten years, had changed completely. The humanitarian idealism expressed in even the most mediocre novels of the pre-1848 period had ceased to be fashionable. The generous but impractical enthusiasm of the socialist philosophies that had inspired them might have been translated into positive action after February 1848; but the chance had been lost, through lack of courage or inexperience. The conservatives seized the initiative again, after suppressing with much bloodshed a popular uprising in the working-class districts of Paris. Nation-wide elections made it plain that the majority of Frenchmen wanted no radical changes. The Church party reasserted itself, while liberal elements in the University were gagged; the capital was purged of working-class activists, either by summary deportations overseas or by their enforced dispersal over the country. Three years later, the few republican institutions that had survived were swept away when the President, Louis-Napoleon, suspended the constitution and had himself proclaimed Emperor.

These events inevitably brought sudden extinction to the novel of social propaganda. Its practitioners either fled the country (like Alphonse Esquiros) or, like George Sand, turned to writing innocuous rustic idylls. The interruption of ordinary commercial life made it, in any case, a bad period for the book trade, and publishers, fearing prosecutions, were wary about what manuscripts they accepted. The point is best illustrated by the well-known story of the mortifying experience the Goncourt brothers had with their first novel. This had been written in the course of 1851 and was due for publication on 2 December. It so happened that the future Napoleon III had secretly fixed on 2 December 1851 (the anniversary of his uncle's coronation as first Emperor of the French) as the date on which he would illegally seize power. His act was bound to remind the French of the *coup* by which Napoleon Bonaparte had, half a century earlier, overthrown the First Republic and made himself master of the country: an event normally referred to by the date in the Republican calendar on which it took place, 'le 18 brumaire' (9 November 1799). Unfortunately for the Goncourts, the title their novel bore was *En 18**. In their publisher's view, it was not improbable, given the authorities' nervousness, that this enigmatic title would be interpreted as a sly allusion to *18 brumaire*; to avoid trouble, he withdrew the advertising posters and sent all but a very few copies of the book to be pulped.

It was in the autumn of the same year (1851) that Gustave FLAUBERT (1821–80), having shortly before returned home after a leisurely tour of Egypt, Palestine and Greece undertaken in the company of his photographer friend, Maxime Du Camp, settled down to write the book which was to take him fifty-six months of uninterrupted labour but which, for the remainder of the century, was to be regarded by critics and the reading public alike as the very prototype of the realist novel.

An interesting, even if not fully authenticated, account of how Flaubert came to write *Madame Bovary* was given by Du Camp in a volume of memoirs published immediately after Flaubert's death. Shortly before the two of them set off on their tour of the Middle East, Flaubert invited Du Camp, together with another close friend, the poet Louis Bouilhet, to come and stay with him at Croisset so that he could read them a piece of work he had just completed. This was a long philosophical drama based on the early Christian legend of St Anthony, the hermit living in the desert whom the devil tempted, by means of voices and visions, to abjure his faith and fall into sin. After the reading, which took several evenings – the work being excessively long – Flaubert asked his friends for their honest opinion. They gave it: frankly, they said, *La Tentation de Saint-Antoine* (*The Temptation of St Anthony*) was fit only to be thrown on to the fire. They criticized it on a number of counts, but chiefly because it was only too evident that Flaubert had allowed himself to be carried away by the excitement the subject had aroused in him: he had not kept control over his material. The result was a patchwork of purple passages and a singular lack of point.

According to Du Camp – and one can believe him here – Flaubert was at first greatly upset by this verdict. He did not in every respect follow his friends' advice: instead of burning *La Tentation de Saint-Antoine* he stowed it away and at a later stage rewrote it as a much shorter, more sober, better shaped work, and finally published it in 1874. In the meantime, however, he did his best to forget all about it: the adventurous trip with Du Camp offered a prolonged holiday from literary labours, and shortly after he returned he started sketching out what was first spoken of among his friends as 'the story of Mme Delamare'.

Delamare was the name of a humble doctor with a practice in the Norman village of Ry, not far from Rouen, which was Flaubert's birthplace and the city where he and Bouilhet had been at school. The most meticulous investigations, undertaken some one hundred years after the events,[6] have brought to light very little solid information about the life of Delamare. We know that his first wife was older than he, that before long he became a widower and remarried, this time choosing as his bride a seventeen-year-old girl called Delphine Couturier. One daughter was born to the couple. Mme Delamare died in 1848, aged only twenty-six, and her husband followed her into the grave a year later.[7] There is no concrete evidence that Delphine committed suicide, or that she had secret love-affairs and fell into the hands of money-lenders. Rumours may have been circulating about some hidden scandal and may have come to Flaubert's ears, but it is equally reasonable to suppose that he invented all this part of the story. At this distance in time, the most we can say is that the facts known to us would have provided Flaubert with the bare essentials of a scenario: the country doctor twice married, and the birth of a child, left an orphan after the successive deaths of the mother and father.

How much or how little of the story was invented by Flaubert is not, perhaps, a question of tremendous significance even though it is one that has constantly fascinated literary historians. What was truly momentous was Flaubert's decision to use a commonplace domestic drama as the subject of his first major work of fiction. The decision could not have been taken without a struggle, for all his instincts urged him in quite a different direction. He would certainly have preferred to devote his time to the retelling of some old legend, like that of St Anthony; as late as 1850 he was still playing with three possible subjects, none of them modern: a history of Don Juan, the legend of Anubis, and the story of a Flemish virgin in the late Middle Ages subject to mystical trances. Alternatively he would have been just as happy to embark on some elaborate work of historical reconstruction such as *Salammbô*, the novel he did actually write after the completion of *Madame Bovary*, a highly coloured romance set in Carthage before the Christian era, with a Punic priestess of the moon as heroine and a barbarian warrior as hero. A romantic at heart, with strong leanings to the lurid, the macabre, the gaudy and the grandiloquent, Flaubert hated his own age, which he regarded as soulless, anaemic and mean-minded; he wanted nothing better than to escape from it, at least in imagination. All the time he was writing *Madame Bovary* he grumbled – mainly in letters to his mistress, the poetess Louise Colet – about the vulgarity of his subject-matter, the platitude of his characters, the difficulty of writing a novel so lacking in incident, of composing dialogue when the tenor of what is being said was so trivial. 'Que ma Bovary m'embête!' – this *cri de cœur* sums up the whole litany.

This book, at the stage I have reached [he was writing in November 1853], tortures me to such an extent (and if I could find a stronger word

I would use it) that it makes me sometimes physically ill. Over the past three weeks I have several times been almost fainting away with pain; at other times I have had difficulty in breathing or felt sick at table. I believe I would have cheerfully hanged myself if my pride hadn't stopped me; it's true that I'm sometimes tempted to send everything to the devil, beginning with the Bovary woman. What a bloody stupid idea it was of mine to have picked on such a subject! God! I know all about the 'torments of art' now.[8]

Some allowance for natural exaggeration must be made, of course – these letters were often written in reply to complaints from Louise, who could not understand why Gustave was giving her so little time and Emma Bovary so much – but there must all the same have been much that was genuine in those laments, otherwise it is difficult to explain why Flaubert should have needed so long to write the book. Proof of the trouble it gave him is there in the countless scored-out passages in the manuscript, versions of paragraphs written and re-written half a dozen times, so that one is almost prepared to agree with Flaubert that the best bits were those that got left out. We know that Flaubert was not, by nature, a laborious writer: the original *Tentation de Saint-Antoine* and earlier unpublished works had been composed with remarkable facility, in long spells of carefree creative verve. *Madame Bovary* marks the point at which the writer suddenly became self-critical. Flaubert's prose style was still far from being as terse, as neutral as it later became, in *L'Éducation sentimentale* and in *Bouvard et Pécuchet*; there are still, in *Madame Bovary*, 'poetic' metaphors, sustained similes with a verbal magic inappropriate in the general context of the narrative. Each paragraph is a little too conscientiously articulated; the sentences flow with an unnatural smoothness, the unerring choice of the *mot juste* gives an uncomfortable impression of artifice. It seems that Flaubert, having resigned himself to the drabness of his subject-matter, decided it was indispensable that the texture should be correspondingly brilliant. The technical problem was to confer beauty of a sort on material totally without intrinsic charm or nobility.

The book was to be about a self-centred young woman, with yearnings for a life of luxury and excitement, who finds herself tied to a hard-working but excessively dull husband, with nothing to occupy or amuse her and nothing to look forward to. Disillusioned with marriage, despising, then detesting her husband, she starts thinking of ways to punish him and avenge herself, not for any positive wrongs – for he is all admiration, indulgence, and dog-like devotion – but for his stupidity, his inadequacy, his lack of fire and spirit: in the last resort, for the vulgar noises he makes when eating his soup. Bored by Charles's monotonously predictable performances in the double bed, she casts her eyes longingly in the direction of the only presentable young man in the village, Léon Dupuis, a notary's clerk who, though attracted to her, is too unenterprising at this stage to press his advantage. Then she meets Rodolphe Boulanger, a local landowner, who guesses her to be ripe for an affair, seduces her without compunction or difficulty and then, alarmed when she talks of elopement, removes himself to Paris to give her time to cool off. This disappointment brings on a nervous breakdown, followed by a phase of religious mania, after which Emma starts sliding rapidly downhill. Her second adultery lacks the sparkle of the first; she compensates by indulging in bouts of wild extravagance, and eventually, to avoid the humiliation of having to admit her debts to her husband, she swallows a few handfuls of arsenic stolen from the local chemist's shop and dies in considerable agony. The story was a sorry one, the setting – the flat farmland of lower Normandy, peopled by shrewd, hard-fisted peasants – was totally lacking in grandeur; everything was sordid and commonplace. But its very banality gave it representative value: as Flaubert himself remarked, the frustrated tears and hopeless sufferings of women like Emma Bovary were concealed behind lace curtains in a score of villages scattered over France in the nineteenth century.

The challenge of the difficulty to be overcome (how could such shabby material be transfigured, so that the finished work would be a literary masterpiece?) partly explains Flaubert's choice: as he told Louise Colet, *Madame Bovary* was a 'tough feat of gymnastics'.[9] But there was another reason why he was originally drawn to the subject: being so remote from him it would, he thought, enable him to maintain artistic detachment. This had never been easy for him. His earlier attempts at fiction, including a first version (unfinished) of *L'Éducation sentimentale*, had been unashamedly autobiographical. The failure of *La Tentation de Saint-Antoine* can be attributed likewise in large measure to the author's over-involvement in the central character:

Flaubert had forgotten the need to re-create the mentality of a fourth-century monk in the pleasure he took in discovering his spiritual affinities with the tormented cenobite. All through his career he was apt to overstep the boundary between empathy with his characters and self-identification with them: in *L'Éducation sentimentale* (1869 version) he gave his hero, Frédéric Moreau, the same great unsatisfied lifetime's passion for a married woman that he himself had secretly nurtured; and in his last, unfinished novel the two copy-clerks, Bouvard and Pécuchet, share many of his intellectual antipathies besides being, like him, antisocial bookworms with a marked preference for the sedentary life.

Madame Bovary appears, at first glance, different from all these other works in that it hardly seems possible to identify any of the leading characters with the author: it was because he felt so detached from them, so alienated by their outlook, that he depicted them with such savage satisfaction. And yet, even though the saying widely attributed to him: 'Madame Bovary, c'est moi', has been shown to be apocryphal, it is not at all fanciful to see in Emma Flaubert's *doppelgänger*. Baudelaire, with his usual perspicacity, was the first to point this out, in the year the novel was published. The author, he said, had tried to achieve the *tour de force* of turning himself into a woman. What had happened was something rather different:

> He could not help infusing a virile blood into the veins of his creation, and so Mme Bovary, in respect of her energy, her ambition, and also her ability to dream dreams, has remained a man. Like Pallas Athene, who leapt fully armed from the brain of Zeus, this bizarre hermaphrodite has conserved all the seductions of a manly soul in her charming woman's body.

Baudelaire was perfectly right. Emma is not lacking in feminine allure. It is not merely her husband and each of her lovers in turn who respond to her powerful sexual charm; she excites even the crabbed old notary Guillaumin, who would like to buy her favours, and Justin, the apothecary's prentice-boy, who worships her silently and weeps on her grave. But she has a man's restlessness, a man's relentlessness and strength of purpose (elsewhere Baudelaire compares her to Lady Macbeth), a man's recklessness. She tends to dominate her lovers – Léon, in particular, is almost completely subjugated by her:

'He did not argue with her views; he accepted her taste in everything; he was turning into her mistress instead of having her as his.' In all these respects, Flaubert fashioned her in his image; but above all he gave her the ability to dream dreams, as Baudelaire says. In some of his early autobiographical works Flaubert describes how at school, when lessons bored him, he would lose himself in reveries, imagining himself in far-off, tropical lands, or fancying himself one of the great criminals of history, Nero . . . or Cleopatra. 'I used to wish I were a woman for the sake of her beauty, that I might, like her, strip myself naked, let my hair drop to my heels, and admire my reflection in the stream.'[10] Emma, with her more practical nature, does not exactly wish herself a man, but she envies men, and when she finds herself pregnant she wishes for a boy. 'The idea of having a male child was like the hoped-for compensation for all her past disappointments. A man is at least free: he can explore passions and foreign lands, overleap obstacles, sink his teeth into the most exotic of delights. Whereas a woman is always held in check . . .'

However, the baby turns out to be a daughter. In spite of the almost symbiotic relationship in which he lived with her for four and a half years, Flaubert was utterly merciless to Emma: her hopes are all dashed, her joys all short-lived. It is partly the fault of woman's condition in a bourgeois society, but, as he saw also, partly her own fault, and his irony is never more biting than when he can denounce her conceit, her self-pity, the conventionality of her ideas, her persistence in worshipping tawdry ideals. It is above all else this finely balanced mixture, where Emma is concerned, of empathy and critical objectivity that has earned the novel its celebrity as the first masterpiece of the realist aesthetic.

Not that Flaubert thought of himself as a realist; indeed, he crossly denied the charge whenever it was made. He wrote to another of his woman friends, Mme Roger des Genettes, at about the time he was finishing *Madame Bovary*: 'People believe that I am drawn to reality, whereas I loathe it; for it was out of hatred for realism that I undertook this novel. But,' he added significantly, 'I detest no less the false idealism by which we are humbugged nowadays.'[11] Realism, as it developed in France in the second half of the century, more and more took on the aspect of a protest-campaign against social hypocrisy – nowhere more visibly, as we shall see, than in the work of Flaubert's closest disciple, Maupassant. That the age of realism should have coincided with the age of cant is not really surprising: in a sense it can be said that the one was invented to furnish a corrective for the other.

In *Madame Bovary* there is one other character besides Emma herself who has become a literary byword: this is Homais, the self-important apothecary or 'dispensing chemist', to use the more flattering description by which he prefers to be known – as, today, do all those of his calling, in accordance with the same polite semantic shift as permits all physicians to refer to themselves as doctors, whether or not they have earned the letters M.D. after their names. Whatever his pretensions to professional status, Homais is a simple tradesman; but, in the economic climate of the time, those who made a living by buying cheap and selling at a profit constituted the ascendant class. So Flaubert was adhering closely to the social reality of the time in showing Homais, together with the travelling salesman Lheureux, who bit by bit obtains title to the whole of the Bovary property, growing steadily more and more prosperous and self-assured. In the end Homais displaces Charles Bovary completely; though quite unqualified, he becomes the sole medical authority in the area; and he is finally awarded the cross of the Legion of Honour.

His actual part in the plot is tiny: it is hardly an exaggeration to say that his sole function is to provide the shop from which Emma can steal the arsenic. But Flaubert gave him a very large place in the novel, probably because Homais incarnates admirably this 'false idealism', this nineteenth-century cant which he told his correspondent he so detested. Homais is smug, pedantic, self-important, prudish. He is respectful of authority, though cunning in circumventing regulations if this is good for business. He has sufficient vision to grasp the potentialities of newspaper publicity and press-campaigns. He has views on art and literature, the views of every thick-skinned, thick-skulled philistine. He basks in the unstinted admiration of his wife – a placid, sexless, timorous creature – and he adores playing papa to his numerous progeny. By a neat touch, Flaubert completed the portrait by making him a freethinker and an anticlerical, forever quoting Voltaire and arguing interminably with the village priest. In creating Homais, the very type of the up-and-coming small French tradesman, later to fill the ranks of the radicals when party politics came into fashion, Flaubert put his finger unerringly on everything that was most ludicrous, but also most sinister, in the emerging class-structure of the country. Such coldly dispassionate observation was, in the long run, far more subtly damaging to the establishment than all the literature of overt social propaganda of the previous decade.

CHAMPFLEURY AND DURANTY

Flaubert had promised Du Camp that *Madame Bovary* should be serialized in his journal *La Revue de Paris*, and the first instalment duly appeared in October 1856. In January of the following year Flaubert had to face a court action on account of the alleged immorality of the book. He won the case, and Michel Lévy brought out the first edition at the end of April 1857. Coincidentally, the first issue of Duranty's literary periodical *Réalisme* was put on sale in November 1856; the sixth and last was dated April–May 1857. Although Duranty was not personally acquainted with Flaubert and failed completely to recognize him as a literary ally (his brief review of *Madame Bovary* in *Réalisme* was both uncivil and unfair), it would be impossible not to regard the conjuncture of these two publications as signalizing the inception of realism as a literary movement. It was in 1856–7 that the word gained wide currency, as a rallying cry or a term of disparagement depending on one's aesthetic and, to some extent, political affiliations.

Its earliest applications had been in the domain of art, specifically in connection with the canvases that Courbet was exhibiting from 1849 onwards. One of Courbet's few defenders, Jules Husson (1821–89), who wrote all his works under the pseudonym CHAMPFLEURY, had used the term 'realism' to denote the style of the revolutionary painting *Enterrement à Ornans*. The word caught on; before long Champfleury's own works were being described, contemptuously, as 'realistic'. Besides his writings on art, Champfleury published in the 1850s a number of stories of provincial life. These novels were not works of art; Champfleury laboured under two major disqualifications – his lack of formal education (he had difficulty with French grammar and syntax) and his poverty, which compelled him to write copiously and hastily for the sake of the money that his books brought in. Aiming at a fairly uncultured public, the lower middle classes, who were on the whole new to literature, he wrote in a simple fashion about characters they could understand; in fact, many of these characters were recognizable copies of the people he remembered in his native town of Laon, beginning with the members of his own family. His themes were as simple as his plots. *Les Aventures de Mademoiselle Mariette* (1851) describes the strains of a love-affair between a writer and his cold-hearted, mercenary mistress. *Les Souffrances du professeur Delteil* (1853) deals with the tribulations of a shabby, middle-aged schoolmaster who cannot keep discipline in class and finally loses his job. An adulterous liaison between the wife of a provincial solicitor and a local landowner who eventually elopes with her provides the focus of action in *Les Bourgeois de Molinchart* (1855), which has been regarded as a first, feeble forerunner of *Madame Bovary*. Daringly, in *Monsieur de Boisdhyver* (1856), Champfleury tells of a young and handsome cleric who runs away with the daughter of a parishioner, while *La Succession Le Camus* (*The Le Camus Legacy*, 1857) has as its protagonist the widow of a rich miser, plundered by her lady-companion. These novels were realistic in the sense that the characters were portrayed with painstaking exactness, and placed in surroundings described in minute and authentic detail. They owed their popularity, which was considerable at the time, to other, less estimable qualities: to the somewhat pawky humour in which Champfleury too often indulged, and to his facile sentimentality.

Edmond DURANTY (1833–80) met Champfleury at one of the regular literary *soirées* presided over by Louise Colet (whose liaison with Flaubert had at this point petered out). The younger man had for some time admired the elder from a distance; this meeting left a profound impression on Duranty. With a couple of friends of his own age he decided to launch the periodical *Réalisme* in order to expound, defend, and propagate his ideas, which were also, in a large measure, Champfleury's, though Champfleury did not join the editorial board and never contributed a single line to the review. The great majority of the articles were written by Duranty himself, though he disguised his authorship of many of them under a variety of pseudonyms. Henri Thulié's most notable contribution was a series of theoretical articles about aspects of the novel (characters, description, plot, style); Jules Assézat, the third member of the trio, played a minor part, and eventually took offence when Duranty refused to accept one of his contributions. His withdrawal from the little team was a major factor in the early demise of the journal, though if one reads the collection through it is fairly clear that the editors were beginning to run out of ideas. The first number contains all the important manifestoes: the later issues were mostly filled with panegyrics on the writers approved of by Duranty and his friends (Restif de La Bretonne, Stendhal, Balzac, and Champfleury) or attacks on their *bêtes noires* (all the romantic poets, but chiefly Victor Hugo). Not all the articles were about literature. The press laws forbade comment on political or other issues of contemporary social interest, but the editors of *Réalisme* did not scruple to speak their minds freely about the art world. The last issue of all included a review, ironically entitled 'Pour les peintres', of the spring exhibition, in which almost every painter in the public eye, including even Courbet, was ferociously attacked.

The editors were united in insisting that the only novelty about realism was the name. Duranty, anticipating Erich Auerbach, traced its genealogy back to Homer. In certain respects the new doctrinaires did no more than formularize and reaffirm what had by that time become accepted practice among serious novelists. Realism in the first instance meant, they said, writing about one's own times; the historical novel was proscribed because it depended not on observation but on imagination. Imagination they considered almost a dirty word, while observation was to be the realist's constant standby – his own observation of the world, and the observations made by others that he overhears. A novel should contain the barest minimum of invention. In the second place, the realist is concerned with the study of ordinary men and women in society, acting and reacting on one another; not with psychological studies of exceptional individuals taken in isolation. A particular social class would be depicted by means of typical characters, those that seem to manifest the greatest number of the features common to their class. Thulié insisted that realism ought not to confine itself to the study of the lower reaches of society; if Champfleury had done this, the reason was simply that he had very properly concentrated on writing about the kind of people he was most familiar with.

Reading these solemn, often awkwardly phrased articles, one might at times be forgiven for imagining the writers were elaborating a syllabus for a school of social scientists rather than guide-lines for a literary movement. A claim they made repeatedly was that realism would serve a socially useful purpose, that the realist novelist was not an entertainer but a teacher, one who 'plays and fulfils the role of educator as others busy themselves being merchants, soldiers, judges; he exhibits the social spectacle, and the nearer he is to the truth, to practical life as it surrounds us, the more *useful* he is to those who read him.' Duranty was not, of course, arguing in favour of didacticism; but he believed – or maintained he did – that one cannot survive in society without a close knowledge and understanding of one's fellow men, and this knowledge and understanding were precisely what the realist, with his trained faculty of observation and deduction, was able to provide.

It followed that the realists were required to express themselves in the simplest possible language, in order to reach the widest possible audience and enlighten the greatest possible number. 'A novelist is bad,' wrote Thulié, 'when he does not say sincerely what he thinks and relate naïvely what he has seen.' Thulié attacked the tendency – which he thought had spread from England – of proscribing certain words in the ordinary vocabulary because they were judged to be vulgar. 'Soon we shall not be able to mention trousers.' He also condemned all efforts to achieve a melodious style at the expense of simplicity and directness. One should write as one speaks; instead of addressing oneself to the 'lettered public', who never constitute more than a tiny proportion of one's potential readership, one should, said Duranty,

make oneself accessible. Workmen, shopkeepers, farm-labourers, all these 'bumpkins', as the *literati* call them, are perfectly capable of comprehending the passions, the foibles, the customs of society (among themselves they make masterly observations about their neighbours), but faced with witty paradoxes, with philosophical systems, with the torments of soul of young men with too much imagination, with tortured phraseology and ideas, with romantic psychology, they remain utterly unmoved.

The realism of Champfleury and Duranty has been called 'plebeian', compared to the 'elitist' or aristocratic realism of Flaubert and the

Goncourts. It was an earnest, high-minded, low-pitched form of writing which avoided the dilemma facing every form of realism – how to reconcile the ordinariness of existence with the ecstasies of art – by pretending that the aim was not artistic in any normal sense: it was instructive. The trouble was, as Duranty discovered, that instruction is about the last thing readers of fiction want. His own novels, though far from dull, were too conscientiously glum ever to achieve popularity. At Champfleury's instances, though with grave misgivings, Poulet-Malassis agreed to bring out his first, *Le Malheur d'Henriette Gérard* (1860), warning the author, however, that he did not expect to cover his costs. Yet it was undoubtedly a more powerful work than any of Champfleury's. Duranty built up the claustrophobic atmosphere of a provincial bourgeois family to a pitch of horror that would hardly be surpassed by François Mauriac. His second novel, and only other one of note, *La Cause du beau Guillaume* (1862), is centred on a liaison between a young townsman and a country girl, the drama deriving from the fiercely hostile reactions of the other villagers. The work is anything but a failure – Duranty achieved in it as convincing a representation of class conflict as had been seen in France since *Les Paysans*. But, of course, as soon as one names Balzac's novel, the enormous gulf between him and Duranty becomes apparent. There is a smallness in Duranty's vision of the world that robs his narrative of true authority. Duranty had talent, honesty, even a sense of drama; what he lacked was the creative touch.

EDMOND AND JULES DE GONCOURT

The oft-quoted phrase, 'history is a novel which happened; the novel is history as it might have happened', is found in the Goncourts' diary under the date 24 November 1861; but earlier, in May 1860, the brothers had already commented on the oddity of their having come to the novel via history (in the 1850s they had published a number of works about eighteenth-century France). 'And yet, we acted quite logically. What are the sources of written history? Documents. And what is the source of the novelist's documentation, if not life?'

Edmond (1822–96) and Jules (1830–70) de GONCOURT were the first novelists in France to make consistent use of documentation – carrying out what the French call an *enquête*, a methodical investigation of a particular aspect of real life – in the composition of a work of realism set in contemporary time. Documentation had, of course, long been practised by the more conscientious historical novelists. Balzac visited Brittany in 1828 expressly to gather material for *Les Chouans*; by talking to the older residents he was able to assemble a mass of authentic details concerning the civil war which had been fought there thirty years earlier and which he intended to use as the background of his book. But when writing about the contemporary scene, novelists had relied on their own private knowledge and had rarely thought it necessary to extend this knowledge in any direction by conducting special inquiries. Following the Goncourts, the naturalists were to develop their procedure into a deliberate technique, taken at times to faintly absurd lengths, as when Zola, wanting to write a novel in which the protagonist was to be an engine-driver, got permission from a railway company to ride from Paris to Le Havre on the footplate of one of their locomotives.

The use of documentation is not without its dangers, and the Goncourts were rather apt to suppose that they were at liberty to introduce any circumstance into their novels, provided they could find it duly authenticated somewhere; whatever could be shown to have happened in reality could safely be shown happening in a work of realist fiction. In the final section of their second novel, *Charles Demailly* (1860), there is a circumstantial account of how the hero gradually loses his hold on his sanity and sinks into a state of hopeless idiocy, having in the end lost even the power of rational speech. In composing this painful episode the brothers relied heavily on one particular medical treatise, compiled by a specialist in diseases of the mind who had had fifteen years' experience as director of the famous asylum of Charenton. They could hardly have found a more authoritative reference book, yet their amateurish use of it destroyed in advance all pretensions to realism; for they proceeded by picking out all the most horrifying pathological manifestations they found described, regardless of the fact that no one patient could possibly have exhibited them all, since they were symptomatic of a great variety of different mental illnesses.[12]

Another mistake sometimes made by the Goncourts was to suppose that they would arrive at 'the truth' by ensuring that their characters were involved in experiences that they had actually heard of people in real life encountering, or that they behaved in a way they had known some real person to have behaved. As keen diarists, they were accustomed to listen to and note down stories retailed in company, particularly when the stories struck them as being a little unusual. Any one of such anecdotes was liable to provide material for a future novel. They worked on the assumption that the best way of arriving at the truth was to refrain from inventing anything.

Unfortunately, all they succeeded in demonstrating was that no realist novel can be constructed by fitting together, in a new pattern, heterogeneous fragments of 'real life' experienced by someone or other. *Germinie Lacerteux* (1864) was based on the story, as they learned it after her death, of the double life led by a housemaid, Rose Malingre, who had been in their employ for years, apparently sober, respectable, hard-working, actually a secret drinker indulging in all kinds of sexual excesses on her 'days off'. The brothers, who had already suspected some irregularities, learned the whole truth from a neighbouring midwife who, out of delicacy, had said nothing during Rose's lifetime. Every detail they discovered of the wretched woman's existence was carefully worked into the novel: Germinie's life is no fiction – except in one respect. To have given her the same employers as Rose had would have been to adhere too closely to the literal ('historical') truth. So the Goncourts fictionalized the situation by allotting the role which, as masters of the household, they had played in reality, to an elderly maiden lady, a woman of rank come down in the world and living on her own with no near relatives. Here again they could flatter themselves they were inventing nothing: all Mlle de Varandeuil's past history, every aspect of her character, even her turns of speeech were directly copied from a cousin of the Goncourts, a certain Mlle de Courmont. What they never stopped to consider was that Rose's story might have been utterly different if her employers had not been a couple of careless bachelors too absorbed in their writing and in fulfilling their social duties outside the house to notice what was going on under their own roof, under their very noses, so to speak. When they made the fictional Germinie the sole servant of a lonely, unoccupied old maid, they changed the situation, they substituted a jigsaw piece that did not fit. This is why *Germinie Lacerteux*, powerful though it is as a study of the disintegration of a human personality, leaves the reader with a slight feeling of puzzlement: the basic circumstances are implausible simply because they were *not* invented. For fear of deserting reality, the Goncourts have sacrificed verisimilitude.

A similar implausibility, attributable to a similar unwillingness or incapacity to invent, underlies the Goncourts' previous novel, *Renée Mauperin* (1864). Here the plot depends entirely, at one crucial point, on the heroine's concealing from her brother her chance discovery that the aristocratic name which he proposes to assume is in fact still borne by a solitary descendant of an ancient family universally believed to have died out. Why did Renée not tell Henri instead of posting a newspaper cutting, with the official declaration of the deed-poll ringed in red, to the very man whose name her brother is unwittingly usurping? The result is a duel in which Henri is killed; and Renée, concealing her part in the disaster, dies of a heart disease brought on by feelings of guilt and remorse.

The unlikeliness of the story matters less, however, in this novel, since the plot merely provides a framework for a composite picture gallery, a set of portraits, some of them caricatural, all of them drawn from life: the originals were all persons known to the Goncourts, whose names occur regularly in their diary. Henri Mauperin, Renée's brother, is the type of ambitious young careerist, always careful to flatter the right people, and unscrupulous enough to seduce the mother of an heiress in order to marry, in the fullness of time, her daughter. There is Renée's older, married sister, a formidable snob; the Abbé Blampoix, an unctuous cleric who doubles as a marriage-broker; and M. Bourjot, a radical before 1830 but a ferocious reactionary now that he has become immensely rich. *Renée Mauperin* is a novel stuffed with sharp social criticism, a broadside directed against the *nouveaux riches* of the Second Empire by a couple of fastidious gentlemen whose great-grandfather had bought his way into the aristocracy just three years before the outbreak of the French Revolution.

There are three characters in the book who are spared the authors' sneers. The first is Denoisel, a bachelor no longer in his first youth, expert at living within his limited means without giving anyone the impression they are limited; Denoisel, the only man outside her family whom Renée fully confides in, is a flattering composite self-portrait of the two brothers. Then there is M. Mauperin, Renée's father, a man of solid worth and delicate sensibility saddled with a stupid wife and three children, to none of whom he is very close except Renée, the youngest. Renée was supposed to represent the 'modern miss' of the 1860s: she is emancipated up to a point – occasionally a bit pert, and fond of using slang. She prefers, understandably enough, to remain the spoilt daughter of the house instead of accepting any of the rather dull young men who come a-wooing. She has also a strong sense of honour, which she grieves to find her brother does not share. The last, pathetic chapters, which show Renée's health gradually failing, while her father makes valiant attempts to pretend she is on the mend, tremble on the brink of sentimentality. It is perhaps only the occasional passage of brutal realism – like the scene in which M. Mauperin attempts the horrible remedy of 'cupping' – that saves this concluding section of *Renée Mauperin* from mawkishness.

A strong interest in disease, in mental and physical degeneration and in the efforts of medical science to deal with these pathological conditions is one of the outstanding characteristics of the Goncourts' work. Sickbeds fascinated them, and if in the popular mind realism has come to be equated with morbidity, the fault is more likely to lie with them than with any other writer. Charles Demailly, as we have seen, passes through all the stages of a mental breakdown and ends incurably insane. Germinie Lacerteux, an alcoholic and a nymphomaniac, dies in hospital of pneumonia, having, on an earlier occasion, only just avoided being carried off by puerperal fever. *Madame Gervaisais* (1869), the last novel the two brothers collaborated over, is about a woman whose brain is turned by religious mania, while *Sœur Philomène* (1861), the short novel that they published after *Charles Demailly* and before *Renée Mauperin*, is set (apart from one long retrospective chapter near the beginning) entirely in a hospital. In the sense that it was the first piece of fiction that involved the brothers in visiting, and then describing, an environment unfamiliar to them, it represented an advance on the mere fictional rearrangement of their own experiences and a first step in the direction of a more objective concept of the novel. The impressionistic pen-pictures of the hospital ward, in particular the night round in the opening chapter, which could almost be taken for a verbal transposition of one of Georges de La Tour's candle-lit scenes, the contrasting callous and uninhibited talk of the medical students over their beer, in general the convincing lugubriousness of the setting must be counted as a major achievement of the new realism; and beyond that, it is difficult not to admire the brothers' painstaking efforts to portray the naïve religious faith of the nursing nun who is their heroine, her struggles to overcome the depression she suffers from at first, and, later, the temptation represented by Barnier, the student doctor with whom she becomes more friendly than she should. The Goncourts must have been aware that they were treading on dangerous ground: in 1861, any novel that could be construed as reflecting adversely on religious faith or institutions ran the gravest of risks of being suppressed. Hence the sister is a little idealized: this, at least, was Flaubert's opinion – Philomène, he said, was a saint, consequently exceptional. 'Why', he asked the brothers, 'did you not place alongside her the ordinary nuns, good sorts straight from the barnyard, as thick-witted as can be and sometimes pretty surly?' Flaubert, who had spent his childhood in a house adjoining the teaching hospital at Rouen, knew what he was talking about.

The lengthy second chapter, a Balzacian 'flash-back' over the nun's origins and childhood, is structurally clumsy but interesting in that it shows the Goncourts tracing with sympathy and imagination the life of a working-class girl. Her father, a locksmith, disappeared when she was three, her mother died when she was four, and the little orphan girl passes into the care of an aunt in domestic service. The mistress of the house spoils her, and eventually she is packed off to a convent school. The child's homesickness and gradual acclimatization are pictured with sympathy and insight; after her first communion she experiences a growing attraction to the religious life which in due time settles into a firm resolve to join the community of nursing sisters. There is nothing harrowing in this story, which is related with tenderness and simplicity, two qualities not often found in the Goncourts.

When in 1864 they wrote their challenging preface to *Germinie Lacerteux*, they referred to *Sœur Philomène* as having been inspired by the same principles as the novel that they were now publishing.

Living in the nineteenth century, at a time of universal franchise, democracy, liberalism, we asked ourselves whether what are called the 'lower classes' have not a right to the Novel; whether this below-stairs society, the common people, ought to remain indefinitely in a literary quarantine, disdained by writers who, till now, have been mute about whatever heart or soul it might possess . . . Today, when the Novel is increasing and extending its domain, when it is taking shape as the truly serious, truly passionate and living form of literary study and social inquiry, when thanks to psychological analysis and investigation it is transforming itself into the moral History of our age; today, when the novel has assumed the tasks and duties of science, it may claim its rights and privileges . . .

These lines, read rather more than a century later, may strike us as both pretentious and misguided; but they contain within them, in the implicit double appeal to the democratic spirit and the prestige of science, the seed of Zola's naturalism, which only Edmond, the surviving brother, was to watch, with a jealous eye, as it developed to full fruition. *Germinie Lacerteux* was, certainly, concerned with the 'lower classes'; and they are viewed dispassionately – not unsympathetically, but not with any marked indulgence either. Germinie's best quality is her deep devotion to her mistress, the decayed gentlewoman, who is pictured as her true support and her good angel, not her exploiter. Those who exploit Germinie all belong to her own class: it is the shopkeepers and artisans who impose on her good nature, provide her with her heartless lovers and reduce her to ruin, shame, and death. The Goncourts' 'lower classes' remind us of nothing so much as a shoal of sharks, turning to rend in blind fury one of their own kind as soon as they sense it to be wounded and defenceless.

The book ends not with Germinie's death in hospital but with Mlle de Varandeuil's shocked discovery of the depths of infamy to which her trusted servant and companion had fallen during her lifetime. But her first reactions, anger and disgust, give way eventually to more charitable reflections. 'She wondered if the poor girl was as guilty as certain others, if she had chosen evil, if circumstances, her bad luck in having the body and the destiny that were hers, if all these things had not made of her the creature that she was, a being compounded of love and suffering . . .' This one sentence, so easily missed, poses rather more acutely than the grandiloquent preface the fundamental problem raised by this, the Goncourts' best work – a problem that the later naturalist novel would also have to wrestle with: the question whether beings of limited education and ability, placed in the crushingly narrow environment of working-class life in the nineteenth century, could truly be held responsible for the evil that befell them. As determinism became, more and more, the central philosophy of the French realist school, the conflict between the hypothetical alternatives of personal responsibility and fatalism was bound to assume larger proportions and take on a deeper resonance.

FLAUBERT: 'L'ÉDUCATION SENTIMENTALE'

The Goncourts' novels, with the exception of the first, *En 18***, all appeared in the 1860s. Just before the Franco-Prussian War broke out in 1870 the younger brother, Jules, died; and although Edmond continued to produce novels down to 1884, these later works lack all the qualities of the earlier ones, either because Jules had always been the brighter spirit or because the habit of collaboration was so strong that once it was broken Edmond found himself unable to achieve anything significant.

A year before the war, on the eve of the downfall of Napoleon III, Flaubert brought out the second of his novels of modern life. Present-day criticism generally rates *L'Éducation sentimentale* as the supreme achievement of the French realist tradition; but recognition came slowly, and throughout the remainder of the century it was neglected by the wider reading public, maligned by the fashionable critics, and treasured only by a select group of literary connoisseurs. Even today it is probable that there are far more who have read and enjoyed *Madame Bovary* than there are who have read and appreciated *L'Éducation sentimentale*.

One charge that no one could lay against Flaubert in 1869 was that of repeating himself. In almost every respect the two novels are quite different. Flaubert had, in the interval, pared his style of the romantic efflorescence that had still characterized it in 1857: he uses fewer similes, the paragraphs tend to be shorter and less consciously structured, as do the sentences within each paragraph. The result is an altogether more taut and businesslike narrative style; Stendhal would surely have preferred it to that of *Madame Bovary*. The cast of characters is larger, as one would expect with the metropolitan setting of *L'Éducation sentimentale*; correspondingly, however, the characters lack the clearly defined outlines of those in the earlier novel, and on a first reading are apt to seem, many of them, vague, shadowy, indistinguishable one from the other. Connected with this, undoubtedly, is the fact that throughout the novel nearly everything is being shown from the point of view of the central character, Frédéric, even though he does not tell the story: like all the realists, Flaubert clung instinctively to the 'omniscient narrator' convention. The indeterminacy and lack of substance of the characters is due simply to Frédéric's inability – through inexperience – to form clearcut judgements about them.

As for the narrative itself, although there are plenty of incidents in *L'Éducation sentimentale*, very few of them impress us as being critical. *Madame Bovary* remains in every reader's mind as a succession of decisive events – Charles's first meeting with Emma, their marriage, the ball at Vaubyessard, the move to Yonville, Léon's departure to Paris, Rodolphe's seduction of Emma, Charles's bungling of the operation on Hippolyte's club-foot, and so on down to Emma's suicide, Charles's belated discovery of her infidelities and his subsequent death. *L'Éducation sentimentale* seems in contrast to be made up of a series of what the modern idiom would term 'non-events'. No one, for a start, dies, except Dussardier, who gets killed almost at the end. Similarly no one marries except, again almost at the end, Deslauriers, who marries Louise Roque whom Frédéric had thought to make his own bride. Both Dussardier's death and Deslauriers's marriage are unexpected, unheralded, and might as easily not have come about. There are at most two major turning-points in the book, one placed at the end of the first part, the other at the end of the second: Frédéric unexpectedly inherits a fortune from his uncle, and he spends a first night with Rosanette Bron. However, this second event could well be regarded as a non-event too, since Frédéric had been counting on taking Mme Arnoux to his love-nest that evening – Rosanette was merely a *pis-aller*.

One could sum all this up by saying that *L'Éducation sentimentale* is pervaded by a sense of aimless drift; it is very like life as Elbert

Hubbard defined it, 'one damned thing after another'; whereas the drama of *Madame Bovary* gives much more the impression of having been organized by an external agency: the author disguised as destiny. Charles Bovary, confronting Rodolphe after he has discovered the other man's treachery, blames the whole tragedy of Emma's death on fate: but this is probably done to avoid blaming himself – he had, earlier, decided that fate must have had a hand in the miscarriage of the surgical operation on Hippolyte. Flaubert was not committed to a fatalistic interpretation of the concatenation of events recounted in *Madame Bovary*, but the role of determinism is all the same strongly emphasized. We are provided with the fullest account of the 'pre-history' not only of Emma but of Charles too, and can see for our-selves how their subsequent behaviour is conditioned by their past. In *L'Éducation sentimentale*, on the other hand, we are given only a few, fairly insignificant facts about Frédéric's boyhood, and we are told nothing at all about Marie's past, not even how she met and came to marry Arnoux; throughout, indeed, her personality remains enigmatic, unexplained since she never explains herself to Frédéric.

Private determinism is replaced in *L'Éducation sentimentale* by the ebb and flow of the tide of history. The later novel gives far more space to historical particulars; it is no chance that an exact date, 15 September 1840, is given in the very opening sentence. With the exception of the last two chapters, which constitute an epilogue and are situated chronologically at approximately the moment when Flaubert was finishing writing the novel, the whole of *L'Éducation sentimentale* covers the period 1840–51: the last eight years of the July Monarchy and the brief span of the Second Republic, or in other words the period of Flaubert's own youth, when he was in his twenties, a student in Paris, precisely like his hero Frédéric. It is true that after 1842, when he fell ill, he spent more time at home and less in the capital, but he returned to Paris in time to witness the revolutionary days of February 1848; in particular he was present, along with Du Camp, at the sack of the Tuileries Palace, so that the account of this event given in the first chapter of Part III is for all intents and purposes that of an eye-witness.[13] The details Flaubert gives of the course taken by the revolution subsequently, in the spring and summer of 1848, are equally authentic from the historical point of view, though they were derived from printed sources (memoirs and newspaper files). The care Flaubert took to sift truth from legend was exemplary: not a single incident, not a single allusion to topical events in his characters' conversation was invented.[14] This historical realism was altogether different from the social realism of *Madame Bovary*, in which references to events of the time are so rare that the novel might almost be said to take place in a historical limbo.

But even though the forms that realism takes in these two books differ so widely, each can be said to explore in its own way the same underlying theme. The real subject of both is disenchantment, the movement from illusion to disillusion, or, in Baudelairean terms, from *l'idéal* to *le spleen*. Each of the two central characters embarks on life with a full complement of romantic preconceptions, and each is taught, by one disappointment after another, how false their first vision of life was. Necessarily, these preconceptions are second-hand. Emma derived hers from *Paul et Virginie*, the Waverley Novels, and various unnamed sentimental romances of the pre-Balzacian age; Frédéric read Goethe for *Werther*, Chateaubriand for *René*, George Sand for *Lélia*, homing instinctively on to the prototypes of sombre, misunderstood romantic genius. Each of the two characters expects to find the way to a paradise of sensual rapture and emotional fulfilment, where passion 'hovers like a great bird with pink plumage in the splendour of poetic skies'. The only difference is that Emma, being as we have seen possessed of a more active, virile temperament, moves from one affair to another, always hoping to light on the ideal lover, while Frédéric, more passive, more 'feminine' in the conventional sense, remains mesmerized by his first passion, from the very opening pages, when Marie Arnoux appears to him on the deck of a river steamer, with the pink ribbons of her straw hat fluttering in the morning breeze, to the very end, when, a quarter of a century later, she pays him a last visit, at dusk, only her eyes visible behind the black lace veil drawn over her face.

Frédéric's constancy does not imply fidelity; indeed, his 'sentimental education' could not have taken place at all if he had remained permanently transfixed in adoration of Mme Arnoux. She represents for him (though for no one else: Deslauriers, for example, judges her 'not bad, though there's nothing extraordinary about her') the Eternal Feminine, more divine than human, to be approached with reverential awe; beyond the reach of his grosser appetites, she is the Beatrice to his Dante. But he finds consolations and diversions: Rosanette, who incarnates carefree, venal sensuality, Mme Dambreuse, whose love promises to unlock for him the secret chambers of wealth and power, and Louise Roque, the untried girl who offers him the same worship as he will give only to Mme Arnoux. These varied experiences make, as the saying is, a man of Frédéric; this is the sense in which Flaubert's title is justified. But, just as Emma's quest for the ideal lover is never fulfilled (to the very end she keeps the picture in her mind of 'a strong, handsome being, valorous in nature, ardent and yet refined, with a poet's heart in an angel's form' whom she might still meet), so Frédéric is never able to possess the only woman he ever really wanted as mistress. At the very end, when years have passed and her hair is white, he suspects that her unexpected visit is a signal to him that her defences are down. He is assailed by the old desire, stronger, more frenzied than ever, but – proof that his education has borne fruit – he quells it: 'at one and the same time out of prudence and so as not to degrade his ideal, he turned on his heel and started to roll himself a cigarette.'

Frédéric resists temptation, while Emma seizes opportunities: this is the cardinal difference between the two characters. In a sense all Emma's dreams come true. She desires to marry, and a husband presents himself; she yearns for a lover, and she has her hour of triumph, seeing herself as one of the 'lyrical legion of adulterous women'; she longs to surround herself with luxuries, and Lheureux provides them – on terms. The trouble is that reality never fully measures up to her inflated expectations. For Frédéric the reverse happens, life compels him to sacrifice the reality and make do with the dream. Typically, on his first visit to a brothel as a schoolboy, he ran away before crossing the threshold, out of 'apprehension of the unknown, a kind of remorse, even the pleasure of seeing at a single glance so many women at his disposal'. But both *Madame Bovary* and *L'Éducation sentimentale*, however differently they end, tend to the same conclusion. Whether or not one's youthful aspirations are realized, the feeling one is finally left with is a frustration born of disenchantment which proves strong enough to drive Emma to suicide, though Frédéric stays alive, vegetating, ruminating on his wasted life. Granted, this reaction is found only among those who have absorbed the virus of romanticism. In both books Flaubert shows us realists – Homais, Martinon – egoists with limited aims who are satisfied with the rewards society is always ready to bestow on those who accept its values.

If the later novel impresses us as being, all said and done, a more important achievement, this is undoubtedly because its scope is so much greater. The most difficult problem facing Flaubert was, as he said, to keep a proper balance between background and foreground, so that the former did not encroach on the latter. He had to find a way of enmeshing the private dramas, spun out of Frédéric's relationships with the dozen or so men and women who play a part in his life, with the great public drama being enacted in France over the period of twelve years spanned by the main action of the novel. The problem was solved by discreetly establishing a whole series of indirect parallels and correspondences between the process of disenchantment as it develops in the course of Frédéric's 'sentimental education' and the great disenchantment of the country after the collapse of the hopes raised by the February Revolution. It is no accident that the occasion when Frédéric comes nearest to making the dream of his love for Marie Arnoux a reality coincides precisely with the outbreak of the revolution, that is, with the moment in time when the socialists came nearest to making the dream of a socialist republic a reality. Mme Arnoux fails to keep the appointed rendez-vous; and so, as we know, did France. Later in the book, Frédéric's vacillations between Rosanette, with her vulgar, lower-class origins, and the 'great lady', Mme Dambreuse, mirror the political waverings of Paris, as the fateful year wore on, between left and right, between a workers' republic and middle-class reaction, while the unattainable Mme Arnoux seems to incarnate the ideal harmonizing of class interests, hope for which was finally dashed at the end of 1851 – which is when the Arnoux family leaves France to enter into indefinite exile.

Similarly, the pairing of Frédéric and his old school-friend Deslauriers, who is the treacherous agent of most of Frédéric's misfortunes, is mirrored, on the political plane, by the coupling of Dussardier with Sénécal. Dussardier, simple-hearted, upright and idealistic, is the mouthpiece of the truly disinterested representatives of the left. Sénécal is the doctrinaire socialist, austere, an imperturbable debater, whose ambition is to establish a progressive society by dictatorial methods. In the end, logically, he throws in his lot with the Bona-partists. The last time we see him and Dussardier together is on the evening of 2 December 1851. The dragoons are galloping down the boulevards, sabres drawn, to clear the terrified inhabitants off the streets. Dussardier, standing on the steps of Tortoni's restaurant, advances a pace or two shouting: 'Vive la République!' – whereupon the nearest policeman, whom Frédéric, horrified, recognizes as Sénécal, runs him through the heart. The Empire has obliterated the Republic, the spirit of violence has extinguished the spirit of generosity: this is how we can spell out the symbolism if we choose – but Flaubert, having shown the incident, closes his chapter without adding a word.

L'Éducation sentimentale qualifies as the supreme masterpiece of French realism not merely on technical grounds – Flaubert's doctrine of impersonality was never better observed than in this novel – and not merely because it fulfils so admirably the aim of every great realist, to paint an exact and comprehensive portrait of the age of which he has the widest personal experience. Its best title to supremacy is, after all, that it stands as an embodiment of the realist critique of whatever runs counter to realism: that is, of romanticism, political idealism, and in general all philosophies of life that wilfully disregard the real conditions of life.

THE DOCTRINES OF NATURALISM

On 3 December 1872 Émile ZOLA (1840–1902) published a long essay on the future of the arts in France which would undoubtedly have attracted more attention than it did, had it appeared anywhere else than in a newly founded anti-government paper which in any case was suspended by ministerial order before the month was out.[15] The points Zola made in this article are worth summarizing, since they include – or adumbrate – most of the arguments he was to develop a little later, in the six-year-long press campaign he conducted in defence of the principles of what he himself had baptized naturalism.

In the first place, says Zola, it is time the arts were given their due. The military disasters of 1870, the threat of a complete breakdown of civil order, which was how many regarded the seizure of power by the Paris Commune in 1871, these traumatic events had resulted in a more severe crisis of confidence than the country had yet known. But France, beaten in battle, isolated diplomatically, facing the threat of financial and industrial ruin, and of class strife graver than that of any other modern state at the time, still remained, as Zola pointed out, supreme in one domain: nowhere in the world were there artists more skilled, writers more accomplished; European culture was still a dependency of French culture. It had been, as Zola readily admitted, an elitist culture, but he was hopeful this would change.

It is not true [he wrote] that the masses are disdainful of these things and refuse to understand them. They have still to be educated, that is the whole point. They have no knowledge of any art except officially approved art, which is no more than infantile picture painting. For the man in the street, art is a form of relaxation for the well-off, a priestly hocus-pocus, a religion he mistrusts. He must be told that art is truth.

Art is in any case a word that Zola dislikes, suggesting as it does conventional image-making, meaningless virtuosity. Life is more important than art, self-expression should replace servile obedience to the accepted canons. Why, in an age of scepticism, should we still pretend to bow down in adoration before aesthetic universals, still continue to pay lip-service to the dogma of transcendental beauty?

People have still not grasped that, if you are no longer sure of heaven, you are bound to believe only in a human art. If the skies are empty, if man denies divine authority, he abolishes the ideal, he has no absolute standard left, all he has is individual creation, the human spirit struggling to give birth. That is the guiding spirit of the modern naturalist school, which alone advocates the abandonment of the ancient fables. The mendacious art that thrives on dogmas and unassailable mysteries is gradually dying away as the tide of science rises; and I am constantly astonished that it has survived so long in the face of the spirit of analytical inquiry which has held the field over the past one hundred years.

Naturalist art, then, should bear the stamp of an individual creator who must be capable of inventing his own rules, without reference to tried recipes and guide-lines. But if it is also to be truthful, then it must be free, it must say what it has to say and refuse amputation even in the name of decency. The naturalists must be prepared to do battle with the hypocritical prudery of the bourgeois public.

I know of drawing-rooms where the hostess receives with every mark of politeness five or six women living in adultery, but where the company utters little shrieks of disgust at the mention of *Mademoiselle de Maupin* and *Germinie Lacerteux*[16] . . . The only anatomists who are tolerated are those who investigate dead civilizations. But to write of contemporary times, and to write about them as men determined to hide nothing, that is a betrayal of the tacit conspiracy of the hypocrites which horrifies our delicate gentlemen, who have just washed their hands and brushed their teeth after their latest bout of debauchery.

The declaration of principles that Zola enunciates here can still stand as a statement of what naturalism meant for him. In the coming years he would change certain emphases, attaching a little less importance to creative originality and considerably more to the function of art as the rival or working assistant of the natural sciences. Parts of the doctrine – like the rejection of historical fiction in favour of bringing the contemporary world into the novel, and the notion of a democratized art, one which would rely on a more broadly based public – were obviously common ground shared with Zola's predecessors, the authors of the theoretical articles that appeared in *Réalisme* in 1856–7. But the suggestion that the moral taboos of the 'polite' classes should be deliberately and ostentatiously flouted – this was new; and what is perhaps most strikingly original of all in this essay is the way Zola links developments in the novel with parallel developments in the art world. At any rate in 1872, naturalism was in his view a movement that was to bring about as many changes in the exhibition galleries of the future as it would in the world of books and on the stage.

Of course realism, when it was first given a name by Champfleury twenty years earlier, had been as much a painter's rallying-cry as one for writers; but in the context of pictorial art, realism had come to be associated almost solely with the work of Courbet, who was in no sense a 'writer's artist' even though he did paint a famous portrait of Baudelaire. In spite of the bridges that Baudelaire himself, and to a lesser degree Théophile Gautier, tried to build between literature and art, there had been under the Second Empire few real contacts between painters and writers. Flaubert, though capable of reacting with great intensity to certain pictures, paid little attention to current art trends, any more than did the Goncourts; if one excepts Gavarni, with whom they were on intimate terms of friendship, they more or less ignored contemporary artists, preferring to dwell on the neglected painters of the previous century, Watteau, Chardin and Fragonard. But Zola, thanks partly to the extraordinary stroke of fortune which gave him Paul Cézanne as his class-mate at Aix-en-Provence, found himself initiated at an early age into the aims and problems of the painter's art, and this fact was of major importance in determining the direction taken by his own. Though he could not claim to have 'discovered' Manet, he was the first critic (in 1866) to insist vociferously that this painter's work represented a significant advance on the accepted formulas of the French school of art. In the same year he defended in the press two unknown artists, Monet and Pissarro, with both of whom he was personally acquainted. What Zola appreciated in the work of Manet and the pre-impressionists was, in part, their efforts to arrive at a truthful representation of the scenes or persons they painted; and, beyond that, their readiness to break with tradition, to innovate, regardless of whether their innovations were acceptable to the critics and the art-buyers.

The outspokenness of his defence of these revolutionary painters gave Zola the reputation – which he was probably not sorry to have won – of a hot-head, a man with no delicacy of feeling, a brutal materialist. The novels he published before the Franco-Prussian War, especially *Thérèse Raquin* (1867), confirmed the view that he was a dangerous man with a perverted imagination. *Thérèse Raquin* is a remarkable work to have appeared when it did; it took realism several steps along the path that the Goncourts had ventured on, less than three years before, with *Germinie Lacerteux*. Zola begins by describing the origins and progress of a guilty love-affair between a Parisian shopkeeper's wife and a clerk working in a railway company, a thick-set, somewhat bovine young man who, infected by Thérèse's neurotic ardour, agrees to murder her husband so that they can marry. But after the drowning of Camille nemesis descends on Thérèse and Laurent: their overstrung nerves make them a prey to horrible hallucinations, mostly connected with the bloated corpse of Camille that Laurent has identified in the morgue; the two lovers turn against one another, and the novel ends with the mutually consented suicide of both.

The violence of this drama was something new in realism, but

Zola compounded his audacity by declaring in the most uncompromising terms (preface to the second edition) that he had written the novel deliberately to show characters devoid of moral scruples because they were totally motivated by their instincts; they were human beings, but they had no souls, they were, properly speaking, human animals. This was taking materialism much further than the Goncourts had, for Germinie never sank so low in depravity that she ceased to feel the pangs of remorse, whereas Thérèse and Laurent appear to experience nothing but bad dreams and a dread of detection. Zola acted in the firm belief that such conscienceless obedience to the promptings of lust and destructiveness was the reality behind the façade of decent, law-abiding behaviour that social conventions had erected. He was trying to look at humanity with the coolly dispassionate gaze of the scientist.

I hope it is beginning to be clear [he wrote in his preface] that my aim has been above all scientific . . . If this novel is read with care, it will be seen that each chapter studies one particular curious physiological case. In a word, I have tried to do one thing: given a vigorous man and an unsatisfied woman, to look for the beast in them, to shut my eyes, even, to anything that is not the beast, to cast them in a violent drama, and scrupulously to note the actions and sensations of these creatures. I have simply conducted on two living bodies the work of dissection that surgeons perform on cadavers.

The analogy established between the novelist and the scientist, particularly the anatomist or physiologist, is one that Zola was to elaborate profusely later on, when he came to write his essay on the 'experimental novel',[17] a notorious piece of special pleading which had been inspired by a reading of Claude Bernard's *Introduction à l'étude de la médecine expérimentale*. Zola never, it seems, noticed the basic fallacy in his argument (or, if he noticed it, he ignored it). The experimental research worker in the natural sciences deals in a reality external to him; he can arrange the conditions of an experiment that he sets up, but has no control over the issue. The creative writer, however carefully he may observe the real world and transpose it in his work, and however scrupulously he adheres to the internal logic of his characters' behaviour, in the last resort invents everything, including the way his characters react to the circumstances in which he has chosen to place them. This is another way of saying that the realist deals always in an interiorized reality. Everything in the world outside has to be filtered through his individual consciousness and processed in the matrix of his individual sensibility before it can emerge as an individually patterned rendering of the reality originally apprehended. If this were not the case, realist art would be uniform, differing only according to its subject-matter; whereas, as our account has amply demonstrated already, there were as many different realisms as there were major realist writers.

'LES ROUGON-MACQUART'

Shortly after the publication of *Thérèse Raquin*, Zola drew up his grand design for a series of novels intended at one and the same time to illustrate how the novelist might continue, in his own sphere, the work of the scientist, and to provide the same social panorama of the Second Empire as Balzac had attempted in respect of the Restoration period. *La Comédie humaine* had been a work both homogeneous and multiple; the numerous constituent stories had been linked together thanks to Balzac's intelligent use of the reappearing character.[18] Similarly, the different novels in Zola's projected cycle would be interconnected, though not by so obviously derivative a device. The bonding element would be the scientific 'hypothesis', as Zola called it: that certain genetic characteristics could be traced through in the life-stories of the offspring of an original coupling and in their offspring's offspring. The workings of heredity had been codified[19]; with a little imagination, a family could be projected of which the various members would illustrate the different mutations of the original hereditary strain.

However, class barriers being what they were in the nineteenth century, to confine himself to a single family would imply studying a single social *milieu*, and Zola's ambitions were large: he wanted to sweep into his net specimens of all the denizens of society at every level, from the ruling class down to the poorest labourers. He thought for a moment of having two families in conflict with each other, one successful, the other unsuccessful. Then a better idea occurred to him: it would be a single family with two branches, one legitimate, enjoying all the advantages of education and inherited property, the other illegitimate, outcasts from the very start. The legitimate branch, the Rougons, would give Zola his opportunity to study the rising middle class; it would include a lawyer who becomes a politician and rises to cabinet rank under Napoleon III; a financier, a company-promoter and stock-exchange wizard; and a man of science, a doctor. The illegitimate branch, the Macquarts, would provide a variety of lower-class types: a farm-labourer, a poor parish priest, a laundress, a railwayman.

The ingrained pessimistic strain in Zola's imagination required further that the history of this family would be one of decline and fall. The Macquarts clearly were destined for nasty and brutish lives, but even the Rougons are not permitted more than a brief phase of prosperity before decay sets in. It is genetic, rather than social catastrophe that awaits them. Either they remain celibate, or else the nemesis of an accelerated degeneration strikes at their children or grandchildren. The Rougon-Macquart family expands in the second and third generations, contracts in the fourth, while in the fifth nothing is left but a few weaklings, idiots or monsters who perish in infancy. What could be called the 'curse of the Rougon-Macquarts' lies way back, with the original founders of the line. The first Rougon, a market-gardener, was a robust if stupid peasant. But his wife, Adélaïde, was a hysteric; in old age she sinks into idiocy and spends the last twenty years of her life shut up in a mad-house. The lover she took after her husband's death, the smuggler Macquart, was an alcoholic; his descendants therefore suffer from a doubly vitiated heredity. No doubt unintentionally, Zola gave a strong moral slant to his interpretation of the working of the laws of genetics, never doubting that because the father drank, the children would inherit a craving for drink, and because the mother contracted an irregular liaison, her daughters and granddaughters would tend to be promiscuous. On the other hand, he showed himself well aware of the complexity and capriciousness of the processes of heredity. Genius being akin to madness, it was perfectly conceivable that the brother of a homicidal maniac might be an artist with quite extraordinary gifts – though even here, the taint in his blood will manifest itself: Claude Lantier, Gervaise Macquart's son, may be an artist of genius, but his genius is 'incomplete', he is incapable of fully realizing his potentialities, and drives himself to death as he wrestles with a task too heavy for him.

Zola subtitled his novel-series 'The Natural and Social History of a Family under the Second Empire'. By the 'natural history' of the family he meant the working out of the genetic disorders due to the sins and excesses of the original progenitors. The 'social history' refers to the other aspect of *Les Rougon-Macquart*, the attempt to rival Balzac's feat and provide a panoramic picture of the society of a given age.

The obvious difference between Zola's attitude to the imperial régime and Balzac's to the monarchies of 1815–48 was that Zola's was that of a left-wing republican whereas Balzac's had been that of a right-wing advocate of absolutism whose chief complaint against the way France was being governed in his day was that too much attention was paid to public opinion. Under the Second Empire Zola's political outlook was that of a convinced democrat, an anti-establishment rebel; he had, indeed, made something of a name for himself as an outspoken polemical journalist in certain opposition papers which were founded in 1868 after the liberalization of the press laws. When he drew up his plans for *Les Rougon-Macquart*, only eighteen months before the unforeseen and unforeseeable collapse of the Empire, it was part of his intention that these novels should form a reasoned indictment of the follies and abuses of the reign of Napoleon III. Zola was to be the Juvenal or the Suetonius of the Second Empire.

If he had hoped to play thereby an active part in discrediting and undermining the régime, he arrived too late on the scene, for the Second Empire had already bitten the dust by the time the first volume of the series was published. The introductory novel, *La Fortune des Rougon* (1871), was written to show how the original schism in the family arose; but it also had a politico-historical theme, since it incidentally described the short-lived resistance in Provence to the *coup d'état* of 1851 when Louis-Napoléon overthrew the constitution and made himself *de facto* dictator of France. Succeeding novels had been planned to denounce some of the more grievous scandals of the reign: the profiteering in land-values incidental on the replanning and rebuilding of Paris by Haussmann; the corruption of the morals of high society, attributed to the profligacy of Napoleon III and his court; the watchful surveillance by the secret police of the defeated republicans, and the occasional swoop to round up the more dangerous of them; the unholy alliance between the government and

the church by which the civil power was able to count on the
ecclesiastical authorities for support and vice versa; the perversion of
parliamentary institutions, the power struggles that went on behind
the parade of debates and votes of confidence. Zola did not abandon
his programme even though the leader of this sorry imperial pageant
had lost his crown and died in exile: the novels published between
1872 and 1876, from *La Curée* (*The Rush for the Spoils*) to *Son
Excellence Eugène Rougon* (*His Excellency*), deal with all those social
and political evils we have enumerated. Their subject-matter was,
as it happened, less dated than might be thought, for they all appeared
at a period when, even though republican institutions had been re-
established, the political climate – largely in consequence of the scare
provoked by the rule of the Commune in Paris between March and
May 1871 – was as blatantly reactionary as ever.

After the moderates' victory at the hustings in October 1877 the
danger of a reversion to right-wing government receded; and in the
Rougon-Macquart novels published between then and 1893 (when
the twentieth volume completed the cycle), the element of political
satire is far less apparent than it had been in the first half-dozen of the
series. Mostly, one is hardly aware of the Second-Empire setting. The
novels depict scenes which might as well have been enacted during
the early decades of the Third Republic: the career of a successful
courtesan (*Nana*, 1880), the expansion of a large departmental store
(*Au Bonheur des Dames* (*The Ladies' Paradise*), 1883), a strike in a
mining district (*Germinal*, 1885), the life of a rural community (*La
Terre* (*The Earth*), 1887), a struggle between two rival banks resulting
in a stock-exchange crash (*L'Argent* (*Money*), 1891). The case of
L'Œuvre (*The Masterpiece*) is particularly revealing. In this novel
(published in 1886) Zola included a fictionalized account of the rise
of the impressionist school of painters, which as a matter of history
straddled the two régimes; the first independent exhibitions by the
impressionists were not held until some time after the war, so that
in this novel the very pretence of a chronological limitation to the
period of the Second Empire is dropped. The novelist's need to have
his say about current and topical matters of interest was greater than
his compulsion to stick to the historical framework originally
envisaged.

ZOLA: FROM REALISM TO SURREALISM

Zola's realism depended for its authenticity chiefly on the fact-finding investigations that he undertook before embarking on a new novel. He read up his authorities; sometimes he entered into correspondence with specialists, such as the engine-driver Lefèvre who was one of his main informants about conditions of work on the railways. But the most characteristic method of documentation was the visit paid, notebook in hand, to the locale where the action of the novel was to take place. There were the tours he made of the new Central Markets in Paris in preparation for the writing of *Le Ventre de Paris*; the visits backstage for the theatre scenes in *Nana*; the trip to Anzin, while a strike was actually in progress, and the descent down one of the mines, before he started on *Germinal*; and the journeys he undertook to La Beauce and to the battlefields of the Franco-Prussian War in order to gather material for *La Terre* and *La Débâcle*. Such conscientiousness was exemplary, but it tended to result in a certain overweighting of the environmental side of the novels, which could have a crushing effect on the characters. Zola was not, in any case, much interested in the creation of compelling human figures, outstanding or mysterious personalities like Manon Lescaut, Gina Sanseverina, Vautrin or Hulot, who keep the reader wondering what extraordinary adventure they will plunge into next. One never encounters, in *Les Rougon-Macquart*, a character with this kind of unpredictability. If one analyses Zola's characters singly, one finds that they are sadly lacking in what is called autonomy. They rarely develop, they seldom if ever transcend their 'given' natures, they never surprise us. The parallel tracks of the railways in *La Bête humaine*, the parallel lines of cables down which the 'cage' descends to the depths of the pit in *Germinal*, are apt symbols of the strict control the novelist exercised over the individuals with whom he peopled his imaginary world.

But this does not necessarily mean that his characters are lifeless. The best of Zola's novels give as strong an impression of a living society as those of any of his predecessors. The individual characters may lack the power to interest us deeply, but the point is that they are never properly shown as individuals (except in a few of the less typical, less successful novels like *Une Page d'amour* or *La Joie de vivre*). They are normally presented as part of a network, as members of a community, and Zola achieves lifelikeness by concentrating on the way they interact. His characters quarrel, argue, fight, or court one another; they are shown working together, eating and drinking together, sleeping together. It is rare for them to withdraw into solitary contemplation; none of them is much given to private daydreaming. This is the fundamental difference between Zola's realism and that of Stendhal or Flaubert, whose characters periodically retire into the inmost chambers of the soul where only the author can watch them. One feels that no one, not even Mme de Rênal, ever understands or draws close to Julien Sorel, so secretive is he, and yet we, the readers, know everything there is to know about his inner life, thanks to Stendhal's revelations. Emma Bovary's daydreams are hidden from everyone, even from her husband, even from her lovers; though, again, not from us. Hence the strongly individual life of these characters, whereas all Zola's lead a fully public life which is public property. He animates them by showing them in conflict or forming alliances, plotting together or confiding in one another. The term 'social novel' takes on a new meaning, applied to Zola.

A community has to have a community centre, which is why Zola took so much care over the details of each of his settings. The topography of Verrières or Yonville cannot matter greatly if the real geography is that of the minds of Julien or of Emma. But the case is entirely different with Zola. We have said that the setting of *Le Ventre de Paris* (*The Belly of Paris*), the third volume of the Rougon-Macquart series, was the Paris provision markets, the 'quartier des Halles'. The opening chapter consists of a lengthy description of the buildings and lay-out, the stalls heaped high with produce, as seen by a tired traveller arriving in the early morning. Florent, the 'hero' of the novel, is an escaped deportee, one of the unfortunate republicans rounded up at the time of the *coup d'état* and shipped overseas to a penal colony. He has returned secretly to Paris, which has been transformed in his absence (the Halles were the first new buildings to be erected under Napoleon III's administration). The description of this novel architecture, of the picturesque labyrinth of streets and the garish display of fruit and vegetables, is thus justified up to a point by the surprise the scene evokes in the returning native; in addition, he is accompanied by a young painter, Claude Lantier, eager to point out to him all the curiosities. This type of opening was used over and over again by Zola. In *L'Assommoir* a bird's-eye view of the working-class district in which the novel is set is conveyed to us through the eyes of Gervaise Macquart, fresh from the provinces, who is observing it in the early morning from a hotel window high above the street. The scene in the bustling foyer of a Paris theatre which provides the setting of the first chapter of *Nana* is rendered as it strikes a young man, Hector de La Faloise, just arrived in town; he is being 'shown the sights' by his cousin. In *Germinal* it is Étienne Lantier's impressions of the mining district and the colliery itself that are given us in lieu of the straightforward, depersonalized description of a locality – a house or a town – that is found not infrequently at the beginning of a novel by Balzac.

The vividness of these opening chapters is enhanced by Zola's normal practice of showing the scene as it strikes someone unfamiliar with it. Such a witness will notice more than one who sees it every day; and his reflections will be those of a newcomer, of the novelist himself embarking on his 'documentary tour'.

As one reads on, it becomes evident that this opening chapter is no isolated piece of descriptive virtuosity, nor a simple setting for the action, as it tends to be, once again, in Balzac. Descriptive passages recur, as different parts of the neighbourhood are explored, or as the aspect of the whole changes according to the time of the day. These repeated studies of the same scene under different lights were, one remembers, a favourite exercise for some of Zola's painter friends, for Monet in particular. Finally it becomes apparent that the environment itself has been given a functional role of major importance. Thus Florent, to return to *Le Ventre de Paris*, finds himself overwhelmingly affected by the Halles, his resolution sapped, his vision blurred. A great uneasiness takes hold of him; even the fervour of his political convictions is weakened by the suffocating presence of all this food, tangible evidence of the new prosperity the Empire has brought to the Parisians but symbolizing, in a wider sense, the willingly consented substitution of affluence for liberty. Later still, the sense of this offensive fatness, conveyed by the piles of vegetables, the festoons of sausages, the pyramids of fruit and the pungent rounds of cheese determines a secondary reaction, and causes Florent to make a further, feeble attempt to overthrow the régime; it fails, of course, and with its failure and Florent's arrest and fresh deportation, the book ends.

The great novelty of *Le Ventre de Paris* was that the material setting of the story, the actual pillars and glass roofs of the Halles, were allowed to play at least as important a part in determining the course of the action as any of the characters. Humanity, in fact, seems in comparison quite powerless, dwarfed, oppressed, given over in bondage to an environment which seems almost literally to have a mind of its own. All Zola's more important, more characteristic novels give the same impression. The huge man-made complexes, buildings or machines, that figure in his books are part of the dramatis personae. The anthropomorphic cast of his imagination may make us think of some primitive skald rather than a frock-coated nineteenth-century writer with a neatly trimmed beard and a pince-nez. The retort for distilling alcohol, in *L'Assommoir*, strikes Gervaise's fancy when she first sees it as a sort of witch, the tubes and pipes like entrails with the venom coursing through them; but the image is repeated until what the reader knows, intellectually, to be inanimate is spoken of as though it were alive and actively malevolent. Whereas for Zola's predecessors, for Balzac in particular, the real furniture of his characters' lives is listed and described in order to give the reader useful information about these characters' status in society, about their habits and hobbies, in Zola these objects that he talks about as though they were demigods or hobgoblins are very often presented as though they were the directing entities ruling the characters' lives. They do not merely symbolize the forces that act on the puny human beings who crawl about in their shadow; they are these forces themselves, in tangible shape, with their density, their sheen, their threshing limbs or heaving flanks, with the glaring eyes or dripping fangs that pertain to the corporeal form they have adopted.

We have seen how Baudelaire proclaimed Balzac a visionary; had he lived long enough to read *L'Assommoir*, *Germinal* or *La Bête humaine*, would he not have recognized in Zola an even more striking demonstration of how realism, pushed beyond a certain point, merges into what Baudelaire himself called *surnaturalisme*? It is not as though Zola ever loses touch with reality or describes what is not there; his gift was to restore the living reality of what is universally registered by the mind or eye but either left unsaid or else expressed as a dead metaphor. It is a fact that an engine-driver – like a yachtsman or a motorist – will always use the feminine gender when referring to his locomotive, as though it were a live mare, or a live mistress. In *La Bête humaine* (*The Beast in Man*) Zola took this fact, this item of reality, and turned the 'iron horse' back into an actual she-animal of gigantic size, which had to be fed and watered, cossetted, urged on or reined in, which could on certain days be docile and on others restive, on which Jacques Lantier, the engine-driver, lavishes greater tenderness and affection than he ever gives to the soft-skinned, blue-eyed mistress who actually shares his bed. And when the time comes, the locomotive can fall sick, be wounded, expire in agony. One winter's day the train is marooned in a snow-drift; the intense cold and damp rob the engine thereafter of its former easy response to the controls, its youthful liveliness; it has become, as Zola says, 'crotchety and cantankerous, like a woman grown old, her chest affected by a bad chill'. When an accident at a level-crossing causes a disastrous derailment, Zola describes to us the engine's entrails spilled, the twin hearts of its pistons beating ever more feebly.

The giantess, disembowelled, ceased to struggle, slipped gradually into a very gentle slumber, and finally fell silent. She was dead. And the heap of iron, steel and brass which she left there, this crushed colossus with its riven trunk, its limbs sprawling, its bruised organs exposed to the light of day, took on the frightful melancholy of a vast human corpse, of a whole world that had lived and from which the life had been suddenly torn, in pain.

In passages like this, Zola's realism reaches out towards surrealism; in others, it seems to be evolving into a crude, popular form of symbolism. In *La Bête humaine* the trains careering swiftly along the tracks stand for the heedlessness of modern technological progress. The mile-deep throat (shaft) of the coal-pit in *Germinal* embodies the inhuman ferocity of capitalism, swallowing down and devouring the miners, its ration of wage-slaves, 'in mouthfuls of twenty, thirty men at a time, with such easy gulps that it did not seem to feel them pass.' Nana's rotting corpse, disfigured by a virulent disease, lying in a luxurious hotel room in the last chapter of the novel, symbolizes the decomposing régime, the Second Empire in its death throes, which had been, like Nana herself, so wanton, so spendthrift, so impudent in the hour of triumph.

Finally, it can be seen how the narrative form in *Les Rougon-Macquart* tends to crystallize in huge patterns which have been called myths. With his powerfully primitive imagination Zola was bound to be attracted to certain legends widespread in the ancient world, even though there may have been no deliberate attempt to re-adapt them. The myths of the fiery hell, of the frozen hell, and of the universal flood are all utilized in *Germinal*, as is the myth of the eternal return in *La Terre*.[20] *La Faute de l'abbé Mouret* (*Abbé Mouret's Sin*), which is of all the volumes in the cycle that which has least to do with realism in any ordinary sense, was in part a planned transposition of the myth of Adam and Eve in the Garden of Eden, including the eating of the forbidden fruit of the Tree of Knowledge and the expulsion from paradise by a jealous God. The whole of *Les Rougon-Macquart*, at least from *Nana* onwards, is strongly marked by the apocalyptic myth of the ultimate catastrophe, the day of judgement or the twilight of the gods, represented, of course, in the narrowly historical sense by the defeat of the French armies by Prussia in 1870. Zola devoted his nineteenth volume (*La Débâcle*) entirely to this disaster, though the twentieth and last (*Le Docteur Pascal*) can be said to be inspired by the contrary myth of renewal which had also informed, though less obviously, certain earlier works in the series such as *La Joie de vivre* and *La Terre*.

Now that the clichés of nineteenth-century criticism have withered away, and the conventional view of Zola as the 'poet of the cesspool', the writer obsessed by bloodshed and lust, poverty, disease and ugliness, has been largely discarded, the true import of his work has had a chance to emerge. Zola carried realism to its extreme limits, so that his successors, if they were to proceed at all, needed to go beyond realism. But his own art, for all the forays he made into surrealism, symbolism, and mythopoeia, remained solidly based on observed reality. He summed up the situation best himself, in a letter written to his disciple Henry Céard just after the publication of *Germinal*, in which he spoke briefly about his tendency to 'aggrandize the truth'. It was, he said, something of which Balzac and Hugo had been guilty as well as he, though in different ways.

We all falsify more or less, but what are the mechanics, what is the mentality of our falsifications? Now I may be wrong in this, of course, but I still think I falsify in the direction of truth. I indulge in hypertrophy of the truthful detail, I leap into the stars from the springboard of exact observation. The truth wings its way to the symbol.[21]

ALPHONSE DAUDET

A striking feature of the French cultural scene, at least since the seventeenth century, had been the tendency of writers to congregate in the capital, where their patrons lived and where, in the nineteenth century, all the most enterprising theatre directors worked and all the best-known publishers and review editors had their offices. The effects of this concentration of the literary talent of a whole nation in one city were not all good; but at least the interchange of ideas was facilitated, there was a certain intellectual excitement in the air to which the native Parisian became so addicted that he could not have lived without it, while foreigners on a visit to Paris (like Henry James) found it both exhilarating and exhausting. Such circumstances favoured too the formation of coteries, *cénacles*, informal literary gatherings, sometimes in the *salons* but often – especially if the writers concerned happened to be unmarried – in cafés or restaurants.

On 14 April 1874 Edmond de Goncourt recorded in his diary a dinner party in town which brought together round the same table four other novelists besides himself: Flaubert, Turgenev, Zola, and Alphonse Daudet. It was the first of a series of such dinners, named the 'dîners des auteurs sifflés' because every participant had written a play which had been hissed off the stage.[22] For the three older men, these parties must have seemed a pallid revival of the much livelier and bigger 'dîners Magny' of the pre-war years. But for Émile Zola and Alphonse DAUDET (1840–97), who belonged to a younger generation, the uninhibited talk over the brandy and coffee represented a privileged initiation into a hallowed fraternity, that of the revered pundits of realism.

These two were born within a few weeks of each other: Zola on 2 April, Daudet on 13 May 1840. Both came from middle-class families which had failed to make good and were slipping down the social ladder: Zola's father, a noted civil engineer, had died when the boy was six, leaving his widow ill provided for; Daudet's father was in the silk trade but ran into severe business difficulties shortly after Alphonse was born. Each of the lads was in his late teens when he made his way to Paris, Daudet in November 1857, Zola the following month. Here they both expected to win literary fame as poets. Zola could not find a publisher for his verse, but Daudet was luckier, though *Les Amoureuses*, a slim volume which came out in 1858, was almost totally ignored by the critics. Zola, who had no useful connections in the capital, endured great poverty for a period; Alphonse Daudet was spared this ordeal, thanks to the help given him by his elder brother Ernest. Both finally landed jobs which brought them a modest income – Zola as publicity manager for Hachette, the book publishers, Daudet as secretary to the Duc de Morny, a public figure very close to the Emperor – and both engaged in freelance journalism, sometimes writing for the same papers: it must have been in the editorial office of one of these that the two first met.

The parallelism of their careers, at least down to their late twenties, would be remarkable were it not that the two young men were entirely typical of their generation. Zola started writing realistic novels a little earlier, at a time when Daudet was still engaged in the fictionalized autobiography (*Le Petit Chose*, 1868) and the humorous story with a strong regional flavour (*Tartarin de Tarascon*, 1872). During and after the Franco-Prussian War Daudet, who remained inside the besieged city, took to writing factual, objective accounts of the scenes he witnessed in the Paris streets.[23] These exercises may have helped to set him on the path to realism, but undoubtedly the contacts he made with the other 'auteurs sifflés', their example, their encouragements and criticisms were equally responsible for the direction in which he developed; for Daudet was an impressionable man, with a great gift for adapting a new formula so that it became acceptable in circles where it might not have been tolerated in its crude state. *Fromont jeune et Risler aîné* (*Fromont Junior and Risler Senior*) was the first novel he wrote which purported to portray contemporary life in the metropolis (it was subtitled 'Mœurs parisiennes'). It concerned a business partnership which comes to grief through the enmity between the wives of the two partners – an unexceptionable plot for a realist novel. Published at the end of 1874, it was very well received and sold widely: an unexpected success which testifies to Daudet's cleverness in producing something that could pass as being thoroughly up-to-date and yet avoided jarring the tastes of his fashionable readership.

Balzac, whom Daudet admired as much as did the Goncourts and Zola, had been the first to use a 'commercial drama' in a novel, and comparison reveals more than one point of similarity between Balzac's *Histoire de la grandeur et de la décadence de César Birotteau* and Daudet's *Fromont jeune et Risler aîné*. In both books a total business failure is threatened, and in both the situation is saved only by the successful application or marketing of a new commercial invention. The difference lies in the attitude of each author to his material, Balzac's view of Birotteau's business manoeuvres being a good deal more balanced than Daudet's assessment of the activities of the house of Fromont and Risler. Daudet accepts without any noticeable reservations the intrinsic rightness of the private-enterprise system as worked by his firm of wallpaper manufacturers. Balzac, on the other hand, had been ironically critical of the process, perfected by Birotteau, of creating a demand for a product of doubtful efficacy (a hair-restorer) and then maximizing the profits that accrued from supplying it. One can widen this analysis to show how, all the way through his career, Daudet constantly recoiled from using realism for the purposes of genuine social criticism. Instead, he quietly underwrote the values of the bourgeois establishment of his day, which, as was only fair, rewarded him by buying his books and showering honours on him. *Fromont jeune et Risler aîné* was 'crowned' by the French Academy, a distinction never bestowed on any of Zola's works any more than it had been on Flaubert's.

Jack (1876), the novel that followed *Fromont jeune*, illustrates even more clearly the confusion of values that constituted a fundamental defect in Daudet's handling of realism. The book starts with an interview between a priest, the director of an expensive private school in Paris, and Jack's mother, who has come to solicit a place for her boy. Her application is turned down on the spot, the headmaster sensing immediately, in spite of the fashionable carriage and rich clothes she is wearing, that this fine lady is, as the saying was, 'no better than she should be'. The most he is prepared to concede is that the boy should attend as a boarder, provided no one catches sight of his mother when she visits her child at the school. 'You must under-stand', he tells her, 'that the institution I am in charge of requires of the families that entrust their children to me an exceptionally high standard of morality.' There is nothing in this scene to suggest that Daudet saw anything to criticize in the priest's priggish and insulting stand. He accepted without question the propriety of the social ostra-cism to which women living in an 'irregular' situation were condem-ned by bourgeois opinion; and even if he does hint that there is something a little harsh in penalizing the offspring of a casual liaison for a 'sin' that the child most certainly did not commit, all the same the blame is not, as Daudet saw it, to be attached to society, but only to the perverse or misguided woman.

This is only one incident, though one that is both typical and signi-ficant. The real subject of *Jack* is a much deeper injustice done to the hero, when he is forced by those in charge of him to become appren-ticed to a trade, a tyrannical act which condemns him to become a manual worker instead of following what is now called a 'white-collar' profession. The boy is befriended by a good-hearted country doctor who, hearing of the plan, tells him to ask his parents 'what you have done to them to make them want to degrade you in this way, make you their inferior'. He then warns Jack's mother: 'To turn your child into a workman is to alienate him from you for all time . . . The day will come when you will blush for him, when you will find that his hands have grown horny, his speech coarse, that your sentiments and his have nothing in common.' In a sense Dr Rivals is right: manual labour, especially in the steel-works to which Jack is sent, was brutalizing and degrading. Workmen did not have full civic rights; they were required by law to carry conduct-books (*livrets*) in which any slackness or any act of insubordination would be noted by their employer. Boys (Jack is twelve when he starts his apprenticeship) were made to work killing hours in conditions where the risks of injury, even of fatal accidents, were unacceptably high. As a realist, Daudet shows us all this, in the chapters of the second part where Jack is learning his trade and then exercising it, as a stoker on a steamship. Yet the implied argument of the entire novel is not that such condi-tions are inhumane and wrong under any circumstances, but that it was wicked to condemn a boy like Jack, not born into the working class, to undergo the toil, fatigue and dangers that were inseparable from factory employment. Daudet's observations were sound, his reporting of them honest; but instead of using his material (as, for example, Zola was to, ten years later, in *Germinal*) in order to call into question the justice of an industrial system based on the unrestricted exploitation of human labour, he narrowed his scope to the consideration of one particular, highly atypical case. The unspoken assumption behind *Jack* was one widely shared by his middle-class readers: that the workers, being a grosser, coarser race of beings, were not greatly to be pitied since they were too insensitive to suffer from the conditions in which they lived and worked; the unpardonable cruelty was to force an intelligent, delicately nurtured child from a middle-class home into their way of life.

Another set of conventional values that Daudet accepted without demur and incorporated into his novels was that which governed the role of women inside and outside marriage. His own experiences almost certainly affected his outlook: an early liaison (with Marie Rieu, to whom the volume of poetry already mentioned, *Les Amoureuses*, was dedicated); then marriage, at the age of twenty-seven, to a strong-minded, intelligent woman, an excellent hostess and herself a writer of distinction capable of criticizing constructively her husband's work. In his novels a triangular pattern recurs with suspicious regularity. It involves a frivolous, pleasure-seeking woman, using her sexual charm to entrap the weak-willed, sensual man and estrange him from his wife, who is presented as a person of unshakeable integrity, not so much jealous of her husband's mistress as offended that he should take one. This is the configuration of the adultery drama in *Fromont jeune et Risler aîné*, in *Les Rois en exil* (*Kings in Exile*, 1879), and in *Numa Roumestan* (1881). But the most interesting novel, from the point of view of what it tells us about Daudet's conceptions of women's proper place in society, is *Le Nabab* (1877). The same triangle can be discerned, but this time the male member is entirely worthy and, moreover, still a bachelor: an attractive and intelligent young man, Paul de Géry is employed by Jansoulet, the 'nabob' of the title, as his private secretary. There are two young women between whom his fancy wavers. One of them, Félicia Ruys, is a highly talented sculptress, the natural daughter of an artist, who, when he died, left her virtually alone in the world and unprotected. She is clear-sighted and has gained, at second hand, a wide-ranging and disillusioning experience of men. Currently, her favours are being sought by two libertines, one the all-powerful Duc de Mora, a character obviously moulded on Daudet's one-time employer the Duc de Morny. Félicia would willingly barter her artist's freedom and independence for the security and protected status of a married woman, and even thinks for a while of Jansoulet, crude, uncultured, and middle-aged though he is. But it transpires that Jansoulet is married. Then she is drawn towards Paul, as he to her; but he is too sensible to think of taking as wife so emancipated a young woman. Instead, he becomes engaged to the eldest daughter of an honest bank clerk. Aline is a stay-at-home, a domesticated, quiet little person who runs her widowed father's household efficiently, caring for and giving lessons to her four younger sisters. Daudet likens her to a queen bee, 'concerning herself only with the hive, never once leaving it to buzz round the flowers in the open air'. The moral is clear: better for a woman to stay indoors, in the warm hive, than to lead any sort of an independent life where she risks becoming the prey of unscrupulous males. So that there should be no doubt about his meaning, Daudet makes Félicia, in despair and exasperation after realizing that Paul is lost to her, yield to Mora's solicitations. The reader is left to imagine her unhappy life thereafter, with her blighted reputation, and no prospect of ever leading a wholesome domestic life.

The five novels that Daudet wrote between 1874 and 1881 must be accounted works of realism since they sprang from a deliberate effort on the author's part to provide just such a picture of contemporary life as had been achieved by his elders, Flaubert and the Goncourts. He used the methods they had perfected, including the *voyage de documentation* (he visited, for instance, the steel-works of Indret, on the Loire, before writing the middle section of *Jack*). His characters were very often based on reality; in *Le Nabab* he transposed the story, which was public property at the time, of a certain millionaire who, having made his pile in Egypt, came to Paris with ambitions to represent the electorate in the Chamber, and within a very short space of time was fleeced of all he had; the original of Jack existed – a young workman whom Daudet helped to a better job in Algeria, where, however, he died of tuberculosis at the time of the Franco-Prussian War. However strained and artificial the plot of *Fromont jeune et Risler aîné*, there are scenes in it which have the ring of authenticity:

the workshop where Sidonie learns how to make necklaces of artificial pearls; a page or two describing a Saturday pay-day in the factory area of Paris; and the account of Désirée's night at the police station after she has tried to drown herself in the Seine. But the realism is, all the same, indisputably superficial; the novels are not slices of life or cross-sections of society, but carefully wrought artifices, often with highly intricate plots, designed to give the impression of realism since realism was in a fair way to becoming modish. The fact remains that Daudet did not really want to discover and lay bare the truth about the society of his time. He wanted to argue certain social theses and this is what he did increasingly as time went on. Already *Numa Roumestan* is almost a thesis novel, a book containing a sustained and astonishingly virulent attack on what Daudet considered to be the shortcomings of the southern French compared to the northerners. In his later novels he increasingly adopted the tone of the preacher. *L'Évangéliste* (1883) is an attack on religious bigotry and a warning against allowing the young and impressionable to fall into the hands of fanatics; *Sapho* (1884) was written to put young men on their guard against designing harpies; and so it went on. It is only fair to say that Zola too, after the completion of *Les Rougon-Macquart* in 1893, fell into the same trap of didacticism, as did Tolstoy during the last forty years of his life. The realist, perpetually studying social problems of one sort or another, is perhaps peculiarly subject to the temptation of offering his own home-grown solutions.

JORIS-KARL HUYSMANS

The naturalist 'school', in so far as it ever existed, was constituted in 1877; on 16 April a much publicized dinner party at the Restaurant Trapp was given in honour of Flaubert, Edmond de Goncourt and Zola by a group of five younger men who included Huysmans and Maupassant. Three years later the same five joined with Zola in composing a collection of short stories on the theme of the recent war. Originally, this volume was to be given the title *L'Invasion comique*; but not all the episodes related were comic, and in any case the Franco-Prussian War was not something to be laughed about; so instead the book was issued as *Les Soirées de Médan*, Médan being the name of Zola's suburban retreat. By implication, the five young contributors were to be regarded as Zola's disciples, though at the time (1880) none of them had given the slightest evidence of possessing literary ability of any sort, excepting only Huysmans.

The books for which Joris-Karl HUYSMANS (1848–1907) is chiefly remembered today, *À Rebours* (*Against the Grain*, 1884) and the series of novels, beginning with *Là-bas* (*Down Yonder*, 1891), which deal with the conversion of the sceptic Durtal to Roman Catholicism, all belong to his post-naturalist period. The works of his first period, with which we shall be concerned here, have suffered undeserved eclipse by having to compete for critical attention with the later ones. They are usually regarded as products of naturalism, and there can be little doubt that in the late 1870s Huysmans was a sincere admirer of Zola's art, though not necessarily of the most 'naturalistic' aspects of it.

He was the first of the group to start reading Zola; an unexpected windfall, a bonus payment from his employers, allowed him to buy copies of *Thérèse Raquin* and the early volumes of the Rougon-Macquart series. His enthusiasm infected his friend Henry Céard, another future *médaniste*, and it was Céard, bolder than Huysmans, who looked up Zola's address and presented himself at his door, telling the astonished and slightly embarrassed author: 'I have read all your books and find them most impressive, which is why I have come to see you.' Zola, once he was satisfied he was not being hoaxed, made his visitor welcome and told him to bring along his friends, particularly Huysmans.[24]

Later in the same year (1876) Huysmans sent a long article entitled 'Émile Zola et *L'Assommoir*' to his Belgian friend Camille Lemonnier, who published it in the literary weekly *L'Artiste* of which he was editor. *L'Assommoir* was currently appearing in serial form and creating a furore; in his article, Huysmans discussed as well all the preceding novels in the series, and offered his own definition of naturalism, in which he faithfully echoed the arguments – and even the terminology – that Zola had used in the preface to *Thérèse Raquin*:

Given, as subjects for study, a man and a woman, we wish to show them acting in an environment that we can observe and render with a scrupulous care for detail; we wish if at all possible to take apart piece by piece the mechanism of their virtues and vices, to dissect the love, indifference or hatred which will result from the temporary or permanent association of these two beings. Grave or gay, we are showmen exhibiting animals!

The passage shows how close, in 1876, Huysmans's ideas were to Zola's. He places the same emphasis on the importance of a careful study of environment, he shares Zola's mechanistic theories of human psychology, he uses the same analogy of surgical dissection to describe the novelist's analysis of behaviour.

The four novels that Huysmans published during his naturalist phase, *Marthe* (1876), *Les Sœurs Vatard* (1879), *En ménage* (1881) and *À vau l'eau* (1882), are, none the less, highly individual creations which could never be mistaken for products of Zola's pen, even though they fully satisfy the naturalist aesthetic as Huysmans himself had formulated it in his 1876 essay on Zola. In fact, Zola was the first to point out publicly[25] that it would be wrong to regard Huysmans as one of his disciples: he had always been an independent, a master in his own right.

Huysmans's individuality emerges in three separate aspects of his work: in his prose style considered as such; in the very special urban background he created for his stories, one of sleazy dance halls, steamy restaurants serving dubious comestibles, noisy bars and poky, inconvenient apartment-houses; and, thirdly, in the black pessimism implicit in his treatment of the relations between the sexes.

His narrative and descriptive style was conspicuously idiosyncratic, emphatically not the neutral, transparent medium of communication which one would suppose might be best suited to a soberly 'scientific' transcription of reality. This style, though owing something to the Goncourts' *style artiste*, was more distinctive and more elaborate than anything they had put their names to. A conscious blending of archaisms with neologisms gave Huysmans's prose an intensely bookish air: no one could call him obscure, but he does not make for easy reading. There is no real comparison with the special language forged by Zola for *L'Assommoir*, which made clever use of contemporary colloquialisms, of the racy back-chat of the denizens of slumland, and so succeeded in being widely understood. Huysmans's style may be judged to distort, over-colour the reality it is supposed to be rendering: this certainly was Flaubert's opinion: 'Rhetoric is turned inside out, but it's still rhetoric,' he told Huysmans. 'It pains me to see a man as original as you ruining his work with puerilities of this sort.'[26] But Huysmans may well have thought that his works would have been altogether too drab if he had to rely solely on his dispirited characters moping in their mundane surroundings. His style can be considered a sort of violent seasoning, a peppery sauce without which the meat, the subject-matter of his novels, would have been unendurably tasteless and unappetizing.

If it is the sign of a great novelist that he can create and make convincing a particular environment, with its sights, sounds and smells, then one cannot deny that in this respect at least Huysmans achieved greatness in these early novels. His street scenes and his interiors are painted with such intensity of feeling that he almost always avoids giving that impression of chilly non-participation which spoils so many carefully observed and exactly pictured scenes in the novels of the Goncourts, for example, and even in *L'Éducation sentimentale*. The fact was that for years Huysmans had inhabited this particular environment; he had hardly known any other. Born in Paris, educated in Paris, he had followed his career as a civil servant in Paris, and it was only during the war and on the occasional brief business trip to Brussels that he had ever left Paris. Like the characters in his novels, he had tramped the streets of the city or traversed it in public conveyances – the horse-drawn buses and trams of the day. Having no proper home of his own he was obliged to dine out most evenings and underwent all the distressing experiences of badly cooked meals and poor service undergone by M. Folantin, the hero of *À vau l'eau* (*Drifting Downstream*), who like him is a government clerk subsisting on an inadequate salary.

Huysmans rarely needed to collect 'documents' for his novels: for the most part he wrote out of personal experience. He had frequented, as an occasional client, the kind of brothel of which his first, unhappy heroine, Marthe, becomes an inmate. At his mother's death he had inherited the bookbinder's establishment from which she had drawn her income, and could therefore describe at first hand the rowdy, cheerful, smelly and stuffy atmosphere which is one of the main settings of *Les Sœurs Vatard* (the two sisters referred to in the title are both bookbinders by trade). From talking to the various working-class girls who temporarily shared his life, he knew how cruelly most of them were exploited at work and could conjure up the reality behind the consecrated phrase: 'sweated labour'.

If in winter you were shut up in draughty rooms like that, heated by coke fires, where already at two in the afternoon they light the gas-jets, which are hung so low they burn your hair and make it fall out; if you had to be there in the stifling heat of the summer, surrounded by a lot of other girls who pull off their dresses to cool themselves, and slip their bubs out of their bodices to see who's got the heaviest and firmest; if on top of all that you had to live through three or four months of short time during the slack season, you'd soon stop laughing.

Jeanne, a dressmaker by trade, forgets to add that she works a twelve-hour day when there is work (from eight in the morning till eight at night) and, even so, never earns enough to keep herself and is forced to live with a man if she is not to starve.

En ménage, which gives us these glimpses of the life of the poor, is not strictly a working-class novel, as was its predecessor *Les Sœurs Vatard*. This earlier work of Huysmans is a mine of information about the way of life of the Paris wage-earners in the early years of the Third Republic: information conveyed not drily, but not, either, with any noticeable accents of pity or indignation on the author's part. Céline Vatard becomes, halfway through the novel, the model, then the mistress, of an unsuccessful artist, Cyprien Tibaille, and it is his disillusioned view of her slatternly habits, her ignorance, her rapacity, her ignominious tastes in entertainment, and her instinctive hostility to whatever she cannot understand or appreciate, that Huysmans conveys to us in the later chapters of the novel. Cyprien is one of several characters that he pieced together out of fragments of self-observation, and this trick of turning the novels into modified autobiographies is a further sign that Huysmans's allegiance to naturalism was not total. Robert Baldick was probably right in saying that *En ménage*, the longest and most ambitious of the products of Huysmans's first period, was 'no typical naturalist work, no sociological study in the Zola tradition, but a personal novel that looks back to Benjamin Constant and forward to Proust'.[27] Cyprien reappears in *En ménage*, but more space is given in this later book to André Jayant, a writer

whose books have been coolly received by the critics, who has few
contacts in the world of letters and no close friends except Cyprien,
with whom he theorizes endlessly about art and women.

En ménage (the title could perhaps best be rendered by a modern
colloquialism, *Shacked Up*) has as its fundamental theme the difficulty
of a reasonably satisfactory relationship between the sexes. In the
opening chapter André and Cyprien are wandering about Paris at
night, the painter holding forth eloquently and endlessly on his
favourite subject, the odiousness of all women, young or not so
young, rich or poor, intelligent or stupid. As if in confirmation of
his friend's uncompromising misogyny, André discovers, when he
lets himself into his flat after parting from Cyprien, that his wife,
thinking he would be spending the night out, has taken the opportunity of going to bed with a stranger. André coolly unlocks the
front door to let the man out, packs his own belongings, and leaves.
Berthe returns to live with her uncle and aunt.

The rest of the book is taken up with André's gradual discovery,
through trial and error, that one cannot live long without women,
but that equally there is no really satisfactory way of living with
them. Visits to brothels do no more than temporarily satisfy certain
physiological needs. A regular, weekly arrangement with a sort of
nineteenth-century call-girl suits him for a while, but it is a poor
substitute for the sympathy and companionship that he craves. Then
Jeanne, the working-class girl with whom he lived for a while before
his marriage, gets in touch with him, and they set up together in his
bachelor flat. But this relatively happy interlude comes to an end.
André is not rich enough to support her, so she has to continue to go
out to work; and when a chance of better-paid employment in
London occurs, she leaves him. The book ends with André weakly
agreeing to take back his wife.

More than anything else, it is the pervasive mood of defeatism in
En ménage that reminds one of Flaubert's *Éducation sentimentale*. It is
not that André is one of fate's playthings, any more than was Frédéric
Moreau; he is not pursued by misfortunes like M. Folantin, the
wretched hero of *À vau l'eau* – this would have made him a mere
caricatural victim, of a kind possible only in a novel as short as *À vau
l'eau*. Far from being constantly dogged by ill-luck, André is really
rather spoilt by fortune. To discover Berthe in flagrant adultery, as

he does, is a tremendous stroke of luck; he has long since grown tired of her, and in the circumstances he can break with her, conserving all the rights of the injured party. After a little trouble, he finds himself comfortable quarters in an interesting neighbourhood, and secures the services of a housekeeper who looks after him reasonably well and does not rob him outrageously. He is lucky in coming across Jeanne again, and even more in finding that, over the five years during which he has lost touch with her, her flesh has kept all the springiness he used to appreciate. But nothing is perfect, or not for long, and André is adept at noticing the imperfections of any situation. Above all, he can never make any progress with his book; married, celibate, or cohabiting with his seamstress, he never finds himself in the mood to settle down to work. His life is undermined by pointlessness. André is a failure, *un raté*, a good enough fellow, but weak-willed, cowardly, mediocre. In a fit of lucid self-examination, at the end of the book, he remembers the comment 'fair' that always appeared on his school reports, and he tells himself that this verdict is applicable to everything he has ever done. 'He had been Mr Everyone, with an insignificant personality, one of those poor fellows who lack even the supreme consolation of being able to rail against an unjust fate, since an injustice presupposes at least some unrecognized merit, some power.'

The reason why Huysmans eventually turned against the realist novel was that his kind of realism inevitably led to this sort of spiritual bankruptcy. Lacking Zola's robust faith in life, in the future of humanity, in the transformation of society that would be brought about by the extensions of scientific inquiry and the applications of scientific discoveries, he unfailingly drifted into the mood of sardonic pessimism which he voiced at the end of *En ménage* and, with even greater bitterness, on the last page of *À vau l'eau*. His next work, the bizarre *À rebours* (1884), presents a hero who is neither working-class nor *petit-bourgeois*, but an aristocrat rich enough to satisfy the strangest caprices; and Des Esseintes very deliberately avoids living in the real world, devoting himself instead to everything that is most artificial, perverse, and unnatural. 'Nature', he proclaims, 'has had her day; the disgusting monotony of her landscapes and skyscapes has finally proved too much for refined and sensitive temperaments.' Not only nature, but naturalism too had had its day, in Huysmans's opinion.

À rebours ushered in a new kind of literature, the literature of aestheticism, decadentism, symbolism. Zola, reading it, realized he had lost a convert; the Abbé Mugnier, seven years later, was to know he had gained one.

GUY DE MAUPASSANT

Although the more old-fashioned histories of French literature make much play with 'masters', 'schools', and 'disciples' (no doubt by analogy with the history of art), it is hard to find a genuine example of one writer teaching another his craft, authorship being an essentially solitary pursuit. The apprenticeship to literature that Guy de MAUPASSANT (1850–93) underwent at the hands of his master Flaubert is one of those rare instances. His mother was the sister of one of Flaubert's closest school-friends, Alfred de Poittevin, an uncle whom young Guy never knew since he was born two years after De Poittevin's premature decease. But Flaubert remained in touch with his dead friend's sister, and when Guy, after the war, took up a post in the civil service, he encouraged the young man to visit him at weekends for informal lessons in the art of literary composition. This tuition went on for several years. Maupassant started by thinking of himself as a poet and dramatist: the poems, of a lightly erotic kind, were in due course published, and a comedy of his called *L'Histoire du vieux temps* was produced in 1879. Flaubert was not well enough to attend, but the initial success won by his pupil delighted him.

Flaubert had introduced him to Zola, and Maupassant started visiting Médan along with the other young writers whom Zola was gathering about him; truth to tell, he appears to have spent more time on the nearby river – he was an indefatigable oarsman – than discussing the niceties of naturalism. We have seen how an after-dinner swopping of war stories led to the decision to bring out a collaborative volume, ultimately called *Les Soirées de Médan*. As soon as it appeared, there was a universal chorus of praise for Maupassant's contribution, a story called *Boule de Suif* which showed more promise and talent than all the others put together. Flaubert was able to read it, and some of the reviews, before a stroke carried him off later that year (1880).

The title of the story (a literal translation would be 'tallow ball') refers to the central character, whose nickname it is. A cheerful prostitute with a thick body, she is one of an assorted coach-load of refugees, fleeing from Rouen before the advance of the Prussians and hoping to reach the coast, and safety, before the enemy arrives. The others include a prosperous business couple, a member of the landed gentry and his lady, a clerk in holy orders and a couple of nuns. They are all mortified to find themselves forced into such disgusting proximity with a girl of her sort, though they unbend when she opens her hamper and offers to share the contents – Boule de Suif is the only one with enough foresight to have brought provisions with her.

Somewhere along the road the coach is intercepted. After due parley, the German officer in charge of the detachment agrees to let the party proceed the following morning, provided Boule de Suif spends the night with him. The unexpected happens: the disreputable tart proves to be so staunch a patriot that she will not hear of pleasuring a Prussian. There follows a scene very typical of Maupassant's sour humour, as the highly respectable citizens of Rouen, representing authority, property and religion, make a concerted effort to argue the girl out of her scruples, realizing that otherwise they will never be able to reach their ship and secure their passage to a neutral country. They plead with her, browbeat her, try to bribe her; the priest urges her that her spiritual duty is to sacrifice herself to the good of all. Maupassant allows his narrative to make his point for him: the *fille publique* has a finer sense of her own dignity and that of her defeated country than any of the upright, uptight cowards who want only to escape in time from the hardships of a military occupation. Having no 'honour' in the cant sense of the term, she has more true honour than any of them.

It would be tempting to interpret *Boule de Suif* as first and foremost a piece of class criticism, especially in view of the final scene: the girl, having given way to the shameless pressure of her compatriots and satisfied the German officer's whim, is seen seated in the carriage the following day with the same group of travelling companions. They are now in the best of spirits and, far from showing any gratitude to their humble deliverer, ignore her as she sits there quietly weeping, and do not even extend to her the ordinary charity which she had spontaneously dispensed to them the previous day; for this time they have provisions, she has none, and they will not share. Maupassant has written a brutal, rather crude satire on the selfishness of the well-to-do, the hypocrisy of the clerical class, the inhumanity, even, of political idealists, represented in this story by a left-wing agitator, Carnudet, who has watched the proceedings sardonically, without taking the girl's side: for, typically, she is a Bonapartist not ashamed to voice her compassion for the fallen Emperor in his misfortunes.

Although many of his subsequent works, and especially his second novel, *Bel-Ami,* could easily be regarded as class satire, with the middle classes – the financiers, the bureaucrats, the clergy – bearing the brunt of his displeasure, it is doubtful whether Maupassant's writing was primarily inspired by so limited an aim. Rather, his quarrel is with the falsity of certain attitudes which he found more widespread in these sections of the community than in others. His mission – in so far as it transcended the mass-production of beautifully manicured short stories – was to deflate the pretensions of people who, as the tell-tale phrase has it, do their best to 'keep up appearances'. The appearance belied by an underlying reality provides the true target of his attacks. This is why many of his best-known stories are set among the shabby-genteel – the people who have to struggle most to 'keep up appearances' in difficult circumstances. He likes to show them at critical moments when the effort to do so is at its grimmest – when, for example, the fear of losing a legacy conflicts with the heirs' sense of proper respect for the dying, or when a family, having vaunted the mythical millions that one of their members is piling up in America, come across him selling oysters on a pleasure steamer bound for Jersey, and are terrified in case this ragged sailor should claim acquaintance.[28] Not all of Maupassant's stories are as bitter as these two. The vein of satire alternates with one of boisterous good humour, but it will almost always be found that the more jovial stories concern villagers and farm-workers – people who have no need to keep up appearances. It is also most often the peasantry who afford instances of the more positive virtues: true fearlessness, implacable resolution.[29]

Maupassant saw himself as the kind of realist whose one merit was that his vision penetrated further than that of the average observer. Had the Curies' discovery been made at the time, he would no doubt have used the analogy of the X-ray. 'The realist,' he stated in one of his rare theoretical essays, 'if he is an artist, will seek not to expound to us a banal, photographic view of life, but to provide a vision more complete, more gripping, more searching than reality itself.' To do this, the realist must be able to select the unique moment of truth, and he must make his point by the use of pure narrative, without analysis or authorial comment. The short story, the form that Maupassant developed single-handedly and on which he imprinted the stamp of his own peculiar genius, did not of course permit any extended philosophical or psychological development; the narrative line had somehow to bear the whole weight of the message. The story-teller, simply by telling his story with the right emphasis, must contrive to penetrate below the surface of the 'banal, photographic view of life' and reveal the underlying, often shocking, often appalling truth, the only truth the realist, 'if he is an artist', can be interested in.

Thus *La Parure* (*The Necklace*, 1880), perhaps the best-known of Maupassant's briefer short stories, picks out two crucial episodes in the life of the heroine, Mme Loisel. She and her husband, a minor government clerk, are invited to a ball. Having no jewellery of her own, she borrows a diamond necklace from her richer school-friend, Mme Forestier, and loses it in the cab on the way home. This is the first episode, from which we are transported, after only a short transition passage, to the second, occurring many years later. In the interval Mme Loisel has grown stout, ugly, careworn and workworn, for in order to pay for the replacement of the lost necklace she and her husband have condemned themselves to a life of grinding poverty and endless toil. Only when meeting Mme Forestier again, at the end of her wasted youth, does she learn that the original necklace was an inexpensive paste substitute; her friend's revelation, coming like a thunderclap, ends the story. Reflecting on *La Parure*, after one has recovered from the shock effect of the 'whiplash ending', one can see that in these half dozen pages Maupassant has taken his usual theme, developed and marvellously orchestrated it: the theme of the deceptiveness of appearances, behind which hides the eternal reality of human vanity. It was vanity that suggested to Mme Loisel she should borrow the necklace in the first place. She was deceived by the appearance of the necklace into believing it to be very valuable; and Mme Forestier, when she lent it, had upheld the fiction by allowing her friend to believe – again, probably, out of vanity – that the diamonds were real. Finally, after losing the necklace, Mme Loisel conceals her carelessness, once more out of pride and the desire to maintain appearances. The famous 'moment of truth' for the two friends comes when it is all too late, when the damage already done is irremediable.

The deeper implications of *La Parure* were probably not grasped by more than a minute percentage of those who read the story when it was first printed in *Le Gaulois*. This was partly because, on the whole, short stories were not accorded serious attention, being regarded at the time as no more than amusing fillers of newspaper columns. Literary critics ignored Maupassant's stories; even when he published collections of them in volume form, reviewers tended to be dismissive, and these volumes sold less well during his lifetime than did his novels. Since Maupassant never discussed his short stories and never published his views on the technique of short-story writing, we must conclude that he shared the common prejudice of the time in favour of the long work of fiction.

Of the six novels he wrote, two only have stood the test of time: *Bel-Ami* (1885) and *Pierre et Jean* (1888). *Bel-Ami* owes its lasting popularity to Maupassant's success in creating the type of the modern society adventurer, the cad who wins through. Georges Duroy's sole qualifications are his ruthlessness and his unfailing sexual charm. That he gets what he wants and goes to the top, without any talents or skills or even competence in a professional sense, with neither money nor connections to help him, might be thought to testify at least to his energy; but in fact the man is, if anything, rather indolent. His success is due simply to the worthlessness and rottenness of the society he sets out to conquer, a society of shady financiers, parasitical media men and corrupt politicians. A comparison between *Bel-Ami* and *Le Rouge et le noir* can be highly instructive. If Duroy is a soulless rascal compared with Julien Sorel, and yet succeeds so much better than he, the reason is that Maupassant's hero has far less to contend with than Stendhal's. Over the period of time separating the two works, French society itself had grown unheroic, morally flabby, ignominiously materialistic. The decline can be observed over the whole range of characters in the two books. The gulf dividing young Sorel from young Duroy is no wider than that dividing M. de La

Mole from M. Walter, or Mathilde from Suzanne. The aristocratic natures which Stendhal could still present as credible types in 1830 have, by 1885, been replaced by a low crowd of profiteers and black-guards.

Pierre et Jean deals with a rather different section of French society. The story is set not in the crowded gas-lit streets of the capital but in the Channel port of Le Havre, with its salty air and sudden fogs. The characters form a tight family circle, where in *Bel-Ami* they had been strangers thrown together by the random cross-currents of business and professional interests. Maupassant has varied his technique too. *Bel-Ami* gave the impression of being constructed by stringing together a series of short stories (as indeed had, even more noticeably, Maupassant's first novel, *Une Vie*). *Pierre et Jean*, however, has been aptly characterized as an extended short story in which the author concentrates on the growth and resolution of a single crisis in human relationships. Yet something links the two novels: both are variants on the same set of interrelated themes, pretence, deception, and betrayal.

There is pretence from the very start in *Bel-Ami* – the pretence that Duroy writes the newspaper articles that he signs, whereas in fact they are the work of Madeleine Forestier. There is pretence over small things – Duroy pretending that his name is really Du Roy de Cartel – and over large things: his pretence that he is in love with Mme Walter, whereas he has seduced her merely in order to worm his way into the household and elope with her daughter, a fantastically wealthy heiress. When he is not concocting pretences of his own, he is trying to penetrate those of others: is Madeleine merely pretending she was faithful to her first husband, Forestier? Betrayals lurk behind all these pretences: Duroy's betrayal of Mme Walter, of Madeleine, her betrayal of him, Mme Walter's of her husband.

In *Pierre et Jean* Maupassant dealt with a rather special form of deception which, in one way or another, recurs so frequently in his stories as to prompt the inquisitive reader to speculate whether the writer may not have considered himself a victim. There is probably no more to it than that the archetypal situation we are speaking of made a special appeal to Maupassant the story-teller, as being fraught with so many different possibilities for different kinds of betrayal. The deception in question is that which takes place inside the family cell. 'It is a wise father', reflects Launcelot Gobbo, 'that knows his own child', and when the child comes to know that the man he thought his father had no part in his begetting; or when the husband suspects his child to be the offspring of some secret affair that his wife has been conducting behind his back; or when (as in the story *L'Héritage*) a childless couple, needing an heir to satisfy the conditions of a legacy, decide, since the husband is evidently sterile, that the wife must take a temporary lover; in all such cases, when the secret is revealed, when the moment of truth arrives, the realist – in Maupassant's sense of the word – finds himself in his element.

Pierre and Jean are brothers; both of them young men, each having completed his studies for the two favoured professions of the French bourgeoisie at this time: medicine and the law. For the moment they are living with their parents, retired folk. The single event that sets in train the sequence leading to final catastrophe is, again, the banal device used in *L'Héritage* of a peculiar and unexpected bequest. A certain M. Maréchal, whom the Rolands knew in the early years of their marriage, dies leaving all his fortune to Jean, the younger brother: an unhoped-for windfall that delights them all.

Apart from the introductory chapter, the whole of the novel is concerned with the slow evaporation of the mist of unreality which Pierre discovers, retrospectively, to have clouded his whole life, falsifying his relations with his brother, his father, and most of all his mother. Since Maupassant presents the events for the most part through Pierre's eyes, we are able to follow him stage by stage through this voyage of bitter discovery. That his father, that stupid but harmless old man, is a cuckold; that his brother is only his half-brother; that his mother was a whore – these painful revelations come not in a flash, but are slowly, inexorably established, chiefly because Pierre is so reluctant to believe the truth when it confronts him. It is so painful that he cannot keep it to himself. He respects his father's peace of mind but is less kind to his mother, who suffers the more because, if Jean the love-child is her favourite, Pierre her first-born is also dear to her. Pierre cannot help himself; even against his better judgement, he must disturb the tranquil self-satisfaction of the others, for he has learned the truth and the truth will out; and having done all the damage he could, hating himself for what he has done, incensed with the injustice of it all (for, after all, of the four of them he is, strictly, the one with the least responsibility for what happened when his mother deceived his father and conceived his bastard brother, and yet he is the one that the others gang up against), Pierre finally decides to leave. He secures an appointment as doctor on a trans-atlantic liner, leaving Jean to the enjoyment of Maréchal's money, of his mother's affection, and the solace of marriage to a handsome young widow for whose hand the two brothers had both been con-tenders. Outwardly, the family remains as before, only rather more prosperous; one son has gone overseas to pursue his career, the other is staying at home and setting up an establishment of his own. Every-thing is, on the surface, perfectly normal. The truth has exploded, but the explosion has been contained.

In a review of Camille Lemonnier's *Le Mâle*,[30] Maupassant in-veighed at length against the unholy complicity he detected between the writers of fashionable novels (those not classifiable as realistic) and their readers.

Have we not invented the odious proverb: 'Not every truth is fit to be told'? We apply it to literature – meaning, then, that it is necessary to tell lies? 'No,' you answer, 'but merely to keep quiet.' That is lying by omission. But for a writer, there can be no halfway house: he must either tell what he believes to be the truth, or tell lies. So, to sum it all up, our literary quarrels can be reduced to the conflict between men's hypocrisy and the sincerity of the mirror.

In so far as the main effort of realism in nineteenth-century France was directed towards the dispelling of myths, towards stripping away the layers of pretence which disguised the ugliness of a self-seeking, materialistic society, then Maupassant may be said to have hit here on the precise formulation of the aims of the movement of which he was the last significantly gifted representative.

Notes

1 In *La Quotidienne*, 12 January 1823; quoted in Marguerite Iknayan, *The Idea of the Novel in France* (Geneva and Paris, 1961), p. 58.

2 See above, p. 38.

3 These are the plots, respectively, of Arnould Frémy, *Les Femmes proscrites* (1840); S. Henry Berthoud, *La Bague antique, 1ère partie: Courtisane et sainte* (1842); and Humbert Pic, *Deux cœurs de femmes* (1843).

4 It is only fair to add that Balzac was equally fierce on husbands who set up irregular establishments: see *Une Double Famille*, *Béatrix*, *La Cousine Bette*, etc.

5 See above, p. 48.

6 Principally by Gabrielle Leleu and Jean Pommier, who incorporated the results of their research in a paper, 'Du nouveau sur *Madame Bovary*', published in the *Revue d'Histoire Littéraire de la France*, Vol. XLVII (1947), pp. 211–44. See also Claudine Gothot-Mersch, *La Genèse de Madame Bovary* (Paris, 1966), pp. 26–36.

7 Flaubert and Du Camp were abroad at the time of Delamare's death, a fact which invalidates Du Camp's statement, in his *Souvenirs littéraires*, that Bouilhet suggested to Flaubert, immediately after the famous St Anthony reading, the idea of using his story in a novel.

8 Flaubert, *Correspondance* (Paris, Conard, 1910), Vol. II, pp. 384–5.

9 ibid., p. 309; and cf. p. 347: 'la *Bovary*, qui aura été pour moi un exercice excellent.'

10 *Novembre*, in *Œuvres de jeunesse inédites* (Paris, Conard, 1910), p. 182.

11 *Correspondance*, Vol. III, p. 85.

12 See R. Ricatte, *La Création romanesque chez les Goncourt* (Paris, 1953), pp. 144–7.

13 See A. François, 'Gustave Flaubert, Maxime du Camp et la révolution de 1848', *Revue d'Histoire Littéraire de la France*, Vol. LIII (1953), pp. 44–56.

14 See G. Guisan, 'Flaubert et la révolution de 1848', and Stratton Buck, 'Sources historiques et technique romanesque dans l'*Éducation sentimentale*', ibid., Vol. LVIII (1958), pp. 183–204, and Vol. LXIII (1963), pp. 619–34.

15 'Causerie de dimanche', *Le Corsaire*, 3 December 1872; reprinted in Zola, *Œuvres complètes*, ed. H. Mitterand (Paris, Cercle du Bibliophile), Vol. X (1968), pp. 973–8.

16 That Zola should mention Théophile Gautier's *Mademoiselle de Maupin* (1835) alongside *Germinie Lacerteux* is, to say the least, surprising: it was a romantic historical novel, not a work of realism, and was largely concerned with the defence of the ideal of classical beauty, which Zola rejected completely. But its secondary theme, to which it owed its notoriety, was the exaltation of pagan sensuality; the ideal world in which Gautier set his romance is one of complete sexual permissiveness.

17 First published in *Le Voltaire*, 16–20 October 1879.

18 See above, p. 60.

19 Notably by a certain Dr Lucas, author of a *Traité philosophique et physiologique de l'hérédité naturelle* (1847–50) – a work more speculative than scientific that Zola read and annotated some time in 1868.

20 See Philip Walker, 'Prophetic myths in Zola', *Publications of the Modern Language Association*, Vol. LXXIV (1959), pp. 444–52, and 'Zola, myth, and the birth of the modern world', *Symposium*, Vol. XXV (1971), pp. 204–20; also J. Borie, *Zola et les mythes* (Paris, 1971).

21 Zola, *Œuvres complètes*, Vol. XIV, p. 1440.

22 Flaubert's *Le Candidat* had had a short and markedly unsuccessful run in March 1874. Zola's *Les Héritiers Rabourdin* was a failure when it was put on in November of the same year. The first performance of the Goncourts' *Henriette Maréchal* (5 December 1865) was ruined by anti-government demonstrations. Daudet's *L'Arlésienne* was so badly received in 1872 that the author gave up writing for the stage, at least for a number of years. As for Turgenev, the first performance of his play *A Month in the Country* was given at the Maly Theatre, Moscow, in 1872. Turgenev was not present, but from reviews sent him in Paris he deduced that the occasion had been 'a fiasco'.

23 A number of these journalistic pieces were revised and republished after the war under various titles: *Lettres à un absent, Contes du lundi, Robert Helmont*.

24 The story has been told, independently, by Paul Alexis, *Émile Zola, notes d'un ami* (Paris, 1882), pp. 181–2, and by Henry Céard, 'Humbles débuts', *Le Journal littéraire*, 10 May 1924, an article partially reprinted as an appendix to Vol. II of Huysmans, *Œuvres complètes* (Paris, Crès, 1928).

25 In a review of Huysmans's *Croquis parisiens* (*Le Voltaire*, 15 June 1880), reprinted in Zola, *Œuvres complètes*, Vol. XII, pp. 619–23.

26 *Correspondance, nouvelle édition augmentée* (Paris, Conard, 1930), Vol. VIII, p. 225. Flaubert was criticizing specifically *Les Sœurs Vatard*. He had similarly accused Zola of using 'inverted preciosity' in the style of *L'Assommoir*.

27 *The Life of J.-K. Huysmans* (Oxford, 1955), p. 59.

28 *En famille* (*Nouvelle Revue*, 15 February 1881); *Mon Oncle Jules* (*Le Gaulois*, 7 August 1883).

29 See *Le Père Milon*, *Le Gaulois*, 22 May 1883.

30 *Le Gaulois*, 4 October 1881. This important text has not been included in any edition of Maupassant's complete works, but E. M. Sullivan has reprinted it as an appendix to his *Maupassant the Novelist* (Princeton, 1954).

FIVE

Realism in Germany,
from the Death of Goethe

BEFORE the unification of Germany in 1871, a widely accepted image of the German was of a poet and philosopher, dreamer and idealist for whom Germany as a political reality existed only through the mystical power of the German language. Since the age of Bismarck's *Realpolitik* this image has been largely replaced in the popular consciousness by a contrary myth, that of the German as the incarnation of bureaucratic, militaristic and scientific efficiency. Not surprisingly, perhaps, the apparent success of Bismarck's policies in the latter part of the century arouses the expectation that his *Realpolitik* will be discovered to have been accompanied by a correspondingly lively development of political realism in the literature of the time, a political realism from which Marx and Engels may possibly have derived their concept of socialist realism. Such naïve assumptions are quickly dispelled by the most cursory study of the history of German literature in the nineteenth century: it soon becomes apparent that the best narrative prose of the period is not outstanding for its realistic portrayal of the social and political problems in the age of Bismarck; one looks in vain in Marx's writings for any detailed definition of realism in the literature or the plastic arts of Germany, while Engels will be found to have drawn most of his basic assumptions about literature from Gutzkow, Börne and the Young Hegelians, none of whose literary works have stood the test of time. So the spectre of communism which was haunting Europe did not haunt German realist narrative, nor for that matter were Bismarck or the political dilemmas of his predecessors matters of direct concern for the German realists.

At first sight, then, Germany seems to be out of step with the rest of Europe and lagging behind the realism of Balzac and even of Sue. Surveys of European realism like Auerbach's *Mimesis* or Becker's *Documents of Modern Literary Realism* pass over German literature in silence as having nothing to offer either in theory or practice comparable with French, English or Russian models. And even standard histories of German literature appeared for a long time to confirm this by stressing that the novel of social or political realism was not to be looked for in German, and by dismissing the literature of the Age of Realism in Germany as something which anyway could not compare with the high art of German idealism. Histories of this kind tended to see German realism in idyllic terms as quiet, rather dull but endearing, the reflection of a pre-industrial, peasant and small-town culture which never achieved anything approaching the stature of realist and naturalist literature outside Germany. Modern criticism, however, by stressing how German realism anticipates twentieth-century narrative forms, has tended to discredit this image of a healthy, solid, contented middle-class literature suitable for school-children, young students and local patriots. Thus, Barker Fairley has had no difficulty in demonstrating that the ideas and literary forms of the supposedly chaotic twentieth century are already present in an apparently conventional novelist like Raabe, while other critics have demonstrated that modern narrative techniques like the stream of consciousness, multiple perspective, and sophisticated time sequences had long ago been anticipated by such 'dull' realists as Otto Ludwig and Theodor Storm.

REALISM AND THE 'YOUNG GERMANS'

German literary historians like to speak of the age up to the death of Johann Wolfgang von GOETHE (1749–1832) as the *Goethezeit*. This is a convenient term, not only because it marks the overwhelming contribution made by Goethe to every literary movement from Storm and Stress onwards, but also because it allows classicism and romanticism, which in Germany did not conveniently follow each other, to be treated together. Goethe's influence did not immediately decline with his death in 1832; indeed, the objective, allusive, ambivalent and symbolic forms of narrative which he displayed in shorter forms like his *Novelle* (1828) or in longer forms like his *Wahlverwandtschaften* (*Elective Affinities*, 1809) were to prove as powerful models for the later realists of the nineteenth century as were his *Wilhelm Meister* novels, the *Lehrjahre* (*Years of Apprenticeship*, 1795–6) and the *Wander-jahre* (*Years of Travel*, 1821). These have sometimes been described as 'realistic' though in general the utopian element prevails, and the reader used to the masterpieces of French realism quickly gives up in despair at the vacuum in which Goethe's characters seem to exist. But the *Bildungsroman* as exemplified by Goethe in his *Wilhelm Meister* novels was to become for Germany the model revealing the full potential of the novel form for the modern world. The *Bildungsroman* ('apprenticeship novel') follows the course of a young man as he enters life, seeks similar souls, experiences love and friendship, comes into conflict with the realities of the world, in short, passes through a variety of experiences by which he gradually matures and finds himself. So worldly a setting might seem to necessitate a realistic frame-work, but in fact this is not so. The hero may seem a Faustian figure whose constant striving means his exposure to all the pleasures and pains that are man's lot on earth, but in general he is passive, letting the world impinge on him instead of attempting to impress his will on the world. Hence instead of conflict there is a striving towards maturity and harmony between the individual and society. In addition, the life of the hero will not exemplify an individual fate; on the contrary, his experiences will be 'typical' and 'symbolic', thereby indicating the general law; his life will not follow an erratic picaresque course, instead it will tend towards an ideal goal. Every experience will be significant and the novel will exhibit a world which is still a meaningful whole.

German novels in this vein are far more didactic and moralistic than were similar works produced elsewhere. The real must always be combined with the ideal, always the opposing forces must be reconciled and tragedy avoided. Significantly, the subtitle of Goethe's *Wilhelm Meisters Wanderjahre* was 'Those who renounce'. The *Lehrjahre* is a work set uncompromisingly in contemporary German society, but the accent is on *Bildung*, the development and cultivation of the self, and not on the experiences which contribute to this development. The writing is characterized by an ironically playful tone that betrays the narrator's casual attitude to the manipulation of reality. The plot progresses by erratic or 'poetic' leaps, following the mood rather than the logical sequence of events. This was the basis on which the novel developed thereafter. When critics complain about the failure of the social novel in Germany they are looking for something which German writers after Goethe consciously rejected. These writers were aware of developments in the novel in other countries; they read, admired, even imitated the historical novel of Scott and the realistic novel of Dickens, but the great model remained *Wilhelm Meisters Lehrjahre*. The Romantics, the Young Germans, the Biedermeier writers, the Poetic Realists all held to the *Bildungsroman* as the German form of the novel and to Goethe as its greatest exponent. When asked for the representative literary novels of the nineteenth century the German critic and historian will automatically name Jean Paul's *Titan* (1800–1803), Immermann's *Die Epigonen* (*The Disciples*, 1836), Stifter's *Der Nachsommer* (*Indian Summer*, 1857), and Keller's *Der grüne Heinrich* (*Green Henry*, 1854). Social novels were written and indeed became so successful that no survey of German realism would be complete without reference to them. But such novels could never compete with the representative novels in *the* representative form.

The first generation of writers to emerge, after 1830, from the political upheavals that culminated in the so-called July Revolution in France, displayed a distinct antagonism towards Goethe. These writers were the 'Young Germans', specifically named as such by the Decree of the Federal Diet of 1835 which put all their works, their publishers, their printers and their distributors under a total ban, because they were 'attacking the Christian religion in the most impudent manner, debasing the existing social order and undermining all propriety and morality'. The writers named in the decree were Heine, Gutzkow, Laube, Wienbarg, Mundt and Börne. Of these names only Heine's is still remembered today. Clearly the Establishment overreacted to the journalistic extravagances of these middle-class liberal reformers. Immermann in his novel *Die Epigonen* noted the essential weakness of the age following the death of Goethe, namely that 'everybody was operating with borrowed ideas'. The Young Germans had views about everything: constitutional democracy, socialism, the emancipation of woman. They would offer an opinion at the drop of a hat, but they had no experience. They were tendentious, contentious, they wrote for all classes of readers, demanding freedom of speech and freedom of the press, but there was no German reality to correspond to their imported abstractions. The issues they raised were important ones, but it fell to others to deal with them properly and exhaustively. The political and social problems they touched on were examined in depth by Marx and Engels, while their criticism of Christianity was consolidated in Strauss's *Das Leben Jesu* (*Life of Jesus*, 1835) and Feuerbach's *Das Wesen des Christentums* (*The Nature of Christianity*, 1841).

Only in the drama did works of real literary merit emerge at this time, but these were due to a young scientist called Georg BÜCHNER (1813-37) who did not want to be associated with the Young Germans. His plays awaken echoes of the 'realism' of the Storm and Stress movement, and such echoes are encountered too in the one piece of narrative prose that Büchner left, the story *Lenz* (1839). His subject was, as the title indicates, the ill-fated Storm and Stress dramatist J. M. R. Lenz (1751-92); the story is important in the development of realism in Germany because it contains the first consistent anti-idealistic aesthetic. Büchner looks for *life* of the kind that can be found in Shakespeare, sometimes in folk songs, sometimes in Goethe. Anything more 'idealistic' is to be consigned to the flames. Unfortunately Büchner was to remain comparatively unknown until the beginning of the twentieth century, and so one powerful platform on which a realist movement might have been based was lost.

Heinrich HEINE (1797-1856) won international renown in his day, but as a poet. His prose, though brilliant, was in the form of the sketch, the memoir or the travel diary. Although he hailed the nineteenth century as the 'Age of Prose', he himself admitted his inability to write a novel and left only fragments of fictional narrative behind, including *Aus den Memoiren des Herrn von Schnabelwopski*. On the other hand, Karl Ferdinand GUTZKOW (1811-78) applied himself to both the theory and the practice of the novel and was in his own time sensationally successful. The work which really launched him on his career was *Wally, die Zweiflerin* (*The Woman who Doubted*, 1835). Doubt, the corrosive force which was so much part of the spirit of the age in religion, morals and politics, is here shown at work in Wally, a sensitive intellectual woman. But if Heine found it difficult to start a novel, Gutzkow found it difficult to stop, and indeed his *Die Ritter vom Geiste* (*The Knights of the Spirit*, 1850-51) seems an almost perfect example of the disease of *Epigonentum* which Immermann had diagnosed as the major affliction of the age that followed the death of Goethe. This novel, Gutzkow's 'political *Wilhelm Meister*', is indeed a poor imitation of its original and, although juggling brilliantly with words and ideas, reveals a dangerous devaluation of linguistic and intellectual currency with no realistic capital to back it up. And yet his theory of the novel, as expounded in the foreword to the first edition of *Die Ritter vom Geiste*, seemed very up-to-date and modern at the time. Gutzkow's contention was that the novel form was entering a new phase. Hitherto, one had had what he describes as the *Roman des Nacheinander*, characterized by the linear development of the narrative, a string of episodes one after the other. As he sees it, this outmoded sequence of artfully entwined events, presenting only incredible, fabulous effects in the romantic manner, needs to be replaced by a method which establishes the links between the individual and the whole on the basis of close attachment to experience and reality, building up a broad picture not from the tension created by deeds and their consequences, but from the stretches of time between such deeds. What the old novel had glossed over by its selective leaping from one event to another must become the area on which the new novel must concentrate. This would be the *Roman des Nebeneinander*, the novel of juxtaposition or things at the same time. In other words Gutzkow proposes a synchronic as well as a diachronic picture of reality: 'The totality of life, the whole age, the whole truth, the reflection of all the light rays of life.'

This is an exciting theory, and critics generally spend most of their time discussing why the novel itself (in nine volumes) falls so far short of fulfilling its promise. One reason suggested is that the German society that Gutzkow attempted to capture was riven by so many contradictions and conflicts in religion, class, and politics that any attempt to reflect such a society must itself become chaotic and contradictory. Certainly this is the effect the novel has on the reader. At the same time Gutzkow's work demonstrates the various problems that literary realism posed the German writer at this time. There was first the problem of language level, one that Gutzkow failed altogether to solve, with the result that his style oscillates alarmingly between a high, rhetorical, 'poetic' literary level and a low, 'realistic' level, without ever finding an acceptable mean. Then there was the problem of factuality and actuality. Gutzkow never quite decided whether his novel should be a *roman à clé*, drawn from real and recognizable political events and personalities of his time, or whether it should select what is 'typical' and true for all time. Hence his novel is partly masked journalism and partly utopian fantasy. Like the other Young Germans before him, he still thought the 'idea' more important than 'reality' and constructed his novel accordingly, making events and people conform with his overall scheme, while at the same time remaining convinced that the sheer mass of realistic genre pictures from various spheres would balance the unreality of the schematic structure. But perhaps the overriding reason why Gutzkow's vast novel of totality fails is its bookishness. It remains almost embarrassingly derivative despite the newness of the theory. The title itself was borrowed from Heine's 'Knights of the Holy Spirit', and there are many other literary echoes. In part this is deliberate, because Gutzkow's novel also attempts a synthesis of all previous novel forms, including the adventure story, the social novel, and the mystery novel *à la* Eugène Sue. But Gutzkow's greatest debt is to Goethe. The novel's political freemasonry of enlightened minds is modelled on the similar secret society in *Wilhelm Meister* and so is utopian rather than real. Gutzkow remains in the shadow of the master.

Going back to the Young German roots from which Gutzkow sprang we may ask with Sengle: 'Were the Young Germans realistic?'[1] The Young Germans, as is well known, attacked Goethe for being a court poet and for failing to take a stand on the issues of the day like the French Revolution. And yet their own novels were no more 'realistic' than Goethe's *Die Wahlverwandtschaften* or *Wilhelm Meister*; indeed Goethe's works easily survived their attacks and continued to influence the German novel in the Age of Realism after 1848. Gutzkow was a perceptive critic, rescuing from oblivion the dramatic works of Grabbe and Büchner; and yet he completely rejected the founders of Anglo-American realism, Walter Scott, Fenimore Cooper, Washington Irving and Charles Dickens. In general this is in line with Young German acceptance of English democracy and rejection of English empiricism and materialism. The Young Germans may have attempted to make literature more political than it had been, but they were still German idealists more concerned with 'art' and 'ideas' than with practical politics. They were, as Magill has said, 'remote from the centres of power in their time and therefore at loggerheads with authority ... Fumbling describes precisely the situation of the Young Germans, astray in an impenetrable ideological fog and mistaking the misty shapes around them for the substance of reality.'[2]

THE BIEDERMEIER WRITERS

Aggressively liberal writers like the Young Germans were by no means the only ones to emerge in the immediate post-Goethe period. In recent years the term *Biedermeier*, originally applied to genre painters like Ludwig Richter, Moritz von Schwind, and Spitzweg, has come to acquire more general currency. M. J. Norst has summed up the associations of the term *Biedermeier* as follows:

It could mean a philistine attitude and a narrow range of artistic endeavour, a lack of intellectual curiosity, a sense of uncritical accept-ance, an exaggerated concern with trivialities. It could also imply domestic tranquillity and virtue, love of 'real' things in a 'real' world because they are a pledge of eternal harmony; in fact that state of innocence in which the German and Austrian *Bürger* was seen to live before the Fall of the Industrial Revolution – his sense of tradition, his social customs. Finally it could be used to express the idea of a period of violent political and social upheaval. [3]

While there has naturally been some resistance to the acceptance of a term with such varied and sometimes contradictory connotations, this has now largely crumbled since the publication of the first two volumes of Sengle's survey *Biedermeierzeit*. The value of the term, as Sengle shows, is that it permits a unified view of the age up to 1848 instead of a fragmented one in which the literary scene dissolves into a *mêlée* of conflicting groups: Young Germans, traditional epigones, and conservative reactionaries. As a result the stature of such writers as Gotthelf, Grillparzer, Stifter, Droste-Hülshoff and Mörike has in-creased instead of being diminished: there need be nothing derogatory now about the term *Biedermeier*.

Equally important, although there is now a clear recognition of the significance of the year 1848, the Year of the Revolutions, as a turning point in German literature as well as in politics, the pre-1848 (or *Vormärz*) period can be seen clearly as part of the developing force of realism in German literature. Gutzkow's sensational novels may have seized the popular imagination, but the works that have endured are those that reacted to the revolutionary tremors of the time by stressing tradition, moderation, and wonder at the beauty and eternal order of God's universe. This has led to their being branded as 'anti-liberal', scorned for being 'uncommitted' at a very critical moment in history, and condemned for the idyllic element in their writing. However, as Norst again points out, the Biedermeier attitude does represent a rejection of the excesses of romanticism and, hence, an approach to realism:

> The attention previously centred on the ego is now focussed on the objective world, the objects within it and the relationship between them. The smallest things are cherished because they, as much as the larger ones, derive their value from a fixed place in the cosmic order and bear witness to it.[4]

Hence, though *detail* in the works of Stifter, Mörike, Droste-Hülshoff and Gotthelf is infinitely careful and precise, it can never become an end in itself because their works reveal a belief in the transcendental: 'everything is at once itself and a reflection of the eternal.' Of the writers of this period Mörike and Droste-Hülshoff are essentially poets, Grillparzer is a dramatist, and only Stifter and Gotthelf produced almost exclusively narrative works in both the shorter form of the novella or the story, and the longer epic form of the novel. However, even the poets and dramatists produced narrative work of remarkable quality. Eduard MÖRIKE (1804–75) wrote a novel, *Maler Nolten* (1832), which is perhaps still too much in the romantic tradition of the artist-hero to be considered realistic, but his shorter pieces, especially *Mozart auf der Reise nach Prag* (*Mozart's Journey to Prague*, 1856), are little jewels.

It is, however, in a tale like *Die Judenbuche* (*The Jew's Beech*, 1842) by Annette von DROSTE-HÜLSHOFF (1797–1848) that one sees most clearly the contemporary dichotomy between romanticism and realism. The author gave her tale the subtitle 'A portrait of the mores in mountainous Westphalia', and indeed her novella reads in part almost like a police report, while the details of cultural history, local habits, customs and traditions make it seem like an anticipatory exercise in the later naturalistic aesthetic based on the determinants of race and *milieu*. Before the story ever starts, an introductory poem makes it clear that this is to be a tale of a poor wretched being of limited capacity, conditioned by heredity and circumscribed by the force of prejudice. This anti-hero, a poor cowherd, is then placed against his class background and the historical traditions of the locality, described significantly as 'a remote corner of the world without factories or commerce, without highways, where a strange face caused a stir and a journey of thirty miles made even the upper-class person something of a Ulysses in the district.' The community is sketched in general terms, the village briefly characterized, the house where the hero was born described, the parents individually intro-duced, and only then does the 'hero' make his appearance. Already the reader will have been struck by the almost naturalistic detail. Friedrich's father has been a 'regular' drunkard as a young man, that is, one who only ended up incapable in the gutter on Sundays and feast-days. But his first marriage ends with his wife fleeing home to her parents, screaming and blood-stained. This great scandal means that Mergel has to comfort himself with more liquor, 'so by that afternoon there was not a single whole pane of glass in the house and until the early hours of the morning he was to be seen lying across his threshold, guiding the neck of a broken bottle to his lips, thereby horribly gashing his face and hands.'

The tale that follows is one of crime and punishment, though the actual moral dilemma facing the young hero arises from the traditional conflict between peasantry and landlords over the right to take wood from the forest. But this is only one side of the story, the rational side. The other is the equally powerful presentation of the forces of dark-ness and evil, and of the natural or supernatural forces to which a man is exposed. Religion and superstition still have an overwhelming part to play, and the story really comes back to the suggestion that a man who is born into a Christian community can never escape from his Christian conscience. There are two elements of *Die Judenbuche* which will recur constantly in the later products of German realist fiction. The first is the scrupulous refusal to succumb to the romantic tempta-tion of the exotic: the hero's twenty-eight years in Algerian slavery are passed over in silence, and the narrative concentrates almost claustrophobically on one individual in one community in a fairly insignificant part of Germany. The second point is that Droste-Hülshoff's story concerns the murder of a Jew. Antisemitism as such is never discussed, but it haunts the pages of the German realists right through to Fontane's *Effi Briest*, in which even the impeccable Innstetten is tinged with Wagnerian antisemitism.

The last words in Droste-Hülshoff's story seem to suggest an Old Testament moral of an eye for an eye and a tooth for a tooth. Much the same might be expected from the works of Jeremias GOTTHELF (1797–1854) who, as his *nom de plume* suggests (he was in private life a Swiss pastor named Albert Bitzius), makes teaching a Christian message his specific aim. What this means in theory is an essentially democratic-conservative position, running counter to the *Zeitgeist* which was leading his flock astray with 'false' ideas of radicalism. What it means in practice can be seen in the best known of his stories, *Die schwarze Spinne* (*The Black Spider*, 1842–6). The scene is presented with such meticulous geographical detail that it can be pinpointed to a farm about ten miles from Gotthelf's own house and church at Lützelflüh in the canton of Bern in Switzerland. Like Droste-Hülshoff, Gotthelf gives a totally convincing picture of the traditional and almost ritual customs of the peasants. The effect is to suggest the dangers of change and the value of continuity. Like Grimmelshausen in the seventeenth century, Gotthelf adopted a convincingly 'realistic' manner, but his tale of the incursion of evil into an earthly paradise is told with such vitality and brio that by the end it reaches the almost cosmic proportions of a total war between the forces of Good and Evil. As a Swiss, Gotthelf commanded a limited audience even among German readers, by reason of the dialect forms he used as well as the special political problems he dealt with. However, he did attain a temporary fame from 1850 onwards when his works were translated into French, and from French into English by, among others, Ruskin (who knew no German, let alone Bernese Swiss).[5] However, it was not until the twentieth century, when the great critical edition of his works appeared, that Gotthelf came to be recognized as a prominent exponent of the 'social' novel in German. Riehl's early description of him – 'Shakespeare as a village priest in the canton of Bern' – is not inapposite.

Franz GRILLPARZER (1791–1872) was, of course, first and foremost a dramatist, but mention must be made of his one great novella, *Der arme Spielmann* (*The Poor Musician*, 1847), whose importance for German literature has been amply demonstrated by J. P. Stern's penetrating analysis in his *Reinterpretations*. We need not be concerned here too much with the nature of its language or the extent to which it does or does not capture the anti-revolutionary spirit of the times. What is important in the context of the problem of realism is the famous passage at the beginning of Grillparzer's highly complex piece of psychological analysis:

Truly, one cannot comprehend the famous unless one has emotionally relived the obscure. From the wrangling of wine-flushed barrow-pushers to the contentions of the gods there runs an invisible but unbroken thread; and in the young serving-maid who half against her will follows her unfortunate lover away from the throng of the dancers, there lie in embryo all your Juliets, Didos and Medeas.

Essentially the claim made here is that there is no difference between the tragic love-affair of an obscure street musician with an insignificant shop girl, and the sorrows of the great lovers of world literature and legend, Romeo and Juliet, Dido and Aeneas, Medea and Jason. German narrative was reaching down the social scale, as Keller was to demonstrate further when he wrote his *Romeo und Julia auf dem Dorfe*.

Adalbert STIFTER (1805–68), undoubtedly the greatest of the authors of the *Biedermeierzeit*, still remains largely unknown outside Germany and Austria, where his reputation has been rising particularly since the end of the Second World War. In the nineteenth century his work was appreciated in England: the *British Quarterly Review* characterized him in 1854 as 'supremely the poet of detail'. The tales contained in *Die Mappe meines Urgrossvaters* (*My Great-Grandfather's Portfolio*, 1841–2), *Bunte Steine* (*Brightly Coloured Stones*, 1853) and *Studien* (1844–50) were known abroad, although Stifter's famous 'gentle law', enunciated in the preface to *Bunte Steine*, does not seem to have caused any stir outside Germany. Novels like *Der Nachsommer* (1857) and *Witiko* (1865–7) were rarely if ever discussed, though the former did elicit the following commentary:

It tells of an attempt to create an earthly paradise ... far removed from the distracting haunts of men, where ... all the ugly details of life are to be banished from sight and knowledge. The attempt succeeds apparently and it would appear that Stifter did not doubt its feasibility, but the effort is too perceptible to the reader. An atmosphere of forced quietism, a calm but deadening air fills this Utopia, which is an Austrian country version of some of our modern pre-Raphaelite experiments.[6]

This makes Stifter's novel sound almost deliberately anti-realistic, and in one sense it was. He did not approve of the introduction of contemporary problems into literature, and, like Gotthelf, he saw himself as standing out against the spirit of the age. Instead of revolution he illustrates organic development, using for this purpose the traditional form of the *Bildungsroman* in which the hero is shown adapting himself step by step to the demands of his environment, and acquiring maturity in the process.

A novel like *Der Nachsommer* which sets out to reveal almost imperceptible growth is bound to be slow, detailed, and at first dull. But Stifter is not merely the nineteenth-century scientist amassing minute observations, he is also the artist who uses these observations to ascertain the natural law and the social law. Nevertheless the whole concept of the passive hero which is fundamental to the German novel in the nineteenth century is one which the non-German reader, accustomed to forceful figures vigorously characterized, finds hard to accept. Otto Ludwig, the best-known exponent of 'Poetic Realism', made the point most clearly, as usual on the basis of the fundamental difference between drama and the novel: the hero of the drama makes his own history, the hero of the novel merely undergoes his.

THE 'POETIC REALISTS'

The change from the realism of the *Biedermeierzeit* (that is, of the period before 1848) to that of the period which follows is not easily characterized, but one essential difference does stand out: the post-1848 generation is one which knew Feuerbach and Strauss. After 1848 there is not a single Christian writer of any stature. Storm, Keller, Raabe, Fontane were more concerned with the things of this earth than with the transcendental. Atheism meant an enrichment of life; to be an atheist implied rejecting the world of ideals and fantasy and instead focusing one's attention on reality. Keller is the writer generally quoted as having responded most fully to Feuerbach's positive atheism, and equally Keller is the author universally regarded as the greatest of the 'poetic' or middle-class realists of the second half of the century. However, the credit for the formulation of the concept of Poetic Realism belongs to Otto LUDWIG (1813–65), although the term itself was one he took over from Schelling.

Realism, Ludwig argues, should not mean an impoverishment of art; on the contrary it should be, as Feuerbach says of atheism, an enrichment of life. Ludwig took great trouble to elucidate this problem of realism in literature. Essentially his approach was that of the crafts-man, and he analysed Shakespeare, Scott and Dickens in an attempt to isolate the techniques involved in creating both the 'real' and the 'typical'. He aimed to steer a middle course between what he felt was the extreme of rhetorical pathos exhibited by Schiller and, on the other hand, mere photographic naturalism. But despite his theoretical studies and his experiments with narrative forms Ludwig remained convinced that drama was the highest form of art and that he was born to be a great dramatist. In this he was wrong. His error meant that he left a limited number of mature works of poetic realism; they include *Die Heiterethei* (*The Merry Lass*, 1854) and *Aus dem Regen in die Traufe* (*Out of the Frying-Pan into the Fire*, 1855), which are scenes from provincial life, and *Zwischen Himmel und Erde* (1856), a long novella or a short novel, whose very title (*Between Heaven and Earth*) is an indication of the poetic and symbolic manner in which Ludwig deals with a potentially realistic topic. In a sense Ludwig, like Gutzkow, is more interesting as a theoretician than a literary practitioner; and yet *Zwischen Himmel und Erde*, despite its almost claustrophobic narrow-ness of vision, is a fascinating example of German realism. Almost existential in the depth of its exploration of human isolation and the difficulty of communication, it does at the same time illustrate the hesitant steps taken by the German novel towards a 'dramatic' form devoid of melodrama. The result is not a work which reflects con-temporary reality nor one that makes us conscious of social processes: political and economic problems play no part in it. On the other hand, as a recent critic has argued, its depth psychology is akin to the psychological realism to be found in Flaubert's *Madame Bovary*, and this alone places Ludwig in the mainstream of nineteenth-century realism.[7]

Despite the attention normally given by literary historians to

Ludwig's extended theoretical studies of realism, it would be wrong to suppose that he became in any way a leader of a school of realists. His extremely diffuse studies took a long time to percolate and, besides, the German realists tended on the whole to avoid theory and each other. The German-speaking lands were still not united; no one city acted as a supreme literary centre; and one can see the particularism of the age reflected in the regionalism of the writing. Each of the German realists tends to be associated with his own corner of the German-speaking lands: Keller with Zürich, Fontane with Brandenburg, and Theodor STORM (1817–88) with Schleswig-Holstein.

His story *Immensee* (1850), which seems to have made a considerable impression on the Victorians, brought Storm an almost embarrassing measure of success; it also illustrates the difficulty of distinguishing between Biedermeier and Poetic Realism. Storm drew freely on Eichendorff, Stifter and Mörike for many of the motifs of his sentimental love story and its 'idyllic' setting, but no matter how derivative and literary his story was, for some reason it harmonized exactly with the secret aspirations of the middle classes in the mid-century. At the same time *Immensee* is the vital key to the 'realistic' style which he was to deepen and enrich in the fifty or so historical, regional, and domestic short stories which were to follow, and which culminate in the tragic tale of *Der Schimmelreiter* (*The Rider of the White Horse*, 1888), written at a time when industrial and urban expansion, themes with which he hardly ever deals, were at last forcing their way into German literature.

The hero of Storm's story *Immensee* is afflicted, like Grillparzer's street musician in *Der arme Spielmann*, with the curse of silence, 'a reticence in the expression of personal emotion', noticeable too in Ludwig's *Zwischen Himmel und Erde* and in the almost English habits of understatement that mark Fontane's novels. Storm's basic artistic principle, which was to become so characteristic of nineteenth-century realist literature in general and of the novella in particular, can best be described as the technique of suggestion and silence. The characteristic feature of such discreet realism is *Verinnerlichung* or progressive inwardness; it is a realism more intensive in its emphasis on the subjective element than extensive in the portrayal of social reality. What is not always fully appreciated is the extent to which, far from being a type of narrative instinctively arrived at, this is on the contrary fully consonant with the guide-lines for the novel laid down by the leading thinkers of the age.[8] Schopenhauer for example saw the task of the novelist as consisting not in the relating of great events, but in making small ones interesting. So he claims a novel will gain in stature in so far as it presents the inner, rather than the outer life. Moriz Carriere too, in *Das Wesen und die Formen der Poesie* (*The Nature and Forms of Poetry*, 1854), explicitly restricts the novelist to 'the realm of the heart with its inwardness' and 'the sphere of private existence'. For him the novel is the artistic form appropriate to the study of individuality in what is, in many ways, a perplexingly prosaic world. And the most important philosopher in Germany after Hegel, Friedrich Theodor Vischer, described the novel as a form based on the spirit of experience, with the whole of the prosaic world order for its theatre of activity. And yet the novelist needed to select those areas of the real which afforded freest play to the ideal. In this Vischer followed Hegel's famous definition of the novel as a form which

presupposes a basis of reality already organized in its prosaic form, upon which it then attempts . . . to make good once more the banished claims of poetical vision. For this reason one of the most common collisions in the novel, and the one most suitable to it, is the conflict between the poetry of the heart and the prose of external conditions antagonistic to it.[9]

All the most important critics from Hegel onwards are united in their acceptance of realism understood as 'what is true to life', while at the same time they continue to insist that it restrict itself to 'the poetry of the heart', with which is associated the need for poetic idealization. What this means in particular cases is readily evident in an author like Storm, who draws the reader into an intensely private world apparently far removed from the turmoils of the age. However, Storm was a minor master only, for his medium was the novella; he never wrote a novel. It may well be that the novella was the form most appropriate for German realism: nevertheless there was always something problematic about the German novella in the age of realism, as can be seen in the case of C. F. Meyer, who showed incredible artistry in the manipulation of the framing-tale and the perspective narrative. As a result his once greatly admired stories are now suspected of excessive formalism, while Storm's have been criticized as sentimental, narrowly domestic, and philistine. More serious still, concentration on the homeland and on particular ethnic and racial qualities made Storm's work a useful quarry for twentieth-century German nationalists, a fate which also overtook Gotthelf, Raabe, and Riehl.

Charges such as these cannot so readily be levelled against Gottfried KELLER (1819–90), one author whom Lukács, in his masterly analysis of the German realists, exempts from his usual strictures because as a Swiss Keller lived in a democratic republic and hence escaped the political reaction which followed the collapse of the 1848 Revolution in the German lands. Switzerland certainly seems particularly rich in realistic talent, having not only nurtured Gotthelf, Keller, and C. F. Meyer but fostered also a strong realist-pedagogical tradition going back to Hebel and Pestalozzi.[10] Attempts have been made to show that the 'Swissness' of Keller is indeed what makes him the master of poetic realism; however, he is clearly in the mainstream of the German tradition. Next to Feuerbach, the greatest influence on him was Goethe, in whose works he saw a love of reality and an awareness of its coherence and depth. Not surprisingly his novel *Der grüne Heinrich* (1854) adheres to the form that Goethe had established; and it is written in the German of Goethe and not in the dialect current in his own canton. *Der grüne Heinrich*, the story of a failed artist who in the end dies from a feeling of guilt and of the impossibility of existing in society, is still a very derivative work in the tradition of the *Bildungsroman* or artist's novel. Much of Keller's own experience has obviously gone into it and there are many episodes of great truthfulness and sincerity. Yet the impression it leaves is of an unplanned, ramshackle composition where the author did not even succeed in solving such technical problems as whether the first- or the third-person narrative should be used. When Keller came to revise the novel some years later, not only did he smooth away the technical infelicities of the first version, but he changed the whole direction of the work. He made his hero abandon his romantic notion of a purely aesthetic existence and settle down as a servant of the state, just as he himself had given up his bohemian artistic life and become an *erster Staatssekretär* in Zürich. There is now no conflict between the artist and society; on the contrary, Keller's moral is that everyone should become a solid citizen performing a useful function in the state, a solution which Lukács argues was open only to Keller as a Swiss in a democratic republic and not to Keller's contemporaries living in Germany under régimes of which in general they could not approve.

Der grüne Heinrich is a significant work, but Keller fails to overcome the inherent limitations of the form he has adopted. Hence his greatest contribution to German realism is not in the novel, nor in the drama, which, like Ludwig, he rated highly but failed to master, but in the novella. Unable to cope with the totality towards which the novel strives, he is at home with the fragment of life, the personal fate of symbolic significance. His stories have a message, they are didactic, but his lessons are offered not directly or tendentiously, as in the work of the Young Germans, but obliquely and discreetly by understatement. A feature of the novella form which made it suitable for the age was the fact that the setting must be the real world, however exceptional the event may be that impinges upon the hero whom fate has singled out. For the Romantics the *Märchen* (fairy-story) had proved a wonderful vehicle for conveying deeper significance in an apparently simple form, and Keller, like his contemporary realists in Germany, never abandoned the *Märchen* completely. Indeed he not only wrote *Märchen* and legends: all his stories have been described as *märchenhaft*. But the word refers only to the 'poetic' tone of Keller's narrative, not to the actual characters or to the settings, which are real enough. His novellas no longer ignore the restrictions of time and place to escape into a romantic world of fantasy; instead they are bound by the necessity for logical and rational motivation, requiring indeed what E. K. Bennett called 'the most careful logical treatment in order to make the unbelievable convince as truth'. But as a writer of novellas he does not offer the unvarnished truth, or reality; his work is given a 'poetic' atmosphere by means of artistic form. An artist in the novella form, like Keller, is not concerned to work up a mass of material, photographically recorded, nor does he attempt anything approaching Duranty's 'exact, complete and sincere reproduction of the social *milieu* in which we live'. The world of the novella can never be more than a significant glimpse carefully selected from the particular perspective of the artist who interprets what he sees and gives it artistic shape. Even the most trivial detail is now made to fit into place and become part of the mesh revealing the 'connectedness of things'.

In this way the aridity of naturalism is avoided and a synthesis arrived at between the real and the ideal, which excludes the extremes of romantic fantasy while retaining its poetic qualities.

One feature of the novella form which Keller exploited to the full is the framework. This becomes more than a simple device for stringing together stories otherwise unconnected. The framework to collections like *Die Leute von Seldwyla* (*People of Seldwyla*, 1856 and 1874), *Züricher Novellen* (1878), and *Das Sinngedicht* (*The Epigram*, 1881) gives the individual stories background and depth. Seldwyla lacks the geographical exactitude associated with, for example, the *Schwarzwälder Dorfgeschichten* (*Village Tales of the Black Forest*) in four volumes (1843–54) by Keller's contemporary Berthold Auerbach, who enjoyed a European reputation at this time. Keller gives his stories a real basis from his own experience but then deliberately generalizes the image, making it a vehicle for all the things he wants to say about his own country. What at first appears to be an 'idyllic' setting turns into an exposé of the emptiness and the philistinism of such an earthly paradise. But the evils of this world, which in themselves would furnish matter for a social novel, are left in the framework: the stories are about characters who *differ* from the average inhabitants of Seldwyla and are therefore more poetic. There is a didactic intention visible in the *People of Seldwyla* but on the whole Keller succeeds in his aim to 'dissolve the didactic in the poetic', while the theme round which his stories revolve is the general one of *Sein und Schein*, true being as opposed to false appearances, and the 'characters' he singles out in his stories are either converted to some form of 'inner truthfulness' or condemned for lack of it.

In the *Züricher Novellen* the connection between the framework and the stories it encloses is much more direct. The problem is a special one – the possibility of being 'original' and the justification for trying to be so. The young man of Zürich, Herr Jacques, has been made uneasy in his mind by reading 'in some pretentious book or other ... that nowadays there are no genuine, original people any more, only ten-a-penny people, people by the thousands all turned out exactly alike'. This is certainly a 'modern' problem. Nineteenth-century man was becoming increasingly aware of the standardization brought about by democratic mass movements and by the growth of an industrialized urban civilization. But quite clearly Keller condemns

Herr Jacques's immature 'originality fever'; and so the stories are told to cure him of it.

It is significant, as well as paradoxical, that the most important genre in Germany in the age of the locomotive should have been the village tale. Regionalism is indeed a feature of German realism. But regionalism brought with it certain problems, not merely, for example, whether the idyllic world of the peasant could achieve epic proportions, but also whether the literary work should be written in the real language of the people, that is, in dialect. Some writers like Gotthelf hovered between the popular idiom of their region and a more elevated literary language. Others, especially northerners like Fritz Reuter, John Brinkmann and Klaus Groth, were more consistent in their acceptance of linguistic realism and wrote only in Low German dialect; of these Fritz Reuter was perhaps the most successful, achieving recognition even in Victorian England. South Germany too had its regional writers, and one must never forget the strong Austrian tradition of regional realism which produced such writers as Peter Rosegger, Ludwig Anzengruber and Ferdinand von Saar – not that they by any means restricted themselves to dialect works. There is one other regional realist whose name is rarely if ever mentioned in histories of German literature, although in his day Leopold von SACHER-MASOCH (1836–95) won wide acclaim as a writer of tales about remote corners of the Austro-Hungarian Empire and was lionized in Paris. Everything that has been said about German realism so far can be said of Sacher-Masoch. He wrote regional tales, Jewish tales, ethnic tales, tales of folklore and history; today, however, he is remembered only because his heroes are often so passive and his heroines so powerful that Krafft-Ebing used his name to coin the word *masochism* in his *Psychopathia Sexualis*. Readers of the story to which reference is generally made, *Venus im Pelz* (*Venus in Furs*), will be amazed to discover how harmless Sacher-Masoch is compared to the infamous Marquis de Sade. This *Venus im Pelz* is only one story in the collection called *Das Vermächtnis Kains* (*The Legacy of Cain*, 1870), of which the first part is devoted to tales of love. The stories from the second part, devoted to property, and the introduction to the whole collection, in which Sacher-Masoch develops his theory of realism in literature, are now seldom studied; and yet he was closer to the great Russians, Gogol and Turgenev, than any of his contemporaries.

It was in the form of the village tale essentially that realism was introduced into German literature. Nationalist critics see the replacement of the literature of the Young Germans, inspired by ideas current in Parisian intellectual circles, by that of the Poetic Realists in terms of a change from rootless, hot-house intellectualism to an honest appraisal of the solid, enduring virtues of the peasantry, just as the National Socialists saw the big-city literature of the Expressionists as decadent and tales of the soil and of tillers of the soil as healthy. It is difficult to decide who was initially responsible for this mythology. Walter Scott had, of course, painted the life of the people in their country setting, combining the historical with the regional, but this was not anything foreign to the German tradition. Early examples of rustic realism include the *Oberhof* story inserted in Immermann's long novel *Münchhausen* (1838–9), Auerbach's *Schwarzwälder Dorfgeschichten* and Gotthelf's peasant stories set in the Bernese countryside. But in this genre Keller surpassed his predecessors. Auerbach was the sophisticated *littérateur* deliberately exploiting the picturesque aspects of peasant life in order to ingratiate himself with his middle-class readership: a sort of German *costumbrista*. Successful though he may have been in accustoming his contemporary public to realism, his stories strike the modern reader as unbearably maudlin and melodramatic. Even the introduction of social problems, to give a semblance of seriousness to his fiction, seems too deliberate and conscious a contrivance. But while Auerbach is little read today, Gotthelf's reputation stands high. Although appreciated in his own time, his works never enjoyed widespread popularity, and it was only with the nationalistic swing of the 1930s and 1940s that his literary stock began to rise. But even Gotthelf's most ardent admirers have to admit that his works, full of vitality though they are, lack artistic shape and frequently suffer from the intrusion of didacticism. Only Keller succeeded in moulding this material into a harmonious form, elevating the village tale to the level of a work of art.

The best example of what he could do with the village tale is

Romeo und Julia auf dem Dorfe (1856). Delius set the story as an opera, *A Village Romeo and Juliet*; this includes an orchestral interlude called *The Walk to the Paradise Garden*, and this is the only part of it that has brought Keller's story into English cultural consciousness. Keller states his intention quite explicitly: to retell the old Shakespearian story but base his version on fact; his source was, indeed, the newspaper account of an actual occurrence. Unlike Auerbach, Keller has no need to resort to sensational treatment to stimulate his reader's interest in the everyday life of the peasant. The story he has to tell might sound sensational: after a night of love on a hay barge the couple commit suicide by drowning! But this is still far removed from the brutally frank eroticism of the naturalist novel: the discreet style of poetic realism ensures that this potentially explosive tale of passion and tragedy does not offend the susceptibilities of even the most prudish reader, and schoolchildren nowadays are regularly given this novella to study. This is not, however, how it was read in England in its own time. The *Westminster Review*, discussing it in 1858, found that the story was characterized by 'a free poetic fancy in the conception and a thorough realism in the execution', but then the mid-Victorian critic warned would-be readers that the dénouement was very strong stuff indeed, suitable for a male audience only and far too shocking for the fair sex and the family circle. Paul Heyse, on the other hand, in the celebrated collection he made of the best novellas of the time (the *Deutscher Novellenschatz*), correctly identified the main features of Keller's style as 'that genuine air of casual comfort and gentleness in the narrative sequence which guides the reader in a smoothly flowing stream past a variety of pictures without rushing him into dramatic whirlpools or breath-taking cascades'. This description fits not only Keller's style but that of poetic realism in general. There never are any dramatic whirlpools or breath-taking cascades, there is no tension, no attempt to build up to a mighty climax. Instead the tone is maintained on an even key and all such potentially romantic themes as childhood, nature, love and death are handled in a realistic but poetic manner which never soars to the heights of rhetoric nor plunges to the depths of vulgarity. The tale Keller has to tell is not only based on a real-life story: it is given exemplary status. But here as always he manages to 'dissolve the didactic in the poetic', and the unformulated message is a moral rather than a religious one. Unlike Gotthelf, Keller is not concerned with life after death. His lovers know that life on this earth is all they have and that they must enjoy it to the full while they can, for there will be no meeting in the hereafter. It is typical of Keller that he does not indulge in social criticism, preferring to accept without fuss the particular social order he finds himself dealing with. The young lovers subscribe uncomplainingly to the middle-class assumption that love needs to be sanctified by marriage, and having defied this convention, they pay the penalty and go to their death.

It is a tragic story, and interesting not only as the supreme example of the village tale but also because the general trend of poetic realism was to avoid tragedy. This is one of the many paradoxes of this paradoxical age. On the one hand it was for long thought that poetic realism stood for something positive and optimistic as opposed to romanticism, for example, which Goethe had described as unhealthy. On the other hand tales of this kind, like Otto Ludwig's *Zwischen Himmel und Erde*, reveal the Poetic Realist's extreme awareness of the problematic nature of the age in which he lived, through which ran a deep strain of pessimism, evidenced by the extraordinary popularity of Schopenhauer's philosophical system about the middle of the nineteenth century. Schopenhauer, in the terms of the title of his best-known work, rejected the world as will and illusion. The consequences of this premise for any subsequent aesthetic of realism were bound to be far-reaching. Certainly the tales of the German realists are steeped in disillusion and marked by an uneasy sense of the unstable nature of the universe. The *Bürger* withdraws into his private world and the novella becomes more and more the expression of his inner predicament and less and less concerned with the notation of external reality. However, his situation is not tragic in any traditional sense: the individual does not rail defiantly against his fate, he does not 'take on' society; instead he resigns himself to his lot. Little wonder, then, that no great tragedies were written at this time, despite the interest shown by most Poetic Realists in the theatre, and that the novella became the substitute for tragedy. Theodor Storm in a famous statement described the novella as the 'sister of the drama', not only because it was the most strictly organized of the narrative forms, but also because like the drama it was capable of dealing with the profoundest problems of human life. More recently Walter Silz in his analysis of *Romeo und Julia auf dem Dorfe* has described the story as a middle-class tragedy, dealing with 'social deterioration and loss of caste and the unhappy consequence thereof in two generations'.[11] The tragedy, of course, does not arise from any conflict between the middle class and the aristocracy, which would have been a meaningless theme for a writer in the Helvetian Republic. Nor is there any suggestion of the kind of tragic situation which Hebbel dealt with in his play *Maria Magdalena* (1844), arising from a clash within the middle class itself, what E. K. Bennett calls 'a conflict engendered of self-criticism'; for Keller obviously has no criticisms to offer of bourgeois society – the lovers' decision to commit suicide is described in the story as one 'which both offends and glorifies middle-class morality'. In *Romeo und Julia auf dem Dorfe* there is, strictly, no conflict: the characters, far from reacting against their situation, meekly accept the suffering it involves. But, as in Storm's *Immensee*, which is also a tale of suffering and resignation, this immediately introduces the risk of sentimentality.

To understand how the German realists avoided this danger involves consideration of another essential element in poetic realism, namely humour. The difference between romanticism and realism in German literature can be summed up as the difference between irony and humour. The Age of Realism was characterized by a spate of definitions of humour, beginning with Jean Paul's. The common element in them all is the mocking feeling for real life and the need for direct contact with it. Humour is felt to rest essentially in a sort of inadequacy between the idea and the expression given to it, between the matter and the form, the sentiment and the tone, the impression produced by the external world and the realist's presentation of it. There are various ways of achieving this effect: the humorist can, for example, enter into minute detail where one would expect some brief generality, or he can take an elevated idea and express it in a very commonplace and down-to-earth way. These are devices ordinarily employed by Jean Paul and copied, in a modified form, by Keller and Raabe. Humour thereby serves to mediate between the ridiculous and the sublime, to reveal the laughable side of anything too high-flown. Any character of more than average pretensions is cut down to size; and conversely the weak, the humble, the helpless are presented as worthy of respect. In this way balance and harmony are achieved, to be disturbed only occasionally when Keller and Raabe imitate too closely Jean Paul's whimsicality and fondness for extended imagery.

Humour of this kind is seldom uproariously funny, arising as it does more often from the general tone of the narrative than from any specific episodes. Hence critics tend to speak of a 'Keller tone' or a 'Fontane tone', implying thereby, incidentally, that there is nothing derivative about such humour. Lesser writers like Freytag or even Ludwig may have been inspired by Dickens, but Keller, Raabe, and Fontane introduced their own personal brand of humour into their narratives.

One feature which all the German realists do share with Dickens, however, is the ability to create memorable comic characters. Sometimes these 'characters' are not much more than caricatures, but often the queer birds and semi-outsiders whom the realists favour are shown to be admirable figures wholly deserving both of the warmth the author feels for them and of the affection they inspire in the reader. Besides viewing their characters humorously, the realists often endow them with the same quality of humour as they themselves display. Such characters have the gift of laughter, the capacity to rise above despair and distress, the faculty of perceiving the essential sadness of things. Characters in a realistic story work through the school of life, see the error of their ways and learn to adapt to reality. The proof that they have passed the test is that they can accept life and its limitations with good humour. Those who fail the test are shown as lacking in an essential quality, but they are not fiercely pilloried as 'philistines', as they might have been had they figured in a romantic work. Humour is an ethical quality, not an intellectual exercise like romantic irony: it establishes the balance between subjectivity and objectivity, allowing the author to take a warm interest in the fate of his characters without ever destroying the illusion of their real existence by the exercise of irony. The intention is to entertain but also gently to point the moral.

THE MIDDLE-CLASS NOVEL

Keller regarded his humorous tale *Die drei gerechten Kammacher* (*The Three Just Comb-Makers*, 1856) as a touchstone for true understanding of his art and was especially pleased when Wagner expressed his delight in it. It provides a good indication too of the level of society and the kind of commercial activity which the German realist favoured. Keller deliberately selected, for its symbolic as well as its realistic implications, the craft of the comb-maker as Ludwig chose that of the steeplejack. In his original design his 'three just men' were to be joiners, but the idea of cutting teeth each one parallel with the next and at an even distance apart seemed to him an appropriate symbol of bloodless righteousness. The journeying craftsmen had formed part of the romantic tradition of the wanderer in Germany, celebrated in countless songs and stories. Keller treats the commercial aspect more realistically, but there is still little trace in his work of the world of the factory and the proletariat proper. The commercial sphere with which German realism deals is perhaps best illustrated through the works of Gustav FREYTAG (1816–95), the title of whose best-known and still widely read novel *Soll und Haben* (*Debit and Credit*, 1855) immediately tells the reader what to expect.

Soll und Haben is an important work, though, judged on purely literary criteria, not an outstanding achievement. Freytag used as epigraph for his book the words of Julian Schmidt, Germany's greatest advocate of realism: 'The novel must seek the German people where they are found at their soundest, namely at work.' Julian Schmidt, co-editor with Freytag of the *Grenzboten*, a middle-class journal of national liberal slant, was deeply conscious of the impact that the revolutionary upheavals of 1848 had had on the German novel. He was convinced that in the post-1848 period the only adequate form for 'a world grown prosaic' was the novel, and as the leading exponent of literary realism he required of the novelist that he should, like the politician, base himself on 'observation of real conditions', and that he should totally reject the empty rhetoric of the previous age. What Julian Schmidt was reacting against was made abundantly clear in his influential *Geschichte der deutschen Literatur im 19. Jahrhundert* (1855), the third volume of which dealt with the contemporary period. This is the volume in which occurs the famous sentence that Freytag used as an imperative for the novel. Gone are the days of romantic fantasies or Young German utopian dreams; instead, Freytag undertakes the gigantic task of showing the German people at work, not of course by depicting the life of the proletariat, but rather that of the man of business.

The period he chose was not quite his own time but one set not too far back in the past, and the type of business he describes is an old-fashioned family one. What Freytag wanted to show in his novel was that a commercial drama could be both enthralling and attractive. The form he adopted was still close to that of the *Bildungsroman*: he traces the biography of a young man who starts as an apprentice in the world of commerce and ends as a highly respected *Grosskaufmann* (wholesale merchant). Wohlfahrt, the protagonist, has all the respectable middle-class qualities, such as honesty, conscientiousness, diligence, and personal initiative. The German *Bürger* emerges as the standard-bearer of social and economic progress, and the crude reality of his life is diluted by a strong dose of idealization. On the whole characterization follows standard racial and national type-casting: the old aristocracy is decadent and incapable of coping with the modern world of finance, the Jews are brilliant but fundamentally unsound, the Poles totally unreliable. Nevertheless the novel is still highly readable; the action-packed Polish sections are very exciting and there is a great deal of humour, though mainly of the Dickensian variety involving curious 'characters'. These are chiefly to be found among the work-people; the middle-class ethos is never held up to ridicule.

Freytag was certainly in the mainstream of middle-class writing in the nineteenth century, but the novelist who was most successful with this type of realism was Wilhelm Heinrich von RIEHL (1823–97). To say that for Germany realism is Riehlism is no mere play on words. In his fiction as well as in his detailed historical surveys he showed how richly rewarding could be a study of the natural history of the people. Riehl was a democrat, but after 1848 a cautiously conservative one. He loved the peasantry, and was fascinated by variations of language and custom from one province or district to another. He stressed the conservative force of family life, centring on the wife and mother. The peasantry and the aristocracy provided in his view the forces of social permanence, while the middle class and the fourth estate were the agents of social change. But the aristocracy, which had once had a part to play, had decayed with the passage of time and was now 'an antiquarian relic, venerable because grey with age'. George Eliot summed up the conservatism of Riehl (and of the German realists) very well when she called him

a clear-eyed, practical, but withal large-minded man, a little caustic perhaps now and then in his epigrams on democratic doctrinaires who have their nostrums for all political and social diseases, and on communistic theories, which he regards as 'the despair of the individual in his own manhood, reduced to a system'; but nevertheless able and willing to do justice to the elements of fact and reason in every shade of opinion and every form of effort.[12]

It was a kind of conservatism which made a strong appeal to the National Socialists, who developed Riehl's idealization of the peasant into a grotesque aesthetic of *Blut und Boden* ('Blood and Soil').

The writings of Riehl, Freytag and Julian Schmidt might suggest that German realism depended exclusively on a middle-class ideology. There were in fact other novelists who viewed the problems of the age from the standpoint of the aristocracy, and, as is well known, Fontane, who came later, had a weakness for the old nobility and loved to portray them in his novels. In general terms, however, it is undeniable that the core of German realism is *bürgerlich* in the sense suggested by Riehl. The lower classes – the factory operatives, artisans and agricultural day labourers – were dismissed by Riehl as the products of a 'decomposition commencing in the organic constitution of society': he regarded them as unsuitable material for literary treatment. In the works of the realists they figure only on the periphery or else are introduced, as in the fiction of social novelists like Gutzkow, only as literary stereotypes. It did not occur to these writers to study them as an emerging social force of the future.

There is one possible exception to this rule, however: the man whom Engels described as the most important poet of the German proletariat, Georg WEERTH (1822–56). His complete works were not available in a collected edition until the centenary of his death, in 1956, which accounts for the fact that Weerth is inadequately appreciated even today. The somewhat exaggerated acclaim that his writings received in certain quarters when they were rediscovered should not obscure the fact that his literary career was a quite remarkable one. He spent some of his most formative early years in Bradford and on the basis of his experience there wrote essays on social and political life in England. He also contributed articles on his travels abroad to the *Deutsche Brüsseler Zeitung* of which Marx and Engels were respectively editor-in-chief and deputy editor. Weerth's major work was the novel *Leben und Taten des berühmten Ritters Schnapphahnski* (*Life and Deeds of the Famous Knight Schnapphahnski*, 1849), the title of which inevitably recalls Cervantes as well as Heine. *Schnapp-hahn* in German means footpad or highwayman, and Weerth was clearly aiming his satire at Prince Lichnowski, a shady nobleman involved in some of the more unsavoury dealings of the Prussian Diet; the novel is a *roman à clé* and suffers somewhat as a result.

Weerth remains a significant though isolated figure on the German literary scene. The proletariat had yet to appear in the mass; the German realist wrote not of the factory worker but of the craftsman, not of the day labourer but of the smallholder. In the village tale he glorified a world which he knew to be fast disappearing under the impact of industrialization and agrarian reform. It is a transitional world caught at the point of change between the old and the new, just as is the business world presented by Freytag in *Soll und Haben*, where old-style commercial values are recorded just before they disappear for ever, to be replaced by a new and harsher economic order.

RAABE

There is still no general consensus of critical opinion about Wilhelm RAABE (1837–1910), an author too little appreciated outside Germany. Like Theodor Storm, who was typecast by the enormous success of the early *Immensee* and had difficulty, almost up to the appearance of his last story, *Der Schimmelreiter*, in persuading his readers that he was capable of anything different, Raabe also lived to regret the astonishing success of his early works and the assumptions they created in the public mind. His immensely popular first novel, *Die Chronik der Sperlingsgasse* (*The Chronicle of Sparrow Street*, 1856), gave him the reputation of an idiosyncratic, sentimental exploiter of nostalgia and neighbourliness in the manner of Dickens. The theme, as the title indicates, is the passage of time, the place is now the big city of Berlin, but the technique is highly sophisticated, involving both the private subjective narrative perspective of the story-teller or chronicler and the objective unfolding of the chronicle, as the street tells its own story. As recent critics have pointed out, *Die Chronik der Sperlingsgasse* is, from one point of view, an old-fashioned work in the style of Sterne and Jean Paul; but it can with equal propriety be regarded as a highly complex product of the modern spirit, anticipating Gide, Butor, and Uwe Johnson. Raabe is not concerned with the city as a phenomenon of modern life; instead his book offers an idyllic enclave and an organic, cosily domestic, literary view of it. The movement of the novel is towards inwardness: what the street reveals is a microcosm of the world past and present. Its qualities are allegorical and abstract rather than realistic.

Raabe's next great success, *Der Hungerpastor* (1864), resembles in manner Freytag's *Soll und Haben*, even down to the conventional contrast between the virtuous German and his tricky Jewish rival. It did not go down well abroad. The *Westminster Review* of 1886 felt that it belonged to a class of fiction unknown in any other language, in which events 'so small as to be microscopic are set forth with the circumstantiality of a *procès-verbal*'. Raabe's *Abu Telfan oder Die Heimkehr vom Mondgebirge (Abu Telfan or The Return from the Mountains of the Moon*, 1868) fared little better. In general the Victorians found Raabe's novels 'too long, too abstract and too complicated', and since then no further attempt has been made to break down reader resistance by risking further translations of later works. This is a great pity, for Raabe is certainly a major writer, and in recent years has been more and more widely recognized as such. He remains, however, despite all arguments in favour of regarding him as 'a modern', very firmly tethered to the traditions of nineteenth-century middle-class realism. His was a life of books, and his books are full of books, so much so indeed that quotation has been singled out as one of the most important elements in his work; but this inner life of the poetry of the heart enters into conflict with an outer world of deepening materialism. That his characters inhabit a world of illusions matters little, since for Raabe man lives by his illusions. He makes few concessions to his readers and his books can be disconcerting. An adventure story will turn out to have little or no adventure and little or no story, historical tales will often abandon history and give up the attempt to re-create reality as it might have been. Instead Raabe rambles on, filling his pages with reflections on the books he has read, with fragments of strange lore, with queer expressions from different languages and lengthy monologues. Yet his novels and stories are only superficially artless. Raabe is one of the great humorists of German realism, and in all these diversions he is merely playing a game in which the reader may join if he chooses. Standing as he does at the crossroads of the past and the future, he is a writer who will always have his circle of devoted adherents but also one who is unlikely ever to achieve general acceptance, let alone mass popularity. Beside his works even those of Thomas Mann, which closely resemble them, seem straightforward and devoid of complexity.

FONTANE

The name of Theodor FONTANE (1819–98) indicates his French Huguenot descent, though there is nothing of the 'French plasticity' of C. F. Meyer about his style. At first he followed his father's calling as a dispensing chemist, but after military service he gave up this trade to become a journalist and theatre critic. He travelled to England more than once, was a war correspondent, secretary to the Akademie der Künste, editor of the reactionary *Kreuzzeitung*, and only gradually developed as an original writer, starting with ballads and travel diaries and graduating to historical fiction and finally novels of life in Berlin and Brandenburg in his own time. His first work of fiction, *Vor dem Sturm (Before the Storm)*, appeared in 1878, and from then on Fontane produced a string of novels, including *Irrungen, Wirrungen (Mistakes and Misconceptions*, 1888), *Unwiederbringlich (Beyond Recall*, 1891), *Frau Jenny Treibel* (1893), *Effi Briest* (1895), *Die Poggenpuhls* (1896), and *Der Stechlin* (1898). Critics vary in their opinion as to which book, in this impressive list, is Fontane's masterpiece. The truth is that he is not the easiest of authors to deal with. As is now being increasingly realized, there is always a marked difference between the outspoken statements which this most liberal of men was prepared to make in private correspondence and the complex ambivalence of the characters in his novels. He never introduces direct social criticism into his books, nor does he convey his message in the form of black-and-white statements of the Freytag variety. He may owe something to the novel of manners as practised by Jane Austen or Thackeray, but he is also a German realist writing in the established manner of the German realists. This he recognized himself and stated explicitly:

Realism in art is as old as art itself, indeed it is more: *it is art*. Our modern tendency is merely a return to the only right road, the recovery of an invalid, which could not fail to take place as long as the organism was still capable of living at all . . . The confusion of empty imagery in the thirties of this century was bound to be succeeded, as necessary reaction, by a period of honest feeling and healthy common sense, a period which we boldly assert is here.

Fontane goes on to define realism as 'the sworn enemy of all pretentiousness and extravagance', and he makes it clear that he will have no truck with those who limit its meaning to 'the naked reproduction of everyday life' especially in its grimmer aspects. Referring particularly to the use of the term by art critics, Fontane observes that

it is not all that long ago that people (particularly in painting) confused wretchedness with realism and imagined that in depicting a dying proletarian surrounded by starving children or in producing those so-called *Tendenzbilder* (Silesian weavers, the game laws and other things of the kind) they had indicated a brilliant tendency for art to adopt. That tendency has the same relationship to genuine realism as raw ore has to metal: the refining process is missing.

And he ended by describing realism as 'the reflection of all real life, all true forces in the element of art'.[13]

The phrase about realism being the 'sworn enemy of all pretentiousness and extravagance' could, as we have seen, be applied confidently to the works of a writer like Gottfried Keller; and in general Fontane's remarks constitute a very adequate description of realism before the advent of naturalist doctrines. The spectacle of a dying proletarian surrounded by starving children, the plight of Silesian weavers and the operation of the game laws are not themes that ever tempted Ludwig, Keller, or Raabe. Like Keller, Fontane wants to transfigure reality; his guiding principles are, like Keller's or Storm's, selectiveness, restraint, and discretion. Fontane called his best-known novel, *Effi Briest*, 'a tale of adultery like a hundred others', and critics have made the inevitable comparison with *Madame Bovary*. But Fontane, as his review of Freytag's *Die Ahnen* in 1875 reveals, must have had little sympathy with Flaubert's aims and outlook. He believed that a novel should avoid everything exaggerated and ugly, that it should address itself to the imagination and to the heart, providing stimulation without excitement; he believed that it should for a spell make the world of fiction seem a world of reality, that it should provoke laughter and tears, hope and fear, but that when he closed the book the reader should be left feeling he had spent some hours among charming and interesting people whose company had afforded him pleasure, enlightenment, and instruction.

As for the subject-matter and chronological setting of the novel, Fontane asserted that the best kind of fiction is that which presents a picture of its own time or of the immediate past. He pointed out that Walter Scott began his career not with *Ivanhoe*, set in the twelfth century, but with *Waverley*, which dealt with the 1745 rebellion and bore the significant subtitle ' 'Tis Sixty Years Since'. All novels of lasting value produced over the previous century and a half had been written in accordance with this general requirement. The great English humorists of the eighteenth and nineteenth centuries depicted their own time; the French novel, despite Dumas *père*, had evolved as a study of contemporary manners and morals. Sixty years was as far back as Fontane was prepared to go, and in his view all historical novels were abominations.

Fontane's works are written in strict accord with this declaration of principles. The name chosen for the heroine of *Effi Briest* may have been intended as a tribute to Walter Scott, the creator of Effie Deans in *The Heart of Midlothian*; indeed, Effi's personal reading list, given towards the end of the novel, confirms that *Ivanhoe* and *Quentin Durward*, as well as Fenimore Cooper's *The Spy*, were novels that Fontane admired. But despite this passing obeisance to the masters of the historical and exotic novel, *Effi Briest*, like Droste-Hülshoff's *Die Judenbuche*, provides a picture of the manners and morals of one particular place at one particular time. Indeed Fontane's novel has the same central theme as Droste-Hülshoff's novella. Not only is the problematical nature of time at the heart of both works, but it crystallizes in both into the specific issue of *Verjährung*, an ambiguous term which can mean either a claim founded on long usage, or a crime which escapes retribution because so much time has passed since it was committed: a statute of limitation, in other words. In *Die Judenbuche* there is a gap of twenty-eight years between crime and punishment; in *Effi Briest* several years have passed before Effi's offence comes to light. Innstetten tortures himself over the problem of *Verjährung*:

If guilt has any meaning at all, it's not tied to any time or place and can't cease to be guilt overnight. Guilt demands expiation: that makes sense. But a time limit is neither one thing nor the other, it's feeble or at least prosaic.

It is significant that in his very first chapter Fontane should refer to Fritz Reuter, the noted exponent of regional realism in the form of dialect literature. Fontane himself eschews dialect, as did all the Poetic Realists, but like them he appreciated the flavour and local colour which a touch of dialect could give to his own prose; this fondness emerges in the lists he gives of evocative place-names: Pichelsberg, Pichelsdorf, Pichelswerder, Kickebusch, Wuhlheide ... The first chapter also introduces the characteristic theme of resignation and renunciation with its echoes of Theodor Storm and Otto Ludwig. These are not the only reminders of Storm, whose stories Fontane knew and admired. It was *Immensee* which first dealt, however discreetly, with the erotic theme of the child bride, and with the question, too, of happiness and the need ultimately to settle for something short of the romantic dream of rapture. Like Storm's and Droste-Hülshoff's tales, *Effi Briest* is full of omens, secret premonitions, guesses and unspoken thoughts. Effi is 'a fantastic little creature' whose mind runs on remarkable imaginings. Her mother warns her from the start that there is a great difference between illusion and reality, and this is indeed one of the lessons she learns in the course of her life. Innstetten on the other hand is a man of character, whose strength is, however, only apparent: a neurotic Wagner-lover, he is almost as much a 'hypochondriac' as Ludwig's Apollonius in *Zwischen Himmel und Erde*, another man paralysed by inherited concepts of honour.

Boredom is as important a theme in *Effi Briest* as it is generally in the literature of nineteenth-century Europe, but even more important is the theme – first fully exploited by Theodor Storm – of the almost existential loneliness of the individual in the domestic circle. The reader never sees Effi on her honeymoon in Capri and Sorrento; almost always she is shown trapped either in a spooky house in Kessin, or in another house in Berlin. She is cut off from the country people, hardly associates with the local aristocracy, and does not have much to do with the local townspeople. The only person she takes to is Alonzo Gieshübler, an artistic apothecary and an *Original*, a character with obvious affinities to Keller's eccentrics and countless similar figures in Raabe. His name splits, like the novel itself, into two parts, one evoking the exoticism of art, the other the commonplace philistine world of daily affairs. Innstetten too, the Prussian bureaucrat, is an Indian or Persian prince to Effi, and in fact not only does Effi live isolated from the outside world like a creature in an oriental harem, but Fontane even suggests the idea to which Hebbel had devoted his play *Herodes und Mariamne*, that the wife should be so much her husband's chattel that her duty is to follow him into the grave should he die before her. A curse of silence bedevils relations between Effi and Innstetten and despite the brilliance and humour of the dialogue in the novel, it is significant that letters play an important part and that Effi's guilt should eventually come to light because she has failed to destroy her correspondence with her lover Major Crampas. One cannot imagine Fontane writing a dramatic discovery or passionate confrontation scene.

The curse is not only the curse of silence but the curse of the past, which can never be lived down. The individual is a member of society and subject to its laws, but ultimately he comes to realize his complete aloneness. This is as true of Innstetten as it is of Effi, who is overcome by a 'feeling of isolation in the world'. There is no escape for Effi, any more than there is for Innstetten, who is incapable of making a new life for himself in another sphere. He has thought of doing so, of course, but he just cannot see himself putting on sackcloth and ashes or acting the dervish dancing himself to death in a welter of self-accusations: 'I've worked out in my mind what else I could best do and that is to leave everything and go where everybody's coal-black and doesn't know anything about culture and honour. Happy people!' But of course he cannot leave and remains bound by 'certain conceptions in people's minds'. As Wüllerdorf puts it, the Congo, palavers and pith helmets are for young lieutenants who get into debt. Innstetten can no more escape and renew himself than can Botho in *Irrungen, Wirrungen*. An aristocrat cannot become 'a cowboy in Texas or a waiter on a Mississippi steamer', he cannot go 'riding along the Sacramento River or out on to the gold fields', he is a member of a particular society and subject to its rules, no matter how meaningless events may have shown them to be. As a novelist Fontane was aware of worlds outside Berlin, just as Keller in the preface to his cycle of stories mentions Australia, California, Texas, Paris, and Constantinople before returning to his tales of Seldwyla. And, needless to say, in this Age of Emigration certain writers had done more than merely name these far-off places. Karl Postl (1793–1864) had long since produced his realistic accounts of life in America (in German and in English), while Friedrich Gerstäcker (1816–72) had travelled as far afield as Australia. Colonial themes were in the air. Ernst Willkomm (1810–86) had devoted his novel *Die Europamüden* (1838) to those who were sick of Europe, while Ferdinand Kürnberger (1821–79) had written *Der Amerika-Müde* (1855) about those who had returned to Europe tired of America. The German realists were well aware of the wide world out there, and some of their stories (Keller's *Pankraz*, Raabe's *Abu Telfan* and *Der Stopfkuchen*) are full of homecomers. But the resulting confrontation only serves to bring into greater prominence the difference between the world 'out there' and the claustrophobic, microscopic world in which the protagonists are trapped. The outcome, as in *Effi Briest*, is more often resignation and acceptance than protest and defiance. This novel does not end with the death of Effi's lover Crampas in the duel with Innstetten, nor with the disillusionment with society that both she and her husband experience. First comes Effi's *Verklärung* (transfiguration, the term always used by the realists when they try to characterize their own approach to reality). Then comes the *Versöhnung* (reconciliation), Effi's acceptance of her fate. Fontane does not altogether avoid the pitfall of sentimentality that always lies in wait for the German realist. In the closing scenes of the book he has Effi's faithful old servant and her dog come back to her, while the priest proclaims that she will go straight to heaven when she dies. The author does, however, fight off the temptation to philosophize or draw a moral, although there are several passages towards the end that serve the purpose of explicit commentary, of which the most significant concerns the need for 'auxiliary structures' to prop up a house which is collapsing. But characteristically almost the last word of the novel, directed against Effi's father, who is constantly accused of uttering them, is *ambiguities, ambiguities*. Fontane is too much a realist ever to see only one side of any question; hence ambiguities, ambivalences, polarities are the hallmark of all his writings.

NATURALISM

As a theatre critic, Fontane was in a very good position to observe the arrival of naturalism on the literary scene in Germany. In general he welcomed the innovations for which the naturalists were responsible, though he did not feel he could follow their example himself. What could happen to a poetic realist who attempted to make the transition to naturalism is best demonstrated in Keller's last novel, *Martin Salander* (1886).

Critics were not slow to point out the similarities between *Der grüne Heinrich* and *Martin Salander*, but how different is the narrative technique! By the time Keller came to write his last work Spielhagen's first essays on the theory and technique of the novel had already appeared. Just as the realistic theory of the novel had approximated it to drama, and Freytag had striven to give *Soll und Haben* a dramatic structure, so too Friedrich SPIELHAGEN (1829–1911) now developed a consistent theory of the objective narrative as a 'dramatic' form. Keller's comments on Spielhagen lack warmth, his suspicions being aroused by the ease and speed with which Spielhagen produced his successful social novels. But Spielhagen's conception of the novel, with its marked Flaubertian overtones, was not unattractive. He was one of the first in Germany to impose on the novel the discipline of form and to give it a solid theoretical foundation. Fontane too was attracted to the theory of the dramatic novel, and his own social novels benefited by the technique which permitted the expression of opinions without the direct intrusion of the author. Keller certainly read not only Spielhagen's theoretical writings but his novels as well, and Spielhagen's *Angela* (1881) provided the 'Excelsior' motif, drawn from Longfellow, which is the basis of *Martin Salander*, where the theme of toiling upwards embraces a complex mixture of idealism, illusion, and mere ambitious social climbing. *Martin Salander* also shows what happens when the balance between objectivity and subjectivity, which is so characteristic of poetic realism, is abandoned and the novel becomes objective in Spielhagen's sense of the word. The story-teller who used to hover between the reader and the story, and whose presence, according to Spielhagen, destroyed the illusion of reality, has disappeared. Explicit appraisal on the author's part of the events related is never allowed, nor does the author introduce his characters and comment on the part they play in the novel. The characters present themselves, just as the facts speak for themselves. The novel becomes dramatic, episodic, progressing by means of action and dialogue instead of narrative and reflective passages. All theoretical discussions, considerations, and explanations are placed in the mouths of the 'actors'. Characterization and psychological motivation are presented by means of interior monologues. Significant repetitions and parallels are now increasingly necessary, not only to reveal the relationship between events and characters, but also to guide the reader in forming a just impression of them. Used in moderation and discretion as by Fontane such techniques and devices could be very effective; used too crudely they risked producing a cold and mechanical work in which the *innere Heiterkeit*, the glow, the gentle warmth so characteristic of poetic realism, was completely lacking.

Martin Salander, which was published the year after the appearance of *Germinal*, shows distinct traces not only of Spielhagen's theories but also of the new conception of the novel evolved by the French naturalists. In so far as Keller was trying to relate the history of a period by showing it reflected in the lives of several members of a single family, he was obviously inviting comparison with Zola's attempt to do the same thing in *Les Rougon-Macquart*. The ambition to embrace the totality of all social conditions in one long work derives from the naturalistic view of the novel as a sociological study. But what struck Keller and many of his contemporaries in Germany most forcefully was not the new naturalist theory of the novel as such, but the way it was applied in practice by the Goncourt brothers and Zola in their choice of material, their apparent predilection for pathological studies of sexual excesses in the lowest classes of society. The discretion exercised by the Poetic Realists in their treatment of carnal love has already been noted. Storm's *Immensee* and Ludwig's *Zwischen Himmel und Erde* work up an atmosphere electric with sexual potential, but the unspeakable is never spoken, and certainly never shown in action. The one exception was Sacher-Masoch, but even his works were more atmospheric than explicit. In *Martin Salander*, however, Keller attempted to portray his hero not only beguiled by false illusions but also succumbing to an 'erotic aberration'. The results were unconvincing; Keller cannot be said to have overcome the difficulties of dealing with the erotic, any more than did his successors. There were to be many German naturalist novels about prostitution, but none to rival *Nana*.

Keller's failure in *Martin Salander* to write a naturalist novel can be taken as symptomatic of the general failure of naturalism to strike roots in Germany outside the world of the theatre. The foreign doctrines were of course known and widely discussed, and the idea of the *roman expérimental* in particular encouraged writers like Heinrich and Julius Hart to engage in a great polemic 'for and against Zola'.[14] However, the literary situation in Germany after the achievement of political unification was an extremely complex one. The writers chiefly attacked by the German naturalists were Geibel, Heyse, Freytag, Dahn, exponents of polished poetry and authors of carefully researched historical plays and novels. The Poetic Realists, on the other hand, were much admired. The Hart brothers proclaimed the young Goethe of *Werther* and *Faust* a source of 'poetry-impregnated truth'; they also acclaimed Keller, who had shown how to 'transfigure primitive, many-faceted nature in the light of the ideal'. The novel had to be rescued from hacks like Spielhagen, Lindau and Heyse; but it was far from clear how this was to be done or who was to do it. Heyse at least is readable even today, while Michael Georg Conrad (1846–1927), who tried to follow in Zola's footsteps and write a cycle of novels about life in Munich, is not. For a time it was thought that a German Zola was emerging in Max Kretzer (1851–1941), who wrote from personal experience of the life of the worker. Again, Arno HOLZ (1863–1929) was a man of considerable talents, and attempts have been made in recent years to have him recognized as a forerunner of twentieth-century word-magic and concrete poetry. However, the so-called 'consistent' or out-and-out naturalism which he advocated proved to have greater potential for the theatre than for prose fiction. In general the new style worked only in shorter narrative pieces; not very many novels were written in German in accordance with naturalist theory. A few were composed by the Austrian Ludwig Anzengruber (1839–89); others by the authoress Clara Viebig (1860–1952), whose *Das Weiberdorf* (1900) shows the psychological and physical effects on the women in a village when they are forsaken by their menfolk, whom economic necessity has driven to seek work in the town.

Bahnwärter Thiel (Signalman Thiel, 1888) by Gerhart HAUPTMANN (1862–1946) invites comparison with Zola's *La Bête humaine*, written later (in 1890). But the similarities are more apparent than real: Hauptmann's Thiel is not a machine like the trains he controls, nor, as is Zola's Jacques Lantier, a beast governed by uncontrollable lusts. Despite its naturalistic trappings, Hauptmann's story owes more to the tradition of symbolic narrative established by the Poetic Realists. In any case, this work was exceptional in Hauptmann's literary output. His true mastery of the themes and techniques of naturalism emerges in his plays. It was in the drama, rather than in the novel, that naturalism made its greatest impact in Germany. After some initial resistance, not all of it from official quarters, the triumph of naturalism on the stage was inaugurated by the first production of Ibsen's *Ghosts* at Otto Brahm's Freie Bühne in Berlin (1889). This was followed by Hauptmann's *Vor Sonnenaufgang* (*Before Sunrise*, 1889), which provoked such a scandal as to ensure at any rate that naturalism would henceforth be a force to be reckoned with in the theatre. Hauptmann went on to write a series of powerful plays – *Einsame Menschen* (*Lonely People*, 1891), *Die Weber* (*The Weavers*, 1892), *Der Biberpelz* (*Beaver Fur*, 1893) – which raised him to a pinnacle of literary fame. He was not, however, the only dramatist of the time to exploit the naturalist formula. Hermann Sudermann (1857–1928) won an international reputation; the leading parts in his plays, like that of Magda in *Heimat* (*Homeland*, 1892), were performed by the greatest actresses of the day, Sarah Bernhardt and Eleonora Duse. Max Halbe, Georg Hirschfeld and others were almost equally successful; only Holz and Schlaf, who tried to apply their brand of 'consistent naturalism' to the drama in *Die Familie Selicke* (1890), failed to attract audiences. It was not just the subject-matter and dialogue but the entire production that tended now to be naturalistic; the new style held sway on the German stage for the next quarter of a century, until it was eventually ousted by the expressionistic reaction against the 'illusion of reality'.

Why naturalism should have succeeded in Germany in the dramatic form while it failed in the narrative is an extremely interesting question. One possible answer is that German literature had known a long tradition of social dramas, so that Hauptmann, Halbe, and Sudermann were able to draw on a rich heritage; their works continued the line started by Lessing's *Miss Sara Sampson* and *Emilia Galotti* and illustrated after him by Lenz's *Der Hofmeister* and *Die Soldaten*, Schiller's *Kabale und Liebe*, Büchner's *Woyzeck* and Hebbel's *Maria Magdalena*. The subject-matter was newer and more daring, but otherwise the naturalistic dramas were not all that startlingly different. The social novel set in the big city had, on the other hand, no antecedents. For a naturalistic novel to become a best-seller it seemed preferable that the author should avoid a metropolitan *milieu*, as Sudermann did in *Frau Sorge* (1887), a novel set in East Prussia which demonstrated that *Heimatkunst* or regional art was by no means dead in the new Imperial Germany. The obvious dearth of naturalist masterpieces in prose fiction has led critics sometimes to attach the label to impressionistic pieces like Arthur Schnitzler's *Leutnant Gustl* (1900), though this would be more accurately described as an early exercise in stream of consciousness than as a work having associations with naturalism. Even a novel like Thomas Mann's *Buddenbrooks* (1900) has been described as 'the one great (partially) naturalistic novel in the German language'.[15] It is only partially naturalistic, presumably, because of its roots in nineteenth-century realism (the very name Buddenbrooks occurs in *Effi Briest*), and also because like Raabe's novels it anticipates the most advanced twentieth-century techniques.

It would be easy, in face of the avalanche of pamphlets, manifestoes, and magazine articles devoted to discussion of French naturalism,[16] to overestimate the impact of this movement on German men of letters. Throughout the nineteenth century German writers and critics had strenuously refused to give their due to such major French novelists as Balzac, Stendhal, Flaubert, and the brothers Goncourt, even though close personal contacts occasionally existed, for example between the Young Germans and Balzac. George Sand was widely acclaimed, but it was Eugène Sue who was imitated. As Remak has put it, German novelists, German critics, and the German reading public 'refused outright to accept the inevitable consequences of the French and industrial revolutions'.[17] It was objected – not surprisingly – that the themes and subjects favoured by French realism testified to the same moral decadence as the French military collapse in 1870 was thought to have demonstrated so dramatically. So once again Idealism was played as the German trump card against Realism, and the beauty of Goethe's *Iphigenie* held up as a model of artistic purity to confound foreign pornographers. Nevertheless it did not really need a Nietzsche to point out that military supremacy did not necessarily denote cultural excellence; only a blind jingoist could find cause for gratification in the pseudo-artistic effusions which followed on the final unification of Germany and the creation of the Empire. The country once again faced the problem of *Epigonentum*, with the full weight of Imperial favour enlisted on the side of neo-romantic and neo-classical eclecticism against realism. A gulf yawned between the establishment art of the new Empire and the reality of the modern industrial state with its special social and political problems.

Germany was certainly ready for a message of the kind that Zola had to offer. The appeal of a creed which placed truth before 'lying convention' explains the intellectual excitement with which naturalism was welcomed in Germany and accounts for the spate of articles that greeted it, the number of groups that were formed to discuss it, the cycles of novels planned to do for Munich and Berlin what Zola had done for Paris. Yet, as we have seen, all this ferment yielded surprisingly few results in terms of original works, and the paucity of naturalist prose fiction cannot be entirely attributed to the lack of a tradition of the socio-political novel in Germany. Another reason may have been that there was still too great a gulf between the literary and the scientific cultures. German science was famous throughout the world both for its theoretical triumphs and for its successes in turning theory to practical use; but German intellectuals were still most reluctant to apply the theoretical concepts of the new positivistic philosophy in their writing, as Zola, or even Goethe before him, had tried to do. At heart they were all inveterate idealists. Darwinism, genetics, and the theory of environmental determinism were all widely discussed topics; the lower orders, down to the dregs of society, became acceptable material for literary treatment, as did too the physiological aspects of sex. But this previously untouched subject-matter formed the basis of no important novels. Always the German naturalists seemed half-hearted or ill at ease. Instead of embarking on creative works, they went on debating such questions as whether naturalism implied a pessimistic or an optimistic view of life. As idealists they were reluctant to accept a deterministic world-view because it implied considerable limitations on the theoretical freedom of the individual. At the same time they indulged in flirtations with socialism, and at least some of them believed in the possibility of changing the social and economic conditions which governed men's lives. Just as they oscillated schizophrenically between optimism and pessimism, so too the German naturalists, while taking a proper patriotic pride in the political power of a united German Empire, turned wistfully to Scandinavia and France in search of new techniques capable of laying bare the grosser deficiencies of their newly industrialized homeland. They dreamed of becoming the prophets of a new Germany, but found themselves denounced by their compatriots for excessive subservience to foreign models.

Yet another possible reason for the failure of the naturalist novel in Germany was simply that Zola's theory of the experimental novel, published in France in 1880, had been discovered too late, at a time when Zola himself was already showing signs of losing faith in the pure doctrine of naturalism as originally propounded. Before naturalism had had time to be properly assimilated in Germany, it was rapidly being superseded by 'a mysticism of the nerves'. Already in 1890 W. Bölsche was writing about what lay 'Beyond Naturalism'; but long before this the German naturalists had been divided in their own minds, congratulating themselves on their 'modernity' while secretly clinging to the past, writing manifestoes demanding a literature of the big city while all the time longing for a return to nature. As it was, far from limiting themselves to the lives of prostitutes and of the industrial proletariat in the slums, they seemed to prefer writing novels about the dilemma of the middle-class intellectual in the modern world, showing themselves to be as obsessed with the problem of genius and the lonely artist as any romantic. If poetic realism hinted at some kind of balance between the extreme subjectivity of romanticism and the absolute objectivity of naturalism, this did not mean that there was always a very noticeable difference between the *Heimatkunst* of the naturalists and the *Dorfgeschichten* of the realists. In practice, as Hauptmann's *Bahnwärter Thiel* demonstrated, the two were all but indistinguishable. And even when an attempt was made to go to extremes and establish a theory of naturalism which would remove any possibility of subjective falsification of reality, the outcome was not a rich harvest of narrative prose; on the contrary, the ultimate limits of naturalism seemed to have been reached.

Collaborating with Johannes Schlaf, Holz, the apostle of 'consistent naturalism', published in 1889, under the Scandinavian *nom de plume* Bjarne P. Holmsen, a collection of three short prose sketches entitled *Papa Hamlet*. This was a demonstration of a new narrative technique designed to record all observable reality second by second, excluding nothing. The result was a phonographic transcription in which direct description was avoided and dialogue prevailed. Prose of this kind aims to create the illusion of total reality; the author nowhere obtrudes to express an opinion, let alone point a moral, which represents an advance even on Spielhagen, in whose novels the point of view is perfectly clear despite the author's withdrawal behind his characters. In writing of the kind exemplified by *Papa Hamlet* the author abdicates all responsibility, leaving the reader as much in the dark as to the meaning of it all as he might be confronted with a Kafka narrative. Clearly with this type of literature there is no possibility of 'epic breadth', no development of character or plot; instead, the impressionistic record simply notes changes in the characters and situations from second to second. It is a technique which replaces narrative either by colloquy, or by soliloquy in the form of the *Gedankenmonolog* or stream of consciousness.

Holz expounded this method in a doctrinal work published in 1891, *Die Kunst, ihr Wesen und ihre Gesetze* (*Art, its Nature and Laws*), in the pages of which occurs the famous formula: 'Art has the tendency to become Nature again. It becomes Nature in so far as the prevalent conditions of reproduction and their manipulation permit this.' This statement is then further reduced to the more scientific formula: art $=$ nature $- x$, where the unknown quantity stands for the technical limitations of the medium adopted. Critics have argued at length over what Holz meant by nature; he himself maintained that he never intended to exclude the artist or to restrict art to the mere imitation of reality. Much more revealing than such theoretical wrangles is a glance at the small volume of narrative prose that Holz and Schlaf did produce, and here it is perhaps significant that the sketch which formed the basis for *Papa Hamlet* is called *Ein Dachstubenidyll* (*Idyll in a Garret*). The title takes us back to the Spitzweg idylls of the Biedermeier artist in the post-romantic world. J. P. Stern's book on the literature of German realism is called *Idylls and Realities*, and it is remarkable how large a part the idyll had to play in German realism. In his story *Der Landvogt von Greifensee* (*The Governor of Greifensee*) Keller even included a sympathetic portrait of Solomon Gessner, one of the first Swiss writers to achieve an international reputation when his idylls were translated into almost every European language. Now the bitterly ironic allusion in *Papa Hamlet* indicates that the modern age is totally unidyllic. But even more striking than the picture of the blighted idyll is the contrast between the sordid reality of the garret and the rhetorical monologues of Thienwiebel the Shakespearian actor. Not only does the technique of consistent naturalism force the story into a dramatic mould; one can say that the characters themselves have stepped out of the world of the theatre. In Germany naturalism, like realism, is obsessed with the theatre and constantly finds its way back to it.

Notes

1 F. Sengle, *Biedermeierzeit* (Stuttgart, 1971), Vol. I, p. 165.

2 C. P. Magill, 'Young Germany: a revaluation', pp. 108–19 in *German Studies* presented to Leonard Ashley Willoughby (Oxford, 1952).

3 *Periods in German Literature*, ed. J. M. Ritchie (London, 1966), Vol. I, p. 154.

4 ibid., p. 160.

5 See H. M. Waidson, 'Jeremias Gotthelf's Reception in Britain and America', *Modern Language Review*, Vol. XLIII (1948), pp. 223–38; and J. S. Andrews, 'The Reception of Gotthelf in British and American Nineteenth-Century Periodicals', ibid., Vol. LI (1956), pp. 543–54.

6 Quoted by J. S. Andrews (*Modern Language Review*, Vol. LIII (1958), p. 542), from *Half Hours with Foreign Novelists, with Short Notices of their Lives and Writings* (2 vols., London, 1880).

7 W. H. McClain, *Between Real and Ideal* (Chapel Hill, N.C., 1963), p. 83.

8 See V. Klotz (ed.), *Zur Poetik des Romans* (1965); R. Grimm, *Deutsche Romantheorie: Beiträge zu einer historischen Poetik des Romans in Deutschland* (1968); H. Steinecke (ed.), *Theorie und Technik des Romans im 19. Jahrhundert* (1970). Source-material on the theory of the novel is collected in E. Lämmert (ed.), *Romantheorie: Dokumentation ihrer Geschichte in Deutschland 1620–1880* (1971).

9 Hegel, *The Philosophy of Fine Art*, tr. F. P. B. Osmaston (London, 1916), Vol. IV, pp. 171–2.

10 See Karl Fehr, *Der Realismus in der schweizerischen Literatur* (Bern, 1965).

11 *Realism and Reality* (Chapel Hill, N.C., 1965), p. 86.

12 *Essays and Leaves from a Notebook* (London, 1884), pp. 235–6.

13 'Unsere lyrische und epische Poesie seit 1848', *Sämtliche Werke*, ed. E. Gross, K. Scheinert, etc., Vol. XXII, p. 9.

14 H. and J. Hart, 'For and Against Zola', reproduced in George J. Becker, *Documents of Modern Literary Realism* (Princeton, 1963), pp. 251–60.

15 Henry Hatfield, *Modern German Literature* (London, 1966), p. 11.
16 The better-known include M. G. Conrad, *Pariser Briefe* (1879–81);
   H. and J. Hart, *Kritische Waffengänge* (1882–4); C. Alberti, *Die
   zwölf Artikel des Realismus* (1889); H. Hart, *Die realistische Bewegung,
   ihr Ursprung, ihr Wesen, ihr Ziel* (1889); Arno Holz, *Zola als Theoretiker* (1890); W. Bölsche, *Hinaus über den Naturalismus* (1890).
17 H. Remak, 'The German Reception of French Realism', *Publications of the Modern Language Association*, Vol. LXIX (1954), pp.
   410–31.

SIX

Realism in
Spain and Portugal

THE SOCIAL AND CULTURAL BACKGROUND

REALISM developed in Spain relatively late in the nineteenth century, paradoxically, since Spain has the best of claims to being considered the birthplace of the modern novel; it was here that the first picaresque novels emerged and, of course, the first masterpiece of the genre, *Don Quixote* (1605 and 1615), was written in Spanish. But after these brilliant beginnings, the novel fell into desuetude until, in an eighteenth century dominated by French culture, it became almost totally extinct in Spain. Throughout the first half of the nineteenth century a lively market existed for fiction, but it was satisfied by translations: of Scott in the first place, but also of certain French authors, principally Victor Hugo, Eugène Sue, George Sand, Dumas *père* and Soulié.[1] One notes that the major realists do not figure in this list: what the Spanish reading public appreciated in these translated works was the exotic element, affording an escape from the unattractive reality of everyday life in Spain. Ironically, certain French romantics, Musset, Hugo, Gautier, Mérimée, were during the same period looking to Spain to provide them with the exotic 'local colour' they required for their own works.[2] In Spain itself, the romantic movement produced nothing more, in the way of prose fiction, than a handful of historical novels, undistinguished imitations of Scott and his French followers. The 1840s saw the development of the *novela por entregas* (serialized novel), corresponding to that of the *roman-feuilleton* in France[3]; these compositions were mostly no more than sentimental, melodramatic tales. There was an undoubted demand for fiction, but as yet no educated public taste. Like the protagonist of Pereda's *Pedro Sánchez*, a story set in Madrid in the early 1850s, the average reader of novels was satisfied with an intricate and eventful plot, full of mysteries, surprises, and dramatic confrontations; a serious and responsible examination of human problems was not looked for in works of fiction and did not, indeed, begin to make an appearance before the publication, in the 1870s, of the first novels of Galdós and his contemporaries Valera and Pereda.

Explanations for the belated flowering of the Spanish realist novel must in the first instance be looked for in the state of the country at the time. Developments which were transforming other European nations during the nineteenth century hardly touched Spain. There was no industrial revolution on the same scale as those that altered the face of England, France, and Germany. The native economy, based on agriculture, could provide neither an adequate home market for industrial products nor sufficient capital to generate industrial development, which was limited to small areas on the country's periphery. Only in Catalonia did a true industrial complex come into being: Barcelona was the only full-scale industrial city, though political control continued to be exercised from Madrid – a circumstance which goes some way to explaining the strength of regionalist sentiment in Catalonia and the Basque provinces. In general, political unrest throughout the first three quarters of the century hampered the formation of a sense of national coherence. In 1840, when, elsewhere, the growth of industry was enabling the middle classes to achieve a dominant position in society, Spain was only just emerging from a series of more or less disastrous national misfortunes: the sanguinary struggles of the War of Independence (1807–14); the loss, felt as a crippling blow materially and morally, of most of her overseas empire (1810–20); then, after the repressive rule of Ferdinand VII (1814–33), the ensuing civil war known as the First Carlist War (1833–9), nominally fought to determine the succession though in reality it was a reactionary counter-revolution.

The period 1856–67 saw some recovery, in spite of regular military uprisings (*pronunciamientos*) and acute political instability as evidenced by frequent changes of government. Even so, Spain was beginning to take on the appearance of a modern state. Thanks in the main to French capital and French engineering skill, the country was provided with a railway system; and there was considerable industrial growth. In 1868 the September Revolution drove Isabel II (Ferdinand VII's daughter and successor) from the throne. The subsequent attempt to set up a radical liberal government was not ultimately successful, the monarchy being restored in 1874. Even so, in the freer atmosphere of these six years, new ideas and fashions of thought were able to percolate from beyond the Pyrenees, inspiring the rising generation of novelists and affecting the trend and content of their work.

The political stability established by the settlement of 1874 enabled the middle classes to consolidate their position and extend their influence, especially in the larger cities like Madrid and Barcelona; since it was the middle classes who for the most part bought and read novels, this social evolution clearly stimulated the growth of this kind of literature. The next dozen years were characterized by fairly rapid economic expansion, with the normal accompaniments of an increase in the numbers of the urban working class, the first stirrings of socialism, and the beginnings of a trades union movement. At the same time the institutions representative of the old order remained extremely powerful. Progressive middle-class Spaniards, well aware that their country was still poor, weak, and backward compared with others, lacked the self-confident optimism usually associated with an emergent bourgeoisie. The whole situation was aptly symbolized by Galdós in the very first novel he wrote that dealt with contemporary society, *Doña Perfecta* (1876): the intense hostility aroused by the radical young civil engineer in the sleepy provincial town to which he attempts to carry his new ideas, and his ultimate failure to achieve anything positive, can be interpreted as epitomizing – as did, in a roughly similar way, Turgenev's *Fathers and Children*[4] – the difficulties of ideological progress in a society still clinging to the old ways and reluctant to be drawn out of its comfortable stagnation.

'COSTUMBRISMO'

It would be a mistake to regard the flowering of the novel in the 1870s as nothing more than a reflex response to a changed socio-political situation. The literary movement known as *costumbrismo* was an important forerunner of Spanish realism. It started as a simple imitation of the French restoration author Étienne de Jouy (1764–1846), whose sketches of contemporary types and customs[5] were translated in the 1820s and imitated by Spanish writers in the 1830s. The movement, although it derived its inspiration from abroad, was intensely nationalistic and traditionalist in character, and is best regarded as a reaction against the dual threat posed by the over-whelming foreign domination of Spanish culture and the en-croachments of industrialization. Even though it might prove im-possible in the long run to avert this double threat to the traditional Spanish way of life, the *costumbrista* hoped at least to leave a detailed record of how the common people of Spain, *el pueblo*, lived and worked.

With one notable exception, Mariano José de Larra (1809-37), the *costumbristas* did not offer a criticism of the social order they described so lovingly. Their general approach, bland and superficial, is best exemplified in the work of Ramón de MESONERO ROMANOS (1803-82) and of his numerous followers, whose articles filled the periodical press in the 1830s and 1840s. *El Semanario Pintoresco Español*, a weekly magazine founded in 1836, became a veritable verbal museum of traditional types and customs. In 1843 and 1844, once again in imitation of a French model, there appeared in in-stalments the extraordinarily popular work *Los españoles pintados por sí mismos*, in which *costumbrismo* took a new departure, adapting the French *physiologie*, with its humorous bandying of pseudo-scientific terminology, to Spanish subjects.[6]

The characteristic form of expression employed by *costumbrismo* was the sketch or brief essay, but the movement did produce one novel. This was *La gaviota* (*The Seagull*, 1849), a rambling composition by a middle-aged lady of Hispano-German parentage, Cecilia Böhl de Faber (1796-1877), who wrote under the pseudonym of Fernán CABALLERO. She originally composed the work in French, feeling that Spanish – more probably, her Spanish – was not up to the task. Considered as a novel, *La gaviota* lacks formal coherence, the writer's guiding principle being to include in her work sketches of every conceivable Andalusian type or custom, the more picturesque the better. The assumption throughout is that all goodness and beauty reside with what is rooted in the soil of Spain, while all wickedness and ugliness spring from what is urban and foreign. (There is clearly some special provision which excludes the authoress from this rule.) But even though *La gaviota* is open to criticism for its primitive technique and its simplistic moral stance, it remains something of a landmark in the history of the Spanish novel; it was the first work since the middle of the seventeenth century in which a genuine attempt had been made to identify and record selected aspects of contemporary Spanish reality.

As a literary movement, then, *costumbrismo* can be seen to have prepared the way for realism by encouraging writers to concern themselves with the national life of their own times. But equally, it can be said to have impeded the development of a genuine realist novel, by fostering an uncritical, uninquiring attitude to social problems and by concentrating on the superficially picturesque aspects of the social scene. Its outlook was narrowly parochial. It was essentially a reactionary movement, in that it carefully excluded from its descriptions of contemporary society everything that did not pertain to an archaic way of life already doomed to change or disappear. The nostalgia that informed it meant that *costumbrismo*, in its own way, was as escapist as the literature produced by the sentimental novelists who vied with the *costumbristas* for popular favour.

For technical reasons, too, *costumbrismo* militated against the development of a true realist tradition. The *costumbrista* was interested not in individual human beings but in abstract types, who by definition were incapable of development. He could rarely sustain a theme or tell a story, for his vision was restricted and fragmentary; Fernán Caballero's brave effort to surmount this disability was totally unsuccessful. The *costumbrista* could not discriminate between the important, the peripheral, and the irrelevant: all details, if picturesque, merited equal attention, for picturesqueness was his sole criterion. His moral position was cripplingly restricted: he was never led to explore moral problems, since his mind was made up in advance on such questions and he was content to assert and illustrate what he took to be immutable moral verities.

'KRAUSISMO'

By and large, in spite of the achievements of romanticism and the efforts of the *costumbristas*, the literary scene in mid-nineteenth-century Spain was depressing to contemplate. Authorship was treated as though it were a harmless hobby; the resultant literature, superficial and cliché-ridden, was a precise reflection of the tastes and ethos of Spanish society in the 1850s and 1860s.

Concurrently, however, there emerged an influential ideological and social movement strongly contrasting with this intellectual vapidity. *Krausismo*, as its name indicates, was as foreign in its origins as any other contemporary current of thought; but its elaboration was a purely Spanish affair. The philosophy of Karl Christian Friedrich Krause (1781–1832), a minor post-Kantian idealist, attracted little interest in his native Germany, but when it was imported into Spain by the Madrid university professor Julián Sanz del Río (1814–69), it made a deep impression on the young middle-class intellectuals who heard his lectures about Krause and other German philosophers and read the book in which he expounded his version of Krause's system (*Ideal de la humanidad para la vida*, 1860). The metaphysics of Krause, presented by Sanz del Río in an obscure and pretentious style which echoed the language in which it was originally clothed, counted far less than the set of attitudes adopted by his young Spanish disciples. A basic tenet was that evil was not inherent to existence, but merely a product of human ignorance; once this ignorance was dispelled, man entered into a state of holy harmony with himself, his fellows, and God (the Absolute Being of *krausista* terminology). The notion that the Divinity could be apprehended by the mere exercise of intellectual faculties was, of course, anathema to the Roman Catholic Church, and *krausismo* came under suspicion from the start as heretical. But the promise it held out of reconciling reason with faith and tempering science with idealism made a considerable appeal to liberal Catholics, and the *krausista* – typically a dedicated reformer, puritanical in his single-mindedness – became a noted figure in Spanish society of the 1860s and 1870s, especially in university circles. Combining, as he did, a deeply religious view of life with a total commitment to intellectual freedom, he argued in favour of liberal ideals in education and became a spokesman for material progress and the advance of science, all in the name of the spiritual progress of mankind. Few educated Spaniards of the time – and therefore few novelists – were untouched by *krausismo*, though it should not be forgotten that the educated intellectuals constituted only a tiny minority of the population; against them were ranged, in tenacious opposition, the embattled traditionalists, who made up a formidable reactionary force not merely by virtue of their numbers but equally by the inflexibility with which they adhered to their beliefs and attitudes. In the last quarter of the century *krausismo* lost some of its importance, though it continued to exert a certain influence on writers from its refuge in the college known as the Institución Libre de Enseñanza, which a group of *krausista* professors founded in 1876 after they had been dismissed from their chairs by the conservative government of Cánovas del Castillo.

Krausismo made a significant impact on the contemporary view of the function of literature. Its adherents held that writing was no frivolous society pursuit, but a serious and responsible activity. They attacked the romantic view that literature ought properly to concern itself with the inner life of the individual: lyric poetry, the customary vehicle for such introspective meditations, was condemned as defective. Instead, the *krausistas* wanted the writer to turn his attention to external reality; they considered drama to be best suited for its reflection. But it is clear that their campaign for literary reform could as well serve to encourage the development of an impersonal, realistic type of novel. Many *krausistas* were active literary critics; and even those who, like Leopoldo Alas, attacked *krausista* rationalism, did in fact express other *krausista* attitudes in their critical writings.

The Age of Realism, when it finally dawned in Spain, can thus be seen as the product of a number of forces working in conjunction: the *costumbrista* movement, which at least suggested to writers that their proper material was the contemporary social reality; *krausismo*, which urged the need for the creation of a literature espousing serious-minded, liberal, and progressive attitudes; and, thirdly, the revolution of 1868, which opened up new avenues of thought and thus renovated the whole cultural and intellectual scene. Each of these developments depended ultimately on the middle classes, who alone could supply the right conditions for a new literature, providing it with its subject-matter, its public, and its exponents – men possessed of sufficient intelligence, education, and initiative to bring about a concrete literary realization of the potentialities of the moment.

THE REALIST NOVELIST AND THE READING PUBLIC

In the ordinary conditions of their working life, the Spanish realist novelists of the end of the nineteenth century suffered certain disadvantages inseparable from the stage of material development society had then reached. They worked, to begin with, for a market so small that their economic base was most insecure. The bourgeoisie who provided them with their staple readership was a far from numerous class. The figure given by Armando Palacio Valdés, of no more than 200–300 regular readers of serious novels, sounds pessimistic[7]; but the public could not, all the same, have been very large, when one bears in mind the fact that as late as 1875, in spite of recent striking advances in popular education, the literacy rate was still only 30 per cent of the population.

The novelist needs to sell his books in order to make a living, but in Spain the widespread habit of borrowing books instead of buying them robbed him of a considerable proportion of his potential earnings. Palacio Valdés introduces his novel *La hermana San Sulpicio* with an urgent plea to his reader not, under any circumstances, to lend his copy to others. One finds the usual railings on the part of authors against the obtuseness of critics and the meanness and unreliability of publishers. Complaints against publishers may have been ill conceived in view of the small sales they could expect to make. It is true that the theoretical readership was coextensive with the Spanish-speaking world; but the existence of a growing Latin-American market helped matters very little, since it was largely supplied by pirated editions originating abroad, particularly in Germany.

Earnings could be swelled by selling serial rights to newspapers, but serious novelists were reluctant to allow their works to appear in instalments except in respectable journals like *La Revista de España*, which did, in fact, serialize several of the novels of Galdós and his contemporaries. Galdós was alone in making a modest living from the proceeds of his writing; he succeeded in doing this partly by acquiring a partnership in the firm that published his novels. Even so, his income was mainly derived not from the works of realism devoted to analysing the society of his time, but from his historical cycle of forty-six novels entitled *Episodios nacionales*. Of the other realists,

Pereda, Pardo Bazán and Palacio Valdés had private incomes; Valera, finding he could not keep body and soul together by publishing fiction, became a diplomat; and Alas scraped a living as a university professor and professional critic. Up to a point, of course, the position was roughly similar in other European countries at the time, where novelists, unless they happened to strike a highly popular vein, were forced to rely on secondary sources of income: Tolstoy and Turgenev derived theirs from their estates, Flaubert and the Goncourts were *rentiers*, Eça de Queirós and Huysmans were in government service, Theodor Fontane earned his living as a journalist.

The difficulties with which the Spanish realists had to contend were not solely of an economic order: they also had to wrestle with ideological opposition. Fiction had always been an object of suspicion to the upholders of moral and religious dogmatism. Censorship, both open and hidden, had largely contributed to the decline of the novel in the late seventeenth century and its virtual disappearance in the eighteenth. Halfway through the nineteenth century, the extraordinary popularity of the *novela por entregas* revived all the old hostility. Trite and inoffensive though they might appear, these stories were eagerly lapped up by a largely female public who delighted particularly in the love interest. Conservatives objected on the grounds that the *novelas* provoked impure thoughts among the young women who read them; and also because the implicit or – often – explicit claim made by the authors that their fictions were 'true histories' was demonstrably false and intended to deceive. We have already seen how this particular moral objection to the novel was clamorously raised in France in the earlier part of the previous century.[8]

Moral denunciation became even more strident when the realists started producing their works. In the first place, their professed aim of depicting all experience implied that they were incidentally claiming the right to represent in detail emotions and activities normally regarded as sinful. Moreover, the ban on authorial comment, an axiom of realism, meant that this sinfulness was not even condemned within the pages of the novel. Thus, not only was immorality shamelessly exhibited, but the motivations of transgressors were presented objectively, so that the reader, understanding why the sinner sinned, was too often inclined to indulgence. In the eyes of conservatives, this amounted, in practice, to condoning evil.

Since conservatism in matters of morality tended to be associated with conservatism in social outlook, the debate about the moral propriety of realistic fiction quickly took on political overtones. Traditionalists would have greatly preferred an idealistic literature, one as far removed from the realities of life as possible; and realism tended to win support from the progressive, liberal wing, if only because it fell under the strictures of the reactionaries. Novelists who, like Pereda, used the techniques of realism but subscribed to traditional moral values found themselves in an anomalous position.

Thus, underlying the debate about realism was the deeper conflict between the 'two Spains' – conservative, Catholic Spain and progressive, liberal Spain; and this conflict itself very often formed the subject of the realist novels, especially during the first decade, that of the 1870s. Hence these earlier novels tended to take shape as 'problem novels' rather than impartial records of the social reality – though, of course, the problems they dealt with did arise out of the social reality. But realism, in this first phase, was more a means to an end than an end in itself. It was only in the 1880s that the priorities were reversed, so that the description of contemporary social reality became the true *raison d'être* of the novel, and the conflicts of values were presented simply as facets of this reality.

PÉREZ GALDÓS: THE NOVELS OF THE FIRST PERIOD

The acknowledged leader of the realist movement in Spain was Benito PÉREZ GALDÓS (1843–1920). He owed this pre-eminence not only to the sheer quantity of his books and their generally high quality, but also to the fact that it was above all in his novels that the bourgeoisie, composed of a variety of different professional groups – bankers and industrialists, doctors and lawyers, engineers and civil servants – could see itself reflected as a single homogeneous class with a common set of values, attitudes, and interests. But Galdós did not merely describe middle-class life; he offered a considered criticism of many of its aspects. His novels cannot be likened to mere mirrors, since it was part of his purpose to educate his readers and promote reforms. Sometimes, indeed, he gives the impression of reserving his deepest sympathies for the lower classes, whom he continues to idealize, as *el pueblo*, in an almost *costumbrista* manner. It was their sense of the mediocrity of their country's achievements, the lowness of its status in the concert of European nations, that provoked the Spanish realists to their disabused reflections on the middle classes from which they themselves sprang and which provided them with their principal subject of study.

Pérez Galdós, who was born in the Canary Isles, came to Madrid in 1862 to start his law studies. He rapidly abandoned them, however, and started writing *costumbrista* sketches and critical articles attacking the empty and hackneyed writing which passed as literature at that time. In the course of a visit to Paris in 1867 he came across Balzac's novels, which he devoured eagerly; the following year the task of translating *The Pickwick Papers* led him to start reading Dickens. His discovery of these two masters opened Galdós's eyes to the possibilities of realist fiction. As he wrote in a review article in 1870:

The middle classes, neglected by Spanish novelists, are the supreme model, the inexhaustible source. The middle classes are the basis of the social order; with their sense of initiative and their intelligence, they are taking over the leadership of society; in their midst is to be found nineteenth-century man, with his virtues and his vices, his noble and tireless ambitions, his reforming zeal, his extraordinary energy. The modern novel of manners will be the expression of all that is good and bad at the heart of the middle classes.[9]

In the light of these remarks it is perhaps a little surprising to find that the first twelve novels published by Galdós, between 1870 and 1875, do not deal with the society of his time but rather with Spain as it was in the early part of the century. What Galdós was trying to do was to reveal the origins of the present state of the country; his *Episodios nacionales* are, therefore, very different from the ordinary romantic historical novel, and he can be observed putting to use in them many of the techniques of realism. They proved highly popular, and established Galdós's reputation; he went on to produce a second series of ten between 1875 and 1879 and, concurrently, published four novels about contemporary Spanish society. Three of these can be described as thesis novels, since they present the same conflict between progressive and reactionary forces, particularly as it affected religious belief. The argument is the same in each of them: Galdós demonstrates how human relationships – specifically, those that link two lovers – can be poisoned by dogmatism and intolerance. As we move, however, from the first of these novels, *Doña Perfecta*, to the last, *La familia de León Roch*, we can observe Galdós groping his way towards increased objectivity and a purer form of realism.

The two unfortunate lovers in *Doña Perfecta* (1876) are Pepe Rey, a young liberal, and Rosario; their plans for marriage are frustrated by Rosario's mother, the lady whose name gives the novel its title, and a priest, Don Inocencio. In the end, Pepe is murdered and Rosario goes mad. This synopsis suggests a quite artificial distribution of the cast between the idealistic youngsters and their wicked, unfeeling seniors; but in fact the author's moral presuppositions are not quite so crudely defined as this. At the beginning, at least, both Doña Perfecta and Don Inocencio are presented as well-meaning people, holding their beliefs quite sincerely; only later, horrified by Pepe's progressive ideas – and Pepe is by no means faultless – do they adopt extreme attitudes and allow themselves to be betrayed into committing vicious actions.

Galdós chose a similarly melodramatic ending for his next novel, *Gloria* (1876–7): this time it is the girl, Gloria, who dies and the young man, Daniel, whose child she has borne, who goes mad. Again it is the girl's rigidly orthodox Roman Catholic family who try to destroy the relationship; their objection to Daniel is that he is a Jew. By making his sympathetic young hero a member of the Jewish faith, Galdós incurred even harsher criticism in the conservative press than he did when *Doña Perfecta* appeared; but in fact the representatives of Roman Catholicism are shown in a rather kinder light in *Gloria*. They act throughout with good intentions; the fundamental wrongness of their attitude is indicated in a more indirect and subtle way than in *Doña Perfecta*. Galdós's effort to avoid too crude a moral dichotomy is shown in his treatment of young Daniel: he is, certainly, an enlightened man, to whom the reader is meant to extend his sympathy; but as an orthodox Jew, he shows himself to be almost as blinkered in his beliefs as the Christians.

The continuing trend towards greater impartiality in the treatment of character is evident in *La familia de León Roch* (1878). The hero is a young *krauṣista* intellectual whose wife, under the influence of her family, turns against him, becoming a bigoted and puritanical religious fanatic. More than in the previous novels, the psychological motivation of this unfortunate conversion is closely and impartially examined, so that Galdós can be seen approaching closer all the time to true realistic objectivity. *La familia de León Roch* has a different setting from the earlier novels just discussed, in both of which the action took place in fictitious small towns on the north coast of Spain; here we are transported to Madrid, where the panoramic view of a great social complex provides an environment more characteristic of the realist manner.

Between *Gloria* and *La familia de León Roch* Galdós produced one other novel, *Marianela*, which is something of an anomaly in his output, being the only lyrical and sentimental novel he ever wrote. The subject is the love of a handsome blind boy for a girl, Marianela, who though spiritually beautiful is unattractive physically. The boy undergoes an operation which restores his sight but destroys the bond of love between him and Marianela. It is a visiting surgeon who performs the operation, just as in *Doña Perfecta* it is an outsider who comes to the small town and wins the love of Rosario, while in *Gloria* the Anglo-German Jew Daniel is brought by shipwreck to the town where Gloria lives. It is thus possible to link *Marianela* with the other novels, since Galdós uses in all three the device of the arrival from outside of the young man who brings modern ideas with him, with upsetting consequences for the established order.

OTHER NOVELISTS OF THE 1870s

The same theme of the effects on traditional provincial life of the arrival of an innovating outsider is prominent in the early novels of José María de PEREDA (1833–1906). Pereda's works of the 1870s nicely complement those of Galdós in that precisely the same problem of the 'two Spains' is treated in them from the opposite viewpoint, that of the convinced traditionalist.

Pereda had begun his literary career as a writer of *costumbrista* sketches about rural life in his home province of Santander, collected in *Escenas montañesas* (1864) and *Tipos y paisajes* (1871). In them he had developed a rather different kind of *costumbrismo* from that which had been made popular by Mesonero Romanos and which Fernán Caballero had introduced into the novel; for Pereda placed much less emphasis on the picturesque than was customary, and was not afraid to depict poverty, squalor and ugliness. Ironically, by the time he came to write novels his attitude had grown considerably less critical towards the traditional ways of life he described; a realist in his *costumbrismo*, he became a *costumbrista* in his realism. Pereda's praise of the old order is quite understandable if one bears in mind the fact that it could undoubtedly be seen at its most attractive in Santander province, where a highly stable patriarchal system functioned smoothly thanks to an active squirearchy that took its responsibilities seriously.

The four novels he published in the 1870s reflect various aspects of the conflict between the old and the new, the emphases being different in each case. *Los hombres de pro* (*Men of Worth*, 1872) is a satirical depiction of the newly rich provincial bourgeoisie, whose ignorance and vulgarity Pereda attacks from his lofty, aristocratic viewpoint. *El buey suelto* ... (*The Solitary Ox*, 1877) is an attempt to refute nineteenth-century attacks on the Christian institution of marriage, particularly those of Balzac in *Physiologie du mariage* and *Petites misères de la vie conjugale*, and to reaffirm the values of family life: it charts the empty existence of a selfish, idle bachelor and its conclusion in a lonely old age. The title derives from a proverbial saying, 'the solitary ox licks himself well', which refers ironically to the allegedly carefree life of the self-centred unmarried man. *Don Gonzalo González de la Gonzalera* (1878) combines the themes of *Los hombres de pro* with a description of the disruptive influence of the 1868 Revolution on the harmonious life of a village in Santander province. Finally, *De tal palo, tal astilla* (*Like Father, like Son*, 1879) seems to be an attempt to refute the thesis of *Gloria*, a novel of which Pereda thoroughly disapproved, judging from the letter he wrote to Galdós shortly after its publication. In Pereda's novel an irreligious outsider falls in love with a devout local girl, but comes to a bad end as a direct result of his lack of religious faith; he commits suicide and the girl's staunch Roman Catholic beliefs are totally vindicated.

In these four novels there is little of that steady development we have noticed in Galdós's early work, apart from a growing interest in physical environment: in the first two, both of them extended fables in which misguided or stupid people come to exemplary ends, Pereda concentrates attention almost exclusively on the protagonists; in the other two he finds room for those extensive descriptions of the country around Santander that constitute a major feature of his mature works. But there is little variation or progress in the ethical standpoint taken up by the author. All four novels present the same simple division between what is traditional and therefore good, and what is modern and therefore evil; and within these opposed categories are subsumed a series of further oppositions, as Pereda contrasts country life with city life to the detriment of the latter, Spanish ways with foreign ways, and the church with the tavern, the church being regarded as the place from which good doctrine is propagated, while from the tavern spread the evil doctrines of liberalism, revolution, and atheism. Innocence is better than knowledge, just as sincerity is to be preferred to deviousness: Pereda's virtuous characters, of both sexes, are immediately recognizable by their tendency to blush at the slightest provocation. A central opposition is between those who belong and those who do not, between natives and outsiders; and the worst outsiders are the natives who have betrayed their breed by going away to the city – Madrid – or travelling abroad, returning later with their heads full of the pernicious nonsense they learnt while away. The theme of the disturbing outsider is more obtrusive in Pereda's novels than in Galdós's; in both authors its importance lies in the fact that it represents, as it were in a microcosm, the situation in the country at large, when as a result of the September Revolution foreign ideas were flooding into Spain and clashing with traditional attitudes. In the novels of Galdós the outsider is treated with great sympathy, while in those of Pereda he is presented as a kind of disease, a foreign body that must at all costs be driven out if society is to survive; for ordinary village people (always judged with lordly condescension in Pereda's novels) are feeble-minded innocents, who follow where they are led, whether along the paths of righteousness or down the slippery slope, and who therefore are only too apt, like naughty children, to turn against their betters if exposed to bad influences. Unlike other *costumbristas*, Pereda idealizes the institution but not those who live under it; he approves of the traditional organization of rural society but not of the ordinary members of that society. The local squire and the parish priest may find favour in his eyes, but his portrayal of the common people is darkened by a peculiarly acute sense of the frailty and wretchedness of man, which was a by-product of his religious convictions.

In Pereda's early novels there is, then, no attempt such as Galdós made to avoid an absolute dichotomy of values. The moral system is completely closed: no character who is included under the liberal/ outsider heading is described with sympathy or understanding, nor are there any serious faults to be found in the leading characters of the traditionalist camp. The only exception to this rule occurs in the last of the four early novels, *De tal palo, tal astilla*, where the irreligious young protagonist is shown to have noble sentiments and to behave in a gentlemanly way: this unusual subtlety is the result, no doubt, of the influence of *Gloria*, combined with Pereda's desire to illustrate the moral that good works are quite irrelevant in the absence of faith.

In none of Pereda's novels is there any interplay between the opposing values; the novels are simply affirmations of the correctness of traditionalism and the wickedness of liberalism. The rigid moral framework of Pereda's novels makes it very hard to see him as even remotely resembling what in other European countries was called a realist. He won his reputation – second only to that of Galdós – as a realist thanks to his detailed descriptions of environment, his accurate reproduction of dialect speech, and the vividness of his scenes of poverty and squalor; and thanks also to his careful avoidance of literary elegance, which often meant in practice resorting to clumsy narrative techniques rather than efficient ones. Not only was Pereda hailed a realist but, still more remarkably, *Don Gonzalo González de la Gonzalera* and all the novels he wrote subsequently were widely regarded as naturalistic works. Such judgements are more revealing of the connotations that realism and naturalism were given in Spain than of the actual qualities of Pereda's writing.

Another novelist who emerged during the 1870s was Juan VALERA (1824–1905), whose previous literary reputation was based on his erudite and wide-ranging literary criticism. In the course of the decade he published five novels, of which the first, *Pepita Jiménez* (1874), is by far the most important and impressive. Set in rural

Andalusia, it tells the story of a young seminarist, Luis de Vargas, who when on the point of taking holy orders falls in love, comes agonizingly to realize the hollowness of his vocation, and gives up the idea of joining the priesthood. Although questions concerning Roman Catholicism are central to it, *Pepita Jiménez* cannot be grouped with the early works of Galdós and Pereda as a 'problem novel'; when some of his readers interpreted it as an attack on priestly celibacy, and associated Valera with Galdós as a liberal and anticlerical novelist, he was quick to refute the allegation. It is a fact that Valera had written not an ideological but a psychological novel; his central concern is with the stages through which his hero Luis passes, as these are revealed indirectly in the letters he writes to his confessor, from an arrogant certainty about his own righteousness into a turmoil of doubt as he gradually becomes aware of what is happening to him. If there is an implicit message in the novel, it is not that the Church is wrong in prohibiting priests from marrying; it is rather – and this is a warning that recurs in many of Valera's novels – that people should not allow themselves to be blinded by their pride into basing their lives on an ill-founded and over-ambitious idealism, but that they should learn to recognize the reality of their own nature and adapt their actions accordingly.

In some ways it could be said that *Pepita Jiménez* is a more realistic novel than any of those mentioned so far: its depiction of life is more objective, in that the author is not striving to bolster the arguments of either side involved in contemporary controversies; all he is interested in doing is to describe human behaviour. Objectivity (in the sense of the lack of explicit moral judgement by the narrator) is facilitated by the use of the letter as a narrative technique: for most of the novel the story is told exclusively in Luis's words, with no external comment or explanation. Yet objectivity in the other sense – the description of external reality 'as it really is' – is necessarily excluded by the use of this device, since the reader has no direct access to characters, events, or scenes: everything is presented through the eyes of Luis, and coloured by his changing moods and states of mind. The depiction of external reality is thus subordinate to the depiction of the inner feelings of an individual. This was the reason, no doubt, why the epistolary form was so popular in the eighteenth century, but was avoided by the realists of the nineteenth century, who normally adopted the narrative viewpoint of an omniscient detached observer. In his elegant, studied, sedate style, too, Valera seems something of an anachronism, and *Pepita Jiménez* can be called a realist novel only in an extremely limited sense. But like the novels of Galdós and Pereda already considered, it can be seen as an important step towards realism, besides being, unlike theirs, a fine novel in its own right.

Valera's other novels of the 1870s provide further evidence of his ambivalent attitude towards realism. In *Las ilusiones del doctor Faustino* (1875) he tells the story of a young man tormented by doubts and emotional frustration; the novel is set in the romantic period, some decades before the time of writing, and the characterization, atmosphere and themes are essentially romantic. *El comendador Mendoza* (1876), similarly, must be judged a historical rather than a realistic novel. In *Doña Luz* (1879) Valera returned to the present, and to the theme of the conflict between profane and divine love. Like Valera's other novels, *Doña Luz* is realistic in its portrayal of highly complex characters and their evolution, and in its critical approach to the theme of idealism in private life. It describes day-to-day happenings in contemporary rural Andalusia, the usual setting for Valera's novels; the viewpoint adopted is that of an omniscient narrator who all the same never makes any pretence of being impersonal or objective. But non-realistic features abound as in all Valera's novels: a consciously elegant style full of learned allusions, which reflects and implies an extensive intellectual ordering of reality, in contrast to the apparently artless, natural, transparent use of language, more characteristic of realism, which aims to give the reader the illusion of being offered direct access to raw, unprocessed reality; a view of man as an individual rather than a social being, and the consequent presentation of the idiosyncratic rather than the typical; and an enduring *costumbrista* fondness for the pleasantly picturesque, which permeates all Valera's descriptions of rural life. Everywhere in his work we find illustrations of his fundamentally anti-realistic belief that art should depict life not as it really is, but enhanced and made more beautiful than it really is: anything sordid and ugly is resolutely barred from his novels, which on the whole give – as they were intended to – not a realistic but an idealized vision of life.

In some ways Valera was the odd man out among the novelists

of the Spanish age of realism. He pursued his own independent course, and he refused to follow the fashions of the time. In the 1870s he showed his independence by refusing to write thesis novels; in the 1880s he was to distinguish himself in a yet more uncompromising way, by ceasing altogether to write novels, at a time when the novel was at the height of its success and popularity in Spain.

During the 1870s one other Spanish novelist besides those mentioned achieved a degree of celebrity: this was Pedro Antonio de ALARCÓN (1833–91), whose career as a novelist had started as far back as 1855, when he published *El final de Norma*. All the novelists of the 1870s and 1880s, without exception, show the influence of romanticism in their works; but in Alarcón's novels romanticism is so all-pervading that their author cannot in any normal sense be considered a realist, even when the term is stretched to accommodate the special circumstances of the Spanish scene. When the realist novel became popular in Spain, Alarcón was one of the traditionalists who attacked it. The short pieces for which he is mostly remembered, *El sombrero de tres picos* (*The Three-Cornered Hat*, 1874) and *El capitán Veneno* (1881), are both romantic historical novels. In *El escándalo* (1875), however, critics have discerned the influence of the new realistic tendency: the novel is about near-contemporary society (it is set in 1861), and has as one of its themes the conflict between the old and the new, particularly as it affects the position of Roman Catholicism, which Alarcón, like Pereda, presents from the point of view of an extreme traditionalist. Apart from this, however, it is totally romantic, in its emphatic style (everything seems to be either fearful, infamous, infernal, or else angelic, heroic, sublime), in its theatrical confrontations, in its intrigue-laden story (concerning the discovery of true love and religious faith by a youthful libertine), and in the cast of characters, all byronic young heroes bearing the weight of a terrible past, the secrets of which are duly revealed as the plot develops. All things considered, *El escándalo* is not a realistic novel but an anthology of all those restrictive and outworn conventions which the realist had to reject in order to be able to give a fresh and convincing portrayal of everyday life in contemporary time.

NATURALISM

By the end of the 1870s it was clear that a change had come over the novel. One of the tasks of the realists seemed, to some extent at least, to have been fulfilled: people were now a little more willing to recognize that a work of fiction could be a vehicle for serious social and ideological comment. Both traditionalists and liberals could now point to recent novels in which a responsible attempt had clearly been made to give artistic expression to their respective beliefs and opinions. The battle for recognition was by no means won – in *La cuestión palpitante* (1883), Emilia Pardo Bazán commented wrily on the contrast between the high status the novel enjoyed in England and the relative lack of critical attention it received in Spain. But some progress had undoubtedly been made; perhaps the novelists now felt that they could relax a little, that they no longer needed to write in such an explicitly high-minded way. What is certain is that from about 1880 the Spanish novelists allowed themselves much more freedom to describe social reality for its own sake; ideological issues tended to be played down.

It was precisely at this time that naturalism burst on the scene. In Spain, as elsewhere in Europe, it immediately aroused impassioned polemics and exerted an influence on literature brief in duration but powerful and decisive while it lasted. Zola's name was unknown in Spain until the uproar consequent on the publication of *L'Assommoir* in 1877 gave him international notoriety; by 1881 naturalism was the principal subject in any argument about literature. The old controversy about the morality of the novel was revived: traditionalists objected even more violently to naturalism than to realism (in so far as they were able to distinguish between the two), because of its deterministic philosophy and its tendency to dwell on the ugly, sordid, and morally abhorrent aspects of life; and naturalism was, inevitably, dismissed as yet another aberration of the progressives. The debate was not helped by widespread uncertainty about the meaning of the word naturalism. Some considered it a simple synonym for realism; others, who regarded it as an intensification of certain undesirable tendencies within realism, formulated the equation 'naturalism = realism + crudeness'; yet others, more careful and accurate in their assessment, saw it as a conscious attempt to apply to literature the discoveries and methods of nineteenth-century science, particularly the biological sciences. In addition to all this, at least three pre-literary meanings of *naturalismo* were still in common usage: 'primitive nature-worship'; 'the close imitation of nature in art'; and 'the scientific study of natural phenomena'. In many of the polemics about naturalism the opponents were quite simply talking about different things.

Among the new Spanish novelists who were to make their name in the course of the next few years, it was Emilia PARDO BAZÁN (1851–1921) who was chiefly attracted to the new literary doctrine. In the collection of literary essays which she published under the title *La cuestión palpitante*, she made a notable attempt to bring some cool commonsense to bear on the matter. A couple of years earlier, in her preface to *Un viaje de novios* (*A Honeymoon*, 1881), the first novel in which she tried out certain naturalist techniques, she had briefly discussed the subject, and suggested an idea which she was to develop more fully in *La cuestión palpitante*, and which commended itself to many others sympathetic to the new literary styles: she argued that realism and naturalism were not to be regarded as novel literary doctrines originating abroad, since they had their roots in classical Spanish literature, especially in works like *La Celestina*,[10] the picaresque novels, and *Don Quixote*. What is more, traditional Spanish realism and naturalism were, she maintained, superior to the modern French varieties because they were more universal; their exponents dealt with all aspects of life, pleasant and unpleasant, whereas their French counterparts directed their attention exclusively to the sordid and the gloomy.

La cuestión palpitante deals comprehensively with the subject of naturalism, setting it in the perspective of European literature, more particularly that of France in the nineteenth century, and it embodies a generally sensible and perceptive critical examination of Zola's theories. Pardo Bazán welcomes the idea of enriching the novel by introducing the latest scientific concepts. She sees, however, that this programme had led in practice to a rigid determinism which a Roman Catholic like herself is bound to find intolerable. But this determinism, she argues, is a consequence of Zola's misunderstanding of basic scientific principles; specifically, of his failure to distinguish between laws that can be tested and proved (like the law of gravity) and mere hypotheses like the Darwinian theory which places man on the same level as the animals, by implication denying him any free-will or soul. Zola's naturalistic doctrine is thus based on a fallacy; his prejudices and short-sightedness commit him to just as unrealistic a representation of life as is offered by the idealists; and Pardo Bazán concludes by reaffirming the supremacy of all-inclusive, objective realism. The lapses from propriety and good taste constitute, in Pardo Bazán's view, unfortunate artistic flaws in the products of naturalism, but their determinism amounts to a cardinal error, a misreading of man's place in the universe. Zola's crudeness is relatively unimportant, for literature has never been respectable, and it was certainly not he who invented indecency, whatever traditionalist critics might like to think.

Pardo Bazán's sane, moderate, reasoned discussion of naturalism – based throughout on an unquestioning acceptance of Church teaching – shocked the traditionalists. She came to be known as a defender of Zola's pernicious doctrines, though all she had done was to offer a careful assessment of their possible merits instead of rejecting them out of hand. But this was quite enough for her to be considered a dangerous radical. The nineteenth-century conflict between the 'two Spains' was not a straightforward confrontation of conservatives and radicals; broadly, the two camps were constituted by, on the one side, diehard conservatives who refused even to contemplate anything that seemed to them to run counter to Church teaching, and on the other moderate conservatives like Pardo Bazán who, while never for a moment questioning Roman Catholic dogma, were at least prepared to think for themselves about new ideas. In fact none of the major Spanish novelists accepted Zola's naturalism without reservation; Pardo Bazán is representative of most of those who were called (and who called themselves) naturalists, and who, like her, disapproved of what was thought of as the obscene element in naturalism and rejected its deterministic philosophy. Naturalism followed the pattern of most movements originating abroad which find their way across the Pyrenees, and undergo extensive modification during the process of acclimatization. The question whether a given Spanish novel is or is not naturalistic (in Zola's meaning of the term) is thus an empty one; all that it is useful, or worth while, to attempt is to discern the specific ways in which Zola's naturalism influenced certain individual works and the Spanish novel as a whole.

As soon as we start considering what naturalism meant in practice for the Spanish novel it is Galdós who, as usual, demands attention first. He was the only established novelist of the time prepared to admit that naturalism might have important contributions to make to the development of the novel in Spain. Pereda, Valera, and Alarcón all made their opposition to the new movement more or less clear, although, with characteristic confusion, Pereda was widely considered a naturalist throughout the 1880s. But all the writers with a genuine claim to be called naturalists were newcomers in the world of letters, with the sole exception of Galdós.

Given the prestige of his name, it is hardly surprising that when in 1881 critics found traces of the impact of the new French fashion on his latest novel, *La desheredada* (*Disinherited*), the discovery caused a certain sensation. Galdós's novel opened with a detailed description of a death in a madhouse; it continued with scenes showing the wretchedness of the life of the poor; and it closed with the heroine's turning to prostitution after she had failed to gain what she considered her rightful social position as a member of the aristocracy. This was a very different story from those of Galdós's four previous novels about contemporary society, in which the unpleasant side of life, where it was described at all, was treated in a much less distressingly detailed and direct way.

In *La desheredada* Galdós placed the same emphasis as Zola did on the importance of heredity and environment as factors in human development; in places he seems explicitly to affirm deterministic principles, as in a description of a group of street urchins: 'Congenital rickets had marked many of the heads with its yellow sign, stamping there a predestination to a life of crime.' The father of the heroine, Isidora, had been driven mad by his excessive social ambitions, and Isidora herself comes increasingly to be dominated by a similar obsession, although not to the point that she loses her sanity. In Isidora's younger brother, Mariano, Galdós is clearly examining the environmental factors that combine to turn an innocent child into a hardened criminal. Generally speaking, the steady moral and social decline of Isidora and Mariano has a sad inevitability about it which contrasts strongly with the impression Galdós had given in his earlier novels that his characters were always in control of their development and were to be regarded as morally responsible for their own actions.

In other ways, however, *La desheredada* seems today a much less naturalistic work than it did to Galdós's contemporaries. Sex is handled gingerly; scenes of squalor are much toned down and never hit the reader as do Zola's. Indeed, there is even a certain *costumbrista* picturesqueness in some of Galdós's descriptions of the poor of Madrid, in which the slightly arch irony that is a characteristic feature of his style is given full play:

The iron-foundry foreman's three sons came along beating time on a sheet of tin, and soon this sweet-sounding orchestra was augmented by the storekeeper's two sons, who joined in playing those delicate Christmas sonatas produced by the delivery of measured blows upon an oil can. These enemies of mankind were dirty little mites. They wore boots that were indecipherable, for there was no sure way of discerning the join between skin and leather. They were all braided from head to foot in mud. If refuse were a decoration, the names of these young gentlemen would assemble all the honorific titles in the book.

Galdós never attempts to present man as a mere phenomenon of flesh, blood, and nerves, to be observed coldly and clinically; he does not for a moment abandon his typically warm-hearted and sympathetic attitude to his characters. The explicitly scientific approach is not absent from the novel; but it is left to the flippant young medical student Miquis to express it, always in a half-mocking way.

La desheredada is probably, however, more extensively influenced by naturalism than any other Spanish novel of the time. It is also a much more realistic novel than any that had been written in the 1870s; it is the culmination of the movement towards full realism that can be traced in *Doña Perfecta*, *Gloria* and *La familia de León Roch*. The effect of naturalism was to accelerate Galdós's development in the direction of a more complete realism. It helped him to abandon the thesis novel and to concentrate rather on the detailed description of human behaviour; and it led him to pay closer attention to material reality and to enlarge his vision in order to include the life of the poor. *La desheredada*, the first of a long series of novels subtitled by Galdós 'novelas españolas contemporáneas', was a decisive step in his career as the leader of the Spanish realist movement.

After Galdós, it was Emilia Pardo Bazán who built up a reputation as a naturalist in the early 1880s. Her first novel, *Pascual López* (1879), is the story of an ambitious medical student, narrated in a quasi-picaresque style by the protagonist, and showing – in spite of its subject-matter – no traces of naturalism. Next came *Un viaje de novios*, already mentioned, which is a curious mixture. Basically it is a feeble romantic novelette, telling of the pure but impossible love of an innocent bride on her honeymoon in France for a young stranger thrown across her path by destiny. This is padded out with lengthy descriptions of French scenes, life and manners, based on the writer's impressions of a journey she had recently made to take the waters at Vichy. Finally there is the occasional passage of naturalistic physiological analysis of character which assorts ill with the rest and which Pardo Bazán appears to have inserted with painful deliberation.

Her next novel, *La tribuna* (*The Orator*, 1882), represents a more co-ordinated and serious attempt to apply naturalist theories and techniques. Zola's influence is apparent in the author's choice of a proletarian heroine, Amparo, employed in a cigar and cigarette factory in a city (based on Corunna) in north-west Spain. The action takes place during the 1868 revolution, and centres on Amparo's seduction by a rich young gentleman, and her revolutionary activities. Working-class life is portrayed less euphemistically than in *La desheredada*; the novel was widely attacked for its 'crudity'. It includes detailed descriptions of the tobacco factory and of the different manufacturing processes conducted in its various departments. The conditions of work are shown for what they are – abominable – and continual stress is laid on the physical effects of poverty and deprivation; the women age prematurely, their children suffer from hunger and disease. Semi-scientific terminology is used in places, as part of an effort to achieve greater objectivity, accuracy and minuteness in description. The characteristic manners and attitudes of the different social classes are closely observed, often with considerable insight, as, for example, in the portrayal of the uneasy relationship between the urban poor and the rural poor. Pardo Bazán makes conscious efforts to analyse every aspect of human motivation, including the more disreputable ones; the role of sexuality is strongly stressed, though the actual occurrence of sexual activity is referred to in such an extremely indirect and delicate manner – as it is in nearly all the Spanish novels of the period – that it is only the most experienced and alert reader who realizes what is supposed to be going on. The taboos of the time could evidently only be defied up to a point.

What separates Pardo Bazán in a more fundamental way from Zola, however, is her explicit and firm rejection of determinism, a rejection which she can be seen putting into practice in *La tribuna* and other novels as she had formulated it theoretically in *La cuestión palpitante*. The message conveyed by the novel is that, however strong may be the pressures of heredity and environment, and however powerful their effect on the minds and bodies of poor people, the human spirit can and does resist these forces. In spite of everything, the factory girls manage to affirm their humanity by stubbornly retaining qualities – especially those of religious faith, gaiety and generosity – which the oppressive material circumstances of their life might have been expected to extinguish. Pardo Bazán maintained that in this respect she was faithfully reflecting the reality of proletarian life in Spain, and she was not mistaken. Spain in the 1880s was not a fully industrialized country – it is noteworthy that the work in the factory in *La tribuna* is still done by hand; the women are not just machine-minders. It is therefore reasonable to conclude that the processes of dehumanization and alienation had made less progress than elsewhere. In Amparo herself the assertion of human resilience is found at its strongest:

her robustness, victorious in its struggle with the environment, had grown in direct ratio to the perils and struggles themselves. If the sedentary nature of the work, the unhealthiness of the atmosphere, and the cold, inadequate and meagre food caused anaemia and chlorosis to wreak havoc in the factory, the individual who was able to triumph over these adverse conditions showed redoubled strength and health.

All the other novels Pardo Bazán wrote in the 1880s – except the more conventional *El cisne de Vilamorta* (*The Swan of Vilamorta*, 1885) – were considered by her contemporaries to be naturalistic. In *Los pazos de Ulloa* (*Ulloa House*, 1886) and its sequel *La madre naturaleza* (*Mother Nature*, 1887) one might be forgiven for supposing that Pardo Bazán was, for once, upholding the principle of determinism: these two novels treat of life in a remote community in rural Galicia, and they show how, despite the feeble reforming efforts of a visiting young priest, the animal side of human nature triumphs at the expense of the spiritual. But even in these gloomy novels the idea is implicit that it is possible for man to withstand the pressures of natural instinct. If the particular characters she describes fail to do this, the reason is that they lack the support of a civilized order and, above all, of religion. In these novels Pardo Bazán illustrates the Augustinian concept of the relations between Original Sin and Grace, as she had expounded it in *La cuestión palpitante*: Original Sin is what pushes men to damnation, and thus corresponds to determinism; Grace is the saving possibility for Christians, which enables them to exercise free will and resist Original Sin. The characters of *Los pazos de Ulloa* and *La madre naturaleza* live in a state of Original Sin, and are therefore powerless to shape their own destinies. The contrary picture is presented in two later novels, *Una cristiana* and its sequel *La prueba* (*The Test*) (both 1890), which show a young Christian woman triumphing, thanks to Grace, over temptation and adversity. But in spite of her strict adherence to the Roman Catholic outlook, Pardo Bazán always retained the anthropocentric concept of life fundamental to realism; and in *La madre naturaleza* she wrote one of the most powerful of all Spanish realist novels. Its ambivalent depiction of nature and life in a rural community as being at the same time innocent and barbarous, exuberant and monstrous, makes it possible for Pardo Bazán's romantic tendencies, her love of impressionistic description, her use of symbolism, and her naturalistic tendencies to co-exist harmoniously in the same novel and to complement one another, where in earlier novels they had often clashed. The romanticism and the impressionism generally correspond to the positive aspects of nature, the naturalism to its negative aspects; in *La madre naturaleza* all three combine to present a convincingly complex account of the relationship between man and a natural environment.

Although he was widely regarded in his day as one of the group of naturalist novelists, it is extremely difficult to see how the writings of Armando PALACIO VALDÉS (1853–1938) can be said to resemble Zola's works in any but the most superficial way; most of them are insubstantial and unskilled little efforts in which, in spite of a few unconvincing attempts at psychological penetration, there is no real exploration of human experience at any level. Palacio Valdés was certainly capable of presenting serious subjects in his novels: in *La espuma* (*Froth*, 1891) he satirizes Madrid high life, and contrasts it with the brutish lives of miners; in *La fe* (*Faith*, 1892) he portrays a saintly young priest who loses his faith under the influence of various nineteenth-century ideologies, but later regains it. The book includes some oblique and mildly irreverent criticism of certain types of worldly priest, though it is far from being the outright attack on the Roman Catholic Church which some have taken it to be. *La hermana San Sulpicio* (*Sister Saint Sulpice*, 1889), his best-known novel, is altogether characteristic of his approach in its presentation of a potentially serious theme in a totally frivolous and evasive fashion. This theme, which Palacio Valdés had used earlier in *Marta y María* (1883), is the conflict between profane and sacred love. The narrator in the later novel is a young medical student who tells how he fell in love with the nun of the title, who turns out to be, however, not a nun at all but a novice; so there are after all no real impediments to her leaving her order and marrying. It is hard to resist the conclusion that the heroine is presented as a nun simply for the sake of the scandal inherent in such a situation, which apart from all else is suspiciously similar to that used by the brothers Goncourt in their *Sœur Philomène* (1861).[11]

Thanks to the element of facile entertainment in his writing, Palacio Valdés won considerable popularity both in Spain and abroad, but even in those novels where he made some attempt to write responsibly he failed: the embryo of an interesting statement about life is time after time aborted, as the author succumbs to the temptation to indulge in thoughtless triviality. Even though he was by no means devoid of talent as a novelist, Palacio Valdés was a quite undisciplined writer; in consequence, one cannot point to a single work of his worthy of serious attention.

THE NOVEL IN THE 1880S (I) GALDÓS

It must be clear by now that, generally speaking, naturalism in Spain amounted to little more than an intensification of realist trends; only in the work of obscure novelists like Eduardo López Bago and Alejandro Sawa, who closely imitated Zola's most extreme style and were condemned as pornographers, can one find writing that would, outside Spain, be recognized as naturalistic. Two of the most prominent characteristics of naturalism were incompatible with powerful forces in the cultural tradition of the Spanish middle classes: the candour with which Zola and his disciples wrote of certain natural instincts and physical functions was regarded as an intolerable flouting of the ordinary decencies; while the determinism fundamental to naturalism was irreconcilable with Roman Catholic doctrine. The influence of naturalism was, nevertheless, considerable; it was no coincidence that the brief period during which it was fashionable (roughly speaking, the decade 1880–90) was also the period during which realism achieved its greatest triumphs in Spain.

During this decade Galdós maintained the position he had established for himself as the leading Spanish novelist. The Madrid world of his *novelas españolas contemporáneas* expanded as fresh works followed *La desheredada* in a steady stream. Galdós loosely modelled this long series on Balzac's *Comédie humaine*, and characters and places recur in various different novels. This technique in itself served to enhance the realism of the series, in that it inclined the reader to accept more readily the fictional world presented therein: as he begins a new novel he feels at home, because the atmosphere and often many of the characters are known to him already. The overlapping structure also overcomes the normal drawback of the arbitrary and unrealistic ending: the story in each of the *novelas españolas contemporáneas* does not so much finish as fade away into the general background of the series as a whole (we learn, for example, in the course of *Torquemada en la hoguera* (*Torquemada in the Fire*, 1889) that Isidora from *La desheredada* is now living with an artist who is dying of tuberculosis).

The society of Galdós's Madrid differs, however, from that of Balzac's Paris in that it forms a friendly, self-contained world, one in which most people are motivated not, as in Galdós's novels of the 1870s, by ideological convictions, but rather by the need to establish relations (usually of love or friendship) with other people, and to find and keep their place in society. Galdós's characters, moreover, succeed in satisfying these needs, even though they may be failures in every other respect. Society emerges, in Galdós's optimistic vision, as one large and – on the whole – happy family; for whatever else may happen, and in spite of all the troubles and suffering in life, which he does not try to gloss over, the complex system of personal relations remains alive and vigorous throughout, always able to cope, adapt, and develop. This serenity derives, up to a point, from Galdós's own temperament, but it is also a realistic reflection of the tight-knit community of pre-industrial Madrid.

The cosy welcome that awaits the reader who penetrates into the world of Galdós's Madrid novels is reinforced by the narrative viewpoint adopted in many of them. Instead of relying on the convention of the external, omniscient narrator characteristic of the realist novel, Galdós often tells his stories from the standpoint of a character who, without being directly involved in the events described, is an acquaintance of some of those principally concerned and thus occupies a position somewhat on the periphery of the action. The narrator puts himself on the same plane as the characters, pretending to know them individually, and also on the same plane as the reader, to whom he acts as personal guide to the world of the novel: the fictional world is thus implicitly equated with the real world. The Galdosian acquaintance–narrator enhances realism in another way: the characters appear to enjoy a degree of autonomy rarely found in novels governed by an external, godlike narrator, where there is no pretence that the author is other than in control of his own created world. In theory, what this device should sacrifice is the greater insight permitted to the omniscient narrator; but Galdós allows himself great licence in this respect, giving in practice as much information about the hidden thoughts and feelings of his characters as any more traditional realist. This anomaly does not strike the jarring note that might be expected: skilful manipulation of the narrative point of view makes it possible for the rules of logic to be continuously and inconspicuously infringed.

The free-flowing, colloquial narrative style of Galdós's novels, with its gentle, friendly irony, contributes much both to the feeling of comfortable and confidential *rapport* between author and reader, and to the overall effect of realism. Galdós's use of everyday language in a seemingly straightforward way led to the mistaken belief that he lacked a sense of style, a view that has only recently been seriously challenged. In fact, as in some of the best realistic writing, the style is only apparently artless, and is quite as capable of intense expression as many a more elaborate literary style. Certainly no other way of writing could have better suited the purposes of a realist like Galdós; in comparison, the self-conscious, studied elegance of Valera's prose undermines realism by constantly drawing attention to itself. Galdós's style is at the same time more serviceable and more subtle.

In this manner Galdós wrote, in the course of the 1880s, nearly all the finest Spanish realist novels. The development of realism in his work was accompanied by a corresponding decline of other features, more particularly of the didacticism and romanticism that had characterized his earlier novels. He was no longer primarily concerned to establish his position but to record human life; and he could now limit and control his romantic tendencies, so that idealistic love between attractive young men and beautiful young women was no longer presented as the most important phenomenon in human life, but rather as one type of personal relationship among many. There were other non-realistic tendencies that Galdós, instead of attempting to eliminate, successfully fitted in to a realistic framework: his liking for fantasy, for instance, which he accommodated in his descriptions of the dreams, daydreams and hallucinations of his characters. Mental abnormality was another subject that fascinated Galdós, and nearly all his novels include characters who lose touch with reality.

Galdós's work develops a panoramic view of society in the Madrid of his day. No section of the population is ignored, but his closest attention is reserved for the middle classes. The theme of social ambition is prominent, and the list of characters who struggle to reach a higher position in society is an extensive one. Mostly they are women: Isidora in *La desheredada*, Irene in *El amigo Manso*, Amparo in *Tormento*, Eloísa in *Lo prohibido*, Fortunata in *Fortunata y Jacinta*, Rosalía in *La de Bringas* ... Such aspirations are often frustrated, and the woman in question shown to have been rather silly to entertain them. A key word in these novels is the curious adjective *cursi*, then a neologism evidently dating from the rise of the new middle class. It is normally applied to someone who makes a fool of himself by unsuccessfully aping the manners of the social class immediately above his own. The point implicitly made by Galdós is that it is less important to be rich and powerful than to establish satisfactory human relationships, regardless of social class, and thus to find a way of reconciling the needs of one's own individuality with the demands of others and of society as a whole. Since the personal dramas that these processes involve occur in all human lives, Galdós had no need to invent – as he had in *Doña Perfecta* and *Gloria* – spectacular occurrences to provide interest. In the manner of a true realist, he concentrated on everyday life, transforming this ordinary material by the depth of the analysis he conducts, and showing that problems and conflicts that might appear petty and commonplace on the surface are as grave and as singular as any, when examined in depth and after due attention is paid to the individual lives they affect.

Having dispensed with the need to hold the reader's interest by describing superficially sensational events, Galdós was able to rely, in his mature novels, on fairly straightforward plotting. Even in the four-volume *Fortunata y Jacinta* (1886–7), generally considered his masterpiece, comparatively little happens. Fortunata, a working-class girl, is the mistress of the wealthy young Juanito Santa Cruz, who is married to Jacinta. Fortunata feels she has more right than Jacinta to be Juanito's wife since she has borne him a child, whereas Jacinta is barren; admittedly this first child did not live. She makes repeated and unsuccessful efforts, which include an abortive marriage, to become 'respectable' like Jacinta; and when she dies, having had a second child, she entrusts it to Jacinta, thus finally achieving a reconciliation with her rival. Other novels have even simpler stories. *El amigo Manso* (1882) concerns a young *krausista* intellectual who comes to realize how mistaken his view of life – and particularly his idealization of the woman he worships – has been. *Tormento* (1884) describes the relationship between a wealthy returned émigré and the woman he hopes to marry, both of whom begin by aspiring to bourgeois respectability and end by rejecting this ideal and deciding simply to live together. *La de Bringas* (1884) is about the wife of a palace bureaucrat, and the trouble caused by her obsessive social ambitions. *Miau* (1888) has as its subject the plight of an unemployed government clerk, who eventually goes mad.

Such novels represent the culmination of Galdós's career as a realist. Yet the realism even of these works was by no means complete, nor, clearly, was it intended to be. It is evident that Galdós was never able to regard his own work with total seriousness, and that he never fully convinced himself that the novel could really be very much more than an agreeable pastime. His fascination with the idea of creating a fictional world to which readers can be induced to react as though it were the real world expressed itself from the very start of his career as a novelist by his habit of teasing the reader by various elaborate pretences, such as that the narrator was none too sure himself about certain factual details in his own narrative. Thus, in the opening chapter of *Torquemada en el purgatorio* (1894) the author poses as a historian who has to collate various conflicting accounts of minor events in the protagonist's life, and he describes his difficulties at some length. A similar effect is created by the narrator's pretence that the characters and events of the novel, and even the manner of their presentation, are matters over which he has no control:

It is, perhaps, most untoward that the first time we meet this interesting couple should be on such a tumultuous occasion as is that of moving house, in the midst of rooms piled up with furniture and belongings and in the heart of a stifling cloud of dust. It's not our fault if the highly respectable person of Don Francisco Bringas appears rather comical as it presents itself to us inside a shapeless old jacket, with an even older cap pulled right down over the ears, the physiognomy disfigured by dust, feet enclosed in ample slippers, crawling about on the carpet . . .[12]

Humour such as this has the effect of drawing the reader's attention to the artificiality of the whole narrative situation. What is normally meant to intensify the realist effect is made to serve an exactly contrary purpose, that of weakening it; attention is called to the artificiality of the techniques the novelist uses and to the spuriousness of his claims to represent reality. All this is clearly done quite deliberately. In Galdós the realist it is possible to discern a significant streak of anti-realism; his novels have the seeds of the anti-novel in them.

The most complete illustration of this aspect of Galdós's art is to be found in *El amigo Manso*, the extraordinary novel he wrote in 1882, immediately after *La desheredada*. Galdós was always experimenting with new narrative techniques, catching his public and critics off balance by producing the unexpected. He wrote *El amigo Manso* in the first person, thereby radically departing from precedent: third-person narrative is the norm in European realism, though a certain number of the Spanish realists adopted the pseudo-autobiography in works published after *El amigo Manso*: Pereda wrote two novels in this form (*Pedro Sánchez* (1883) and *Peñas arriba* (1894)) and it was adopted too by Palacio Valdés in *La hermana San Sulpicio* (1889) and by Emilia Pardo Bazán in most of her novels. But *El amigo Manso* is not a straightforward first-person novel. The protagonist–narrator, a teacher of philosophy named Máximo Manso, begins by proclaiming in the first words of the novel: 'Yo no existo' ('I do not exist') – as resolutely anti-realistic an opening as could be imagined. The first chapter goes on to insist on the fact that the narrator is in no sense a real person, but merely a figment of the author's imagination, an illusory being who inhabits 'these regions of the idea' but who, paradoxically, has an independence and autonomous existence as such (all the supposedly original features of Unamuno's famous 'existential' novel *Niebla* (1914) are to be found in *El amigo Manso*).

I am – to put it in obscure language so that I may be better understood – a devilish artistic condensation, a creature of human thought (*Ximia Dei*) which, if it can lay its hands on a little style, starts imitating with its aid the works that God has wrought with matter in the physical world; I am a new edition of those falsifications perpetrated by man which, since the very beginning of the world, have been put on sale everywhere by people that I (totally failing in my filial duty) call wastrels, and that the masses, in their innocent kindness, call poets and other such things. I am a chimera, the dream of a dream and the shadow of a shadow, the suspicion of a possibility . . .

As the story moves towards its end and Manso comes to realize more clearly that all the standards on which he has based his whole existence are quite irrelevant to the actual business of living, he falls ill and dies; and the final chapter elaborates another sense of the novel's opening words: we are now asked to believe that everything we have been reading was composed in the other world. Not only is Manso a fiction invented by Galdós; he is a fiction that has, by dying, departed even from the fictional world that Galdós provided for him. Moreover, even when supposedly 'alive', he had never properly lived in this world because his value-system had come between him and the business of living. He is thus at three large removes from reality. It need hardly be stressed how, at every turn and on every level, *El amigo Manso* seems deliberately to set at naught the fundamental assumptions of realism and perversely to tear to shreds most of the time-honoured conventions which the realist novelist had used in order to give the illusion of reality.

This was Galdós's most daring experiment; but *Lo prohibido* (1884–5), also a story related by the protagonist–narrator, *La incógnita* (1888–9), which uses the epistolary form, and its sequel *Realidad* (1889), composed in dramatic dialogue form, offer further examples of novels which, in their mode of narration, are non-realistic. One can discern an increasing tendency in Galdós's work towards the pure dialogue form, unaccompanied by narrative, descriptive, or explicative passages. This form is encountered in individual chapters of earlier novels, such as *La desheredada*, *El doctor Centeno*, and *Tormento*, and Galdós's later production came to be dominated by dialogue novels like *El abuelo* (*The Grandfather*, 1897), dramatizations of earlier works (*Doña Perfecta* (1896) being the most successful), and original plays, beginning with *La de San Quintín* (1894). Galdós was a writer who could never for long remain satisfied with one set of literary conventions; instead of casting his novels in the moulds created by previous writers he was constantly breaking and re-forming them. To study Galdós's literary production is to realize the truth of Frank Kermode's assertion: 'The history of the novel is a history of anti-novels.'[13]

THE NOVEL IN THE 1880S (II) PEREDA

Of the three other novelists who had become prominent by 1880, only Pereda continued writing regularly; Alarcón's last published novel, *La pródiga*, came out in 1881, and Valera was thought to have given up writing novels until he resumed in the 1890s. Pereda followed Galdós in his adoption of a colloquial, confidential style (though in Pereda's case its simplicity really is a question of artlessness); in his use of a factual historical and geographical background in order to reinforce the impression of realism in his novels; and in his abandonment of the thesis novel in favour of the description of reality for its own sake – though the difference here is that in Pereda's novels this change cannot be attributed to his having developed, like Galdós, a more open and tolerant attitude, but is due rather to the fact that the thesis previously preached more or less directly is now simply taken for granted. On this basis Pereda wrote novels most of which described life in his home province of Santander among farm-workers, most notably in *El sabor de la tierruca* (*The Flavour of Rural Life*, 1881) and *Peñas arriba* (*Up Among the Crags*, 1894), and among fishermen, in *Sotileza*[14] (1884) and *La puchera* (*Fish Stew*, 1889).

The world of Pereda's rural novels is one of traditional ways of life intimately bound up with and dependent upon God's nature; it is therefore inevitable that these novels should reject the anthropocentric view of life held by Galdós and by the realists in general. For this reason they suffer from a shortcoming which would normally be fatal: Pereda is at his weakest when he attempts to portray individual human beings, to describe their actions as individuals and to analyse the relationships between them. In most of his writing, however, he obviously felt compelled by current literary conventions, however foreign these conventions were to his outlook and however ill-suited to render the quality of life he was describing, to try and create characters with distinctive individual personalities and make them interact in such a way as to produce recognizable intrigues, especially romantic love intrigues of – in practice – a singularly unoriginal, mechanical, and stilted sort. *Peñas arriba*, Pereda's last novel, is also one of his best because in it most of the characters are simply mono-lithic and archetypal representations of the way of life being described: the mountains are credited with more independence than the people who inhabit them and who are content to remain in harmony with nature. Pereda's nature descriptions are as often dynamic as static, and natural phenomena are regularly anthropomorphized; human beings, on the other hand, are frequently described in terms of inanimate objects, as at the beginning of *Peñas arriba*, where the ailing patriarch Don Celso refers to himself as an old oak tree whose roots are tearing loose from the soil, and as a decrepit house which depends on props to keep it standing. The story of *Peñas arriba* is suitably slow and simple, and petty intrigue is almost completely excluded. It concerns a young city gentleman summoned against his will to a remote mountain community presided over by his aged uncle; the young man is slowly brought to realize the superior moral values of the patriar-chal system, and finally decides to take over his uncle's position and leave the city for good. In *Peñas arriba*, where the literary conse-quences of an ultra-conservative world-view are worked out in full, and both the idiosyncratic individual character and the complex intrigue are rejected as contradictions of that world-view, Pereda wrote a novel which expressed his ideas completely and coherently: a novel which admittedly has little to do with conventional realism except in so far as it presents itself as an accurate and detailed record of a certain way of life; and a novel whose literary values the modern reader has great difficulty in appreciating since these values rest on assumptions largely alien to contemporary thought.

Pereda was fully aware of the limitations of the type of regionalism that inspires most of his novels. In an attempt to break free of these limitations, he wrote two novels about life in the capital, *Pedro Sánchez* (1883) and *La Montálvez* (1887), and a third, *Nubes de estío* (*Summer Clouds*, 1891), concerned with the bourgeoisie and minor aristocracy of Madrid on summer holiday in Santander. These are the only novels in which Pereda deals directly with the new society instead of dwelling on the traditional order that this new society was displacing; they alone can be properly assessed according to the canons of nineteenth-century realism. To the reader familiar only with Pereda's better-known novels of country life, *Pedro Sánchez* comes as something of a revelation. It takes the form of the memoirs of a man from one of those northern villages that provide the normal background of Pereda's novels, a man who was attracted to Madrid as an innocent youth, made a name for himself in the 1854 revolution of Espartero and O'Donnell, contracted a disastrous marriage with the daughter of one of the aristocratic families of the capital, went into voluntary exile and finally, many years later, returned a sadder man to his native village. Pereda's two best novels thus complement each other: *Pedro Sánchez* embodies the drama of the villager confronted with city life, *Peñas arriba* that of the city-dweller confronted with village life. Although in *Pedro Sánchez* Pereda remains the same country-lover, distrusting city life, that he shows himself to be elsewhere, he is unusually restrained and detached in the way he handles his material. This enables him to depict city characters and manners, and the countryman confronting them, in a satisfying realistic manner; the attacks on modern urban civilization are the more effective for appearing to be reasonable and well-based. Perhaps because of the intrinsic interest of its subject-matter – the bustling city in the midst of revolutionary turmoil – this novel has none of the flat, insipid dullness that threatens most of the rural novels. Its characterization takes far more account of the real complexity of human beings than is usual with Pereda; the story he tells rings true and has not that air of desultory contrivance typical of so many of his other narratives; and the whole structure is skilfully arranged to achieve greater coherence and unity at every level.

Pereda was not able to maintain this quality of artistic achievement in the other novel he wrote with an urban setting, *La Montálvez*. The hostility he felt for Madrid steeps every page of this exemplary tale of a society woman and her empty, immoral life; the book is little more than a heavy-handed satire of the vanity, hypocrisy and wickedness that Pereda saw as inseparable from metropolitan society. In its explicit, insistent, and predictable moralizing, which never allows the story or the characterization any independent development, *La Montálvez* represents an unfortunate regression to the manner of Pereda's novels of the 1870s.

THE NOVEL IN THE 1880s (III) ALAS

The culminating achievement of Spanish literary realism is represented by *La Regenta* (1884–5), a work of extraordinary power by Leopoldo ALAS (1852–1901) writing under the pseudonym Clarín. Previously, the only fiction he had published had been short stories: he was the principal Spanish exponent of the genre until the 1890s, when Pardo Bazán took it up with great success. The short story did not undergo quite the same extension in nineteenth-century Spain as it had known in other European countries. It had been revived by the Spanish romantics, and Alarcón's cultivation of the short story from the 1850s onwards demonstrated that his talents were better suited to the brief than to the extended narrative. In spite of this precedent and the example of the *costumbristas*, whose articles came close to being short stories, little more of value was produced during the realist period. This is not to say that short stories were not written – the expansion of the newspaper and magazine industry created a demand for them in Spain as elsewhere in Europe – but on the whole it was the less talented writers who supplied this demand. Galdós fought shy of the short story (though one or two that he wrote have been found); after Alas, Palacio Valdés was the most distinguished short-story writer of the time. Alas, always writing much too quickly, as he was the first to realize, in order to meet the deadlines set by his editors, poured out a steady stream of stories, most of which fail to engage the interest of the modern reader because of their rigid polemical approach. Nearly all of them hammer home the same point, that the only true values are the spiritual ones, which rationalistic and materialistic nineteenth-century civilization was in danger of undermining. It is a curious reflection on the prevailing confusion of political and ideological thought that the writer who constantly expressed such reactionary sentiments should have been universally considered, and should have considered himself, a man of advanced liberal attitudes: simply, it seems, because in his critical writings – Alas was perhaps the foremost literary critic of his day – he was prepared to think for himself about important subjects instead of dutifully quoting church doctrine. In each of his short stories, the evidence is so obviously slanted in order to accommodate his own views that the reader is bound to react by rejecting the story both as polemic and as literature, on the grounds that life is manifestly not nearly so simple as Alas would have us believe. Only in some of his longer stories, like *Pipá* (1879), *Superchería* (1889–90) and *Doña Berta* (1891), does artistic creativity begin to assert itself against moral dogmatism. But it seems that he needed, like Cervantes before him, the broad canvas of the long novel before he could reveal to the full his exceptional talents as a writer of fiction. It remains something of a paradox, even so, that the same man who composed these trite and repetitive little moral fables should have also produced *La Regenta*, where the complexity of human experience is explored so deeply and convincingly. It is almost as if in the short stories he was attempting to provide reassuringly simple answers for the troubling problems which in *La Regenta* he is content to expose rather than solve.

Among these problems, one of the most intractable was that of the mutually exclusive interpretations of human behaviour represented by the alternatives of determinism and free will. We have seen how this issue was faced and resolved by Pardo Bazán. Alas, in the preface he wrote to *La cuestión palpitante*, argued that naturalism was not necessarily deterministic, positivistic, or pessimistic. In *La Regenta* he expressed his ideas on this subject in a fuller and more convincing fashion. In a general sense the story runs along deterministic lines. The heroine, Ana Ozores, is a sensitive and intelligent young woman married to a retired magistrate. In the oppressively dull and mediocre provincial town where she lives with her husband, Ana searches in vain for self-fulfilment, and when finally she succumbs to the local philanderer she shows herself to be of no finer nature than her neighbours. The portrayal of human nature is blackly pessimistic; a peculiarly sordid and often perverse type of sexuality is seen to pervade life, although Alas usually evokes it even more allusively than do Pardo Bazán or Galdós; but this very indirectness only adds to the sense of perversity. The material environment always presses very heavily indeed; mental states are generally given physical causes – Ana's occasional feelings of mystical fervour, for example, occur like Emma Bovary's when she is physically weak, convalescing from illness; and we are shown how ultimately futile is her struggle against the forces that press in on her. In all these ways *La Regenta* presents the deterministic case very fully. On the other hand, the characters are by no means mere puppets, their movements totally controlled by heredity and environment. They remain self-aware and in control, to the extent of deliberately calculating the results of an action before they embark on it. Of course they often miscalculate, and in stress lose their self-control. Ana, for example, makes conscious choices at key points throughout the novel, choices which often lead her into courses of action that conflict with her fundamental urges; on the other hand there are occasions when she loses this self-control and acts spontaneously. It is on one of these occasions that she allows herself to be seduced, but Alas makes it perfectly clear that this outcome was in no way predestined. In few novels has the conflict between free will and determinism, idealism and materialism, Grace and Original Sin been dramatized so completely as it is in *La Regenta*. Alas offers us in the pages of his book a complete case for determinism and a complete case against it, the two opposites being brought together and interwoven in a continuing dialectic within the overall structure of the novel.

La Regenta, which has only recently come to be recognized by critical opinion for the masterpiece it is, displays a more intense and serious realism than is to be found in any other Spanish novels of the period, although, like many serious works of literature, it is predominantly comic in tone. The orthodox realistic technique of the omniscient narrator who is able to see into his characters' minds and present their view of what they witness is exploited with virtuosity and yields the fullest possible picture of a society and of the individuals who make it up, in a vast series of complementary perspectives all co-ordinated in complex patterns. The language of *La Regenta* is the source of its intensity; and this also is the consequence not of radical departures in new directions but rather of the full utilization of the potential inherent in established methods. Alas perfected the normal realistic style of apparent linguistic simplicity which conceals an underlying complexity of meaning: a style in which what is implied is usually more important and revelatory than anything that is explicitly stated. It is a style which is itself an expression of the narrator's fundamentally critical attitude and of one of his principal themes, the deceptiveness of superficial appearances, the need to penetrate these before the truth can be apprehended. The mordant irony that pervades the novel also draws attention constantly to the gap between appearances and reality. And Galdós's fondness for narrating by means of conversations in direct speech is replaced in *La Regenta* by accounts of characters' thoughts – which often contradict what they say – expressed in *style indirect libre* ('free indirect discourse'). This is only one of the respects in which Alas betrays his very considerable debt to Flaubert, the first writer to make extensive use in his novels of this device.

All this is achieved in *La Regenta* with a sureness in the handling of narrative techniques that would be remarkable in any novelist, let alone in one who is writing his first novel and who has chosen to go about it in such an ambitious way. Yet *La Regenta* was not well received, and it has continued in relative obscurity until quite recently; so far, it remains untranslated into English. The bleak vision it gives of life and the unflattering portrait it paints of man are not easy to countenance. Its extraordinary artistry was simply not noticed by contemporaries; the subtle handling of its complex themes made it a work far in advance of its own time. Its failure to achieve the recognition it deserved, together with Alas's declining health and the pressure of his work as a critic and teacher, explains why he did not persevere with his plans for further works of fiction. His only other published novel was *Su único hijo* (*His Only Son*, 1890), the introductory section of an intended trilogy; it tells the story of an ineffectual little man (Bonifacio Reyes, one of a number of humble heroes, treated with great sympathy here and in Alas's short stories), whose life is a total failure but who ultimately finds fulfilment in fatherhood – even though this fatherhood is illusory, for the child his wife bears is the son of another man with whom she has been conducting an adulterous liaison. *Su único hijo* is the ultimate expression of one of the central themes of Alas's short stories: the rejection of material reality and of rational thought. What is implied is that Bonifacio is a father if he believes himself to be one, notwithstanding all concrete evidence to the contrary. The book is quite without the complexity and depth of *La Regenta*, and the reader who turns to it after Alas's great novel can only be disappointed.

THE DECLINE OF REALISM

The move away from realism in the Spanish novel started at the end of the 1880s. At this time the vogue of the Russian novel was eclipsing that of the products of French naturalism among Spaniards who followed the literary fashion; in 1887 Pardo Bazán produced her assessment of this latest development in *La revolución y la novela en Rusia*. In 1887, too, the economic boom that had coincided with the flowering of Spanish realism ended, and a period of industrial depression followed. Pessimism was intensified, to reach its eventual climax in 1898, the year of crisis when national morale sank to its lowest ebb after the defeat sustained in the war with the United States and the consequent loss of Cuba, Puerto Rico and the Philippines. But even before these disasters had overwhelmed the country, a mood of dejected self-concern had replaced the outward-looking period of growth, just as protectionism replaced the free-trade policies that had been practised for some years. The change in the political and economic climate was paralleled by a corresponding modification of the tone adopted by the novelists, as their 'open' vision of man as a social being receded and was replaced by the 'closed' vision of him as a creature facing alone and unaided the problems of existence. The essential, if tempered, optimism of a Galdós, based on the assumption that social man is supreme, and that whatever happens social relationships will triumph, wilted before the more pessimistic outlook characteristic of the new group of writers, who emerged towards the end of the century and who came to be called the Generation of 1898. The very different kind of literature they produced was inspired by an overriding introspective concern with the problems of the individual being and with those of Spain, conceived as an individual entity; the viewpoint adopted was that of an extreme philosophical idealism, expressed in articles, essays, poems, plays and anti-realistic novels.

But even in the work of novelists like Pardo Bazán and Galdós a shift of interest can be detected away from social reality and towards the intimate problems of the individual, especially religious problems. For neither of these two writers did this development represent an abrupt change of direction, but rather a confirmation and intensification of trends discernible embryonically in earlier work. All Pardo Bazán's 'naturalistic' novels of the 1880s had, as has been noted, a firm Roman Catholic basis; and Galdós too, in all his novels, had expressed a constant preoccupation with the problem of religious faith.

Between 1889 and 1895 Galdós published his series of four novels about the spiritual and social progress of a miser, Torquemada.[15] To this period also belongs *Angel Guerra* (1890–91), in which Galdós traces the development of deep religious feeling in a young revolutionary intellectual. Although the critical observation of society remains an important feature of all these novels, the new tendency manifests itself in the pronounced emphasis given to the study of the inner life and spiritual predicament of the main characters. In Galdós's next three novels, *Nazarín* (1895), *Halma* (1895), and *Misericordia* (1897), the religious theme is totally dominant: these novels serve to convey the author's conviction that life should be based on a personal, non-institutional faith, an all-pervading, sincere and Christ-like love for all men.

The novels published by Pardo Bazán after 1890 reveal a similar growth of interest in psychological problems. The characteristic form is an account by the protagonist–narrator of his spiritual life; the device of the unreliable narrator is handled with mastery, just as in some of Pardo Bazán's earlier novels full use had been made of the technique of the omniscient narrator. Her characters are now exceptional people with unusual personal problems, whereas previously, as a realist, she had been primarily interested in characters who were representative of various social groups and classes. The series begins with *Una cristiana* and its sequel *La prueba* (both 1890), which tell of an irreligious young man who is converted to Christianity by the example of the life of saintly suffering endured by the young woman he admires; it culminates in *La quimera* (*The Chimera*, 1905) and *La sirena negra* (1908), both characterized by a remarkable depth of psychological portrayal. To this period too belong the short stories that Pardo Bazán wrote in quantity, and in which she arguably reached her highest peak of achievement as a writer. Full of interest as her novels are, most of them embody passages of extremely doubtful relevance to the whole: an indication of the difficulty she found in sustaining a central theme throughout a lengthy narrative without resorting to 'padding' under various guises. Her talents seemed well suited to the restrictive form of the short story, and her writing in this genre shows a new density and terseness. Her stories cover an extra-ordinarily wide range of subjects and themes, and are written in a diversity of styles. They still await proper critical recognition.

Not all the novelists we have considered followed the trend towards the religious novel. Two in particular show no noticeable variation in the course of their careers. Palacio Valdés continued – and was to continue for some time to come, though with steadily declining popularity – to produce his insubstantial, superficial fictions. It is true that *La fe* (1892) is concerned with the spiritual predicament of an individual; but it exhibits all the normal features of the author's writing, and cannot by itself be said to indicate a general move in a new direction. Neither did Valera show any disposition to renew his manner. After a long absence from the literary scene he started writing again, at the age of seventy, and produced three more novels in the space of four years: *Juanita la larga* (*Lanky Joan*, 1895), *Genio y figura* (1897), and the fantasy *Morsamor* (1899). The first is the most important of the three: set in rural Andalusia, it is a simple but well-told story of a woman's search for fulfilment in love, in which although (as in earlier novels) profane and religious love are juxtaposed and the former shown to triumph, there is none of the total preoccupation with religious problems that characterizes Galdós's novels of the 1890s.

And so the Age of Realism drew to its close in Spain. Realism had been a brief, though intensely active phase, starting considerably later than elsewhere and ending only a little later; and the Spanish novelists were by no means disposed to accept unreservedly all the methods and implications of the movement. Yet its importance for the development of modern Spanish literature was immense. The continuing influence of Galdós, in particular, can be seen in the work of many novelists writing in Spanish in the twentieth century, Latin American as well as peninsular; even the novelists of the 'Generation of 1898', who in many respects embody a reaction against the realism of Galdós and his contemporaries, were in fact indebted to their predecessors; and the work of successful modern writers like Gironella represents, for better or for worse, a return to a realism very much after the fashion of the novelists of the 'Generation of 1868'.

REALISM IN PORTUGAL: THE 'GENERATION OF 1870'

At a dinner-party described by Eça de Queirós in his masterpiece, *Os Maias*, a bare-armed baroness, seated near the young hero, asks him what the latest news is from the capital. 'I don't think there has been any news in Lisbon, *senhora*,' drawls Carlos de Maia, 'since the death of Senhor Dom João VI in 1826.'

The history of Portugal in the nineteenth century, and the historical background, therefore, of Portuguese realism, were perhaps a little less uneventful than this foppish sally suggests. The ruinous struggle known in our history books as the Peninsular War left the country in almost as devastated a condition as Spain. Prince John of Bragança (the Senhor Dom João referred to above), who had been in charge of the affairs of the kingdom since his mother lapsed into a melancholy madness in 1792, succeeded to the throne only in 1816, when Queen Maria finally died. During the first few years of his reign, however, he was an absentee monarch. With the court and government, he had sailed from Lisbon to Rio on a wet November day in 1807, just before the invading French army under Junot reached the Portuguese capital; and even though Wellington succeeded in driving the last French troops out of Portugal in 1811, the future John VI preferred to remain in Brazil for the next ten years. When he finally returned to take up the reins of government in his rightful kingdom, he left his son Pedro to administer the extensive Portuguese dominions in South America. But the Brazilians had no desire to revert to the subordinate status which had been theirs before the war, and in 1822, a bare fifteen months after John VI sailed back to Portugal, the young prince, his heir, was acclaimed 'constitutional emperor' of an independent Brazil.

The two countries continued to be ruled by members of the same royal house until 1889, when the Brazilians threw out the first Pedro's son, Pedro II, and proclaimed a republic. Meanwhile the home country had been undergoing tribulations similar to those that afflicted neighbouring Spain throughout the greater part of the century. Liberal constitutions were set up by liberal monarchs, only to be abrogated by despotic ones. There were bouts of civil war and military rule. There were quarrels with Great Britain over the slavery issue or, more precisely, over Palmerston's policy of having Portuguese merchantmen searched by units of the Royal Navy to make sure they were not carrying slaves. There were other clashes between the same two powers – officially allies since 1386 – over the control of Mozambique and, later, of Nyasaland. The state's finances, badly upset by the loss of revenue from Brazil, were further dilapidated by internal strife and maladministration; by 1890 Portugal was close on bankruptcy, and its foreign creditors – Germany in particular – were threatening to satisfy themselves by seizing Portuguese possessions in Africa. And all this time, little or nothing had been done to check the twin evils that were weighing most oppressively on the country's spirit: the grossly uneven distribution of wealth between landowners and peasantry, and the tyrannical obscurantism of the Church.

For a people with so remarkable a past history as the Portuguese, this period could hardly have been viewed as anything else than one of calamitous decline and decadence. The best sons of Portugal at this time – men like the Romantic poet and dramatist Almeida Garrett (1799–1854) and the historian Alexandre Herculano (1810–66) – saw it as their overriding duty to help in the regeneration of Portugal through their writings and, where possible, through active participation in the political life of the country: Garrett, after his return from exile in 1837, became a deputy and (in 1852) Foreign Minister. In due course, the same patriotic desire to rescue Portugal from the hopeless lethargy in which she seemed to be sunk was to inspire the realists during the last three decades of the century. It may be noted, incidentally, that wherever it made its appearance in Europe, realism was always a national movement, in the sense that none of the writers concerned, with the single exception of Stendhal, ever paid any attention to what went on outside the national frontiers; many of them, indeed, were regionalists, confining themselves to studying the life and customs of a small area inside the national territory. This was, of course, an inevitable consequence of the requirement, central to the realist aesthetic, that a writer should seek his material exclusively within the society of which he had direct and personal knowledge. But in Portugal the realists examined the present condition of their country and assessed its probable future with an anxious concern which went far beyond objective, 'scientific' curiosity. Their primary aim was the same as that of realists everywhere in continental Europe, to 'tell the truth'; but this truth-telling mission was not merely salutary – for the Portuguese, it was crucial. They had to be told the truth about themselves because the truth alone could save them from ultimate disgrace and degradation. Authentic patriots, said Eça de Queirós, wish neither to flatter nor to deceive their countrymen.

They don't tell her that she is great because she took Calcutta, but that she is small because she has no schools. They shout the harsh, the brutal truth to her without remission: You are poor – work! You are ignorant – study! You are weak – arm yourself!

Thus, the fervid patriotism that filled the breasts of the Portuguese realists was no self-centred chauvinism. They spoke little of Vasco da Gama or of Camoens, but much of Hegel and of Proudhon. The programme of the lecture course organized at Lisbon by Antero de Quental, Eça de Queirós, Oliveira Martins and others in 1871 – the so-called 'Conferências Democráticas do Casino' – was cosmopolitan in its scope, even though aiming to set in train a national revival. The declared intention was

to link up Portugal with the modern movement, thus enabling it to draw nourishment from the vital elements on which civilized humanity thrives; to make an attempt to understand the present situation in Europe; to start a public debate on the great question of the political, economic, and religious transformation of Portuguese society.

Because of its geographical situation in the extreme south-west corner of Europe, with a narrow hinterland and a relatively long coast-line, Portugal had always depended more on sea-routes than on communications overland for its contacts with the rest of the civilized world; hence, no doubt, its centuries-old love-hate relationship with that other great maritime people, the English. This has to be understood in order to appreciate the extraordinary revolution brought about in the intellectual life of Portugal by an apparently minor event, the opening of the first railway line between Paris and the old university city of Coimbra in 1864. Eça de Queirós later recalled, in an obituary written for his friend Antero de Quental, who committed suicide in 1892, the 'mental tumult' into which Coimbra was plunged as packing-cases full of new books arrived by train from the great Paris publishing houses, Hachette, Hetzel, Michel Lévy, Charpentier:

> Every morning brought its revelation like a new sun. It was Michelet who rose, and Hegel, and Vico, and Proudhon; and Hugo turned prophet, chastiser of kings; and Balzac with his perverse and languid world; and Goethe, vast as the universe; and Poe, and Heine, and I believe even Darwin, and how many others! Into this nerve-ridden, sensitive, *pallid* generation – like Musset's, having been conceived like his during the civil wars[16] – all these marvels dropped like logs on a fire, making a great crackling and sending up clouds of smoke. And at the same time, over the peaks of the Pyrenees now, morally speaking, levelled, we were touched by the great enthusiasms to which Europe was thrilling and which we adopted on the spot as our own: the cult of Garibaldi and resurgent Italy, a violent sympathy for partitioned Poland, a love of Ireland, green Erin, the Celtic emerald isle, mother of saints and bards, trampled underfoot by the Saxon . . .

One of the first-fruits of these 'revelations' was Antero de Quental's *Odes Modernas* (1864), a collection roundly condemned on its appearance by the *doyen* of Portuguese romanticism, the famous blind poet Antonio Feliciano de Castilho, a man now in his sixties and exercising the same kind of dictatorship of letters as did Hugo in France after his return from exile. But Quental did not accept the rebuke meekly: in a resounding pamphlet entitled *Bom Senso e Bom Gosto* (*Good Sense and Good Taste*) he hit out at Castilho, accusing the old man of wasting time on frivolous exercises in versification while the rest of Europe was in the throes of a cultural and intellectual revolution. Castilho's sycophantic entourage was ridiculed in a second pamphlet, *Teocracias Literárias*, written by Teófilo Braga (1843–1924), another young poet whom Castilho had attacked.

Though essentially a quarrel among poets, this polemical battle demonstrated the feverish desire of the younger generation to 'join Europe' and escape from the stifling provincialism into which Portuguese literature had sunk in the mid-nineteenth century. Romantic subjectivity was to be henceforth proscribed. Quental wanted poetry to become 'the Voice of the Revolution'; Braga took Hugo as his inspiration and modelled his *Visão dos Tempos* on the French poet's *Légende des Siècles*.

Over the next few years political events outside Portugal acted as an intoxicating stimulus to this hot-headed group of Coimbra students and graduates. In 1868 there was the September Revolution in Spain; in 1870 came the downfall of the Second Empire and the proclamation of a republic in France; and there followed, for a few months in 1871, the rule of the Commune in Paris. The original Coimbra group joined up with new converts in Lisbon, who included J. P. de Oliveira Martins (1845–94), the historian, later to become a socialist deputy and even, at a critical moment, Finance Minister; the poet Guilherme de Azevedo (1839–82), a disciple of Antero de Quental; and J. D. Ramalho Ortigão (1836–1915), who, with the help of Eça de Queirós, launched a monthly satirical journal called *As Farpas* (*The Darts*, or *Banderillas*), which ran very successfully from 1871 to 1883 and served to disseminate the ideas of the group throughout Portugal. It will be noted that Eça was the only future novelist in this group, though at the time he was known only for an uncharacteristic series of prose poems, published in the *Gazeta de Portugal* (1866–7), and subsequently in book form under the title *Prosas Bárbaras*.

It was the programme of lectures announced, and in part delivered, at the Casino in Lisbon – the Conferências Democráticas already mentioned – that first brought the group to public notice. In the first lecture, Antero de Quental attributed what he called the 'decline of the Peninsular peoples' to the retrograde influence of the Roman Catholic Church and to the habit of drawing wealth from conquered territories overseas instead of building up home industries. To reverse these trends, nothing short of a revolution would do; his ringing conclusion ran: 'Christianity was the Revolution of antiquity; the Revolution is nothing more than the Christianity of the modern world.' Nor was this mere rhetoric: at this time, Quental was deeply engaged in the effort to found a branch of the International among the working people of Lisbon.

Eça de Queirós gave the second lecture, on realism (*O Realismo na Arte*). In it he combined an attack on the anachronism of romanticism with an attempt to define the true function of the artist in modern society; he concluded that this function consisted in portraying the social reality objectively, in the hope that knowledge of the truth would help to promote reforms. More specifically, his view that heroes in fiction were outmoded, that the novelist should present man as 'a result, a conclusion and a product of the circumstances that have evolved him', and should concern himself exclusively with type characters illustrative of social trends and institutions – all this indicates how Eça's thought was developing along the orthodox realist pattern. One imagines he must have been reading Taine with marked attention.

The third lecture was never given. It had been planned to deal with the new, secular view of the historical person of Jesus, as developed by Strauss and Renan. But the authorities banned it. The protests that were raised in the press and even in parliament testify to the widespread interest that this short-lived venture had aroused.

EÇA DE QUEIRÓS

One of the strangest facts about the career of José Maria de EÇA DE QUEIRÓS (1845–1900) was that so little of his adult life was actually spent in Portugal, the country he satirized and denounced and for which he so clearly experienced all the nostalgic tenderness of the resentful exile. Shortly after the affair of the Casino lectures he joined the consular service, and thereafter lived mainly abroad; he was sent first to Havana and then to Newcastle, where he remained from 1874 to 1888. His *Cartas da Inglaterra* (*Letters from England*), based on this long experience, constitute a fascinating documentary account of Victorian society during the heyday of imperial splendour. Then Eça made an advantageous marriage and settled in Paris for the remaining twelve years of his life, though he also travelled in North America and the Middle East. He counts, with Stendhal and Turgenev, as the most cosmopolitan of the European realists.

As a writer, he asserted that he owed everything to the French culture he had absorbed:

My novels are fundamentally French, as I am French myself in almost every respect – barring a certain genuine bedrock of lyrical melancholy, which is a Portuguese characteristic, a depraved taste for *fado* singers, and a proper fondness for cod with onions. In everything else I am a provincial Frenchman. It could not have been otherwise: in the university campus and the Largo do Rossio [in Lisbon], I received my education and educated myself thanks to French books, French ideas, French turns of speech, French sentiments and French ideals.[17]

Much scholarly attention has, in fact, been devoted to tracing the numerous borrowings from French authors of opinions, phrases, motifs and attitudes which are discoverable in Eça's writings. It is sometimes said that his very style was contaminated by a species of linguistic osmosis, that he wrote a kind of Franco-Portuguese as Joseph Conrad a kind of Franco-English. However this may be, his realism is of purely Portuguese application, as becomes rapidly apparent as soon as one turns to the handful of novels that have given him his international reputation.

The first, which caused considerable scandal on publication, was *O Crime do Padre Amaro* (*The Sin of Father Amaro*, 1875). The basic situation exploited here by Eça, a love-affair between a priest, vowed to celibacy, and a virgin, might have been suggested by any one of a number of literary sources, the first English (M. G. Lewis's *The Monk*, 1796), the rest all French. Hugo's *Notre-Dame de Paris* (1831) showed an archdeacon (Frollo) consumed with lust for a gipsy girl (Esmeralda); Lamartine's *Jocelyn* (1835), a narrative poem, dealt with the unconsummated passion of a seminarist, ordained during the Revolution, for the girl Laurence. There had been more recent variations on the same theme: Barbey d'Aurevilly's *Un Prêtre marié* (1865) and Ernest Daudet's *Le Missionnaire* (1869). What appears certain is that *O Crime do Padre Amaro* owes nothing to Zola's *La Faute de l'abbé Mouret*, in spite of the similarity of the titles and the parallelism of the plots: the two novels, by an odd coincidence, were published in the same year. Nevertheless, the comparison is instructive. For a start, it cannot be denied that Eça's novel conforms much more closely with the accepted norms of realism. Whereas Zola chose a remote, primitive hamlet for his setting, the environment picked by Eça is the busy town of Leiria, with its shops, offices, cafés, and its cathedral. The description of the clerical community, and of the admiring flock of feminine penitents (*beatas*) who minister to the canons, the deacons, the reverends of every degree, owes nothing to Eça's literary models, everything to his personal observations. In the second place, Amaro bears not the slightest resemblance to Serge Mouret, in whom Zola wanted to portray a victim of Roman Catholicism, a man reduced by prayer and fasting to impotence and imbecility. The Portuguese priest is masterful as well as ingratiating; ambitious for sexual as well as social triumphs; a man who hankers after the good old days when, thanks to the Inquisition, the Church and all her servants were feared and unquestioningly obeyed throughout the length and breadth of the land.

Then again, the intrigue between Amaro and Amelia is much more realistically motivated than the fairy-tale romance between Serge and Albine which occupies the middle section of *La Faute de l'abbé Mouret*. Even though his anticlericalism was probably quite as strong as Eça's, Zola did not dare show a tonsured priest actually forgetting his vow of chastity; he got over the difficulty by giving Serge a 'brain-fever' in consequence of which he loses his memory and is then free to seduce Albine as it were 'innocently'. By contrast, Amaro is at all stages completely aware of what he is doing; his casuistry convinces him that his 'sin' is venial, commonplace and – provided it remains hidden – of no great account. He discovers the attraction he exerts over the pretty eighteen-year-old girl in the house where he lodges, and soon realizes that she is as eager for his embraces as she is reluctant to submit to those of the gawky clerk to whom she has been promised in marriage. Possibly Eça's boldness in describing the erotic imaginings of a supposedly innocent virgin was even more startling, at the time, than his outrageous exposure of the libidinous longings of his all too handsome, all too virile *senhor paroco*; certainly the account given, in the middle chapters of the book, of the love-making between this pair in a borrowed room above that of a mute, bed-ridden hysteric, aware of the sacrilegious coupling taking place but powerless to denounce it – this showed greater audacity in a certain kind of realism than any other author, in Portugal or anywhere else, was prepared to risk at the time.

On the whole, it would seem wrong to count Eça among the adherents of French naturalism. One cannot doubt that he was deeply impressed by the creative achievement represented by *Les Rougon-Macquart*. There is, in *Os Maias*, an admiring authorial allusion to

those powerful and vigorous works published in thousands of copies; those harsh analyses that had taken Church, Royalty, Bureaucracy, Finance and all the sacrosanct subjects, brutally dissected them and displayed their diseased organs like corpses in an amphitheatre; those new styles that were so precise and malleable and caught the very beat of life in the act, the line, the colour . . .

But though ready enough to pay homage, Eça was never a member of the small band of disciples that Zola had in Portugal, who included Júlio Lourenço Pinto (1842–1907), author of a number of novels and of a treatise on naturalism (*Estética Naturalista*, 1885); Francisco Teixeira de Queirós (1848–1919), who took a medical degree at Coimbra and whose fiction was written strictly in accordance with the tenets of positivism; and Abel Acácio de Almeida Botelho (1854–1917), the title of whose novel-series, *Patologia social*, speaks for itself.

It was not Zola but Flaubert who commanded Eça's literary allegiance, a fact that emerges clearly enough in his second novel, *O Primo Basílio* (*Cousin Bazilio*, 1878), which could fairly be described as an adaptation of *Madame Bovary* to a Lisbon setting. Superficially, at least, the resemblance is flagrant: Eça's heroine is linked to her husband by nothing stronger than a community of material interests; her only refuge from the deadly tedium of conjugal life is to indulge her taste for romantic novelettes, and she falls an easy prey to the first unscrupulous philanderer who presents himself. Just as Flaubert surrounded Emma with a few types representative of middle-class dreariness, so Eça included, among the *habitués* of the house, an empty-headed, self-important poet, symbolizing the world of 'official' literature, and the unforgettable Councillor Acácio, typifying the politician thrown up by parliamentary democracy.

If one were to try and single out one particular theme as being closest to the heart of nineteenth-century realism, it would surely be that of the 'woman taken in adultery'. A simple list of the works in which it figures affords proof enough of the horrid fascination it held for middle-class novelists in every country: beginning with *Madame*

Bovary, such a list would have to include Tolstoy's *Anna Karenina*, Fontane's *Effi Briest*, Alas's *La Regenta* and, in Portugal, besides *O Primo Basílio*, J. L. Pinto's first novel, *Margarida* (1879). The matrimonial state being the cornerstone of respectable middle-class society, the bourgeois realist's deepest anxieties were roused by anything that could constitute a threat to its stability. Both Flaubert and Eça saw the most dangerous of such threats in the pervasive influence of neo-romantic literature. As realists, they were offended by the oblique, disguised eroticism of these outwardly decent love-stories: as males, they feared the corrupting effect of such fiction on the bored, ill-educated womenfolk of their class. 'If vice continued,' argues one of Eça's mouthpieces in *Os Maias*, 'it was because an indulgent and romantic society gave it names which beautified it, idealized it. What scruples could a woman have about cuddling and kissing an outsider between conjugal sheets, if all the world sentimentally called this romance, and the poets sang its praise in gilded strophes?'

If *O Primo Basílio* counts as Eça's version of *Madame Bovary*, *Os Maias* (*The Maias*, 1880) has some title to being considered the equivalent of *L'Éducation sentimentale*. The two works both cover a vast canvas; each is peopled by the same confusing medley of characters, every one bent on his own private, futile concerns, among whom stand out a couple of inseparable companions, Carlos and Ega in *Os Maias* as Frédéric and Deslauriers in Flaubert's book. Political issues do not bulk as large in *Os Maias* as in *L'Éducation sentimentale*, for obvious reasons: Eça had no revolution to narrate. Instead, Carlos and his clever friends lounge around waiting for one to happen. 'The only thing to do in Portugal is to grow vegetables until there is a revolution which will bring to the surface some of the strong, living, original elements that are imprisoned in its depths.' Sometimes they talk nostalgically of the distant past when the Portuguese nobleman would stride aboard his caravel, sword in one hand, the cross in the other. But today, as an up-and-coming young deputy explains to Ega,

we've done the same as you literary people. In the old days literature was all imagination and fantasy and ideals. Now it's reality, experience, positive facts, documents. Well, here in Portugal politics are following the realist trend. In the time of the Regeneradores and the Históricos, politics meant progress, liberty, verbiage. We've changed all that. Today it's plain fact – money, money! Filthy lucre!

But if Carlos de Maia and the elegant parasites who surround him leave politics to the plunderers, conversely the sentimental, not to say erotic aspects of the novel obtrude rather more than they do in *L'Éducation sentimentale*. The hero, quite unlike the namby-pamby Frédéric Moreau, is a handsome, wealthy offshoot of the aristocracy whom all women find irresistible; he finds them merely importunate, until he falls in love at last with a mysterious Maria Eduarda, supposedly married to a certain Senhor Castro Gomes whose business affairs have taken him to Brazil. The lady, who offers suspiciously little resistance to Carlos's suit, turns out not only not to be married to anyone but – by a malicious trick of fate – to be his own sister, lost to view and believed dead. This contrivance, depending on a most exceptional train of events and a thoroughly unconvincing sequence of coincidences, raises doubts about whether *Os Maias* can properly be held to qualify for admission to the category of realist novels. The incest motif was probably intended to have some kind of allegorical significance: perhaps his passion for his sister is Carlos's way – or rather Eça's – of making manifest his chronic narcissism; or perhaps again the business is meant to represent the predicament of the old Portuguese aristocracy, condemned to inbreeding on a spiritual, if not on a crudely genetic plane.

There is no doubt that the decadent aristocracy made a far stronger appeal to the artist in Eça de Queirós than the peasantry or the factory-workers, who are strikingly absent from his works; in this sense he links up in a very obvious way with post-realists like D'Annunzio and Proust. However, it is probably true to say that it was decadence itself, the pure phenomenon of degeneration, that fascinated him, much more than the question of the social role, if any, still open to the hereditary nobility in the modern industrial world. His last novel, *A Ilustre Casa de Ramires* (*The Illustrious House of Ramires*), was published in 1900, the year of his death and, as it happens, the year when Thomas Mann published *Buddenbrooks*, another study of the decline of a wealthy and powerful family. Eça stresses the contrast between the pusillanimity of his hero Gonçalo and the fearlessness of the Ramireses of olden times, using the rather facile device of quoting long extracts from the historical novel that Gonçalo is composing about his bloodthirsty medieval ancestors. The impoverished landowner breaks his word to his tenant farmer and trots away, abashed, when insulted by the village bully. Then he returns to his study to celebrate, in flowery prose, the feudal sense of honour of the earlier Ramireses and their bestial battle-fury. This irony is not sustained to the end, however; by a sudden reversal, Gonçalo is nerved to horsewhip the bully, breaks off his engagement to a rich butcher's daughter and achieves an unconvincing apotheosis on the final page. This is a very different ending from the epilogue of *Os Maias* when Carlos and Ega, returning to Portugal after a three-year absence during which they have journeyed right across the world, find Lisbon as depressing a city as ever; or rather, as Carlos says, 'it's not the city, it's the people. They're so ugly and grubby and lazy and shabby, all yellowish and bandy-legged . . .' The difference in the way the two books end may have something to do with Eça's sensitivity to the charges made by many critics in Portugal that *Os Maias* showed an unpatriotic spirit. In fact, the difference is not as great as might appear: though he was forced to acknowledge, in the end, that merely to reflect a sordid reality does not suffice to bring about the wished-for transformation, still, his love for his country, for the land itself and its tranquil, imperishable beauty, remained as strong as ever, proof against every disappointment that his countrymen could inflict.

Notes

1 Frédéric Soulié (1800–1847), an extremely prolific writer of sensational novels. He came into prominence with *Les Mémoires du
Diable*, serialized in *Le Journal des Débats* in 1841.

2 Musset's *Contes d'Espagne et d'Italie* (poems) appeared in 1830.
Hugo wrote two successful verse plays with Spanish settings,
Hernani (1830) and *Ruy Blas* (1838). Gautier's *Voyage en Espagne*
was published in 1845. Mérimée's story *Carmen*, the source of Bizet's
opera, dates from 1847.

3 See above, pp. 146–8.

4 See above, pp. 110–12.

5 *L'Hermite de la Chaussée d'Antin* (1812–14), *L'Hermite en province*
(1824).

6 The eight-volume collective work, *Les Français peints par eux-
mêmes* (to which Balzac contributed), appeared in Paris in 1840–42.
Balzac's *Physiologie du mariage* had been first published, anony-
mously, in 1828.

7 *Epistolario a Clarín* (Madrid, 1941), p. 32.

8 See above, pp. 19–20.

9 Quoted by J. F. Montesinos, *Galdós* (Madrid, 1968), Vol. I, p.
32.

10 Properly called *La tragicomedia de Calisto y Melibea*, this was an
early novel in dialogue form (the first edition is dated 1499) about
a procuress and her clients.

11 See above, pp. 170–71.

12 *Tormento* (Madrid, 1968), pp. 19–20.

13 *The Sense of an Ending* (New York, 1967), p. 131.

14 'Sotileza' is the nickname given to the heroine of the novel by the
fishing community in which she lives. A dialect word, it refers to
the fine thread employed to tie fishing hooks on to the line, and is
applied to the young woman as a derisive comment on the airs and
graces she gives herself.

15 viz. *Torquemada en la hoguera, Torquemada en la cruz, Torquemada
en el purgatorio, Torquemada y San Pedro*.

16 The reference is to Chapter II of Alfred de Musset, *Confession d'un
enfant du siècle*: 'Pendant les guerres de l'Empire, tandis que les maris

et les frères étaient en Allemagne, les mères inquiètes avaient mis au monde une génération ardente, pâle, nerveuse.'

17 Letter to Oliveira Martins, 10 May 1884; quoted in Hernani Cidade, *Século XIX: a revolução cultural em Portugal e alguns dos seus mestres* (Lisbon, 1961), pp. 94–5.

SEVEN

Realism in Italy

THE SOCIAL AND CULTURAL BACKGROUND

On 11 October 1891, after the unveiling of a monument to Alessandro Manzoni, a select audience which included the mayor and councillors of Lecco, together with other civil and religious authorities, gathered in the Teatro Sociale to hear a lecture given by Gaetano Negri, a former mayor of Milan and a well-known critic, writer and politician. 'Manzoni', said Negri, 'was a worshipper of truth. Truthfulness became for him the guiding principle, the standard, the aim of art. He was the first and the greatest of all *veristi* because he was the most genuine of them.'[1]

'Le vérisme italien, oui, oui, je comprends: c'est mon naturalisme', Zola is reported to have said when meeting Verga briefly in 1894 in Capuana's flat. The terms *verismo, realismo, naturalismo* were used a little haphazardly in the course of the long, acrimonious, and rather fruitless controversies waged in the last quarter of the nineteenth century between the admirers and imitators of Manzoni and the admirers and imitators of Émile Zola: controversies which in many respects were reminiscent of the protracted quarrel between classicists and romantics in the first half of the century.

In view of this, to claim that Alessandro MANZONI (1785–1873) was the first *verista* may appear surprising, but there were very good reasons why such a view should have been put forward by an established speaker at an official celebration. It was not an uncommon view. Francesco De Sanctis had authoritatively stated, in a course of lectures given in 1871–2, that the basis of Manzoni's art was 'positive reality . . . natural, positive, and historical truth, which today people call *realism*', and that the descriptive passage which opens *I promessi sposi* (*The Betrothed*, 1840–42) seemed 'written by a geographer or a naturalist rather than by a poet, such is the precision of its local colour down to the smallest details'.[2] The same novel was defined 'a masterpiece of realism' five years later by Felice Cameroni, a critic highly sympathetic to naturalism.[3] Cameroni's friend Emilio Quadri ended his essay *Il realismo in letteratura* (1878), written in defence of Zola's Italian disciples and in particular Cesare Tronconi, by quoting approvingly Manzoni's words on narrative art: 'be it prose or poetry, the author must have usefulness for his aim, interest for his means, and truth for his subject-matter'. The belief that an unbroken thread connected Manzoni's romantic realism to late-nineteenth-century *verismo* was to become, with minor qualifications and shifts of emphasis, one of the tenets of twentieth-century literary criticism, in the works of Russo, Marcazzan, Sapegno and others.[4]

It had a basis in fact: not so much in the claims made by most romantic writers, Manzoni included, that art should be true to life (for, after all, such claims had been made by artists from time immemorial), as in Manzoni's concrete achievements. As a writer he was always inspired by democratic ideals, which took the form of a conscious striving towards more realistic forms of art and acceptance by a wider readership. It is important all the same to distinguish between Manzoni's artistic beliefs and the ideological implications of his work. His paternalism may have been revolutionary at a time when ruthless exploitation and oppression of the lower classes was the rule, but it was nevertheless rapidly becoming outdated in an age of growing industrialization and urbanization which generated a new and more appropriate corpus of social and political thought. Manzoni had wanted art to become more responsive to the requirements of society as a whole and to take fuller account of its needs; but his own novel, in which he realistically described the wide gap between the powerful (who happened also to be rich) and the humble (who seemed destined to be poor) implied that the proper course for the underprivileged was to cultivate the Christian virtues of resignation and political non-involvement. Hence it was open to bourgeois ideologists to interpret his work as supporting the view that social divisions are inherent to a stable social order, and that the lower classes should be content with their lot and leave politics to their betters. Manzoni became thus the prophet both of popular democracy and of a solidly bourgeois Risorgimento founded on the exploitation of the workers and their *de facto* exclusion from civil and political rights. He was claimed as patron on the one hand by Roman Catholic writers and conservative critics, and on the other by the new breed of realist novelists and radical intellectuals; thoroughly disgusted by the reactionary overtones of Manzonianism, the latter group argued that the master had displayed a far more radical and progressive approach than his degenerate followers, who had therefore forfeited all claim to his spiritual inheritance.

This ambiguity long bedevilled literary criticism, torn between the condemnation of Manzonian ideology as voiced by Luigi Settembrini and Antonio Gramsci among others, and the inescapable fact that Manzoni was a true artist, an influential innovator, the only great novelist to emerge from pre-Risorgimento Italy, hence the fountain-head and term of reference of all that was subsequently attempted and achieved by Italians in the field of narrative writing. Unless the structural reasons for this ambiguity are clarified it can only continue to generate fruitless controversy, as it has for so long in the past; but such clarification cannot be achieved without a proper understanding of the relationship between art and society. The question posed by this relationship has often been wrongly asked in the past, as if one could speak of the kind of art individuals produce within a society without reference to the kind of art society as a whole can use and consume; the two things are not necessarily the same. The nature of the relationship must not be construed, except in the most loose and metaphorical sense, as a comparison between levels of achievement: firstly because there is no objective scale of aesthetic achievement to which one can relate measurable data of economic and social development; secondly because any aesthetically based definition of achievement would 'load' the definition of art, which must be kept value-free if the whole question is not to be begged; and thirdly because 'levels', however defined, just do not occur on parallel and separate planes. The purpose of the inquiry can only be, in the last resort, to throw some light on the internal dynamics of culture in its widest sense, not to explain how or why great art comes into existence.

Ever since the beginning of the seventeenth century Italy had been suffering from economic stagnation and political decline, aggravated by the protectionist and colonialist policies of the European powers who exercised control over extensive portions of the country. This political and economic subservience to foreign domination had lasted a long time, and although since the fall of Napoleon the general situation had improved, especially in Lombardy and Tuscany, it was still, relatively speaking, an unhappy one. The unification of the country, a mere administrative device bringing under one government widely different regions, each with its peculiar economy, resources, administration, laws, customs, currency, and even weights and measures, could not but turn several badly balanced parts into one big unbalanced whole. In several parts of Italy, furthermore, especially in the South, unification turned out to be just a thinly disguised annexation by the kingdom of Piedmont, with all the attendant disadvantages of a harsh military occupation which the new central government hoped would quickly deal with local unrest. Soon after unification and until January 1870 large areas of Southern Italy were placed under martial law, while up to 120,000 soldiers conducted a savage campaign of repression against guerrilla-type formations of peasants, a struggle responsible for more casualties than all the other Risorgimento wars put together.[5] There is ample evidence to suggest that national unity was more a literary concept than a deep aspiration of the Italian people, most of whom remained totally indifferent to, and unaffected by, an event in which they played no significant role.[6] Fear of the centrifugal forces that threatened the new state forced the ruling class to strengthen its newly acquired powers by ruthlessly enforcing centralization and suppressing even the most legitimate and reasonable aspirations to local self-government. By keeping regionalism in chains, this policy paradoxically kept it alive. If some people preferred to be 'taken over' by the Piedmontese, it was often because of the old rivalry between their town and the nearest regional capital, from which they might otherwise have been governed. The new state's refusal to grant even minimal local autonomy not only did nothing to encourage the growth of civic responsibility among the new Italians, but in addition ensured that every petty local dispute was inflamed out of all proportion by being transferred to the central parliament and debated there.

In fact the only unitary tradition common to the whole peninsula, at least ever since a language based largely on literary Tuscan had replaced Latin as a means of communication between cultivated people, was the literary tradition. Literary Italian had become the recognized means of expression and interchange among the intellectuals, who constituted, however, a tiny minority in a largely illiterate mass of people speaking some two score mutually incomprehensible dialects. It was a learned tongue which came to resemble in many respects the Latin it had displaced, and by the beginning of the nineteenth century had turned into a dead, fossil language rarely used in speech even by those who used it in writing, suitable for refined literary purposes and as a *lingua franca* for people with different native languages, but severely deficient in the lexical areas concerned with the nomenclature of flora, fauna, household and farm implements, and in the terminology needed by commerce, industry, science and technology.[7] Since it was, however, the one common element in an otherwise fragmented culture, it enjoyed a prestige totally out of proportion to its effective penetration and cultural role. Its relative stability through time, due, as had been the case with Latin, to the simple fact that dead languages do not change, was interpreted as the sign of an inherent purity and beauty which had to be preserved at all costs. Consequently many, even among the romantic writers who were in favour of social and political reform, consciously or unconsciously resisted linguistic change and, with the notable exception of Manzoni, failed to bring new life to their literary medium.

In this way the Italian literary tradition came to be looked on as the symbol of a national unity still to be achieved and, as is often the way with symbols in which men place a superstitious trust, hoping thereby to bring into being the state or condition that they symbolize, it was seen first as the means through which the unification of the country could be accomplished, and later as one of the principal agents of its accomplishment. In other words, it was believed that one needed only to promote 'good' literature and to teach everyone the standard language for a new, united, reformed Italian society eventually to emerge. This curious theory lies behind the extraordinary claims made by both *manzoniani* and *veristi* for the educational value of what they were writing. Even if it were true that literature has the power to alter the course of history, such an effect could hardly be expected in a country where, as in Italy, the vast majority of the population could neither read nor write. In 1871 only 16 per cent of the inhabitants over six years of age in Southern Italy were classified as literate, which does not necessarily mean that they read literature, or even newspapers.

The figures were rather better in Central and Northern Italy: about 25 per cent and 45 per cent respectively.[8] Not much improvement could be looked for so long as the conditions of social inequality and economic exploitation persisted that made illiteracy endemic.[9] And the number of peasant riots, protest marches, and strikes which took place in the new united Italy and were often brutally repressed by the army and police afforded ample evidence of the persistence of those very evils that the Risorgimento should have eliminated once and for all.

The distinction between the production of art and its consumption is particularly relevant to literature. Leaving aside for the moment the question of access to, and appreciation of, art in general, it is obvious that literature, unlike the other arts, demands special skills not only for its production but equally for its consumption. Anybody can look at painting, sculpture, and architecture, or listen to music, and gain something from the experience; but in countries with a high rate of illiteracy, the appreciation of literature is necessarily restricted to a small minority. Although there is no absolute reason why writers should not produce great art even in a culturally backward country (and in speaking of their 'art' we must be understood as using the word to imply a value-judgement), it is obvious that the lack of an adequate readership will severely inhibit the art of literature (using the word now in its value-free sense). This inhibition works in the first instance by reducing the total output of books. Just to give one example, a rough computation of the number of titles in the *Catalogo generale della libreria italiana* under the entry *romanzo* (which includes novels and short stories, both by Italian authors and in translation) gives a figure of about 3,500 titles for the period 1847–99. The corresponding figure deduced for France (where the literacy rate averaged about 70 per cent) over a slightly longer period (1840–99) is about 25,660 titles. Moreover, these comparative figures take no account of the number of copies printed and sold, usually higher in France than in Italy, where runs of over 5,000 copies were the exception, and most books were printed in editions of between 500 and 1,000 copies. Another way in which illiteracy has a debilitating effect on the art of literature is that in the absence of a mass readership, a rift opens up between the writers and their public; authors no longer have full access to the rich cultural storehouse of experiences, ideas, emotions, and shared aspirations on which they necessarily draw when writing their books, while this storehouse itself is impoverished by the lack of readers' 'feed-back'. A vicious circle develops, resulting in a universal lowering of the level of culture within the community.

The tendency was, then, for Italian writers to form a restricted, elitist caste of intellectuals, using an artificial language, cut off from the rest of the population and therefore insensitive to their needs. Deprived of the rich cultural nourishment provided by a broadly based audience drawn from every level of society, they were faced with a limited number of options. They could pretend that their small *coterie* of intellectuals represented the whole of society; or they could turn elsewhere – to the past, or to foreign cultures – for stimulation; or finally they could attempt to break out of the charmed circle in which they dwelt in isolation, and try and make contact with the common people. One has here the structural matrix of Italian literary history in the past two centuries, generating distinct and opposite trends: extreme inbreeding and parochialism, but also overdependence on cultural imports from abroad (from France, in the special case of *verismo*); traditional classicism but also romantic cosmopolitanism; 'going to the people' but also being totally unsympathetic to the people. It is well to recognize that, while these different trends are clearly distinguishable, they were only apparently contradictory, in that they all arose out of an identical cultural and social situation which writers by themselves could do little or nothing to change. As Olindo Guerrini remarked in 1878, generalizing from the special situation in Italy: 'Art never modified the aspirations of a people or a society, but the opposite ... Art does not make revolutions but follows and supports them.'[10] Thus one should not be surprised to find classical and romantic, or romantic and naturalistic traits existing side by side in Italian writers; to see them wavering between adherence to their indigenous tradition and dependence upon foreign ideas; to observe their inevitable progress from literary radicalism to political conservatism. It is perhaps clearer now why Manzoni could be claimed as a leader by novelists militating in opposite camps; and also why nearly all subsequent Italian novelists claimed to be realists, or used naturalistic methods even if they claimed otherwise; and finally why, with only a few exceptions, none of them succeeded in creating a truly realist art.

REGIONALISM AND 'VERISMO'

It is as well to bear in mind that the terms 'realism' and 'realistic', and to a lesser extent *naturalismo* and *verismo* with their related adjectives, can be and have been used to fulfil two separate functions: they work both as simple statements of literary policy and intention, and as criteria of artistic achievement (it is in this sense that all great art can be said to be realistic). It is particularly important to keep this distinction clear when one is reading Italian literary critics, for many of whom *verismo*, in the first sense, is a movement which, in the second sense, curiously turns out to have a membership of one (Verga) or two at the most (if we include Capuana); and also when one is dealing with writers like Verga, who is at his realistic best as a story-teller when he is being demonstrably inconsistent with his theoretical veristic principles.

What makes a work of art great is the author's skill not so much in 'imitating reality' as in making the process of representation appear convincing, appropriate and inevitable. For example an impressionist painting, which not only embodies the representation of a landscape, but in addition stands as a concrete demonstration of the historical possibility of representing it in that particular way – such an impressionist painting imparts a richer 'feeling' of the landscape than one could hope to experience viewing it as a simple observer. All fiction has the art of writing and the skill of reading among its subjects, and the writer and reader among its protagonists. Like any other social activity, art has a social function; and it follows that the artist has a social duty, which is to make his work socially relevant *as art*; this he cannot do without exploring and extending the possibilities of representation, in other words without renewing form. The artist has power over reality through form, and has power over form insofar as he realizes that it is only through manipulating form that he can acquire power over reality. This helps one to understand why it should have been primarily through a painstaking reappraisal and reworking of formal techniques that the realists set about expressing their new social awareness, their new vision of the world. Most of them declared their aims to be social rather than formal and technical; their primary purpose was to influence the course of events; but anyone who insists loudly on his ends as a way of justifying his means cannot fail all the same to be passionately concerned about the means. It is, however, more profitable to justify one's means by achieving one's ends than to try to achieve them by endlessly discussing one's means, which is what many *veristi* did in Italy in much the same way as the naturalists were doing about the same time in Germany.[11]

In fact the whole controversy for and against *verismo* was the literary extrusion of an underlying and far more momentous debate between the radical and conservative parties in Italian politics, neither of which had the sense to see that no political issues could be seriously discussed so long as discussion was limited to the educated upper and middle classes, and so long as the working illiterate masses that constituted the majority of the Italian people were deprived of their social and political rights. (Compulsory free education for all children between the ages of six and nine was instituted only in 1877; in vast tracts of the country it was hardly enforced and remained an unimplemented reform until the beginning of the present century. Universal suffrage for literate male citizens was introduced only in 1912, and that did not help much.) It is true that in a country traditionally saddled with all sorts of legal and religious restrictions on the freedom of opinion, some political battles had to be fought in disguise on the field of literature. Victories of one faction or the other, whatever their literary significance, were politically and socially irrelevant, however, since the battles never amounted to more than skirmishes between different detachments of the same ruling-class army. Whether to be *manzoniano* or *verista* or both was a side-issue; the real scandal was that a bourgeois pastime was masquerading as the national literature, that a ruling-class culture pretended to be the national culture, when three quarters of the population were not merely uneducated but illiterate, while only a minority of the remaining quarter ever read books. What was unrealistic was to shut one's eyes to the absurdity of such a pretension, to refuse to see it for what it was – one symptom among others of the same social injustice and class exploitation that *veristi* writers were all too ready to denounce.

The fact that it had become possible to speak of 'Italian' literature since the Renaissance, when the Tuscan standard became universally accepted and a new generation of writers like Tasso and Guarini adopted it, means only that, for the first time, all writers in the peninsula had a common medium of expression at their disposal and more or less fixed terms of linguistic reference whereby to solve technical and stylistic problems; it does not mean that, from then on, all literature became 'national' in language, tone, or tradition. Paradoxically, the adoption of a national standard gave regional dialect literatures their first opportunity to establish themselves with standards of their own. Most Italian authors, including for instance Alfieri, Parini, and Manzoni, wrote dialect poetry at some stage or other in their careers; and some poets, like Carlo Porta and Giuseppe Gioacchino Belli, acquired a national reputation through their use of dialect, thereby disproving the contention that dialect constituted an inferior medium, unworthy of great art. Even literature in the standard language had always come under the influence of regional cultural traditions. Finally, the Risorgimento and the new state to which it gave birth, by promoting, however slowly and inadequately, literacy, social mobility, and economic growth, by making freedom of expression appear a legitimate goal, by bringing common people from widely separate areas into personal or cultural contact, not only created through unity a great awareness of diversity, but also brought to light the underlying wholly regional texture of non-aristocratic culture, tendentiously rejected by the cultural establishment, and often misrepresented even in the recognized dialect literature. It should be noted that ever since the French Revolution, radical intellectuals had made periodical attempts, constantly frustrated by the authorities, to accommodate popular dialects to cultural life, by using them in schools as a teaching medium, in churches for preaching sermons, and in the popular press.

There are, then, sound historical reasons why *verismo*, being sympathetic to Risorgimento ideals of social reform, should have manifested such marked regionalist tendencies. However, the widespread myth of an exclusively southern *verismo* devoted to exposing the wretched condition of the peasantry needs to be revised. One of the basic limitations of realism is that reality cannot be represented wholly and completely, and both the area (content) and the manner (form) of representation must be chosen by the artist. Because of the realistic dogma of absolute objectivity, this inherently subjective choice must appear to be made in accordance with objective criteria. What needed to be understood was that the artist's task was not so much to look at reality – this had been taken for granted for a long time – as to observe it with a fresh eye, picking out, as Degas said, its 'less-known' aspects, which could be seen and expressed independently of 'that knowledge of form which sustains the artist like a crutch . . . and, as it were, dictates to the eye what it must see'.[12] Thus 'realistic' took on the meaning of 'unusual', though in the rather special sense of not having a usual form of artistic representation; in the ordinary sense one could hardly conceive of less unusual subjects than those chosen by most realists – commonplace situations in the lives of ordinary people. In Italy the few literate readers of fiction were comparatively well-to-do urban dwellers living in the northern half of the country, where the literacy rate was higher and where, incidentally, there was a greater concentration of publishing houses with famous names like Pomba, Bocca, Sonzogno, Vallardi, Treves, Zanichelli, Barbera, Salani. By the mid-sixties the book market had considerably expanded. Cheap paperbacks were flooding the book-shops, and in Milan alone fiction readers were catered for by no fewer than five specialized magazines, while several other newspapers and reviews published novels by instalments (*romanzi d'appendice*) in their *feuilletons*. Ladies and gentlemen in boudoirs and drawing rooms had long been accustomed to see, reflected in the products of romantic realism, flatteringly idealized images of themselves or their betters. It was a change for them to read stories about the lives of penurious labourers in the south: this is what constituted, in their case, one of Degas's 'less-known' aspects of reality. And since critics and arbiters of taste, as well as the novelists themselves and their readers, all belonged to the same class, it is hardly surprising that *verismo* took on this peculiar social and geographical bias.

In addition the Italian 'honest Dicks and Dolls', nearly a century and a half later than their English counterparts, were beginning to read Cesare Cantù and Giulio Carcano in the kitchen. Whether realism counts as cause or effect here, the recruitment of this new class of reader was perfectly in keeping with its social aims. In 'going to the people', novelists not only paid lip-service to those ideals of social commitment which the enlightened minds of Carlo Tenca, Carlo Cattaneo, Ippolito Nievo and others had seen as offering a solution to the intellectual crisis of the age; they were, besides, cornering a lucrative market, tapping an important source of revenue. The needs of these humble readers were very modest: to escape in imagination from below stairs to the upper regions of the house; to exchange the dull and grey routine of working-class life for a rosy world of make-believe in which the petty bourgeois lived like the rich, and the rich were as refined and sophisticated as the titled gentry; and vicariously to experience that sense of security that comes from contemplating at a distance the wretchedness of others. The extraordinary gap between literary Italian and the language, or languages, spoken by ordinary people meant that the writers catering for this market were compelled to abandon the old formal traditions if they wanted to win over their new readers. Outworn images and metaphors, the crutches on which both authors and readers had leaned for centuries, had to be replaced by words and expressions which, if they were to be understood by the honest Dicks and Dolls, must be taken from their immediate experience. This was no doubt well within the scope of *verismo*, but the danger was that truth now came to be identified not only with the prejudices of the novelist, but also with the limited outlook of the low-brow reader. This kind of popular literature, supplemented by countless translations from the French, for the most part ill-written versions of indifferent originals, could hardly be expected to break new ground; nor did it.

One further point is worth mentioning in this connection. It was not just the rural proletariat of the south that fiction writers had previously ignored; they had had nothing to say either about the urban middle classes, the northern peasants, or the new industrial proletariat. And beyond this, if the primary requirement of the realistic method was to look at reality with fresh eyes (the realist concentrated on the 'less-known' only because the 'less-known' was easier to view without preconception), then it could be argued, as indeed it was, that the traditional picture of the upper classes and the aristocracy needed to be scraped clean of the century-old crust of idealization and done again.

Besides the 'standard' regional *verismo* with its settings mostly in Southern Italy, there are therefore two more types to be taken into account – a commercial *verismo* mainly but not exclusively supported by low-brow readers, and profiting by the development of cheap paperbacks and of the *feuilleton*; and a *verismo* that tries to explore other environments than the South and to analyse other classes than the lowest. It would be difficult otherwise to understand why authors like Capuana, Verga, and Matilde Serao, who were so successful in the first, 'standard' variety, should have tried to extend their repertoire to take in other and different subjects.

'SCAPIGLIATURA'

In the period extending from the unification of Italy to the end of the century, the literary scene is so full of variety, with writers of such different types and talents competing for attention, that it is only for the sake of convenience that this period can be referred to as the age of *verismo*. We can observe, working side by side, the ageing but still productive Niccolò Tommaseo (1802–74), moralist, poet, lexicographer and novelist, whose *Fede e bellezza* (*Faith and Beauty*, 1840) contained in embryo many of the ideas later developed by psychological and decadent novelists; the *doyen* of the romantic poets, Giovanni Prati (1814–84), whose poem *Edmenegarda* had been regarded as scandalously realistic when it appeared in 1841; the young, fiercely anti-romantic Giosué Carducci (1835–1907); Cletto Arrighi (pseudonym of Carlo Righetti, 1830–1906), one of the leaders of the *Scapigliatura*; the great literary critic Francesco De Sanctis (1817–83); the dramatist Giuseppe Giacosa (1847–1906); the two major *veristi*, Luigi Capuana (1839–1915) and Giovanni Verga (1840–1922), and the two chief *anti-veristi*, Antonio Fogazzaro (1842–1911) and Emilio De Marchi (1851–1901). Verga and Capuana were still writing when Gabriele D'Annunzio and Italo Svevo brought out their first novels.

Arrighi completed the final draft of his novel *La Scapigliatura e il 6 febbraio* in 1861; in the same year Ippolito NIEVO died at the early age of thirty. Nievo, who, had he lived, might have become one of the greatest minds of the new Italy, must count as the only great novelist that the Risorgimento produced. Narrative truth, which for Manzoni and his followers signified the projection of the author's class-bound ideology on to a providential and teleological view of history, emerged for Nievo out of a rendering of the whole of human experience, individual, social, economic, political, set against a vast fresco of Italian history extending from the end of the eighteenth century down to his own time. *Le confessioni di un Italiano* fell rather flat when it was posthumously published in 1867: the mood of the nation, after Italy's disastrous defeats in the Third War of Independence, was hostile to heroics, and readers had no desire to be reminded of past glories nor, *a fortiori*, of past mistakes. The novel occasionally shows too clearly the shaping hand of the author to qualify as realistic; there are too many contrived meetings, recognition scenes and *coups de théâtre*; yet the marvellous first ten chapters, the finely observed characters (La Pisana is one of the very few real women in Italian literature), the sharp etching of certain episodes (like Carlino's interview with Napoleon) are worthy of the greatest traditions of realism; and the work as a whole gives a better idea of what it was like to live, love, and fight in the years of the Risorgimento than did many a contemporary book of memoirs.

For Cletto ARRIGHI, on the other hand, the riots in Milan against the Austrians on 6 February 1853, to which the title of his novel refers, afforded no more than a pretext to describe

a certain number of people of both sexes, between twenty and thirty-five years of age, no more; nearly always very intelligent and ahead of their time, free as Alpine eagles; ready to do good as well as evil; restless, troubled, and troublemakers; who, either because of some terrible contradiction between their constitution and their status, that is to say between what they have in their heads and in their pockets, or because of certain social influences by which they are affected, or even because of their eccentric and disorderly way of life, or finally because of a thousand and one other causes and effects . . . deserve to be classified as a new and peculiar subdivision of the great social family.[13]

Whence it can be seen that protest or *contestazione* by the young, their scorn for bourgeois morality, and, judging by the word *scapigliatura* (*scapigliato* means 'dishevelled'), their long and rumpled hair as a sign of non-conformity are phenomena by no means restricted to our own times.

La Scapigliatura was the name given to a group of artists, some of them active in more than one medium of expression, like the poet-painters Emilio Praga (1839–75) and Giovanni Camerana (1845–1905), whose sketches are reminiscent of those of Victor Hugo; the poet-composer Arrigo Boito (1842–1918), well known for his friendship with Eleonora Duse and for the librettos he wrote for some of Verdi's operas; the writers Igino Ugo Tarchetti (1839–69) and Carlo

Dossi (1849-1910); and others, like the painter Tranquillo Cremona, the sculptor Giuseppe Grandi and the the composer and conductor Franco Faccio, besides, of course, Arrighi himself. The Horatian tag, *ut pictura poesis* ('as in painting, so in poetry'), was one of the favourite maxims of this group: Dossi maintained that it was Cremona who taught him how to write. Not many years before, Champfleury, Duranty, and their friends, writers like themselves or artists like Corot and Daumier, had joined Courbet in a lively discussion group which met in the Brasserie of the rue Hautefeuille in Paris; and Escudier had developed, in an article published in *Le Réveil* on 13 February 1858, an ingenious analogy between contemporary writers and painters.[14] The mentor of the *Scapigliati*, Giuseppe ROVANI (1818-74), used to hold forth on aesthetic questions before his friends in the garden of an inn, sipping wine. In 1857 the *Gazzetta Ufficiale di Milano* began serializing a monumental novel by him, entitled *Cento anni*. The finished work, in five volumes, vies with Balzac in its scope, in the wealth of historical details it includes, in the perceptive description of urban life at all levels of society, and the way in which the consequences for a whole host of major and minor characters of the initial chance occurrence (the theft by the groom Galantino of the will of a wealthy Milanese nobleman) are followed through over a long span of years (the period from 1750 to 1849).

It may well be that Rovani's synaesthetic theories, elaborated in concert with his group of artistically gifted friends, had the ultimate effect almost of creating a united front of the arts against everything that was not art, with the manifest risk that art would drift away from its social moorings. The creative efforts of the *Scapigliati*, lacking the centre of gravity that social relevance might have afforded, became fragmented; their initial cohesion was shattered by the centrifugal force of their acute individualism. Their protest, similar to that of their contemporaries in other parts of Europe (the Young Germans, the *Bousingos* in France), arose out of the disillusionment consequent on the failure of so many revolutionary and socialist movements from 1830 onwards to produce a genuine transformation of social and economic structures. This disillusionment was more pronounced in the economically and socially more advanced areas, where the contrast was more marked between the expectations and aspirations of the intellectuals and the degree of conformity and subservience demanded by the inner logic of bourgeois progress; it made itself felt especially among those writers who were born too late to take an active part in the revolutions, and too early to benefit from being gradually integrated in the expanding structures of organized culture (education, entertainment, publishing, journalism) and make a living out of them. There was therefore nothing fortuitous in the fact that it was at Milan that the *Scapigliatura* germinated, flourished, and faded away during the sixties; it is true, none the less, that writers sympathetic to the vision and aims of the protest movement can be found also outside Milan: Giovanni Faldella in Piedmont, Alberto Cantoni in Mantua.[15] In their loathing for everything bourgeois, the *Scapigliati* found it necessary to break with the Manzonian tradition and its ideological mystifications; on the other hand their anti-social instincts prevented them from achieving an authentic realist art. They could escape this contradiction only by adopting postures of aesthetic preciosity, extreme political and social indifferentism, or, as a last resort, complete nihilism. Tarchetti, who had been an acute observer and critic of the distorting disciplines of military life, took refuge in mysticism; Boito cultivated a dazzling poetic virtuosity, and Dossi a refined lexical aestheticism; Praga drowned his sorrows in alcohol; Camerana committed suicide. As for Arrighi, he ended by jumping on to the Zola bandwagon, with *Nanà a Milano* (1880), and joining the 'commercial' *veristi*, whose leader was Cesare TRONCONI (1836?–1894?). Tronconi's ostentatiously veristic novels, *Passione maledetta* (*Accursed Passion*, 1875), *Madri . . . per ridere* (*Make-believe Mothers*, 1877), *Delitti* (*Crimes*, 1881), caused quite a stir; several literary critics took sides for and against his 'school', engaging in protracted polemics. It is an interesting fact that people spoke in the 1880s of a *scuola di Tronconi* for the novel, and a *scuola di Stecchetti* for poetry (Stecchetti being the pen-name under which Olindo Guerrini was publishing his veristic verse); but one never finds mention of a *scuola di Verga*.[16]

POPULAR REALISM

The slight literary value of the products of popular realism in Italy accounts for its relative neglect by literary historians. Even Professor

Paul Arrighi, whose monumental study gives valuable information and critical comments on authors often ignored by other scholars, could not really be expected to devote time and space to the *romans pour femmes de chambre* published in the *Piccola biblioteca galante*, or the titillating stories in the *Biblioteca degli adulti*, or to novels such as *Morta d'amore* by R. A. Porati (six reprints by 1885), *Gli amori di una kellerina* (*The Loves of a Barmaid*) by Mario Mariani (1888), the anonymous *Notti d'amore nell'acqua, sul prato, nell'alcova* (1887), or the large number of books subtitled *romanzo sociale* or *romanzo storico-sociale*, and the proliferating *romanzi d'appendice*. Various common misinterpretations of positivistic science, Taine's essays and Zola's novels, had given currency to the notion that human behaviour was explicable in terms of physiological motivation and of the conditioning factors of heredity and environment; the progress of medicine, popularized by Paolo Mantegazza, had given everybody a smattering of symptomatology and of primitive sexology; the works of Parent du Châtelet, Frégier, Buret and later of Cesare Lombroso and his school had provided disturbing glimpses into the murky lives of the 'dangerous classes', which, oddly enough, were apparently to be equated with the working classes[17]; journalists had described exotic lands and customs (the age of realism being also the age of colonialism); women were slowly becoming emancipated. And so the shelves of bookshops were crammed with novels figuring 'blood-thirsty tigresses' and 'velvet panthers' (usually princesses of Russian origin), aristocrats whose tainted blood represented the ultimate distillation of ancestral debauchery, men driven to crime and women lured into prostitution by the injustice of society, chaste and beautiful girls threatened by death in various pathological guises, or by various sinister fates even worse than death, all caught up in the 'great whirlpool of life'. The language of these novels was just as cliché-ridden as that of the contending school: only the clichés were different. The *Scapigliati* of the previous generation had at least had the courage to proclaim the 'death of Manzoni' (who was still very much alive) and the overthrow of bourgeois morality. These *veristi*, on the other hand, did not have the courage to market their wares for what they were, cheap, mass-produced goods: which, in an age when industrial mass-production was on the point of establishing itself, would have been a justifiable, significant, and almost prophetic gesture.

They excused their sensationalism by appealing to the principles of bourgeois morality: they claimed to be writing their books not with the improper aim of exciting sensuality but with the salutary purpose of performing a much needed exercise in social therapy.

And yet, as Giovanni Faldella wrote, 'even in the *feuilletons*, which are considered no better than rubbish, there is often something to admire. Not only the clever imagination displayed in putting together and pulling apart the pieces of an attractive narrative device, but, more than that, there are innocent victims to be pitied, murderers to be discovered, punished and booed like stage tyrants . . . And all this shows an everlasting popular reservoir of rough-and-ready morality.'[18] Faldella's words are particularly applicable to the works of Francesco MASTRIANI (1819–91), one of the most prolific writers of his time – his output comprised 107 novels, 263 short stories, 248 articles, 49 poems and 40 plays – and possibly one of the least appreciated. The character of Leopoldo X, in the fifth and sixth volumes of *I vermi* (*The Worms*, 1863–4), the journalist, teacher, and writer who, for all his honest toil and tireless efforts, cannot earn himself a living, is certainly autobiographical. Knowing from personal experience how difficult it was to make enough money to buy food and keep a roof above one's head, Mastriani was well placed to describe working-class characters, with whom his ties were always close even though he was a highly educated professional man, widely read, and better versed in French and English than many of his more famous contemporaries. Unlike Eugène Sue, from whom he took the idea of describing *I misteri di Napoli* (1870), he is never patronizing. Unlike Frégier, one of his sources for *I vermi* (subtitled 'Historical studies on the dangerous classes in Naples'), he understood quite well the reasons why the working classes should be the dangerous classes: crime was not the manifestation of normal instincts inexplicably perverted, nor the effect of corrupt frequentations, but the result of unbearable social conditions. Unlike many *veristi* who complacently explained poverty and destitution as the melancholy but inevitable consequences of adverse circumstances causing an initial 'fall from grace' and subsequent moral degradation, he was concerned with the scandalous and intolerable fact that, in the *normal* order of things, honest hard-working men and women could not earn a living wage and that therefore 'honest existence for those without private means was impossible'. Like Champfleury, who thought that 'le public du livre à vingt sous c'est le vrai public' – that the real readers were the shilling-a-volume public – Mastriani wrote to reach, and teach, the largest possible number of literate workers. He expressed, simply and in a language they could understand, such emotions as they could share, such ideas of social justice as they could grasp and strive after. He was not interested in writing for the critics. But it is time more modern critics took a serious interest in him.

As for those forms of *verismo* that were not specifically devoted to peasant life in South Italy, space permits only a short and superficial survey. Mention must be made in the first instance of Girolamo ROVETTA (1851–1910), one of the chief exponents of bourgeois naturalistic drama, who in addition wrote several novels, among them *Le lagrime del prossimo* (*The Neighbour's Tears*, 1888) and *Baraonda* (*Hurly-Burly*, 1894), showing the urban middle classes ousting by devious and corrupt methods a degenerate aristocracy from its commanding social position; in these books he adhered scrupulously to the methods outlined by Zola in his *Roman expérimental*. Such methods were by this time beginning to influence authors unsympathetic to the veristic movement, like Emilio DE MARCHI (1851–1901), who endeavoured to write realistic novels and even *feuilletons* in which no concessions were made to immorality and bad taste – De Marchi's works provide an interesting example of the direction in which the Manzonian tradition was able to evolve in the changed historical and cultural conditions of the late eighties and early nineties. Other regional writers include Mario PRATESI (1842–1921), whose novels *L'eredità* (*Heredity*, 1889) and *Il mondo di Dolcetta* (*Dolcetta's World*, 1895) paint a somewhat claustrophobic and depressing picture of life in the Tuscan province; and, also from Tuscany, Renato FUCINI (1843–1921), author of popular sketches of country life – *Le veglie di Neri* (*Neri's Vigils*, 1883), *All'aria aperta* (*In the Open Air*, 1897) – which are sometimes humorous and moving, but more often uneasily poised between caricature and patronizing sentimentality. Perhaps one of Fucini's most interesting works was the factual account of his visit to Naples and of the wretched life led by most of its inhabitants; published under the title *Napoli ad occhio nudo* (*Naples seen with the Naked Eye*, 1878), this book was a revelation for many northerners. Another exposure of the social evils suffered by the poor of Naples, *Il ventre di Napoli* (*The Belly of Naples*, 1884), was written soon after the cholera epidemic of 1883 by Matilde SERAO (1856–1927), whose journalistic talents gave her a reputation perhaps not fully justified by the literary qualities of her work. She is at her best when describing with genuine human sympathy the lives of simple working people (*Telegrafi dello stato* (*State Telegraph Offices*, 1895) and *Il paese di Cuccagna* (*Land of Plenty*, 1891)) but becomes hopelessly novelettish and shallow when she is trying to deal with passions and emotions as experienced higher up the social scale (*Fantasia*, 1883; *La conquista di Roma*, 1885). Federico DE ROBERTO (1861–1927), a friend and biographer of Verga, wrote several volumes of fiction between 1887 and 1920, but he is chiefly remembered for *I Vicerè* (*The Viceroys*, 1894), a novel of Sicilian life among the nobility and the upper classes at a time of social and political change. *I Vicerè* is like one of those large paintings full of interesting detail which repay close and careful study but which, looked at from a distance, appear rather crowded and patchy; some vivid streaks of colour here and there only serve to emphasize the general starkness and bleakness of the picture. De Roberto was only marginally a *verista*; quite early on in his career he turned towards decadent psychologism.

LUIGI CAPUANA: FROM 'VERISMO' TO IDEALISM

'To Giovanni Verga and Luigi Capuana, famous writers, great hearts and powerful minds, the first and best champions of the experimental novel in Italy!' By the time this dedication appeared on the front page of an essay by Augusto Lenzoni, interestingly enough written *against* the experimental novel (*Contro il romanzo sperimentale*, 1886), Verga and Capuana had established themselves as the leading *veristi*. Lenzoni would have probably been surprised if he could have foreseen then that about ten years later Capuana would have abjured naturalism, while Verga would have stopped publishing altogether. Today the importance of Capuana appears limited to his critical work, largely, if not exclusively, because of the impact it made on Verga; and Verga stands out from the herd of minor *veristi* precisely because, in his artistic practice, he was often able to go beyond the theoretical principles he had learned from his friend.

Both Verga and Capuana came from reasonably well-to-do families who provided them with the kind of education it was possible to obtain in Sicily under the Bourbons, where to have read Voltaire and Rousseau was still something of an achievement, while government censorship prevented the sale of most worthwhile books published on the Continent.

It is some indication of the unpromising outlook of Sicilian culture after the unification that both Capuana and Verga felt the need to leave the stagnant atmosphere of Catania and move up north to Florence, the new – temporary – national capital. Luigi CAPUANA (1839–1915) has left us a description of his literary apprenticeship in an autobiographical preface to one of his volumes of short stories.[19] He had already written a few plays, a short story, and several pieces of theatre criticism for the *Rivista Italica* and *La Nazione*, he had heard of Shakespeare, Victor Hugo, Dumas and Poe, but the first time he encountered the name of Balzac was in 1867 when, in an essay on the modern novel by Luigi Buonopane, he came across the following rhetorical question: 'What shall we say of the empty Dumas, the frivolous Balzac [*il leggerissimo Balzac*], the lewd De Kock?' Understandably reluctant, at first, to read such a worthless author, Capuana fortunately listened to the advice of a fellow journalist from Milan, and plunged into *La Comédie humaine*, which fired him with enthusiasm. From Balzac he moved on to other French writers, among them Flaubert, the brothers Goncourt, and Zola. The poet and critic Enrico Nencioni got him to read Taine, and thanks to the painter Telemaco Signorini he discovered Diderot. He read De Sanctis's *Saggi critici*, published in 1866, and all the Neapolitan critic's subsequent essays (*Nuovi saggi critici*, 1869; *Storia della letteratura italiana*, 1870–71) on the relationships between science and art, on Darwinism, realism, and Zola. By 1868, however, Capuana had already left Florence for his native Mineo, where he was soon entirely taken up with administering the family estate and with local politics: not so fully, however, as to lose all touch with continental culture.

1868 was when Angelo Camillo DE MEIS (1817–91), Professor of the History of Medicine at the University of Bologna, published *Dopo la laurea* (*After Graduation*), a lengthy, indigestible book written in the form of an exchange of letters between Filalete, a philosopher and scientist, and Giorgio, a young graduate in medicine rather disillusioned with the soulless positivism taught him during his degree course. The book was the first of a series of systematic attempts made in Italy in the second half of the nineteenth century to rid positivism of its dangerous radical potential and turn it into a safe ideology; the hope was that the internal contradictions of bourgeois culture could be reconciled so that the class which had just won political supremacy might also go on to achieve cultural hegemony. What De Meis was trying to do was to reduce the inevitable tension arising from the conflict between the basic moral, social, and aesthetic categories – still largely founded on the old metaphysical concepts of the Good, the True and the Beautiful – and the negation of these absolutes under the steady, relentless criticism offered by the new experimental sciences: but he would have needed the intellectual equipment of Benedetto Croce to do it successfully. He borrowed from Hegel the idea of sketching a 'natural history of the Spirit', seen as a succession of forms, each with its life-history of birth, development, and death, 'in which is reflected the rhythm of the total history of the universe'. The details of this dialectical succession are obscure and often contradictory, for De Meis was engaged in the impossible task of trying to preserve 'forms' like religion and art which, in the terms of his own system, were at some stage or other inescapably doomed to extinction. The clearest part of his argument, for Capuana's purposes, was that in which he discussed the development of literary forms. As Religion and Art tend towards pure thought, and fantasy, no longer sustained by religious faith, withers away, Poetry also disappears. The Spirit, divided between art and science, poetry and prose, and unable as yet to give birth to a poetic science, creates for the time being prosaic poetry, that is, the novel. The novel, as epic prose, replaces the epic poem, and is bound to evolve into increasingly historical, positive and reflective forms. Only a short step was needed to take De Meis from this most recent stage of the evolution of the novel to the theory of the *roman expérimental* that Zola expounded in 1880. It was a step, however, that De Meis seemed reluctant to take. He rejected the idea that his book, the story of a young man's spiritual development, might be considered a work of fiction, and added: 'The novel of science, the extraordinary story of reason: can there be a more absurd combination? Of course not . . . This seems, however, to be the course taken by the novel in general.'[20]

De Meis's book was just what Capuana needed to bring together and reconcile in his mind all the varied cultural influences to which he had been subjected in Florence. Ideas implanted by De Meis and De Sanctis were to bear fruit when Capuana was persuaded by Verga to join him in Milan, to which city he had moved in 1872. There Capuana published a volume of short stories, *Profili di donne* (*Sketches of Women*, 1877), a naturalist novel dedicated to Zola, *Giacinta* (1879), which unleashed a scandal, and a collection of critical essays, the first series of *Studi di letteratura contemporanea* (1880). The preface to this work, embodying a summary of his aesthetic theories, is preceded by two quotations, one from De Sanctis, explaining the indissoluble unity of content and form in a work of art[21] (the matrix of the later Crocean idea of the unity of intuition and expression): the other a prediction drawn from De Meis of the progressive absorption of art into scientific thought (an idea, incidentally, with which De Sanctis disagreed). The reason why two critics so different in importance and outlook should be quoted by Capuana side by side, and their influences mingle in his critical work after 1872, is that the dangerous ethical and political implications of De Sanctis's critical approach to bourgeois culture needed to be watered down with a strong dose of 'scientific' idealism. Cultural history would then appear to be conditioned not by social development and class structure, but by 'natural laws of the spirit', which would take it safely out of the political sphere. Capuana's syncretistic operation, conducted in accordance with French precedents, and its failure can be summed up as follows. To accept the proposition that Art was a synthesis of content and form involved accepting that the personality of the artist should diminish in importance. If art forms evolved through history, the last stage in the evolution of literary forms would be the scientific novel. The theory of artistic impersonality and objectivity as elaborated by the French realists fitted beautifully as a link between the two propositions. The operation looked convincing enough, but it had serious flaws. The concept of form appeared in two guises: on the one hand it was an element in De Sanctis's synthesis of form and content (both autonomous, since neither can prevail over the other); and on the other hand it appeared as the form this synthesis takes throughout its alleged historical evolution, in the framework of De Meis's theory of literary genres (but it is inherent to the concept of genre that the content should condition the form). This ambiguity allowed Capuana both to write veristic works in which, as we have seen, the choice of a certain content was crucial, and, later, to maintain the autonomy of form and content against excessive naturalistic determinism. He attempted to preserve the freedom of art by arguing that, while the writer was allowing his work to be conditioned by scientific ideas, he was actually creating a fictional world unaffected by chance, 'almost truer than reality itself', and epistemologically more valuable. However, if poetic reality is different from reality proper and if 'it does not matter whether a character really existed so long as it receives life from the writer's powerful imagination' (the idea will reappear in Pirandello's *Six Characters in Search of an Author*), then the whole of the naturalistic theory of the 'human document' becomes totally irrelevant.

These flaws are reflected in the quality of Capuana's narrative work, caught up between the writer's aspiration to use a new aesthetic theory in order to penetrate reality, and his failure to see that the theory itself was unworkable, being nothing but the product of a class ideology which was trying to ignore its inner contradictions by turning away from social and political reality. Thus Capuana treats his 'human documents' – much as the Goncourts treated theirs – as pathological cases; and once they are safely removed from history and society to the antiseptic atmosphere of the experimental novelist's laboratory, it becomes impossible to see what on earth they are supposed to document. In common with most men of his period, he was attracted to emancipated and sexually uninhibited women, both the lower-class sensual animal types who haunted the libidinous imaginations of naturalistic writers, and the upper-class educated ladies, an increasingly common type in real life. But at the same time Capuana persisted in cherishing the old romantic ideal of the pure, chaste, and faithful love-object. As for his actual love life (of which one finds echoes in *Il marchese di Roccaverdina*, 1901), this was more consistent with the feudal ethos than with scientific positivism. In this way he was able to counter the threat of authentic female emancipation, which would have destroyed the security of his male-dominated Sicilian world, and the consequence is that the women in his short stories (in *Profili di donne*, 1877; *Homo!*, 1883; *Fumando*, 1889) are stereotypes endowed with no reality.

No wonder that Capuana ended by disclaiming his early allegiance to Zola and considering *verismo* as just one among many other contemporary 'isms' (*Gli ismi contemporanei*, 1898). His revised versions of *Giacinta* (of which he made at least two, in 1886 and 1889) and the subsequent novels *Profumo* (*Perfume*, 1890) and *Rassegnazione* (*Resignation*, 1907) show how far he had moved away from *verismo*. It would be wrong to see this apostasy as a piece of inconsistency; on the contrary, it is clear evidence of Capuana's constant adherence to the ideas of his time, which were slowly evolving away from realism towards neo-Catholic spiritualism with Fogazzaro, decadent psychologism with D'Annunzio, and neo-idealism with Croce.

GIOVANNI VERGA: FROM 'VERISMO' TO REALISM

The all-important date in the literary life of Giovanni VERGA (1840–1922) (his personal life, apart from his liaison with Dina di Sordevolo and the interminable legal wrangle over *Cavalleria rusticana*, was rather dull and commonplace) was 1874. By then Verga had been living nearly two years in Milan. He was a reasonably successful novelist: his *Storia di una capinera* (1871), about a young woman forced to take the veil against her will and pouring out her anguish and frustrated love in highly emotional letters, was selling well, for reasons probably totally at variance with the author's intentions – he had wanted to write a romantic story, not an anticlerical pamphlet. He had been presented to Countess Maffei, whose *salon* had since 1834 provided a rendez-vous for all the most famous literary, artistic and political personalities of the time. In 1873 he had published two more novels reflecting his experiences during his earlier sojourn in Florence from 1869 to 1871; these were *Eva* and *Tigre reale* (*Royal Tiger*), which in the ensuing years were to be acclaimed, or decried, by a variety of critics and writers as examples of *verismo*. Ten years later a Sicilian critic, Antonino Velardita, mentioned in the same paragraph Zola, Tronconi, and Verga, 'who insisted on demeaning himself by following their fashionable school',

and then went on to condemn *Eva*, 'whose refined lust is more seduc-
tive and more dangerous than the loathsome lust of Nana'.[22] If
Verga's production had continued on similar lines, he would rate
today with Rovetta, Pratesi, and Serao; and of Capuana much less
would be heard.

But in 1874 the publisher Brigola brought out *Nedda*, subtitled
'Bozzetto siciliano' ('Sicilian Sketch'), the sad and squalid story of a
young olive-picker, her nasty and brutish life, and her short, inarticulate and ill-fated love for Janu, a poor wretch like herself. Its
language was simple and direct, with no rhetorical turns of phrase,
quite different from the assortment of literary clichés and colloquialisms, southern speech forms and Tuscan words used by Verga in his
previous novels. There were critics who, on the strength of this,
announced Verga's 'conversion'; many others have followed suit
down to the present time. But 'conversion' to what? If *verismo* is to
be taken in a eulogistic sense to mean great realistic art, then, true
enough, Verga had been converted to *verismo*; but there would then
be no *verista* but he, and what name should we give to all the others?
If on the other hand one uses the word in the value-free historical
sense we have accorded it hitherto, then as the author of *Eva* and
Tigre reale Verga had been an acknowledged *verista* almost since the
start of his literary career. The preface to *Eva*, with the lip-service
it paid to plain unvarnished truth, its moralizing strictures on bourgeois hypocrisy 'in an atmosphere of banks and industrial enterprises',
its references to art as the expression of society, was a typical veristic
preface reminiscent of Gautier's to *Mademoiselle de Maupin* and the
Goncourts' to *Germinie Lacerteux*. But was there a conversion at all?
Apart from its greater literary distinction, there was much in *Nedda* –
not least the descriptions of the Sicilian landscape – strikingly reminiscent of Verga's earlier work. In 1875 he published *Eros*, its subject
the empty and futile life of a dissolute young nobleman, compounded
of capricious passions and unrealized ambitions, to which a conventional suicide puts a conventional end. The following year *Nedda*
reappeared in the same volume as a number of other veristic short
stories, no better and no worse than Capuana's. In 1882, one year
after his masterpiece *I Malavoglia*, Verga published *Il marito di Elena*
(*Helen's Husband*), as good a veristic novel as they came, but no more.
Various attempts have been made to explain away *Eros* and *Il marito*

di Elena. They are certainly better than the 'pre-conversion' novels, but their superiority is due not so much to a radical change of aesthetic principles as to the normal development of the veristic novel towards greater refinement in psychology. Attempts have been made to trace in them the theme of the 'defeated by life' (*i vinti*), outlined by Verga in the preface to *I Malavoglia*; it is true that both their protagonists are defeated by life – but so were all the protagonists of Verga's previous novels, so are Fogazzaro's characters too and even D'Annunzio's supermen. To be 'defeated by life' is a natural subject for bourgeois *verismo* as we have outlined it so far: unable to free himself from his class ideology and to understand and express reality, the *verista* can achieve nothing more significant than to celebrate consciously and conscientiously his own defeat by chronicling the defeat of his characters.

Verga, however, whether because of the deficiencies in his education, the absence of militancy in his make-up, or his psychological reluctance to jump on to bandwagons and join the crowds, was less amenable than Capuana to ideological indoctrination. Whereas Capuana held his reactionary ideas with deep conviction, Verga's middle-class prejudices were perfunctory and superficial. He managed therefore to free himself occasionally from the straitjacket of veristic theory, so that his artistic practice, fortunately, does not always accord with his theoretical utterances.

Of these the first, the preface to *Eva*, points up one of the basic ambiguities of *verismo*. Verga begins by making the point that every society has the art it deserves; the corrupt society of his time had produced an art which was the expression of its tastes. But at the end he attributes to this corrupt art a moralizing function, and confers on it the power to judge the very society by which it was debased. The confusion arises from the fact that Verga is here attributing two conflicting meanings to the word 'art': that of an article of consumption, tailored by the tastes of the consumer, and that of an autonomous spiritual activity. One way out of the contradiction was to put as great a distance as possible between the creative activity as such and the ordinary concerns of those destined to consume its products; in other words to answer affirmatively the question the Goncourts had asked in the preface to *Germinie Lacerteux*, 'whether what are called the lower classes have not a right to the novel', and stop writing about the lives of the usual consumers of fiction, well-to-do members of the middle classes.

The second major theoretical statement by Verga is found in *L'amante di Gramigna* (1870) by way of a dedication to the novelist Salvatore Farina. Here Verga formulates his view of artistic impersonality, but in a characteristically ambiguous way. He had by then accepted the naturalistic theory of the *document humain* (whereas formerly he professed not to care whether *Eva* was considered 'a dream or a true story'); and under the tutelage of Capuana he had adopted De Meis's idea of 'the death of the novel'. The ambiguity lies in the fact that he begins by describing the creative process as a minute scientific analysis of the mechanism of passions, but ends by presenting it as a 'mystery', and its finished product as a natural, spontaneous, autonomous work of the spirit.

Like Capuana, Verga is impaled on the dilemma, how to introduce an objective scientific methodology into the production of works of narrative art while preserving the autonomy of art as an organic unity of content and form. This explains how at this stage in his career he fluctuated between aesthetically inferior novels consistent with veristic theory, and a more liberated, more spontaneous creation which no longer catered for the usual upper- and middle-class consumers of novels any more than it used them for its subject-matter. It also explains why by 1907 *Storia di una capinera* had gone through twenty-two reprints, *Eva* through thirteen, but *I Malavoglia* through only five.

About 1878 Verga started to plan and compose a large, complex narrative work embracing several generations and a variety of different social environments, in accordance with precedents set not only by *La Comédie humaine* and *Les Rougon-Macquart* but also by Rovani and Nievo. He originally intended to call this cycle *The Tide* (*La Marea*); it was to consist of five separate novels, which between them would provide a panorama of Italian life from the highest ranks of society to the lowest. This time Verga, again thanks to Capuana, had fallen under the influence of Edmond de Goncourt, who in his preface to *Les Frères Zemganno* (1879) had argued that realism could never achieve all its potentialities unless it found the strength to break out of its self-imposed limitations in subject-matter and deal as confidently with the upper classes as it had with the lower. There are precise textual correspondences between Capuana's article on Edmond de Goncourt (1879) and Verga's preface to *I Malavoglia* (1881), embodying his last important theoretical statement. In Capuana and Verga, much more clearly than in Goncourt, the basically sound idea that it was the business of realism to investigate all aspects of reality, if it was to be worthy of its name, was justified by those same class prejudices that caused realism to concentrate 'scientifically' (that is, a-politically and in a patronizing spirit, with a few exceptions) on the working classes. Human passions and emotions were interpreted along positivistic lines as a mechanism, the delicacy and complexity of which was directly proportional to class status (one is reminded here of what was said of Paul Bourget's heroines, who needed an annual income of 100,000 francs to gain the right to psychological complexity). It followed that the higher the social standing of the main characters, the greater the challenge for the writer. Hence Verga's repeated attempts to meet this challenge even after he had produced his masterpieces; hence too, sensing how superior they were to anything else he had written or could ever write, his final disillusionment and failure. He never finished *La Duchessa di Leyra* (the third novel in the series) and never started on the others. There is a sense in which one could say that *I vinti* (the new title given to the series in place of *La marea*) was completed by other writers: the life of the Sicilian gentry was described by Federico De Roberto in *I Vicerè* (1894); political life by Matilde Serao and Antonio Fogazzaro in *La conquista di Roma* and *Daniele Cortis*, both published in 1885; and life at the top among the leisured classes by Gabriele D'Annunzio in *Il piacere* (1889). Verga soon scrapped *Padron 'Ntoni*, the first novel in his series, and began afresh. The first draft does not seem to have survived, but one may guess the reason for Verga's dissatisfaction by looking at *Fantasticheria* (1879), a short story containing the germ of the novel-to-be, in which the characters are patronizingly sketched from a sympathetic upper-class standpoint, and the Sicilian landscape is described in a style reminiscent of *Eva* and *Tigre reale* (Verga included it the following year in *Vita dei campi* (*Life in the Fields*), together with some of the best of his Sicilian stories). The final draft was given the title *I Malavoglia* and turned out to be a masterpiece, at variance at every single point with the principles enunciated in its preface. The psychology of the characters is infinitely more subtle and complex than in Verga's other novels, in spite of the mechanistic and hierarchically structured model of humanity on which it was allegedly based. Its language and style, every sentence bearing the indelible imprint of its author, are hardly compatible with Verga's theory of impersonality. The novels of *I vinti* were to be genetically and structurally connected; as far as can be seen, such connections had been planned only between *Mastro-Don Gesualdo* (the projected second novel) and the others, but no character in *I Malavoglia* appears to be related to any of those in the other novels. The cycle was designed to illustrate the drive for social betterment, in its consecutive aspects of struggle for basic material needs, for superfluous wealth, for social status, for political power, and for the pleasures of life. In *I Malavoglia*, however, the struggle for material needs is presented merely as an unavoidable accompaniment to working-class life, not as a driving force to social betterment; it is connected with simple survival, not with ambition. In fact the moral of the story is that men will not discover their true human dignity through social climbing, but only through loyalty to their particular social class, social environment, and work (one is tempted to say, through a keener sense of class solidarity). Therefore, although the series is entitled *The Vanquished*, the Malavoglias, as a family, are victorious. Unlike Renzo and Lucia in Manzoni's novel, they do not need to move on to a higher social plane in order to survive.

In developing his cycle, however, Verga was obliged to place greed and ambition, the mainsprings of social *arrivisme*, firmly in the foreground. The themes of home life, family loyalty and love, so important in *Vita dei campi* and *I Malavoglia*, were replaced in the *Novelle rusticane* (1883) by darker topics: the obsession with private property and gain (*La roba*), selfishness (*Il Reverendo*), shameful compromises (*Pane nero*), and murderous class hatred (*Libertà*). Humour, which in the earlier stories arose naturally out of the circumstances of life, derives in this new collection from a sour awareness of human stupidity. Hence the pessimism and melancholy which compose the dominant mood of *Mastro-Don Gesualdo* (1889), caused by the collapse of every illusion; the home is revealed as an empty shell, the family as a group of strangers, wealth as a useless acquisition, status as leading to isolation and loneliness. If *I Malavoglia* is a masterpiece, irrespective of literary theories and labels, *Mastro-*

Don Gesualdo is certainly the highest achievement of Italian *verismo*, the highest level of awareness a writer could reach of the contradictions of society in the light of the prevailing ideology. Verga could never rise above his achievement in *I Malavoglia*, and his limited culture and experience allowed him to explore no further up the social scale than he did in *Mastro-Don Gesualdo*. The third novel of the series was never written, and Verga spent the last thirty years of his life in increasingly bitter silence.

Verismo dragged on a little longer, but its days were numbered. Born out of the faith that the Italian middle classes placed in the solidity and four-squareness of reality, and out of their conviction that providence had entrusted them with the mission to build, shape, and control such a reality which they alone could understand and describe in full, it soon began to crumble under the impact of the world-wide crisis in values which led up to the First World War.

Notes

1 G. Negri, *Opere*, Vol. IV (Milan, 1909), p. 70.

2 F. De Sanctis, *La letteratura italiana nel secolo XIX*, Vol. I (Bari, 1962), pp. 47–8.

3 *Il Preludio*, 15 September 1877. See Paul Arrighi, *Le Vérisme dans la prose narrative italienne* (Paris, 1937), p. 5, n. 5.

4 See Luigi Russo, *Giovanni Verga* (Bari, 1966), pp. 57–60; Mario Marcazzan, 'Dal Romanticismo al Decadentismo', pp. 765–7 in *Letteratura italiana: le correnti*, Vol. II (Milan, 1956); Natalino Sapegno, 'Appunti per un saggio sul Verga', p. 256 in *Ritratto del Manzoni ed altri saggi* (Bari, 1961).

5 See Franco Molfese, *Storia del brigantaggio dopo l'unità* (Milan, 1964).

6 See Denis Mack Smith, *The Making of Italy, 1796–1870* (London, 1968), and D. Beales, *The Risorgimento and the Unification of Italy* (London, 1971).

7 Maria Corti, 'Il problema della lingua nel Romanticismo italiano', pp. 163–91 in *Metodi e fantasmi* (Milan, 1969).

8 Svimez, *Statistiche sul Mezzogiorno 1861–1953* (Rome, 1954), pp. 770–72. See also C. M. Cipolla, *Literacy and Development in the West* (Harmondsworth, 1969).

9 See Dina Bertoni-Jovine, *Storia dell'educazione popolare in Italia* (Bari, 1965).

10 Olindo Guerrini, *Le rime di Lorenzo Stecchetti* (Bologna, 1966), pp. 196–7.

11 See above, pp. 258–60.

12 Quoted by Linda Nochlin, *Realism* (Harmondsworth, 1971), p. 20.

13 This passage is quoted from Cletto Arrighi's introduction to *La Scapigliatura e il 6 febbraio*.

14 René Dumesnil, *Le Réalisme et le naturalisme* (Paris, 1968), p. 15.

15 The standard history of the movement is Gaetano Mariani, *Storia della Scapigliatura* (Caltanissetta–Rome, 1967). Useful analyses of the works of Praga, Boito, Tarchetti, Camerana, Dossi in Jørn Moestrup, *La Scapigliatura: un capitolo di storia del Risorgimento* (Copenhagen, 1966).

16 Paul Arrighi, op. cit., p. 180.

17 Paolo Mantegazza, *Fisiologia del piacere* (Milan, 1874) and *Fisiologia dell'amore* (1875). Alexandre-Jean-Baptiste Parent du Châtelet, *De la prostitution dans la Ville de Paris considérée sous le rapport de l'hygiène publique, de la morale et de l'administration* (Paris, 1836). Honoré-Antoine Frégier, *Des classes dangereuses de la population dans les grandes villes et des moyens de les rendre meilleures* (Paris, 1840). Antoine-Eugène Buret, *De la misère des classes laborieuses en Angleterre et en France* (Paris, 1840). Cesare Lombroso, *L'uomo delinquente* (Milan, 1876) and *Sull'incremento del delitto in Italia e sui mezzi per arrestarlo* (Florence, 1879).

18 Quoted by Augusto Lenzoni, *Contro il romanzo sperimentale* (Verona, 1886), p. 16.

19 'Come divenni novelliere', in *Homo!* (Milan, 1888).

20 *Dopo la laurea* (Bologna, 1868), pp. 250–51.

21 De Sanctis, 'Settembrini e i suoi critici', in *Saggi critici*, Vol. II (Bari, 1965), p. 306 n.

22 Antonino Velardita, *Il verismo in filosofia, letteratura e politica* (Piazza Armerina, 1883), pp. 164–7.

Conclusion:
the Decline of Realism

A point that emerges very clearly from a comparative review of the European novel in the nineteenth century is the extent to which writers in France appear to have monopolized public interest in almost every other country. It was the French version of the social novel that permeated everywhere, though admittedly its most distinguished exponents were not always those whose works were most widely read. If Balzac inspired a few thoughtful spirits – Capuana in Italy, Pérez Galdós in Spain – devotees of Stendhal remained thin on the ground until almost the end of the century; and the broad mass of the European reading public resorted for preference to less intellectually demanding story-tellers, George Sand, Eugène Sue, Frédéric Soulié and Dumas *père*. But it was undoubtedly the case that a novelist, if he did not write in French, suffered from a grave initial handicap in the struggle to attain an international reputation. Even the greatest had to content themselves with a purely local celebrity while they watched their compatriots greedily devouring the products of lesser writers from France: thus it was not until the mid-eighties that the major novels of Tolstoy and Dostoyevsky were translated into French, at a time when works by Flaubert and even Zola had long since been translated into Russian.[1]

The reasons for this imbalance are partly historical. The hegemony of French culture on the continent of Europe, established the previous century, had still scarcely been challenged. Even in the absence of translations, French writers commanded a wider audience among educated people abroad than writers of any other country, thanks to the fact that in 'polite society' French was the one foreign language that was universally understood. And beyond this, setting aside questions of intrinsic literary merit, it was a fact that the French realists had always been fractionally more 'advanced', more daring, than the realists of any other country. This was as true for Zola and his school at the end of the century as it had been for Stendhal and Balzac fifty years before. We have seen something of the disturbing impact, in Germany as much as in Italy and the Iberian peninsula, which naturalism and the theory of the experimental novel made when exported from France; if this effect was more muted in Russia the reasons were, once more, historical. The assassination of the Tsar by a group of nihilists in 1881 was the signal for a period of renewed political reaction, so that throughout the reign of Alexander III (1881–94) writers avoided, for prudential reasons, the kind of social topic that naturalism specialized in. Realism came to be replaced by introspection and melancholy, and, as the towering constructions of Tolstoy and Dostoyevsky receded over the horizon, the most gifted fiction writers of the eighties and nineties, V. G. Korolenko (1853–1921), V. M. Garshin (1855–88), and Anton Chekhov (1860–1904), concentrated on exploiting the short-story form with the opportunities it offered for poetic word-painting and the delicate evocation of mood and atmosphere. Realism was to reappear in the Russian novel at the turn of the century, notably in the works of Maxim Gorky (1868–1936), but it was a realism which owed little to Zola, Maupassant, or any other of the French naturalists. With Gorky, almost for the first time in literary history, the novel was used to express a distinctively lower-class attitude towards the middle-class establishment. The disciples that Gorky gathered around him, after his final return to Soviet Russia in 1931, helped him set up a new tradition of 'socialist realism' very different in ideological approach from the predominantly bourgeois realism that this volume has been concerned with.

Outside Russia, where history took a different course, major exponents of the novel almost without exception discarded the principles which had governed this form during the nineteenth century. Realism is a term which fits none of the *chefs de file* of twentieth-century narrative prose. In turn, writers as diverse as D'Annunzio, Gide, Alain-Fournier, Unamuno, Pérez de Ayala, Italo Svevo, the later Thomas Mann, Julien Green, Hermann Hesse, Kafka, Broch, and Piovene wrote allegorical, poetical, mystical, symbolical, psychological or autobiographical novels, but ceased on the whole to use fiction as it had been primarily used down to 1890 approximately, that is, to reflect and criticize the social order of their day. What we shall attempt to do in these concluding pages is to suggest reasons why the formula which had stood the European novel in such good stead for most of the nineteenth century should in its very last decade have been rejected as no longer serviceable.

The collapse of confidence occurred first in France where, it might have been thought, the realist tradition was most firmly implanted and had shown most vigorous growth. In the event, however, the doctrines of literary naturalism, after exciting the keenest interest and excitement abroad, fell into such sudden disrepute in the very country where they had originally been formulated that the enthusiasts who had made it their business to propagate them in Germany, Italy, Spain and Portugal found themselves disconcertingly overtaken by events: only eight years after she published her work of interpretation and apologetics, Pardo Bazán's 'cuestión palpitante' had ceased to excite anyone, while Arno Holz's *Zola als Theoretiker* came out at a time (1890) when Zola himself had tacitly abandoned his former theoretical dogmatism.

Literary historians usually cite the so-called 'Manifeste des Cinq contre *la Terre*' of 18 August 1887 as the first clear sign of a reaction against naturalism. The five young writers who signed this manifesto (printed, with maximum publicity, in the columns of *Le Figaro*), all self-proclaimed disciples of Zola, declared solemnly that having read *La Terre*, or as much of *La Terre* as had appeared by that time in instalments,[2] they wished it to be known that they no longer considered themselves as belonging to his 'school'. What had chiefly alarmed and disgusted them was the brutal savagery and excessive preoccupation with sex that this latest addition to the Rougon-Macquart series exhibited. There was nothing new in such accusations: they had been levelled at Zola by conservative critics like Fernand Brunetière and refined dilettantes like Anatole France for at least ten years previously; and when, in his popular treatise *Le Roman russe* (1886), E.-M. de Vogüé had wanted to recommend Gogol, Tolstoy, Turgenev, and Dostoyevsky to the French public, the principal argument he used was that, in contrast to the French realists, the great Russians were men of soul and sensibility, compassionate to their characters and above all careful of their readers' sensibilities. But the 'Manifeste des Cinq', although it added nothing of substance to earlier criticisms, did succeed in attracting unusual attention since it seemed to show that a rift was opening up between the middle-aged naturalists and the younger generation.

Any remaining doubts about the strength of the reaction against naturalism inside France were dispelled in 1891. This was the year in which a journalist on the staff of the *Écho de Paris*, Jules Huret, circularized over sixty men of letters – poets, philosophers, critics and dramatists as well as novelists – asking them whether, in their view, naturalism was now defunct. The replies, published between 3 March and 5 July, seemed to show that hardly anyone, even among its former adherents, retained any faith in the movement. Later the same year Léon Bloy lectured in Copenhagen on 'Les Funérailles du Naturalisme', while Jules Case, author of half a dozen gentle novels of country life, published a series of articles in *L'Événement* of which the first was entitled 'La Débâcle du réalisme', the remainder purporting to analyse the causes of the 'débâcle'. With the downfall of naturalism, some observers were inclined to think that the novel itself was in danger of extinction: Édouard Rod expressed the fear 'the novel had no future, no immediate future at least . . . for the reason that it has had too splendid a past', while Lucien Muhlfeld was only a little less pessimistic: 'The novel is certainly not on the verge of disappearing, but it stands in great need of renewal.'[3]

These prognostications were not idly made: it really did seem as though the novel as it had been practised for the last couple of centuries was going into eclipse. Zola went on writing fiction, using the tried techniques (documentation, minute description, summary characterization) until he died suddenly in 1902; but his aims in the last ten years of his life were quite different from those that had inspired him during the period of his maturity. His writing became increasingly didactic, prophetic, even idyllic; and the utopian fantasies he was composing towards the end, like *Fécondité* (*Fruitfulness*, 1899) and *Travail* (*Work*, 1901), had no discernible connections with realism even though Zola kept all his old superstitious belief in the mission of positivism to regenerate the French nation. The friends and disciples who had been associated with him in earlier days had either died in the interval (Maupassant in 1893, Edmond de Goncourt in 1896, Alphonse Daudet the year after), or had long since apostasized, like Huysmans who, on the opening page of the novel he published in 1891, *Là-bas* (*Down Yonder*), had denounced Zola through the mouth of his character Des Hermies for having 'incarnated materialism in literature . . . glorified the democracy of art'.

If naturalism, materialism, and the 'democracy of art' were so violently assailed and universally repudiated in republican France, it is hardly surprising that in the monarchical states elsewhere on the continent, what some had at first saluted as a new direction in literature, big with future promise, turned out to be little more than a brief fashion soon discarded. Successive chapters in this book have shown how in Germany naturalism never really struck roots except in the drama; in Spain, the political crisis of 1898 discouraged further attempts to examine the flaws of Spanish society in the light of realism; while in Italy, neither Capuana nor Verga persisted long in their efforts to acclimatize the experimental novel in the peninsula, leaving it to D'Annunzio, whose *Il trionfo della morte* (*The Triumph of Death*) was published in 1894, to inaugurate a totally different literature of luridly erotic psychologism.

So abrupt and widespread a desertion of a literary tradition like realism admits of no simple explanation. It is not enough to refer to the general reaction against rationalism which had been gathering momentum throughout the second half of the nineteenth century under the impulse of such varied writers and thinkers as Schopenhauer and Gobineau, Wagner and Dostoyevsky, Nietzsche, Ibsen, and Rimbaud; for one still has to explain why conditions appear to have been so propitious just at this time for so radical a revolt against reason, for the abandonment of the creed of social and scientific progress and the development of a pessimistic, frequently mystical or nihilist art in place of the dispassionate, objective portrayal of reality which had seemed to offer so much.

There is almost certainly some connection between the disintegration of realism and the decline of self-confidence among the middle classes at the end of the nineteenth century. We have seen how, during the first half of the eighteenth century, realism evolved in response to the unexpressed need for a new kind of literature capable of illustrating the values and aspirations of a middle class which had still to assert its supremacy. A hundred years later, by which time all the apparatus of the nation-state, political, economic, industrial and cultural, had fallen under the control of the successful bourgeoisie, realism acquired a new function: it became critical and deflationary, like the slave in a Roman triumph walking behind the victorious general, reminding him that he was mortal. Even so, it is important to note that it remained in every sense a bourgeois literature, created by members of the same class as it was directed against. Scarcely one among all the writers who made their reputation during the age of realism came from the working classes, which, given the absolute monopoly of education and leisure enjoyed by the moneyed section of the population, is hardly surprising. But the effect was that the realist novelist, if he wanted to be something more than a tame apologist for middle-class 'virtues' like Freytag or Daudet, had to voice the troubled conscience of the rich, expose their hypocrisy, denounce their greed and selfishness, explode the myths by which they justified their enjoyment of privilege.

A critical realism of this sort was tolerable so long as the middle-class establishment continued to feel reasonably secure. But a vague mistrust of the future, an uncertainty as to how long it would prove possible to contain the increasingly militant forces of the under-privileged, both in the cities of Europe and throughout the vast tracts of Asia and Africa administered by Europeans, began to spread ripples of uneasiness even as industrialization intensified and colonial empires expanded. There were portents of a cataclysmic future: the publication of the Communist Manifesto in 1847, the founding of the First International in 1864, the unprecedented outbreak of class warfare represented by the bloody suppression of the Paris Commune in 1871; then, in all industrial countries of Europe, the growth of the trades union movement, the organization of social democratic parties with representation in the national parliaments, and in the 1890s the ineffectual but still ominous outbreaks of anarchist violence. It can hardly be denied that this changed situation constituted a factor in the realists' reluctance to persevere in their role of licensed satirists, while the middle-class public grew increasingly averse to reading harrowing accounts of the 'seamy side' of life in slums, factories, and impoverished villages. Instead, it looked to its writers to provide an imaginary refuge from reality, it applauded any and every experiment in escapism, from historicism to occultism, from airy symbolism to the grossest forms of decadent eroticism.

A somewhat different, though equally plausible explanation of the transformation that overtook the literary scene in the 1890s emerges from a consideration of the aims of realism on a more narrowly technical level. Ever since Balzac set the example, serious novelists had seen it as their primary mission to furnish as complete and accurate a description as possible of the way the society of their time was constituted, how it functioned, what were the relations of the individual to the community, how customs and social conventions arose, whence they derived their compulsive authority. Long before Zola proclaimed the novelist to be a social scientist, his predecessors had been dignifying their activities by using scientific terminology to describe them: they claimed to be writing *studies* rather than works of imaginative fiction; they *analysed* social problems; they collected data by diligent inquiry and *research*. In all this they were doing no more than duplicating in an amateurish sort of way the work that was being undertaken, concurrently and simultaneously, by a small group of men engaged all through the nineteenth century in laying the foundations of twentieth-century academic sociology. The time was bound to come when it would occur to the more thoughtful of their readers that the functions the realists were performing in this respect might be more reliably discharged by sober specialists who would have no interest in weakening the force of their findings by wrapping them up in the distracting packaging of art. Some such a conclusion must have been reached at the extreme end of the century. It was in 1895 that Émile Durkheim, the man who did more than anyone else to chart the future course of sociological inquiry, published his seminal work *Règles de la méthode sociologique*; its appearance thus coincided with the great wave of public reaction against literary naturalism. Three years later Durkheim launched the first periodical entirely devoted to the new science: this was *L'Année sociologique*, the forerunner of a great number of academic journals in the same field.

The word 'sociology' had been coined by Auguste Comte in 1830 (it does not appear in English until 1843). Comte regarded sociology as the most complex of the six main categories of human knowledge, the others being mathematics, astronomy, physics, chemistry, and biology. But he insisted that it was a true science, not a branch of speculative philosophy, and should therefore be pursued like any other science by means of multiple observations on the basis of which laws might eventually be formulated. These ideas were not all that dissimilar from Balzac's, and it is interesting to note that Balzac (1799–1850) was an exact contemporary of Comte, who was born in 1798 and died in 1857. Again, like Balzac, Comte was a political reactionary who never had a good word to say for the French Revolution and, in due course, showed himself a stern critic of the February Revolution of 1848.

Comte's principal successor, Frédéric Le Play (1806–82), was also a conservative, a staunch defender of bourgeois institutions. The work which first made him famous, *Les Ouvriers européens*, came out in 1855, at a time when the polemics stirred up by the new school of realism were reaching their climax in France, as much in the domain of art and art criticism as in literature. Le Play made use of the same techniques – factual inquiry or 'documentation' – that the realist novelists were beginning to resort to, though no doubt he applied these techniques more objectively and less impressionistically than did, for example, the brothers Goncourt. Starting from the premise that the smallest observable social unit was the family, Le Play decided to investigate its nature by analysing a series of typical working-class family budgets. He elicited the details he required by means of short questionnaires, a method of investigation which was refined and elaborated by his followers, notably Paul Bureau and Edmond Demolins.

Finally we may mention Gabriel Tarde (1843–1904), who belonged to the same generation precisely as Émile Zola (1840–1902), though his first important sociological work, *Les Lois de l'imitation*, was not published until 1890. Tarde's view of humanity as being largely composed of semi-passive automata, responding fairly predictably to stimuli reaching them from outside, was not very different from the picture Zola projects in *Germinal* and *La Débâcle*, though there is no evidence that the two men had any close intellectual contact.

Thus we can observe the curious spectacle, in France at any rate, of a small body of systematic researchers carrying on, in relative obscurity, the same sort of work as the novelists were trying to accomplish amid much greater publicity and ultimately with less solid results from the standpoint of objective truth. Once it became clear that the sociologist was better equipped for the task of investigating and explaining social phenomena, the novelist had no option but to leave it to him to get on with the job; and one of the principal pretensions of realism was destroyed.

Possibly a more fundamental reason than either of the two already given for the discredit into which nineteenth-century realism eventually fell was that it became more and more difficult to believe in the bare possibility of achieving genuine objectivity in the novel. Critics and creative writers alike had come to consider objectivity or impersonality as the great criterion by which realism should be assessed, although none of the realists ever quite forgot that the picture they presented of external reality was inevitably coloured up to a point by the preconceptions to which, as observers, they could not help being subject; their duty, as they saw it, was to minimize and as far as possible eradicate the personal element which compromised the truthfulness of their rendering of reality. Even conservative critics hostile to naturalism seem to have assumed that the more objective a writer's approach to his material, the higher he was to be rated. For Vogüé, what was admirable in Tolstoy was his 'unequalled lucidity and powers of penetration for the scientific study of the phenomena of life', his 'clear, quick, analytic view of everything that is on earth, both inside man and outside'; in short, the 'plain, unvarnished reproduction of the realities of middle-class life' that even his earliest ventures into realist fiction had provided.[4] Zola called Flaubert's *Éducation sentimentale* 'a verbal report dictated by the facts' ('un procès-verbal écrit sous la dictée des faits'), and proclaimed it to be 'the model of the naturalist novel . . . No one will go further in the direction of real truth, I mean that down-to-earth, exact truth which appears to be the very negation of the art of the novel.'[5] In *Pot-Bouille* (1882) Zola did his best to imitate Flaubert's flatness, but he was only too mournfully aware how seldom he came anywhere near the 'scientific' objectivity that he professed to regard as the highest quality of prose narrative. 'It is certain that I am a poet,' he confessed to one of his Italian correspondents (Giuseppe Giacosa) in 1882, 'and that my works are constructed like great musical symphonies . . . All that does not lessen my ardent desire for scientific certainty. The trouble is, being a man of my time, I am bathed in romanticism up to the waist.'[6]

All this can be summed up by referring once again to the quasi-algebraical formula enunciated by Arno Holz: art = nature − x, where x stands for the limitations of the medium. The best efforts of the realists were devoted to reducing the value of x to zero, in which case the equation would read: art = nature. Admittedly, art could never be nature, it was always, in Zola's phrase, 'nature seen through a temperament'; but the more transparent the interposed 'temperament', the more satisfactory would be the resultant art-product. This was tantamount to saying that the closer art came to resembling the reality it purported to reproduce, the better. The ideal would be not just *trompe-l'œil*, but *trompe-cerveau* as well.

This was the slightly absurd position reached by the theoreticians of realism at the end of the century. If art was to be valued according to the perfection with which it duplicated reality, it would seem to follow that the most valuable aesthetic experience available to anyone would be to sit in rapt contemplation of reality itself. And we are back – the wheel having turned full circle – with Dr Johnson's level-headed objection, quoted in our first chapter: 'If the world be promiscuously described, I cannot see of what use it can be to read the account: or why it may not be as safe to turn the eye immediately upon mankind, as upon a mirror which shows all that presents itself without discrimination.'

If the novel were not to remain stalled, it was clearly imperative that novelists should retreat from this doctrinal cul-de-sac and see what else they might find to do besides composing dispassionate factual accounts of miscellaneous social environments. Of course, the realist tradition did not die away completely: it continued to evolve, not only in Russia, as we have already seen, but elsewhere as well, in England with Arnold Bennett, John Galsworthy, and Somerset Maugham, in the United States with Frank Norris, Theodore Dreiser, and Upton Sinclair, and in Spain and Portugal with Blasco Ibañez and Ferreira de Castro. But the characteristic art of the more forward-looking masters of prose narrative in the twentieth century owed very little to realism; its roots can be traced, rather, to a searching critique of the objective, pseudo-scientific norms of the preceding age.

The basis of this critique is to be found, in its most persuasive formulation, not in any treatise on aesthetics but in the concluding sections of Marcel Proust's seven-part masterpiece, *À la Recherche du temps perdu*. This work had been sketched out and partly written in the years immediately preceding the First World War, and although its publication was not completed until 1927, some years after Proust's death, it is reasonable to suppose that many of the ideas put forward in the final volume, *Le Temps retrouvé* (*Time Regained*), reflect an intellectual position that Proust had reached much earlier.

Proust's great novel does not represent as complete a break with traditional realism as do, for example, the frankly surrealistic or 'absurdist' narratives of Franz Kafka, which were written at approximately the same time. One can find in *À la Recherche du temps perdu* a detailed and no doubt scrupulously accurate account of upper-class society during the so-called 'belle époque'; the characters were partly modelled on people with whom the author was personally acquainted; and it should not be overlooked that the two French writers Proust most admired were the memorialist Saint-Simon and the father of the French realist novel, Honoré de Balzac. All the same, in the frighteningly ballooning mass of critical exegesis and commentary that now surrounds *À la Recherche du temps perdu*, surprisingly little is devoted to the historical aspect of the work, that part of it which is concerned with reflecting the society of Proust's own time. One reason is that Proust himself made it very clear that to read his novel as though it were a work of literary realism in the traditional sense would be to fall into the worst kind of critical error.

In a passage occurring fairly early in *Le Temps retrouvé* Proust shows his Narrator reading a volume of the celebrated diary of Edmond de Goncourt. One particular passage is transcribed: it is not, of course, a genuine extract – Proust was astonishingly good at composing pastiches of other men's work, and he gives here an extremely clever imitation of the peculiar style affected by the Goncourts in their *Journal*. The passage in question interests the Narrator because it embodies an account of a fashionable party at which he remembers having been present himself. What staggers him is that the diarist has noted so many circumstances and recorded so many remarks of which he, the Narrator, must have been completely oblivious at the time, since they correspond to nothing he remembers witnessing; he realizes that if he had 'written up' this social gathering, he would perhaps have gone into as much detail as De Goncourt, but the observations he made would have been of quite a different nature – reflective rather than reflecting.

Thus people's reproducible surface charm escaped me because I lacked the ability to remain on the surface; I was like a surgeon who sees under the satiny skin of a woman's stomach the hidden disease that is devouring it. It was a waste of time for me to dine out: I could not see the guests because, under the impression I was looking at them, I was in fact X-raying them ... But did that rob my portraits of all value, since I was not offering them as portraits? If, in the domain of painting, one portrait demonstrates certain truths about volume, light, or movement, does this mean that it is necessarily inferior to another portrait, totally unlike it, of the same person, in which countless details omitted in the first are scrupulously recorded, so that one would conclude from this second portrait that the model was enchanting, whereas one would have judged her from the first to be a fright . . .?

What Proust is implying here is a great deal more than the truth of the old proverb that 'beauty is in the eye of the beholder'; he is subtly challenging the premise of any art based on the belief that there can be such a thing as a 'neutral viewpoint', or such a person as a 'disinterested observer'. When one notes the difference between one's personal experience of an event and someone else's written testimony concerning the same event, one has either to decry the value of the testimony, or to conclude that one's own powers of observation are grossly deficient.

There is, however, a third possibility: which is that each observer is as good as the other, but that each genuinely sees a different spectacle; that there is no one 'external reality', but that each of us lives in his own subjective universe, which is admittedly affected by what goes on outside, but is structured in addition by all the experiences he has undergone throughout his life, experiences which have determined the particular cast of his mind and the special quality of his imagination. This is, in fact, the conclusion the Narrator reaches many years later, at a period when he is deeply preoccupied with the question whether the kind of novel he wants to write will have any documentary or 'real' value. In a flash of illumination, he sees that all phenomena external to us are never perceived in themselves, in their objective reality, but that their appearance is invariably contaminated by the mood we happen to be in when we observe them. The writer is therefore obliged, if he wants to be truthful, to include in his transcription of reality all the fine filigree-work of desire or repulsion that his own mood had attached to a person or scene when first encountered. 'Every impression is two-ended, one half embedded in the object, the other half – which only we can know – extending into ourselves.' It is this 'other half' that the realists neglect or conceal, whereas they ought to accord it their full attention. Realist art as it has been practised hitherto, says Proust, can never yield more than a useless copy of what the eye sees, what the intellect knows is 'out yonder'. What is really apprehended is often something quite different – richer and more mysterious.

He is not, however, arguing in favour of a totally private, esoteric or hermetic art; for the writer must not remain enclosed in the impenetrable world of his own subjectivity. His duty is to translate into terms understandable by the reader the reality that lies within him. If he can do this, he will have succeeded in giving his reader some inkling of the qualitative difference existing between the various impressions of the same reality that different human beings receive, and thus will have made it possible for him to enter into the consciousness of another of his fellow beings, miraculously overleaping the seemingly impregnable barrier of incommunicability.

It would, of course, be absurd to claim that Proust represents in any sense an 'advance' on Balzac or Tolstoy or even, for that matter, on lesser artists such as Flaubert, Fontane, Pérez Galdós or Giovanni Verga. Post-realist art could only develop as a reaction against realist art, and since in the long run any art has to develop and transform itself if it is not to stagnate and wither, it would have been impossible for Proust, as it would have been impossible for Gide, Kafka, Joyce, or in our own day Beckett and the *nouveaux romanciers*, merely to bring up to date the art of their nineteenth-century predecessors. If the age of realism had not retreated into history, and if its art had not been supplanted by something new, the twentieth century would not have been the explosively dynamic age it is.

Notes

1 Versions both shortened and unabridged of the early Rougon-Macquart novels were published in Russia as early as 1872–3, so that Zola found himself a best-selling author in Moscow and St Petersburg even before he had attained that status in Paris; see E. P. Gauthier, 'Zola's Literary Reputation in Russia prior to *L'Assommoir*', *French Review*, Vol. XXXIII (1959), pp. 37–44.

2 The serialization of *La Terre* in the newspaper *Le Gil Blas* (which, according to custom, preceded its publication in volume form) was not completed until 16 September 1887.

3 Rod, writing in *Le Gaulois*, 25 May 1891; Muhlfeld in *La Revue blanche*, December 1891; both quoted in Michel Raimond, *La Crise du roman: des lendemains du naturalisme aux années vingt* (Paris, 1966), p. 51.

4 *Le Roman russe* (1886), pp. 282, 292. In a foreword written for his translation of Tolstoy's *Three Deaths*, Vogüé observed (*Revue des Deux Mondes*, 15 August 1882): 'Bien avant qu'on eût inventé chez nous et réduit en formule la littérature dite *naturaliste, impressionniste*, M. Tolstoï avait été conduit, non point par une théorie, mais par la nature de son esprit, à photographier la vie dans ses plus cruelles réalités, dans ses plus fugitives nuances.'

5 *Le Voltaire*, 9 December 1879. See Zola, *Œuvres complètes*, Vol. XII (1969), pp. 606–9.

6 ibid., Vol. XIV (1970), p. 1426.

Chronological Table

	General including United States and Great Britain	France	Russia
1812	U.S.–British War (1812–14)		Defeat of Napoleon's 'Grande Armée'
13	J. Austen, *Pride and Prejudice*		
14	Scott, *Waverley*	Abdication of Napoleon. Treaty of Paris. Louis XVIII King	
15		The 'Hundred Days' (7 March–18 June) Battle of Waterloo	
16	J. Austen, *Emma* Scott, *The Antiquary*	Constant, *Adolphe*	
17	J. Austen d.	Mme de Staël d.	
18	Scott, *The Heart of Midlothian*		
19	Scott, *Ivanhoe* First steamship crossing of Atlantic		
1820	Formation of Holy Alliance		
21	Scott, *Kenilworth* Greek War of Independence (1821–7)		
22			
23	Scott, *Quentin Durward* Promulgation of Monroe Doctrine	Military intervention in Spain	
24	Byron d. Trades unions legalized in G.B.	Charles X King	
25	Foundation of University of London First railway (Stockton and Darlington line)		Decembrist Revolution Nicholas I Tsar
26	Cooper, *The Last of the Mohicans*		
27	Battle of Navarino	Stendhal, *Armance*	

Germany and Austria	Spain and Portugal	Italy
	Ferdinand VII King of Spain	
	John VI King of Portugal	
Founding of Zollverein		
Schopenhauer, *Die Welt als Wille und Vorstellung*		
Goethe, *Wilhelm Meisters Wanderjahre*		
E. T. W. Hoffmann d.	Proclamation of Brazilian independence Spain cedes Florida to U.S.	
Jean Paul d.		
	Central and S. America lost to Spain Pedro I of Brazil succeeds (as Pedro IV) to throne of Portugal. Constitution granted	
		Manzoni, *I promessi sposi* (first version). Foscolo d.

Chronological Table

	General including United States and Great Britain	France	Russia
28	Scott, *The Fair Maid of Perth*		
29		Balzac, *Les Chouans*	
1830	Kingdom of Belgium established	French take Algiers July Revolution. Louis-Philippe King Stendhal, *Le Rouge et le noir* B. Constant d.	Insurrection in Warsaw
31		Balzac, *La Peau de chagrin* Hugo, *Notre-Dame de Paris*	Partitioning of Poland
32	Reform Bill (U.K.) Scott d.	Balzac, *Le Curé de Tours* G. Sand, *Indiana*	
33		Balzac, *Eugénie Grandet*; *Le Médecin de campagne*; *La Muse du département*	Pushkin, *Eugene Onegin* (written 1823–31)
34		Balzac, *Le Père Goriot*; *La Recherche de l'absolu*	Pushkin, *The Queen of Spades*
35		Balzac, *Le Lys dans la vallée* Stendhal, *Lucien Leuwen* (written 1834–5, published posthumously)	Gogol, *Mirgorod*
36		Balzac, *L'Interdiction*; *La Vieille Fille*	Pushkin, *The Captain's Daughter*
37	Accession of Queen Victoria Dickens, *Pickwick Papers* Morse invents electromagnetic telegraph	Balzac, *César Birotteau* G. Sand, *Mauprat*	Pushkin d.
38		Balzac, *Une Fille d'Ève*	
39	Invention of photography	Balzac, *Béatrix*; *Le Cabinet des antiques*; *Le Curé de village* Stendhal, *La Chartreuse de Parme*	
1840	Introduction of penny post	Balzac, *La Rabouilleuse*	Lermontov, *A Hero of our Time*
41		Balzac, *Ursule Mirouet*	Lermontov d.
42		Stendhal d. Balzac, *Avant-propos* to *Comédie humaine*	Gogol, *Dead Souls*

Germany and Austria	Spain and Portugal	Italy
Goethe, *Novelle*		Monti d.
Hegel d.	Pedro IV of Portugal re-nounces throne of Brazil in favour of his son	Gregory XVI Pope
Goethe d.		Pellico, *Le mie prigioni*
	Ferdinand VII of Spain d. First Carlist War (1833–9)	
	Maria II Queen of Portugal	
Gutzkow, *Wally, die Zwei-flerin*		
Immermann, *Die Epigonen*		
		Leopardi d.
Büchner, *Lenz*	Isabel II Queen of Spain	
Frederick William IV King of Prussia		
Droste–Hülshoff, *Die Juden-buche*		

	General including United States and Great Britain	France	Russia
43		Balzac, *Illusions perdues* (1837–43) Sue, *Les Mystères de Paris*	
44		Balzac, *Les Paysans*	
45		G. Sand, *Le Meunier d'Angibault* Sue, *Le Juif errant*	
46		Balzac, *La Cousine Bette*	Dostoyevsky, *Poor Folk; The Double*
47	*Communist Manifesto* published	Balzac, *Le Cousin Pons*	Goncharov, *An Ordinary Story* Herzen, *Who is Guilty?*
48	C. Brontë, *Jane Eyre* E. Brontë, *Wuthering Heights* Thackeray, *Vanity Fair* Dickens, *Dombey and Son* Californian gold rush	February Revolution. Abdication of Louis-Philippe Louis-Napoleon elected president of Second Republic Chateaubriand d.	Belinsky d.
49		Military expedition to Rome	Dostoyevsky sentenced to exile
1850	Dickens, *David Copperfield* Hawthorne, *The Scarlet Letter*	Balzac d.	
51	Melville, *Moby Dick* Hawthorne, *The House of the Seven Gables* Crystal Palace Exhibition	Coup d'état of 2 December	
52	Stowe, *Uncle Tom's Cabin*	Napoleon III Emperor	Turgenev, *Sketches from a Hunter's Album* Tolstoy, *Childhood* Aksakov, *A Family Chronicle* Gogol d.
53	Dickens, *Bleak House* Commodore Peary visits Japan (end of Japanese isolation)	Champfleury, *Les Souffrances du professeur Delteil*	Outbreak of Crimean War
54	Dickens, *Hard Times*		

Germany and Austria	Spain and Portugal	Italy
Gotthelf, *Die schwarze Spinne*		Pius IX Pope
Grillparzer, *Der arme Spielmann*		
Franz Josef Emperor of Austria Suppression of Bohemian and Hungarian revolts A. von Droste-Hülshoff d.		Proclamation of Roman and Venetian Republics
	Fernán Caballero, *La gaviota*	Battle of Novara Victor Emmanuel King of Piedmont Restoration of Papal power in Rome
Storm, *Immensee*		
Gutzkow, *Die Ritter vom Geiste*		
Stifter, *Bunte Steine*	Pedro V King of Portugal	
Keller, *Der grüne Heinrich* Gotthelf d.	Garrett d.	

	General including United States and Great Britain	France	Russia
55	Charlotte Brontë d.	Champfleury, *Les Bourgeois de Molinchart*	Tolstoy, *Sevastopol Sketches* Alexander II Tsar
56	Paris Peace Congress	Champfleury, *Monsieur de Boisdhyver* *Réalisme* (periodical) Nov. 1856–May 1857	Crimean War ended Turgenev, *Rudin*
57	Indian Mutiny	Flaubert, *Madame Bovary* Champfleury, *La Succession Le Camus* E. Sue d.	
58	Transatlantic telegraphic communication established		Aksakov, *Childhood Years* Pisemsky, *A Thousand Souls*
59	Darwin, *The Origin of Species* G. Eliot, *Adam Bede* Meredith, *The Ordeal of Richard Feverel*		Goncharov, *Oblomov* Turgenev, *Home of the Gentry* Tolstoy, *Family Happiness* Dostoyevsky, *The Village of Stepanchikovo* Aksakov d.
1860	Sack of Winter Palace, Peking	Duranty, *Le Malheur d'Henriette Gérard* Goncourts, *Charles Demailly* Savoy and Nice ceded to France	Turgenev, *On the Eve*
61	American Civil War breaks out Dickens, *Great Expectations*	Goncourts, *Sœur Philomène* Expeditionary force to ·Mexico	Emancipation of the serfs Dostoyevsky, *Notes from the House of the Dead*; *The Insulted and Injured*
62		Hugo, *Les Misérables* Flaubert, *Salammbô* Duranty, *La Cause du beau Guillaume* Annexation of Cochin-China	Turgenev, *Fathers and Children*

Germany and Austria	Spain and Portugal	Italy
Freytag, *Soll und Haben*		
Mörike, *Mozart auf der Reise nach Prag*		
Ludwig, *Zwischen Himmel und Erde*		
Keller, *Romeo und Julia auf dem Dorfe*		
Raabe, *Die Chronik der Sperlingsgasse*		
Stifter, *Der Nachsommer*		
	Spanish invasion of Morocco	Battles of Magenta and Solferino
Schopenhauer d.	Sanz del Río, *Ideal de la humanidad para la vida*	Garibaldi's Sicilian campaign
		Unification of Italy
	Luiz l King of Portugal	Arrighi, *La Scapigliatura e il 6 febbraio*
		Nievo d.

	General including United States and Great Britain	France	Russia
63	Abolition of slavery in U.S.	Renan, *La Vie de Jésus*	Tolstoy, *The Cossacks*
	Battle of Gettysburg		Chernyshevsky, *What Is To Be Done?*
	Thackeray d.		Polish rising crushed
64	First International founded	Goncourts, *Renée Mauperin*; *Germinie Lacerteux*	Dostoyevsky, *Notes from Underground*
	Hawthorne d.		
65	American Civil War ended		
	Assassination of Lincoln		
66		Withdrawal of French troops from Mexico	Dostoyevsky, *Crime and Punishment*
67	Alaska purchase	Zola, *Thérèse Raquin*	
		Baudelaire d.	
68		Daudet, *Le Petit Chose*	
69	Suez Canal opened	Flaubert, *L'Éducation sentimentale*	Dostoyevsky, *The Idiot*
	Completion of Union Pacific railroad	Goncourts, *Madame Gervaisais*	Tolstoy, *War and Peace* (1863–9)
1870	Dickens d.	Franco-Prussian War	
	Invention of typewriter	Napoleon III abdicates	
		Proclamation of 3rd Republic	
		J. de Goncourt d.	
71		Commune of Paris	
		Zola, *La Fortune des Rougon*	
72	G. Eliot, *Middlemarch*	Zola, *La Curée*	Dostoyevsky, *The Possessed*
		Daudet, *Tartarin de Tarascon*	
73		Zola, *Le Ventre de Paris*	
74	Creation of Universal Postal Union	Daudet, *Fromont jeune et Risler aîné*	
75		Zola, *La Faute de l'abbé Mouret*	Dostoyevsky, *A Raw Youth*
		Republican constitution adopted	

Germany and Austria	Spain and Portugal	Italy
Raabe, *Der Hungerpastor*	Pereda, *Escenas montañesas*	Mastriani, *I vermi*
Ludwig d.	Saavedra d.	
Prussia defeats Austria (Seven Weeks War)	Herculano d.	Venice transferred to Kingdom of Italy
Institution of Dual Monarchy (Austria and Hungary)	Estébanez Calderón d.	Nievo, *Le confessioni di un Italiano*
Marx, *Das Kapital* (first vol.)		Garibaldi repelled at Montana
Stifter d.	September Revolution (Spain). Abdication of Isabel II	De Meis, *Dopo la laurea*
Sacher-Masoch, *Das Vermächtnis Kains*		Rome made capital of Italy
Proclamation of German Empire	'Conferências Democráticas', Lisbon	Verga, *Storia di una capinera*
Grillparzer d.	Pereda, *Los hombres de pro*	Mazzini d.
Formation of 'Drei-Kaiser-Bund'	First Spanish Republic	Manzoni d.
		Verga, *Eva*; *Tigre reale*
	Alfonso XII King of Spain	Verga, *Nedda*
	Alarcón, *El sombrero de tres picos*	Rovani d.
	Valera, *Pepita Jiménez*	
	Eça de Queirós, *O Crime do Padre Amaro*	Tronconi, *Passione maledetta*
	Alarcón, *El escándalo*	

General including United States and Great Britain	France	Russia
76 Bell's first telephone	Daudet, *Jack* Huysmans, *Marthe* G. Sand d.	
77 James, *The American*	Zola, *L'Assommoir* Flaubert, *Trois Contes* Daudet, *Le Nabab*	Tolstoy, *Anna Karenina* (1873–7) Russo-Turkish War (1877–8)
78 Congress of Berlin. Bulgaria granted autonomy. Cyprus ceded to G.B. Hardy, *The Return of the Native*		
79 Meredith, *The Egoist* James, *Daisy Miller*	Huysmans, *Les Sœurs Vatard*	
1880 G. Eliot d.	Zola, *Le Roman expérimental; Nana* *Les Soirées de Médan* Flaubert d. Duranty d.	Dostoyevsky, *The Brothers Karamazov* Saltykov-Shchedrin, *The Golovlyov Family*
81	Flaubert, *Bouvard et Pécuchet* Daudet, *Numa Roumestan* Huysmans, *En ménage* French protectorate established over Tunisia	Dostoyevsky d. Pisemsky d. Assassination of Alexander II Alexander III Tsar
82	Zola, *Pot-Bouille* Huysmans, *À vau l'eau*	
83	Maupassant, *Une Vie*	Turgenev d.
84 Mark Twain, *Huckleberry Finn*	Zola, *La Joie de vivre* Huysmans, *À rebours* Daudet, *Sapho*	
85 Berne Convention on international copyright	Zola, *Germinal* Maupassant, *Bel-Ami* Hugo d.	Garshin, *Nadezhda Nikolayevna* Korolenko, *Makar's Dream*
86 Stevenson, *Dr Jekyll and Mr Hyde*	Zola, *L'Œuvre* Vogüé, *Le Roman russe*	Tolstoy, *The Death of Ivan Ilyich*
87	Zola, *La Terre*	

Germany and Austria	Spain and Portugal	Italy
	Galdós, *Doña Perfecta*	
	Pereda, *El buey suelto*	Capuana, *Profili di donne*
Keller, *Züricher Novellen* Gutzkow d.	Galdós, *La familia de León Roch* Pereda, *Don Gonzalo* Eça de Queirós, *O Primo Basílio*	Fucini, *Napoli ad occhio nudo* Leo XIII Pope
	Valera, *Doña Luz* Pereda, *De tal palo, tal astilla*	Capuana, *Giacinta*
	Eça de Queirós, *Os Maias*	Verga, *Vita dei campi* Arrighi, *Nanà a Milano*
	Galdós, *La desheredada* Pereda, *El sabor de la tierruca*	Verga, *I Malavoglia*
Formation of Triple Alliance (Prussia–Austria–Italy)	Pardo Bazán, *La tribuna* Galdós, *El amigo Manso* Mesonero Romanos d.	
Wagner d. Marx d.	Pardo Bazán, *La cuestión palpitante* Pereda, *Pedro Sánchez* Galdós, *Tormento; La de Bringas*	Verga, *Novelle rusticane* Serao, *Il ventre di Napoli* De Sanctis d.
	Alas, *La Regenta* Pinto, *Estética Naturalista*	Serao, *La conquista di Roma* Fogazzaro, *Daniele Cortis*
Sudermann, *Frau Sorge*	Pardo Bazán, *Los pazos de Ulloa* Galdós, *Fortunata y Jacinta*	

	General including United States and Great Britain	France	Russia
88		Maupassant, *Pierre et Jean*	
89		Champfleury d.	
1890		Zola, *La Bête humaine*	
91	Hardy, *Tess of the D'Urbervilles* Wilde, *The Picture of Dorian Grey*	Huysmans, *Là-Bas* Rimbaud d.	Goncharov d. Franco-Russian alliance
92		Zola, *La Débâcle*	
93		Zola, *Le Docteur Pascal* (last of *Rougon–Macquart* series) Maupassant d.	
94	Stevenson d. First motor-cars constructed	Dreyfus sentenced for treason Assassination of President Carnot	
95	Crane, *The Red Badge of Courage* First public cinema shows	Confédération Générale du Travail established	
96	Hardy, *Jude the Obscure*	E. de Goncourt d.	
97	James, *The Spoils of Poynton*	A. Daudet d.	
98		Mallarmé d. Zola, *J'Accuse!*	
99	Outbreak of Boer War Hague Peace Conference James, *The Awkward Age*		Tolstoy, *Resurrection* Gorky, *Foma Gordeyev*
1900			

Germany and Austria	Spain and Portugal	Italy
Accession of Kaiser Wilhelm II Storm, *Der Schimmelreiter* Fontane, *Irrungen, Wirrungen* Hauptmann, *Bahnwärter Thiel* Storm d.	Galdós, *Miau*	Rovetta, *Le lagrime del prossimo*
Holz and Schlaf, *Papa Hamlet*	Palacio Valdés, *La hermana San Sulpicio* Pereda, *La puchera* Luiz I King of Portugal Proclamation of Republic in Brazil	Verga, *Mastro-Don Gesualdo* D'Annunzio, *Il piacere*
Keller d. Bismarck dismissed by Kaiser	Alas, *Su único hijo* Pardo Bazán, *Una cristiana*; *La prueba*	
Fontane, *Unwiederbringlich* Holz, *Die Kunst, ihr Wesen und ihre Gesetze*	Galdós, *Angel Guerra* Alarcón d.	Serao, *Il paese di Cuccagna*
	Pereda, *Peñas arriba*	De Roberto, *I Vicerè* Rovetta, *Baraonda*
Fontane, *Effi Briest* Freytag d. Sacher-Masoch d.	Valera, *Juanita la larga*	Fogazzaro, *Piccolo mondo antico*
Riehl d.		
Fontane d.	Spanish–American War. Spain loses Cuba, Puerto Rico, Philippines	
Mann, *Buddenbrooks* Nietzsche d.	Eça de Queirós, *A Ilustre Casa de Ramires* Eça d.	

Bibliographies

NOTE: The bibliographies are intended as a guide for further reading, not as a compendium of source works. Only the more recent English translations of the novels etc. discussed in each chapter are included: those that have appeared in the Penguin Classics or Modern Classics series are marked with an asterisk.

CHAPTER I. REALISM AND THE NOVEL:
THE EIGHTEENTH-CENTURY BEGINNINGS

On the general topic of realism, two important essays should be noted: Harry Levin, 'Romance and Realism', in *The Gates of Horn* (New York, 1963), and René Wellek, 'The Concept of Realism in Literary Scholarship', in *Concepts of Criticism* (New Haven and London, 1963). There are some interesting ideas in Damian Grant's short monograph *Realism* (London, 1970); another recent and more extended treatment of the question will be found in J. P. Stern, *On Realism* (London, 1972).

The standard work on the eighteenth-century English novel is Ian Watt, *The Rise of the Novel: studies in Defoe, Richardson and Fielding* (London, 1957). Diana Spearman, *The Novel and Society* (London, 1966), and Alan McKillop, *The Early Masters of English Fiction* (Lawrence, Kans., 1956), are also worth consulting on the subject.

There are two principal studies of the French scene: Vivienne Mylne, *The Eighteenth-Century French Novel: techniques of illusion* (Manchester, 1965), and Georges May, *Le Dilemme du roman au XVIIIe siècle: étude sur les rapports du roman et de la critique* (New Haven and Paris, 1963). English Showalter, *The Evolution of the French Novel, 1641–1782* (Princeton, 1972), has a useful chapter, 'The Individual against Society in the Eighteenth-Century French Novel'. On the specific subject of the pseudo-memoir, see Philip Stewart, *Imitation and Illusion in the French Memoir-Novel, 1700–1750: the art of make-believe* (New Haven and London, 1969). Peter Brooks, *The Novel of Worldliness* (Princeton, 1969), deals particularly with the novelists' attitude to society during this period of French literature.

The fullest account of the epistolary novel in Europe is Godfrey Frank Singer's *The Epistolary Novel: its origins, development, decline and residuary influence* (Philadelphia, 1933); but since Singer fails to do justice to the achievement of Laclos, his book needs to be supplemented by referring to an up-to-date study such as Dorothy Thelander, *Laclos and the Epistolary Novel* (Geneva, 1963). A more specialized treatment of realism in the epistolary novel is provided in H. R. Picard, *Die Illusion der Wirklichkeit im Briefroman des 18ten Jahrhunderts* (Heidelberg, 1971).

Translations
PRÉVOST: **Manon Lescaut*, tr. L. W. Tancock, 1949.
LACLOS: **Les Liaisons dangereuses*, tr. P. W. K. Stone, 1961.

CHAPTER 2. REALISM IN THE AGE OF ROMANTICISM

Recent studies of Stendhal in English include Victor Brombert, *Stendhal: fiction and the themes of freedom* (New York, 1968); Gilbert D. Chaitin, *The Unhappy Few: a psychological study of the novels of Stendhal* (Bloomington, Ind., 1972); F. W. J. Hemmings, *Stendhal, a study of his novels* (Oxford, 1964); and Margaret Tillett, *Stendhal: the background to the novels* (London, 1971). A useful short English introduction to Stendhal's most popular work is John Mitchell, *Stendhal: 'Le Rouge et le noir'* (London, 1973). French works of criticism are numerous, but the only book specifically devoted to Stendhal's realism is in Italian: Mario Bonfantini, *Stendhal e il realismo* (Milan, 1958).

The most authoritative account of Balzac's works in any language is H. J. Hunt, *Balzac's 'Comédie humaine'* (London, 1959). Shorter introductory works in English include Samuel Rogers, *Balzac and the Novel* (Madison, Wis., 1953), and F. W. J. Hemmings, *Balzac: an interpretation of 'La Comédie humaine'* (New York, 1967). Among works in French, particular mention must be made of Félicien Marceau, *Balzac et son monde* (Paris, 1955; tr. *Balzac and his World*, London, 1967), a detailed study of the social stratification of Balzac's fictional world; André Wurmser, *La Comédie inhumaine* (Paris, 1964), which illustrates the standard Marxist approach; and J.-H. Donnard, *Balzac: les réalités économiques et sociales dans la 'Comédie humaine'* (Paris, 1961), an examination of the reliability of Balzac's fiction as a guide to the actual situation in France at the period. Among more recent studies, two works by Pierre Barbéris are particularly noteworthy: *Balzac et le mal du siècle* (2 vols., Paris, 1970) and *Mythes balzaciens* (Paris, 1972). V. S. Pritchett, *Balzac* (London, 1973), adopts a broadly biographical approach.

Louis Maigron, *Le Roman historique à l'époque romantique* (Paris, 1912), remains the only general study of Scott's influence in France, though H. J. Garnand, *The Influence of Walter Scott on the Works of Balzac* (New York, 1926), and K. G. McWatters, *Stendhal lecteur des romanciers anglais* (Lausanne, 1968), may be consulted specifically in connection with the two French novelists principally dealt with in this chapter.

Translations
CONSTANT: **Adolphe*, tr. L. W. Tancock, 1964.
STENDHAL:
  NOVELS
    Armance, tr. Gilbert and Suzanne Sale, 1960.
    *Scarlet and Black, tr. Margaret Shaw, 1953.
    Lucien Leuwen, tr. H. L. R. Edwards, 1951.
    *The Charterhouse of Parma, tr. Margaret Shaw, 1958.
    Féder or the Moneyed Husband, tr. H. L. R. Edwards, 1960.
    Lamiel, tr. T. W. Earp, 1951.
  NON-FICTION
    Rome, Naples and Florence, tr. Richard N. Coe, 1959.
    Love, tr. Brian Rhys, 1959.
    Life of Rossini, tr. Richard N. Coe, 1956.
    Racine and Shakespeare, tr. Guy Daniels, 1962.
    A Roman Journal, tr. Haakon Chevalier, 1959.
    Memoirs of an Egotist, tr. T. W. Earp, 1949.
    *The Life of Henry Brulard, tr. Jean Stewart and B. C. J. G. Knight, 1958.
    Memoirs of a Tourist, tr. Allan Seager, 1962.
BALZAC: **The Chouans*, tr. Marion Crawford, 1972.
  *Domestic Peace and other stories, tr. Marion Crawford, 1958.
  At the Sign of the Cat and Racket, tr. Clara Bell, 1955.
  The Wild Ass's Skin, tr. Ellen Marriage, 1961.
  *Eugénie Grandet, tr. Marion Crawford, 1955.
  The Country Doctor, tr. Ellen Marriage, 1957.
  *Old Goriot, tr. Marion Crawford, 1951.
  The Lily in the Valley, tr. Lucienne Hill, 1957.
  The Bankrupt (César Birotteau), tr. Frances Frenaye, 1959.
  *Lost Illusions, tr. Herbert J. Hunt, 1971.
  *A Harlot High and Low (Splendeurs et misères des courtisanes), tr. Rayner Heppenstall, 1970.
  Beatrix, tr. Rosamond and Simon Harcourt-Smith, 1957.
  *The Black Sheep (La Rabouilleuse), tr. Donald Adamson, 1970.
  *A Murky Business, tr. Herbert J. Hunt, 1972.

Cousin Bette, tr. Marion Crawford, 1965.
Cousin Pons, tr. Herbert J. Hunt, 1968.

CHAPTER 3. REALISM IN RUSSIA,
TO THE DEATH OF DOSTOYEVSKY

English readers will find Russian realism given its proper context within
the evolution of Russian nineteenth-century literature in the elegant
and expressive, but now rather dated, *History of Russian Literature* by
D. S. Mirsky (London, 1949). More specific in its treatment of realism
is Ernest J. Simmons, *Introduction to Russian Realism* (Bloomington,
Ind., 1965), which contains essays on Pushkin, Gogol, Dostoyevsky,
Tolstoy, Chekhov, and Sholokhov. For the relationship between
Russian realism and the European tradition, seen admittedly from a
Marxist standpoint, the reader should consult Georg Lukács, *Studies in
European Realism* (London, 1949).

The connection between Russian realism and the novel has been
studied by English and American critics primarily as part of the history
of the nineteenth-century Russian novel. Henry Gifford has provided
an admirable short guide to the most characteristic features of the novels
of Pushkin, Lermontov, Gogol, Goncharov, Turgenev, Tolstoy,
Dostoyevsky and others in *The Novel in Russia* (London, 1964). A fuller,
more idiosyncratic, stimulating and densely written study is F. D. Reeve,
The Russian Novel (London, 1967). Brief, lucid introductory essays on
the principal nineteenth-century authors are to be found in A. F. Boyd,
Aspects of the Russian Novel (London, 1972). *The Rise of the Russian
Novel* (Cambridge, 1973) by Richard Freeborn offers analytical studies
from *Eugene Onegin* to *War and Peace* and demonstrates how the form
of the Russian novel evolved from imitative beginnings to the point
when, in the 1860s, it established itself as part of the European tradition.

On Pushkin the only important monograph in English is John
Bayley's *Pushkin, a Comparative Commentary* (Cambridge, 1971). On
Lermontov's prose the best work in English is John Mersereau, *Mikhail
Lermontov* (Carbondale, Ill., 1962). Gogol has attracted several inter-
preters largely because his work has received such attention in Russian
criticism. The most stimulating studies are Vladimir Nabokov, *Nikolai
Gogol* (New York, 1944), and Vsevolod Setchkaroff, *Gogol, his Life
and Works* (London, 1965). Victor Ehrlich's *Gogol* (New Haven, 1969)
offers insights which tend to be obscured by the dense style.

Pisemsky is studied in Charles A. Moser, *Pisemsky, a Provincial
Realist* (Cambridge, Mass., 1969). André Mazon's monograph, *Un*

maître du roman russe: Ivan Gontcharov (Paris, 1914), is still valuable, but J. Lavrin's *Goncharov* (Cambridge, 1954) provides an excellent short guide in English. Alexandra and Sverre Lyngstad's *Ivan Goncharov* (New York, 1971) is informative but uninspiring. On Turgenev Henri Granjard's *Ivan Tourguénev et les courants politiques et sociaux* (Paris, 1954) is very helpful; in English there is Richard Freeborn, *Turgenev, the Novelist's Novelist* (Oxford, 1960).

The most stimulating work in English devoted to Tolstoy is John Bayley, *Tolstoy and the Novel* (London, 1966). R. F. Christian's *Tolstoy* (Cambridge, 1969) is excellent, as is his *Tolstoy's 'War and Peace': a study* (Oxford, 1962). Isaiah Berlin's *The Hedgehog and the Fox* (London, 1953) is an important study of Tolstoy's philosophy of history. A pioneer Russian study available in English translation is D. S. Merezhkovsky, *Tolstoy as Man and Artist* (London, 1902). There is also reference in this book to Dostoyevsky and it has become fashionable to treat them as twin poles in the evolution of Russian realism, as does George Steiner in his *Tolstoy or Dostoevsky* (New York, 1959).

The three most informative and stimulating studies of Dostoyevsky in English are K. Mochulsky, *Dostoevsky, his Life and Work* (Princeton, 1967); Donald Fanger, *Dostoevsky and Romantic Realism* (Cambridge, Mass., 1967), which includes a discussion of Gogol's treatment of urban themes; and Richard Peace, *Dostoyevsky: an Examination of the Major Novels* (Cambridge, 1971), which explores in particular Dostoyevsky's concern with Russian sectarianism and his use of linguistic symbolism. Edward Wasiolek, *Dostoevsky: the Major Fiction* (Cambridge, Mass., 1964), is a general guide to Dostoyevsky's novels. On Dostoyevsky's humour there is Ronald Hingley, *The Undiscovered Dostoyevsky* (London, 1962); on his concern with aesthetics, particularly his interpretation of realism, there are R. L. Jackson, *Dostoevsky's Quest for Form* (New Haven, 1966), and Sven Linner, *Dostoevskij on Realism* (Stockholm, 1967). For those interested in a fuller appreciation of Dostoyevsky's work as a novelist, the University of Chicago has published English translations of the notebooks to the major fiction. René Wellek has edited an interesting selection of criticism in English in *Dostoevsky: a Collection of Critical Essays* (New York, 1962).

Translations
PUSHKIN: *★Eugene Onegin*, tr. Babette Deutsch, 1964.
  ★The Queen of Spades; The Negro of Peter the Great; Dubrovsky; The Captain's Daughter, tr. Rosemary Edmonds, 1962.
  The Complete Prose Tales, tr. Gillon R. Aitken, 1966.

LERMONTOV: *A Hero of our Time*, tr. Paul Foote, 1966.
GOGOL: *Mirgorod: Four Tales*, tr. David Magarshack, 1969.
  **The Diary of a Madman; The Nose; The Overcoat; How Ivan Ivanovich
    Quarrelled with Ivan Nikiforovich; Ivan Fyodorovich Shponka and
    his Aunt*, tr. R. Wilks, 1973.
  *Dead Souls, tr. David Magarshack, 1961.
PISEMSKY: *One Thousand Souls*, tr. Ivy Litvinov, 1959.
GONCHAROV: **Oblomov*, tr. David Magarshack, 1954.
TURGENEV: **Sketches from a Hunter's Album*, tr. Richard Freeborn,
    1967.
  *Home of the Gentry, tr. Richard Freeborn, 1970.
  *On the Eve, tr. Gilbert Gardiner, 1950.
  *Fathers and Sons, tr. Rosemary Edmonds, 1965.
  Smoke, tr. Natalie Duddington, 1949.
  Five Short Novels (*The Diary of a Superfluous Man; Rudin; First Love;
    A King Lear of the Steppes; Spring Torrents*), tr. Franklin Reeve,
    1961.
  Youth and Age. Three Short Novels (*Punin and Baburin; The Inn;
    The Watch*), tr. Marion Mainwaring, 1968.
TOLSTOY: **Childhood; Boyhood; Youth*, tr. Rosemary Edmonds, 1964.
  *The Cossacks; The Death of Ivan Ilyich; Happy Ever After, tr. Rose-
    mary Edmonds, 1960.
  *War and Peace, tr. Rosemary Edmonds, 1957.
  *Anna Karenin, tr. Rosemary Edmonds, 1954.
  *Resurrection, tr. Rosemary Edmonds, 1966.
  Ivan the Fool and Other Tales, tr. G. Daniels, 1966.
DOSTOYEVSKY: *Poor People and A Little Hero*, tr. David Magarshack,
    1968.
  The Dream of a Queer Fellow, tr. S. Kotelian and J. M. Murry, 1960.
  A Gentle Creature and other stories, tr. David Magarshack, 1950.
  Netochka Nezvanov, tr. Ann Dunnigan, 1971.
  Memoirs from the House of the Dead, tr. Jessie Coulson, 1956.
  *Notes from Underground and The Double, tr. Jessie Coulson, 1972.
  *Crime and Punishment, tr. David Magarshack, 1951.
  *The Gambler; Bobok; A Nasty Story, tr. Jessie Coulson, 1966.
  *The Idiot, tr. David Magarshack, 1955.
  *The Devils, tr. David Magarshack, 1953.
  The Adolescent, tr. Andrew R. MacAndrew, 1972.
  *The Brothers Karamazov, tr. David Magarshack, 1958.
  The Diary of a Writer, tr. Boris Brasol, 1972.

The minor French novelists of the period 1830–48 have been studied in D. O. Evans, *Le Roman social sous la Monarchie de Juillet* (Paris, 1939), and J. S. Wood, *Sondages 1830–1848. Romanciers français secondaires* (Toronto, 1965). The most informative work on Sue is still Nora Atkinson, *Eugène Sue et le roman feuilleton* (Paris, 1929).

E. Bouvier, *La Bataille réaliste, 1844–1857* (Paris, 1913), remains a useful guide to the early history of the realist movement. Some interesting documents have been collected in B. Weinberg, *French Realism: the critical reaction 1830–1870* (New York, 1937). The life and work of Edmond Duranty are exhaustively studied in M. Crouzet, *Un méconnu du réalisme: Duranty* (Paris, 1964).

There are numerous critical studies of Flaubert in English, quite apart from the detailed biography by Enid Starkie, *Flaubert: the Making of the Master* and *Flaubert the Master* (London, 1967 and 1971). Closest to the point of view adopted in this chapter is Anthony Thorlby, *Gustave Flaubert and the Art of Realism* (London, 1956). Other books worth consulting are Margaret Tillett, *On Reading Flaubert* (London, 1961); Victor Brombert, *The Novels of Flaubert: a study of themes and techniques* (Princeton, 1966); and R. J. Sherrington, *Three Novels by Flaubert: a study of techniques* (Oxford, 1970). Alison Fairlie, *Flaubert: 'Madame Bovary'* (London, 1962), is an indispensable monograph on Flaubert's first novel. Less rewarding is Peter Cortland, *The Sentimental Adventure: an examination of Flaubert's 'Éducation sentimentale'* (The Hague and Paris, 1967). Cortland is also the author of *A Reader's Guide to Flaubert* (New York, 1968).

Robert Baldick, *The Goncourts* (London, 1960), covers the whole of the brothers' fictional work in a brief space. A recent work in French by an Italian scholar throws fresh light on the novels of the Goncourts' 'realist' period: this is Enzo Caramaschi, *Réalisme et impressionnisme dans l'œuvre des frères Goncourt* (Pisa and Paris, 1971).

Accounts of naturalist theory and the naturalist movement in France can be found in various readable introductions: Pierre Cogny, *Le Naturalisme* (Paris, 1953), a sound, factual exposition, and P. Martino, *Le Naturalisme français* (Paris, 1969), an updated version of a book originally published in 1923. A short but penetrating book which takes in German as well as French naturalism is Lilian Furst and Peter Skrine, *Naturalism* (London, 1971).

The most complete study of Zola in English is F. W. J. Hemmings,

Émile Zola (2nd ed. Oxford, 1966). For an enlightening discussion of the early works, see J. C. Lapp, *Zola before the Rougon-Macquart* (Toronto, 1964). Some of the individual novels of the Rougon-Macquart cycle have been separately examined, e.g. R. B. Grant, *Zola's 'Son Excellence Eugène Rougon'* (Durham, N.C., 1960); E. M. Grant, *Zola's 'Germinal': a critical and historical study* (Leicester, 1962), and R. H. Zakarian, *Zola's 'Germinal': a critical study of its primary sources* (Geneva, 1972); R. J. Niess, *Zola, Cézanne and Manet: a study of 'L'Œuvre'* (Ann Arbor, 1968); Martin Kanes, *Zola's 'La Bête humaine': a study in literary creation* (Berkeley and Los Angeles, 1962).

Murray Sachs, *The Career of Alphonse Daudet* (Cambridge, Mass., 1965), is a sound account which makes no excessive claims for its author. Writers on Huysmans tend to neglect the novels of his naturalist period in favour of the later (neo-Catholic) fiction; but the first chapter in Pierre Cogny, *J.-K. Huysmans à la recherche de l'unité* (Paris, 1953), is worth consulting. For English readers the most useful studies of Maupassant are E. D. Sullivan's two books: *Maupassant the Novelist* (Princeton, 1954) and *Maupassant: the Short Stories* (London, 1962).

Translations

FLAUBERT: *November*, tr. Frank Jellinek, 1967.
  The First Sentimental Education, tr. Douglas Garman, 1972.
  *Madame Bovary, tr. Alan Russell, 1950.
  Salammbo, tr. Robert Goodyear and P. J. R. Wright, 1962.
  **A Sentimental Education*, tr. Robert Baldick, 1964.
  *Three Tales, tr. Robert Baldick, 1961.
  Bouvard and Pécuchet, tr. T. W. Earp and G. W. Stonier, 1936.
E. and J. de GONCOURT: *Germinie*, tr. Jonathan Griffith, 1955.
  Pages from the Goncourt Journal, tr. Robert Baldick, 1962.
  The Goncourt Journals, 1851–1870, tr. Lewis Galantiere, 1969.
E. de GONCOURT: *Elisa*, tr. Margaret Crosland, 1959.
  The Zemganno Brothers, tr. Leonard Clark and Iris Allam, 1957.
ZOLA: *Thérèse Raquin, tr. L. W. Tancock, 1962.
  Madeleine Férat, tr. Alec Brown, 1957.
  Savage Paris (Le Ventre de Paris), tr. David Hughes and Marie-Jacqueline Mason, 1955.
  A Priest in the House (La Conquête de Plassans), tr. Brian Rhys, 1957.
  The Sin of Father Mouret, tr. Sandy Petry, 1969.
  His Excellency, tr. Alec Brown, 1958.
  **L'Assommoir*, tr. L. W. Tancock, 1970.
  A Love Affair (Une Page d'amour), tr. Jean Stewart, 1957.
  *Nana, tr. George Holden, 1972.

Restless House (Pot-Bouille), tr. Percy Pinkerton, 1953.
Ladies' Delight, tr. April FitzLyon, 1960.
Zest for Life, tr. Jean Stewart, 1955.
*Germinal, tr. L. W. Tancock, 1954.
The Masterpiece, tr. Thomas Walton, 1950.
Earth, tr. Margaret Crosland, 1962.
The Beast in Man, tr. Alec Brown, 1956.
*The Debacle, tr. L. W. Tancock, 1972.
Doctor Pascal, tr. Vladimir Kean, 1957.
DAUDET: *Letters from my Mill*, tr. Alec Brown, 1962.
Sidonie (Fromont jeune et Risler aîné), tr. Charlotte Haldane, 1958.
Sappho, tr. Alec Brown, 1959.
HUYSMANS: *Marthe*, tr. Robert Baldick, 1958.
Downstream (À vau l'eau), tr. Robert Baldick, 1956.
*Against Nature (À rebours), tr. Robert Baldick, 1959.
Down There (Là-bas), tr. Keene Wallace, 1972.
MAUPASSANT: **A Woman's Life*, tr. H. N. P. Sloman, 1965.
*Bel-Ami, tr. H. N. P. Sloman, 1961.
Pierre and Jean, tr. Martin Turnell, 1962.
The Master Passion (Fort comme la mort), tr. Marjorie Laurie, 1958.
*Boule de Suif and other stories, tr. H. N. P. Sloman, 1946.
Madame Tellier's Girls and other stories, tr. Alec Brown, 1960.
Mademoiselle Fifi and other stories, tr. Denis George, 1962.
*Miss Harriet and other stories, tr. H. N. P. Sloman, 1951.
*The Mountain Inn and other stories, tr. H. N. P. Sloman, 1955.
*Selected Short Stories, tr. Roger Colet, 1971.

CHAPTER 5. REALISM IN GERMANY,
FROM THE DEATH OF GOETHE

The modern revival of interest in German realism was sparked off by
R. Brinkmann, *Wirklichkeit und Illusion* (Tübingen, 1957); Brinkmann
has since edited a collection of essays by various scholars entitled *Zur
Begriffsbestimmung des literarischen Realismus* (Darmstadt, 1969). Fritz
Martini published his vast historical survey, *Deutsche Literatur im bürger-
lichen Realismus 1848–1898* (Stuttgart), in 1962. This was followed by
Fritz Sengle's *Biedermeierzeit: Deutsche Literatur im Spannungsfeld
zwischen Restauration und Revolution, 1815–1848* (Stuttgart, 1971), the
first of three projected volumes. No comprehensive study exists in
English to match Martini and Sengle. J. P. Stern, *Reinterpretations*
(London, 1964), has a chapter on antecedents and comparisons, but

discusses only Stifter and Fontane among the narrative writers. His more recent *Idylls and Realities* (London, 1971) similarly consists of a series of perceptive but disparate studies which now include Keller and Raabe.

Young Germany has never been a popular field of study: however, a certain amount of material has recently been made available in J. Hermand, *Das Junge Deutschland, Texte und Dokumente* (Stuttgart, 1966); see also, by the same author, *Der deutsche Vormärz* (Stuttgart, 1967). A welcome study of the prose fiction of *Das junge Deutschland* is Jeffrey L. Simmons, *Six Studies on the Young German Novel* (Chapel Hill, N.C., 1972).

Essential as sociological guides to the period are E. K. Bramsted, *Aristocracy and the Middle Classes in Germany, Social Types in German Literature 1830–1900* (London, 1937), and Eda Sagarra, *Tradition and Revolution, German Literature and Society 1830–1890* (London, 1971). French critics have been particularly interested in the German social novel, witness J. Dresch, *Le Roman social en Allemagne 1850–1900* (Paris, 1913), and P. P. Sagave, *Recherches sur le roman social en Allemagne* (Paris, 1960), which deals mainly with Goethe, Freytag and Fontane. A survey of the vast literature on the *Bildungsroman* can be found in Lother Köhn, *Entwicklungs- und Bildungsroman: ein Forschungsbericht* (Stuttgart, 1969). R. Pascal, in the first part of *The German Novel* (Manchester, 1957), deals with the *Bildungsroman*, and in the second part with Gotthelf, Raabe, Fontane, etc., while E. K. Bennett and H. M. Waidson have written a *History of the German Novelle from Goethe to Thomas Mann* (Cambridge, 1961). Walter Silz, *Realism and Reality* (Chapel Hill, N.C., 1965), includes excellent studies in the German Novelle of Poetic Realism. The problem of the Novelle has provoked a vast critical literature in German, in some respects quite out of proportion with its importance in the context of European literature. The best surveys are Benno v. Weise, *Die deutsche Novelle* (2 vols., Düsseldorf, 1962), and Richard Thieberger, *Le Genre de la nouvelle dans la littérature allemande* (Paris, 1968). German naturalism has never roused much critical interest though there are some signs of a revival, with E. Ruprecht, *Literarische Manifeste des Naturalismus 1880–1892* (Stuttgart, 1962), and U. Münchow, *Deutscher Naturalismus* (Berlin, 1968). The terms Realism, Biedermeier and Naturalism are discussed in *Periods of German Literature*, ed. J. M. Ritchie, Vol. I (London, 1966). Vol. II (London, 1968) deals with works by Stifter, Fontane, Holz and Schlaf.

Critical studies of individual German authors of the nineteenth century are available in English in *German Men of Letters*, ed. A. Natan (6 vols., London, 1961 ff.). Annette von Droste-Hülshoff has been studied biographically by Margaret Mare (London, 1965), but the fullest account of *Die Judenbuche* is given in the edition by H. Rölleke (Bad Homburg, 1970). For the most recent literature on Gotthelf see Karl Fehr, *Jeremias Gotthelf* (Metzler, 1969). The outstanding single study of this novelist is H. M. Waidson, *Jeremias Gotthelf* (Oxford, 1953). The only extensive work on Stifter in English is Eric A. Blackall, *Adalbert Stifter, a Critical Study* (Cambridge, 1948). The best account of Ludwig's theory and practice of poetic realism (after that given by Brinkmann in his *Wirklichkeit und Illusion*) is W. H. McClain, *Between Real and Ideal* (Chapel Hill, N.C., 1963). W. J. Lillyman, *Otto Ludwig's 'Zwischen Himmel und Erde'* (The Hague, 1967), is the only full-length study of this work.

Theodor Storm has been extensively studied outside Germany, especially in the United States: see E. O. Wooley, *Studies in Theodor Storm* (Bloomington, Ind., 1943); E. A. McCormick, *Theodor Storm's Novellen: Essays on Literary Technique* (Chapel Hill, N.C., 1964); and C. A. Bernd, *Theodor Storm's Craft of Fiction* (Chapel Hill, N.C., 1966). For an idiosyncratic English view of Storm see also T. J. Rogers, *Techniques of Solipsism: a study of Theodor Storm's narrative fiction* (Cambridge, 1970).

J. M. Lindsay, *Gottfried Keller, Life and Works* (London, 1968), makes this great Swiss writer unnecessarily dull. Much better, for English readers, is B. A. Rowley's *Keller: 'Kleider machen Leute'* (London, 1959). Gilles Deleuze, *Présentation de Sacher-Masoch, le froid et le cruel* (Paris, 1967), has been translated into English. The standard work on Riehl is Viktor von Geramb, *W. H. Riehl, Leben und Wirken* (Salzburg, 1954). Barker Fairley is responsible for a magnificent study, *Wilhelm Raabe: an Introduction to his Novels* (Oxford, 1961), which was immediately translated into German. The subsequent Raabe revival is assessed in H. Helmers, *Wilhelm Raabe* (Metzler, 1968), and in the collection of essays edited by the same author, *Raabe in neuer Sicht* (Kohlhammer, 1968).

One of the first studies of Fontane was Kenneth Hayens, *Theodor Fontane, a critical study* (London, 1920). For Fontane's politics see Joachim Remak, *The Gentle Critic Theodor Fontane: German Politics 1848–1898* (Syracuse, N.Y., 1964). Specifically dealing with the problem of realism in Fontane are Peter Demetz, *Formen des Realismus: Theodor Fontane* (2nd ed. Munich, 1966), and Josef Thanner, *Die Stilistik Theodor Fontanes. Untersuchungen zur Erhellung des Begriffes 'Realismus' in der*

Literatur (The Hague, 1967). More comparative in treatment is R. Osiander, *Der Realismus in den Zeitromanen Theodor Fontanes* (Göttingen, 1953). For Schnitzler, see Martin Swales, *Arthur Schnitzler, a critical study* (Oxford, 1971).

While there are countless studies of Hauptmann's drama, little has been written about his naturalistic prose, but see *Bahnwärter Thiel* and *Fasching*, ed. S. D. Stirk (Oxford, 1966), with a thirty-page introduction. The great defender and editor of Arno Holz is Wilhelm Emrich: see 'Arno Holz und die moderne Kunst' in his *Protest und Verheissung: Studien zur klassischen und modernen Dichtung* (Frankfurt a. M., 1960).

Translations

GOETHE: **Elective Affinities*, tr. R. J. Hollingdale, 1971.
  Wilhelm Meister. Apprenticeship and Travels, tr. R. O. Moon, 1947.
  *The Faithful Ghost, tr. F. J. Lamport, in the *Penguin Book of German Stories*, 1974.
BÜCHNER: **Lenz*, tr. F. J. Lamport, in the *Penguin Book of German Stories*, 1974.
MÖRIKE: *Mozart's Journey to Prague*, tr. Leopold von Loewenstein-Wertheim, 1957.
DROSTE-HÜLSHOFF: *The Jew's Beech*, tr. Lionel and Doris Thomas, 1958.
GOTTHELF: *The Black Spider*, tr. H. M. Waidson, 1958.
GRILLPARZER: *The Poor Fiddler*, tr. Alexander and Elizabeth Henderson, 1969.
STIFTER: *Rock Crystal*, tr. Elizabeth Mayer and Marianne Moore, 1945.
  Limestone and other stories, tr. David Luke, 1968.
  The Recluse (Der Hagestolz), tr. David Luke, 1968.
LUDWIG: *Between Heaven and Earth*, tr. Muriel Almon, 1964.
STORM: *Immensee*, tr. Ronald Taylor (with BÜCHNER, *Lenz*, tr. Michael Hamburger, and KELLER, *A Village Romeo and Juliet*, tr. Ronald Taylor), 1966.
  The White Horseman and Beneath the Flood (Aquis submersus), tr. Geoffrey Skelton, 1962.
  Viola Tricolor, tr. B. Q. Morgan, and *Curator Carsten*, tr. Frieda M. Voigt, 1956.
  *St George's Almshouse, tr. G. W. McKay, in the *Penguin Book of German Stories*, 1974.
KELLER: *Green Henry*, tr. A. M. Holt, 1960.
  People of Seldwyla and Seven Legends, tr. M. D. Hottinger, 1929.
  A Village Romeo and Juliet, tr. Paul Bernard Thomas, 1955.

Martin Salander, tr. Kenneth Halwas, 1964.

SACHER-MASOCH: *Venus in Furs*, tr. H. J. Stenning, 1965.

FONTANE: *Beyond Recall*, tr. Douglas Parmée, 1964.

★Effi Briest, tr. Douglas Parmée, 1967.

A Suitable Match, tr. S. Morris, 1968.

HAUPTMANN: *★Thiel the Crossing-Keeper*, tr. John Bednall, in the *Penguin Book of German Stories*, 1974.

SCHNITZLER: *★Lieutenant Gustl*, tr. Sheila Stern, in the *Penguin Book of German Stories*, 1974.

CHAPTER 6. REALISM IN SPAIN AND PORTUGAL

On the general nineteenth-century literary background the best recent work is *A Literary History of Spain* (ed. R. O. Jones): *The Nineteenth Century*, by D. L. Shaw (London, 1972). For the history of the period see A. R. M. Carr, *Spain 1808–1939* (Oxford, 1966). S. H. Eoff, *The Modern Spanish Novel* (New York, 1961), is not, as its title might suggest, a comprehensive survey but a series of essays comparing individual Spanish novels with foreign ones; the works dealt with include Pereda's *Sotileza*, Galdós's *Fortunata y Jacinta*, Alas's *La Regenta* and Pardo Bazán's *Los pazos de Ulloa*.

Galdós has attracted a great deal of critical attention. J. F. Montesinos presents the results of a lifetime's work in *Galdós* (3 vols., Madrid, 1968 ff.). S. H. Eoff, *The Novels of Pérez Galdós* (St Louis, 1954), is an interesting but partial study of his depiction of the relationship between the individual and society. R. Gullón's *Galdós, novelista moderno* (Madrid, 1960) and *Técnicas de Galdós* (Madrid, 1970) contain important analyses of Galdós's narrative techniques. Gustavo Correa, *Realidad, ficción y símbolo en las novelas de Benito Pérez Galdós* (Bogotá, 1967), explores the relationship between illusion and reality in Galdós's novels: and his *El simbolismo religioso en las novelas de Galdós* (Madrid, 1962) studies his presentation of religious themes. M. Nimetz, *Humor in Galdós* (New Haven, 1968), is worth consulting for this aspect of the work. J. E. Varey has published (London, 1971) a useful study of *Doña Perfecta* in the series *Critical Guides to Spanish Literature* (ed. Varey and Deyermond).

A fundamental, if dated, work on Pereda is J. M. de Cossío, *La vida literaria de Pereda, su historia y su crítica* (Santander, 1934). J. F. Montesinos, *Pereda o la novela idilio* (Mexico, 1961), is more critical and more interesting. Among books on Valera the three most useful are perhaps J. Krynen, *L'Esthétisme de Juan Valera* (Salamanca, 1946), A. Jiménez,

Juan Valera y la Generación de 1868 (Oxford, 1955), and J. F. Montesinos, *Valera o la ficción libre* (Madrid, 1957). Both Alas and Pardo Bazán, still, astonishingly, await adequate treatment in book form. On Alas's short stories there is Laura de los Ríos, *Los cuentos de Clarín* (Madrid, 1965), and the *Critical Guides to Spanish Literature* mentioned above include a textual analysis of *La Regenta* by J. D. Rutherford (London, 1973). In addition, A. Brent, *Leopoldo Alas and 'La Regenta'* (Columbia, Mo., 1951), and E. J. Gramberg, *Fondo y forma del humorismo de Leopoldo Alas* (Oviedo, 1958), make some worthwhile points. Carmen Bravo Villasante, *Vida y obra de Emilia Pardo Bazán* (Madrid, 1962), is a biographical study in which little of interest is said about the novels themselves; D. F. Brown, *The Catholic Naturalism of Emilia Pardo Bazán* (Chapel Hill, N.C., 1957), is not as sound or as complete as it might have been.

A reliable account in English of the work of Eça de Queirós has still to appear. Recent studies in Portuguese include Álvaro Lins, *História literária de Eça de Queirós* (3rd ed. Lisbon, 1960); J. G. Simões, *Eça de Queirós* (Lisbon, 1961); and Djacir Meneses, *Crítica social de Eça de Queirós* (Rio, 1962).

Translations

CABALLERO: *Gaviota: Sea Gull*, tr. Joan MacLean, 1966.
GALDÓS: *Doña Perfecta*, tr. Harriet De Onis, 1960.
　Disinherited Lady, tr. Guy E. Smith, 1957.
　Torment, tr. J. M. Cohen, 1952.
　The Spendthrifts (La de Bringas), tr. Gamel Woolsey, 1962.
　*Fortunata and Jacinta, tr. Lester Clark, 1973.
　*Miau, tr. J. M. Cohen, 1963.
　Compassion, tr. Toby Talbot, 1962.
VALERA: *Pepita Jiménez*, tr. Harriet De Onis, 1965.
ALARCÓN: *The Three-Cornered Hat*, tr. H. F. Turner, 1965.
EÇA DE QUEIRÓS: *The Sin of Father Amaro*, tr. Nan Flanagan, 1962.
　Cousin Bazilio, tr. Roy Campbell, 1953.
　The Maias, tr. Patricia McGowan Pinheiro and Ann Stevens, 1965.
　The Mandarin and other stories, tr. Richard F. Goldman, 1966.
　The Relic, tr. Aubrey Bell, 1954.
　The Illustrious House of Ramires, tr. Ann Stevens, 1968.
　The City and the Mountains, tr. Roy Campbell, 1955.
　Letters from England, tr. Ann Stevens, 1970.

CHAPTER 7. REALISM IN ITALY

The basic work for any study of Italian *verismo* is still Paul Arrighi, *Le Vérisme dans la prose narrative italienne* (Paris, 1937), which should be supplemented by Roberto Bigazzi, *I colori del vero: vent'anni di narrativa, 1860–1880* (Pisa, 1969). Giulio Marzot's account of literary controversies for and against *verismo, Battaglie veristiche dell'Ottocento* (Milan, 1941), is also useful. Marzot has a chapter on *verismo* in *Questioni e correnti di storia letteraria*, ed. Umberto Bosco (Milan, 1965). Two interesting attempts at a sociological analysis of recent Italian literature, with chapters relevant to *verismo*, are Alberto Asor Rosa, *Scrittori e popolo* (Rome, 1965), and Gianfranco Vené, *Il capitale e il poeta* (Milan, 1972). The best and most up-to-date account of the period 1861–1900 is to be found in Vol. VIII of the *Storia della letteratura italiana*, ed. E. Cecchi and N. Sapegno (Milan, 1968); it includes essays by Sergio Romagnoli on Nievo, Carlo Muscetta on De Sanctis, Giulio Cattaneo on veristic prose, and Giorgio Cusatelli on the Scapigliatura. There are studies of Pratesi and Fucini in Luigi Baldacci, *Letteratura e verità* (Milan and Naples, 1963), and of Mastriani in Antonio Palermo, *Da Mastriani a Viviani* (Naples, 1972).

The following monographs on individual authors of the period can be recommended: Vittorio Spinazzola, *Federico De Roberto e il verismo* (Milan, 1961); Carlo Alberto Madrignani, *Capuana e il naturalismo* (Bari, 1970); Luigi Russo, *Giovanni Verga* (Bari, 1966), and Vitilio Masiello, *Verga, tra ideologia e realtà* (Bari, 1970). There is an English biography of Verga by Alfred Alexander, *Giovanni Verga, a Great Writer and his World* (London, 1972), but it does not add significantly to Giulio Cattaneo, *Giovanni Verga* (Turin, 1963), which gives a better insight into Verga's literary work.

Translations

MANZONI: *The Betrothed*, tr. Bruce Penman, 1972.
NIEVO: *The Castle of Fratta* (*Le confessioni di un Italiano*, first five chapters), tr. L. F. Edwards, 1957.
DE ROBERTO: *The Viceroys*, tr. A. Colquhoun, 1962.
VERGA: *The House by the Medlar Tree* (*I Malavoglia*), tr. E. Mosbacher, 1950.
  Mastro-Don Gesualdo, tr. D. H. Lawrence, 1923.
  Little Novels of Sicily, tr. D. H. Lawrence, 1925.
  Cavalleria Rusticana and other stories, tr. D. H. Lawrence, 1928.
  The She-Wolf and other stories, tr. Giovanni Cechetti, 1958.

Index

Index

Index